Tourism and Visual Culture, Volume 1

Theories and Concepts

FSC
www.fsc.org

MIX
Paper from
responsible sources
FSC® C013604

Tourism and Visual Culture, Volume 1

Theories and Concepts

Edited by

Peter M. Burns, Cathy Palmer and Jo-Anne Lester

University of Brighton, Eastbourne, UK

www.cabi.org

CABI is a trading name of CAB International

CABI Head Office
Nosworthy Way
Wallingford
Oxfordshire OX10 8DE
UK

Tel: +44 (0)1491 832111
Fax: +44 (0)1491 833508
E-mail: cabi@cabi.org
Website: www.cabi.org

CABI North American Office
875 Massachusetts Avenue
7th Floor
Cambridge, MA 02139
USA

Tel: +1 617 395 4056
Fax: +1 617 354 6875
E-mail: cabi-nao@cabi.org

A catalogue record for this book is available from the British Library, London, UK.

Library of Congress Cataloging-in-Publication Data

Tourism and visual culture volume 1: theories and concepts / edited by Peter M. Burns, Cathy
Palmer and Jo-Anne Lester.
     p. cm.
  Includes bibliographical references and index.
  ISBN 978-1-84593-609-9 (alk. paper)
1. Tourism. 2. Visual communication. I. Burns, Peter (Peter M.). II. Palmer, Cathy.
III. Lester, Jo-Anne. IV. Title.

  G155.A1T679 2010
  306.4'819–dc22

                   2009045338

ISBN-13: 978 1 84593 609 9

Commissioning editor: Sarah Hulbert
Production editor: Fiona Harrison

Typeset by AMA Dataset, Preston, UK.
Printed and bound in the UK by CPI Antony Rowe

Contents

Contributors

Antonioni, Stefania, University of Urbino 'Carlo Bo', Faculty of Sociology, Department of Communication Sciences, Media, Languages and Spectacle, Via Saffi, 15-61029 Urbino (PU), Italy. E-mail: stefania.antonioni@uniurb.it

Asensio, Mikel, Departamento de Psicologia Basica, Universidad Autonoma de Madrid, Spain. E-mail: mikel.asensio@uam.es

Baker, Clive, Faculty of Business, Sport and Enterprise, Southampton Solent University, East Park Terrace, Southampton, Hampshire SO14 0YN, UK. E-mail: Clive.baker@solent.ac.uk

Baker, Kathy, Department of Geography, King's College London, Strand, London WC2R 2LS, UK. E-mail: kathy.baker@kcl.ac.uk

Bartoletti, Roberta, Facoltà di Sociologia, Università degli Studi di Urbino 'Carlo Bo', Via Saffi, 15-61029 Urbino (PU), Italy. E-mail: Roberta.bartoletti@uniurb.it

Buddhabhumbhitak, Ketwadee, Naresuan University, Phitsanulok, Thailand. E-mail: ketwadeeb@hotmail.com

Cardeira da Silva, Maria, Center for Research in Anthropology, Universidade Nova de Lisboa, Av. de Berna 26-C, 1069-61 Lisboa, Portugal. E-mail: m.cardeira@fcsh.unl.pt

Costa, Teresa, Escola Superior de Hotelaria e Turismo do Estoril, Av. Condes de Barcelona, 2769-510 Estoril, Portugal. E-mail: Teresa.costa@eshte.pt

Du Cros, Hilary, Institute for Tourism Studies, Colina de Mong-Há, Macao, SAR, China. E-mail: Hilary@ift.edu.mo

Dumont, Elisabeth, Université de Liège, 1, Allée des Chevreuils, B52/3, B-4000, Liège 1, Belgium. E-mail: 4elisabethdumont@qmail.com

Dunn, David, Dean of School, Drama and Creative Industries, Queen Margaret University Edinburgh EH21 6UU, UK. E-mail: dunn.dr@btinternet.com

Gemini, Laura, University of Urbino 'Carlo Bo', Faculty of Sociology, Department of Communication Sciences, Media, Languages and Spectacle, Via Saffi, 15-61029 Urbino (PU), Italy. E-mail: l.gemini@soc.uniurb.it

Higgins-Desbiolles, Freya, School of Management, University of South Australia, North Terrace, Adelaide, SA 5000, Australia. E-mail: Freya.HigginsDesbiolles@unisa.edu.au

James, Kevin, Department of History, University of Guelph, Guelph, Ontario, N1H 2X5, Canada. E-mail: kjames@uoguelph.ca

Mazzoli, Lella, University of Urbino 'Carlo Bo', Faculty of Sociology, LaRiCA Via Saffi, 15-61029 Urbino (PU), Italy. E-mail: mazzoli@uniurb.it

Moir, James, School of Social & Health Sciences, University of Abertay Dundee, Kydd Building, Dundee DD1 1HG, UK. E-mail: J.Moir@abertay.ac.uk

Mortari, Manuel, Departamento de Psicologia Basica, Universidad Autonoma de Madrid, Spain. E-mail: manuel.mortari@uam.es

Paschen, Jana-Axinja, The Australian Centre, School of Historical Studies, University of Melbourne, 137 Barry St, Carlton, VIC 3053, Australia. E-mail: j.paschen@pgrad.unimelb.edu.au

Power, Lisa, Faculty of Business, Sport and Enterprise, Southampton Solent University, East Park Terrace, Southampton, Hampshire SO14 0YN, UK. E-mail: lisa.power@solent.ac.uk

Roberts, Les, The University of Liverpool School of Architecture, Leverhulme Building, Abercromby Square, Liverpool L69 3BX, UK. E-mail: Les.Roberts@liverpool.ac.uk

Stoetzer, Sergej, Institute for Sociology Technical University, Darmstadt, Residenzschloss, D-64283 Darmstadt, Germany. E-mail: sergej@urban-images.net

Wijesinghe, Gaythri (Gee), School of Management, City West Campus, University of South Australia, Adelaide, Australia. E-mail: gayathri.wijesinghe@unisa.edu.au

Willis, Peter, School of Education, Mawson Lakes Campus, University of South Australia, Adelaide, Australia. E-mail: Peter.Willis@unisa.edu.au

Author Biographies

Stefania Antonioni took her PhD in Communication Studies at the Faculty of Sociology, University of Urbino 'Carlo Bo'. Teaches Sociology of Tourism at the same Faculty, is a member of the Research Lab for Advanced Communication (LaRiCA), member of the International Visual Sociology Association (IVSA) and member of the Italian Association of Sociology (AIS).

Mikel Asensio has a PhD and is professor at the Universidad Autonomia de Madrid. He was awarded the 'Extraordinary Bachelor's Degree Prize' and the 'National Research Award'. He also cooperates with other universities and institutions, in Spain and abroad, such as, Autonomia de Barcelona, Sevilla Valencia, Zargoza, Granada, Villadolid, Girona, UNED and Complutense, Exeter (UK), Sinaloa (Mexico), Central de Venezuela, Buenos Aires (Argentina), FLACSO (Argentina) and Catolica de Uruguay, University of Wisconsin, Milwaukee Public Museum, the School of Architecture Research and Urban Design, the Smithsonian Institute's Institutional Studies Office, the Colorado State University in Fort Collins (USA). He has been academic coordinator, together with the Columbia University, of the Open Exchange program, financed by MOMA and featuring MOMA itself, the Witney Museum, the National Museum of Design, the Brooklyn Museum of Art, the New Museum, the African American Museum of Art, the Reina Sofia, the Caixa-Forum, the Fundacion Miro, the Artium and the Centro Gallego de Arte Contemporaneo. He directed Spanish research projects DGICYT, CIDE and Plan Regional, and European projects SOCRATES, SENECA, LEONARDO, etc. He has also directed the national teams of two EU sixth framework programme-funded European projects: APPEAR (Accessibility Projects, sustainable Preservation and Enhancement of Urban Subsoil Archaeological Remains) and PICTURE (Pro-Active Management of the Impact of Cultural Tourism upon Urban Resources and Economies). Academically, he has fulfilled the positions of Vice Dean, Master Director, International Agreements Director and National coordinator of the 'Heritage and Education' European Exchange program. He was also the Evaluation Coordinator for the Area of Humanities and Social Sciences of the *Direccion General de Investigacion de la Communidad de Madrid*, and External Evaluator of the National Agencies of Spain, Cataluña, Colombia, Argentina and Venezuela. He has also been vice-president of the Asociacion Española de Meusologos (AEM) for several years. He has published more than one hundred books, chapters and articles on Museology, Education and Psychology issues, some of them noteworthy such as Nuevos Escenarios en Educacion: Aprendizaje informal sobre el patrimonio, los museos y la ciudad' (2002); Planification en Musologia: el caso del Museu Maritim (2001); Aprendizaje del Arte (1998). During the last 5 years he has directed consulting, assessment and planning projects for the following institutions: *Museo de la Biblioteca Nacional* (2006); *Museo del Ejercito* (*Ministerio de Defensa*, 2004); *Parques Nacionales* (*Ministerio de Medio Ambiente*, 2004-2006); *Museo de la Salud* (*Ministerio de Sanidad*, 2003); *Museo del Traje* (*Ministerio de Educacion y Cultura*, 2003); *Parque Minero de Almaden* (*Ministerio de Fomento*, 2002-2004); *Casa Museo de El Greco* (*Ministerio de Educacion y Cultura*, 2002); other works and programs for the *Fundacion La Caixa*, *Museu Maritim de Barcelona*, *Museu d'Historia de la Ciutat de Barcelona* and other museums run by *Junta de Extremadura*, the *Comunidad de Madrid* and the *Junta de Galicia*.

Clive Baker, Senior Lecturer in Business Strategy. Clive joined Southampton Solent University after a career in local government. He is currently undertaking research in the Leisure and Tourism sector with particular reference to Military Museums. This has developed from his interest in Military history.

Kathy Baker is currently Senior Lecturer in the Department of Geography at King's College London. Kathy graduated from King's with a BSc in Geography in 1971 and a PhD from the School of Oriental and African Studies (SOAS), University of London, in 1975. The research for her PhD focused on the impacts of the Green Revolution on rural livelihoods in western Uttar Pradesh, North India. The growth of tourism in India and in parts of West Africa has led to new research interests on the impact of tourism on livelihoods of the poor. Kathy's research interests in tropical agricultural development and tourism are closely linked with her teaching. Kathy is currently Co-ordinator of the MA Environment and Development, and the MA Tourism, Environment and Development. She is Course Director for the University of London External Programme in Geography, and has been a member of the Central Research Fund (Panel C) of the University of London from 2000 to 2006.

Roberta Bartoleti is Associate Professor, Faculty of Sociology, University of Urbino (Italy). She gained her PhD in sociology and social research at University of Bologna in 1995. She has been researching the sociology of culture, communication and consumption since 1990 and since 1999 has been teaching sociology of consumption, cultural globalization and sociology of communication at University of Urbino. Her present research is on consumption in a cultural perspective analysis of cultural objects, and the connection between memory, consumption memory and social web consumption practices and social network sites and virtual worlds.

Ketwadee Buddhabhumbhitak graduated from the School of Tourism, The University of Queensland, Australia. Her area of research interest is the relationship between a society and tourism, particularly tourist psychology and behaviour. This chapter relates to the backpacker market. Currently, Ketwadee is a head of Tourism Major at Naresuan University, Phitsanulok, Thailand.

Maria Cardeira da Silva is an anthropologist interested in Arabic and Islamic contexts, and in Anthropology of Tourism. She has conducted intensive ethnographic fieldwork in the medina of Salé, and more recently and briefly in Aljadida and Azzamor (Morocco) and in Ouadane (Mauritania). Since 1986, she has taught Anthropology of Islamic Contexts, Anthropology of Tourism and Anthropology and Human Rights at the Universidade Nova de Lisboa. She is the author of *Um Islão Prático* (*A Practical Islam: Women's Daily Performances in Urban Moroccan Context*, 1999; Celta) and editor of *Outros Destinos* (*Other Destinations. New Sites for Tourists, New Fields for Anthropology*, 2005; Livros Horizonte).

Teresa Costa works as lecturer of EFL at ESHTE – Estoril Higher Institute for Tourism and Hotel Studies. Her field of research is poetry and painting, *ekphrasis*. She concluded her masters on William Carlos Williams in 2003. Her interests further include public art and industrial heritage.

Hilary du Cros arrived in Macao from Australia in 1999, and has been engaged by several universities in Southern China researching tourism and cultural issues. Over half of her 75 publications deal with this region and most notable are those on World Heritage, cultural tourism, postcolonial issues and cultural heritage management. Hilary has recently published a book with Yok-shiu F. Lee on *Cultural Heritage Management in China* (2007) and is also known for her collaboration with Bob McKercher for *Cultural Tourism: The Partnership between Tourism and Cultural Heritage Management* (2002).

Elisabeth Dumont has worked as a senior research officer at the University of Liège, working on different projects related to tourism, heritage, cultural expressions and sustainable development. Among others, she co-ordinates an EU 6th framework programme funded project (13 partner institutions) called PICTURE, focusing on the Proactive management of the Impact of Cultural Tourism upon Urban Resources and Economies and is the editor of a Strategic Urban Governance Framework for Cultural Tourism. She specifically focuses on the relationship between tourism and development, on cultural contacts and changes and on quality of life. She also knows the other side of the coin as she worked in the private sector related to culture. For instance, she took part in the launch of a start-up selling cultural products over the Internet and worked as a marketing and business development manager for a major publishing company. She has volunteered across the world and still does in a local cultural centre. She is now specializing in tourism and conflicts in South America.

David Dunn worked as a television programme maker for 30 years, directing and/or producing a range of dramas and documentaries for STV, ATV, Central and BBC before returning to the Academy to study for a PhD on Television Representations of the Tourist Destination, which he was awarded by the University of Birmingham in 1998. He has taught video direction and production at the Universities of Wolverhampton, Salford and Paisley (now the University of the West of Scotland). He now works at Queen Margaret University Edinburgh where he is Dean of the School of Drama and Creative Industries. His research interests, on which he has published extensively, include: The Tourist Gaze and the Television Camera's gaze; Lifestyle Television; Alexandria and the Mediterranean; Writing about Food; Food Tourism on Television; Television Drama and Adaptation; Soap Opera and Place.

Gayathri (Gee) Wijesinghe's research and teaching interests focus on the philosophical, historical, anthropological, social, cultural and psychological dimensions of Tourism and Hospitality studies. She has been teaching at the University of South Australia since 1998 in a number of core areas in Tourism and Hospitality Management. She is currently the Course Co-ordinator and Lecturer for the undergraduate course Managing the Hospitality Experience and the postgraduate course Festivals and Events. Her PhD thesis explored the everyday experiences and challenges of hotel receptionist work. This led to subsequent explorations of the cultural and emotional dimension of tourism/hospitality work, sexuality in host–guest relations, explorations of hospitality through the 'gaze' of the guest, and the pedagogy of tourism and hospitality experience. Gee works in the 'expressive' tradition with a preference for qualitative research. She is also affiliated to the Centre for Research in Equity, Education and Work (CREEW).

Laura Gemini is Researcher at the University of Urbino 'Carlo Bo', Faculty of Sociology, member of the Research Lab for Advanced Communication (LaRiCA), Professor of Sociology of Tourism and Theory and Practices of Contemporary Imagery, member of the International Visual Sociology Association (IVSA) and member of the Italian Association of Sociology (AIS).

Freya Higgins-Desbiolles is a lecturer in tourism in the School of Management of the University of South Australia. She holds academic degrees in politics and international relations. She came to academia after 10 years working in the development arena with NGOs such as the US Peace Corps, Community Aid Abroad in Australia and the Global Education Centre of South Australia. Her research in tourism has included a focus on the concerns of host communities, the impacts of tourism, Indigenous tourism and justice through tourism. She has recently worked with Indigenous Australian communities and Palestinians on projects fostering the use of tourism for community benefits. She has served as an advisor to the Ecumenical Coalition on Tourism and has been a member of the boards of the International Institute for Peace through Tourism (Australia chapter) and the Responsible Tourism Network.

Kevin James is Associate Professor of History at the University of Guelph, Canada. His research interests lie in 19th-century Scottish and Irish social and economic history. The author of *Handloom Weavers in Ulster's Linen Industry, 1815–1914* (Four Courts Press, Dublin, 2007), his current projects explore the history of tourism in Killarney, Ireland, and history of the hotel trade in Victorian Ireland. He also has a long-standing interest in public history, and appears in Canada on History Television's hit show *Ancestors in the Attic*.

Lella Mazzoli is Full Professor of Sociology of Communication at the Faculty of Sociology of the University of Urbino 'Carlo Bo', Director of LaRiCA (Research Lab for Advanced Communication) at the University of Urbino, Director of the institute for the vocational training to journalism and member of the Italian Association of Sociology (AIS).

James Moir is a senior lecturer in sociology at the University of Abertay Dundee (Scotland) with a research interest in the application of discourse analysis within visual sociology. This has extended to such topics as representations of body language within reality television programmes; the visual representation of opinions via graphical information in print and broadcast media, and the visual aesthetic of mass produced good in terms of environmental impact. His contribution to this volume maintains this interest by considering the visual nature of tourism as a constructed perceptual-cognitive practice in which 'seeing the sites' is the outcome.

Manuel Mortari works as a Research Officer at the Universidad Autonoma de Madrid, on different projects related to the planning and assessment of heritage enhancement projects. He has a Bachelor's degree in History of Art from La Sapienza University of Rome and a Master's degree in Museology from the Ecole du Louvre of Paris. Before starting his research activity, he worked in the Fine Arts sector as Coordinator of International Art Exhibitions, freelance journalist and art restorer. During the last three years he has joined the Spanish team ascribed to the EU sixth framework programme-funded PICTURE project, as Research Officer working on issues related to tourism, heritage and visitor studies in several Spanish and European case study cities. His experiences in different fields have equipped him with a broad and multidisciplinary array of tools, making him a versatile researcher specialising in Fine Arts and heritage conservation and management.

Jana-Axinja Paschen is currently completing her doctoral thesis on German tourists' experiences of Self and Other in the Australian desert at The Australian Centre, University of Melbourne, Australia. Drawing on psychoanalytical and anthropological understandings of how subjectivity is constituted, her research focuses on issues of collective and individual identities, identity and space, particularly the non-representational aspects of human experience and relationships with the material world. Her research interests also include the geographies of home and wilderness, Indigenous knowledges, postcolonial and cultural theories. She has taught subjects in Australian studies that have a focus on human–land relationships.

Lisa Power is Senior Lecturer in Tourism at Southampton Solent University where she teaches on a range of heritage and attractions management units at undergraduate level. Her research interests lie in cross-cultural interaction and cultural representation and she has recently published papers on creating space for cultural contact through student field trips to The Gambia, West Africa. She is currently undertaking research into Tour Guides and their role as cultural brokers. Her interest in military tourism stems from family connections with the Royal Marines.

Les Roberts is a postdoctoral researcher based in the School of Architecture, University of Liverpool. His research explores the broad intersection between ideas and practices of space, place and mobility, particularly in relation to film. This has formed the basis of a number of publications, with his more recent work focusing on the critical relationship between film, cartography and urban space. Les is currently working on a jointly edited volume on urban landscapes and the moving image to be published by Palgrave in 2010, as well as a monograph on film, mobility and urban space. As part of his current research, Les is conducting ethnographic work amongst amateur filmmakers and community groups in Liverpool and Merseyside and developing an interactive digital map of Liverpool's urban landscape in film, using Geographic Information Systems (GIS) technology.

Sergej Stoetzer, educationalist and urban sociologist, is a PhD-candidate at the Institute for Sociology, Darmstadt University of Technology. His professional background in academia includes research and lectures at the Institute for Sociology as well as research at the institute for higher education research Wittenberg. He completed his studying in Halle a.d., Saale and Berlin. Outside academia, he has worked on urban panoramic photography and with computer vendors developing sophisticated IT-technology for outdoor and industrial appliances. His research areas are sociology of space/place, perception of urban space, visual methods, tourism, architecture and the use of technology in these fields of science.

Peter Willis is senior lecturer in education at the University of South Australia specialising in the education and training of adults. His main research areas at present concern transformative and 'second chance' learning among adults and the relationship between religion, spirituality and civil society. He is particularly interested in ways in which social science in its theorizing can find appropriate and vivid ways to engage with and represent human lived experience with its quest for meaning and interpersonal connection. Before his academic career, he worked initially as a religious missionary priest and then an adult educator in community development and cultural awareness education with Aboriginal and non-Aboriginal people in the outback Kimberley area of North Western Australia and in Central Australia. He wrote about these and subsequent experiences in two books. The first, Patrons and Riders: Conflicting roles and hidden objectives in an Aboriginal Development program (Queensland: Post Pressed) is a critical reflection on the relationship between missionaries and Aboriginal people in the Kimberleys. The second, Inviting Learning: An exhibition of risk and enrichment in adult educational practice (London: NIACE) explores the lived experiences of Adult Education practice in different contexts in Australia over more than 20 years.

Acknowledgements

_____

I would like to thank two friends and research companions, Jo-Anne Lester and Cathy Palmer, for their support and encouragement during this book project. Editing a book is a messy task, dealing with different locations, cultures and software! I would also like to thank Merz for her hard work in providing the organization for the tourism and visual culture conference held at the Centre for Tourism Policy Studies, Dr Jenny Shackleford who provided invaluable editorial support during the final months of preparation and finally Sarah Hulbert, commissioning editor at CABI, who has been a strong supporter of the project from the start: we remain indebted to you!

Peter Burns,
Brighton,
October 2009

Introduction

Peter M. Burns, Cathy Palmer and Jo-Anne Lester
University of Brighton, Eastbourne, UK

We are crammed with stimuli. Capitalism plus electronics have given us our new habitat, *our forest of media.*

(Hughes, 1980, p. 324, italics added)

About Tourism

The Robert Hughes quote from his 1980 tour de force, *The Shock of the New*, made a somewhat prescient point that applies even more in the early 21st century than it did when he wrote it some three decades ago. Taking a cue from a more recent cultural icon (if not commentator), Madonna assures us that 'we live in a material world', and it is argued in this book that tourism is an image-rich cultural and commercial part of the material world (and the ironic double meaning Madonna attaches to her epigram). One only has to consider the rapid transition from the 20th-century passive consumption of visual materials (photographs, brochures, TV documentaries and postcards) to the greater interactivity of the 21st century such as home-made videos, manipulable digital images, interactive websites and the like. This introduction makes it clear that economics, planning, impact studies and even anthropology are not enough to explain tourism in late capitalist systems. In this sense, the time is right to claim that tourism studies have come of age.

If intellectual and cultural acceptance is a signifier of such a 'coming of age', then travel and tourism has clearly arrived: in late 2005 (at London's Hayward Gallery), a group of some 70 artists were invited to articulate their experience of travelling through various countries and cultures at an exhibition, 'The Universal Experience: Arts, Life and the Tourist's Eye'. With credentials such as these, it is hardly surprising that a discrete group of colleagues researching and teaching tourism give high status to visual evidence. Avgerinou and Ericson (1997, p. 287) develop the general argument about the value of visuality a little further:

> Whether we acknowledge it or not, we live in an era of visual culture, in the so-called 'bain d'images', which influences enormously our attitudes, beliefs, values and general lifestyle. The images inundating our environment, be it private or public, come in different forms and through several channels of visual communication. The almost ubiquitous TV set is not the only one to blame. Films, Advertising and New Technologies of printing and reproduction are also responsible for this flood of visual messages.

What is addressed here is that amidst our increasingly visual milieu as highlighted by Avgerinou and Ericson (1997), there exists a rich seam of visual evidence in its various forms that can inform our understanding of tourism as a sensual undertaking dominated by visual imagery. The contributors to this book are specifically interested in how visuality can be embraced not only in research and critical reflection, but also in teaching and learning, and how awareness of visuality as a recurring and dominant theme in tourism can be enhanced and used to best effect.

At a practical level, advertising agencies rely on a variety of print and broadcast media, i.e. visual images, to promote products, cityscapes and landscapes and, uniquely in the case of tourism, ethnoscapes in the form of people's lifestyles and daily routines. On the consumer side, other forms (souvenirs, postcards) contribute to personal social toolkits essential in placing the touristic experience, in shared memory banks (Burns and Lester, 2003). Despite the fact that there has been significant recognition of the importance of visual data in tourism,[1] there are many aspects of 'the visual' in tourism that are empirically under-researched (Feighey, 2003) and as Burns and Lester (2003) have previously posited in quite forceful terms, it is nothing short of astounding that visual images are not used more as both research data and as teaching material within tourism.

Academia's understanding of it as an industry and social phenomenon is nuanced, complex and draws on sufficiently interesting theoretical bases to reinforce the idea proposed by Adrian Franklin (2004), that tourism is a 'relentless force' that is 're-ordering society'. In his view, the way we act in our everyday lives is becoming more like that of a tourist: wanting to live near easily available Italian or Vietnamese food, the urge to take photos of the most mundane subjects, going out for drinks mid-week and not just at weekends . . . it may not exactly fit everybody's personal profile but the data tell us that the service economy is expanding in ways that stretch far beyond the needs of holidaymakers: we are all tourists now! In an essay by the eminent sociologist Zygmunt Bauman (2005) provocatively called 'tourists and vagabonds', he describes tourism as 'the only acceptable form of human restlessness', which in a way has

to be a precursor to his idea of 'liquid modernity' in which society and technology changes so fast we never have time to catch up and assimilate new ways of being before the next idea comes along. Francesco Bonami, who curated the 2005 Hayward exhibition mentioned above, even goes so far as to say 'Whether we travel or not, the modern world increasingly forces us to conform to modes of behaviour that mimic the rituals and structures of tourism and the psychology of the tourist.'

If we accept the premise outlined at the start of this introduction, that tourism is a form of mobility framed by sets of cultural, economic and political phenomena, with its meanings and applications loaded with ambiguities and uncertainties (Franklin and Crang, 2001), then we also have to accept that the rapid growth of the Internet, multimedia and digital images has exposed tourists and host communities to a bewildering array of interpretations and histories of place and culture. So, this book is not so much the nuts and bolts of how the industry works as a sector, but is intended to explore the more nuanced debates about what tourism means in modern/postmodern society. The first question to arise (and one that is not sufficiently addressed) is simply 'why is there so much tourism?' This seemingly disarming question can be answered in several ways. First, a basic history of tourism will offer us economic and circumstantial answers related to increased post-war leisure time, cheap holidays and the potent mix of technology, willingness to travel 'abroad' and the money to do it. Second, more economic answers related to post-war and post-colonial national development initiatives and market diversification including interventions from the World Bank and various donor agencies. However, in more recent times we have entered the more complicated arena of seeking answers related to the social (rather than economic) drivers of tourism where the general consensus is that for the advanced economies, it is an integral and essential part of the postmodern condition.

The 'smoothie' produced by blending diverse elements from politics, culture and ideology

---

[1]See Chalfen, 1979; Uzzell, 1984; Albers and James, 1988; Dann, 1988, 1996; Edwards, 1996; Crang, 1997; Markwell, 1997; Morgan and Pritchard, 1998; Markwick, 2001; Pritchard, 2001; Echtner, 2002; Garlick, 2002; Echtner and Prasad, 2003; Burns, 2004; Scarles, 2004; Palmer and Lester, 2007.

can at one level be described as the world's largest industry (if that is to be believed) but at a more profound level as part of our *everyday* existence.

We clearly need to see tourism as more than a supply chain ending in deckchairs and ice creams. It is part of the mass-mediated, post-industrial, postmodern society that has spawned tourists who seek instant gratification in the dreamscapes, landscapes, ethnoscapes and heritagescapes[2] created and provided by the tourism sector.

The place of tourism in visual culture, as spectacle, voyeurism, metaphor or phantasmagoria, is well established but seemingly so embedded that it is somewhat neglected or overlooked in what might be described as a problem of ubiquity – both of images and tourism itself. Tourism, as a prime manifestation of social change, has the ability to act as a vehicle for showing how visual discourses of leisure can be located in 'the practices, politics, and poetics of cultural and visual representation' (Schwartz and Ryan, 2003, p. 4). There is no such thing as unmediated tourism and certainly no possibility of unmediated corporeal, digital or mechanical images. It is no coincidence that photography and tourism have, in many respects, a shared chronology and history not only in respect of their development over time, but also in the patterns of commoditization, liquidity and common occurrence in post-industrial, postmodern societies. By going someplace else to compare ourselves with others, we re-affirm our own identity and in so doing take comfort in our 'search for happiness' (de Botton, 2002, p. 9). This volume has a strong common core running through it: tourism's visual culture. It brings together a collection of cutting-edge methodological applications, innovations and original empirical works to examine some important implications for society through its engagement with tourism.

In describing his first foray into analysing tourism via the gaze in early 1990, Urry makes the point that he underestimated the growing significance of both globalization and in particular, the Internet (in its form as a global phenomenon). 'Indeed' he says, 'the Internet had only just been invented and there was no indication how it would transform countless aspects of social life.' Picking up on Roland Robertson's sociological take on globalization, Urry goes on to say 'Overall the 1990s have seen remarkable "time-space compression" as people across the globe have been brought "closer" through various technologically assisted developments.' There is increasingly, for many social groups, a 'death of distance' (Cairncross, 1997), while Bauman describes the shift from a heavy, solid modernity to a much more fluid and speeded-up 'liquid modernity' (2000). Both Cairncross's and Bauman's concepts resonate through tourism studies.

Tourism is an essentially visual experience: we leave our homes to travel to see places, thus adding to our stock of personal knowledge about and experience of the world in the hope of finding novelty, renewal or our authentic selves in the company of like-minded others. These social practices were contextualized and developed by John Urry (2002), who took 'the aestheticisation of consumption' (2002, p. 15) as an overarching theme to consider the importance of tourism as both an agent and signifier of social change in a postmodern world.

The Rhetoric of the Image

In a discussion on the political ideology of aesthetic idealization, Bernard Edeleman describes photographic images as a 'legal fiction' (Mitchell, 2003, p. 57), while Kember (2003, p. 202) expresses some angst over the photographic realism 'Computer manipulated and simulated imagery appears to threaten the truth status of photography even though it has already been undermined by decades of semiotic analysis.' For any discussion on the visualities arising from tourism and tourists, Kember makes a crucial point about how photography mediates and intervenes in an understanding of the world. Walter Benjamin would recognize these arguments as rooted in the Frankfurt School's concern with 'the relation between public spheres of debate and activity and the private, and also

---

[2]These 'scapes are of course inspired by Appadurai's 1996 work on globalization.

with the social role of art' (Wells, 2003, p. 15) and Benjamin's particular preoccupation with 'the nature of photography as a creative act' and the social consequences of 'the mass reproducibility of images' (Wells, 2003, p. 15). It can be seen that in a style increasingly characteristic of tourism studies, a variety of disciplines and theoretical standpoints are brought to bear on this collection of essays themed around tourism and visuality.

Structure of the Book

Taking a cue from Susan Sontag who said 'Photographs, which cannot themselves explain anything, are inexhaustible invitations to deduction, speculation, and fantasy' (1977, p. 23). This book explores, in various ways, the relationship between tourism and visuality. In so doing, the 17 chapters contribute to what has become a growing interest and body of knowledge defining the contours of the visual culture of tourism.

Kathleen Baker for example discusses how the changing nature of the gaze has affected the evolution and use of the hill stations of India. Created during the British colonial era, the hill stations not only offered a refuge from the heat of the summer they also provided a temporary refuge from the Other; a refuge that was essentially English in both character and form. After close on 60 years of independence, Baker shows how the gaze of a different type of visitor continues to influence and mould the hill station experience.

The undercurrent of nostalgia in Baker's chapter leads us into the chapter by **Roberta Bartoletti**, which offers a fascinating exploration of what she refers to as 'memory tourism', a form of tourism arising out of the commodification of nostalgia. Drawing upon the analysis of visual data and literary text and the findings from observational research undertaken at sites in Switzerland and former East Germany, Bartoletti sets out the social and cultural context supporting the emergence of this form of tourism. Memories of travel are also explored by **Teresa Costa**, who examines the travel-related narrative within the work of the American painter Edward Hopper. An enthusiastic traveller, many of Hopper's paintings reflect his travel experiences by depicting travel aspects such as transport, hotels and scenic landscapes. In discussing selected paintings, Costa highlights the link between painting and photography, between the painter's gaze and that of the photographer. Recognition of the canvas/photograph link causes Costa to pose and explore an interesting question, how far can the tourist gaze be rendered in paint?

The painted image moves to the printed image in **Kevin James**'s chapter on late 19th-century guidebooks and travelogues. James highlights the role of such artefacts in prefiguring the Irish landscape for promotion to the domestic tourist market in Great Britain. James discusses how visual images and text were specifically employed to enable parallels to be drawn between Ireland and more fashionable resorts of the time such as Germany, Norway and Switzerland. Visual imagery was further used to make comparative links between Ireland and other destinations within the UK, e.g. the English Lake District, Wales and the Scottish Highlands. Through his discussion, James illustrates how efforts to promote Ireland in this way were influenced by the political and economic imperatives of the day. Following on from the contemplation of landscape, **Jana Paschen** presents a fascinating, multi-layered reading of place through her examination of Uluru, a sacred Aboriginal site located in Central Australia. Through interviews and observation, Paschen reveals how the tourists she encountered learnt to appreciate other ways of seeing and understanding the landscape. In so doing, the seeming universality of Western knowledge production is challenged by the older, mythical approach to knowledge production of Aboriginal culture.

A focus on landscape moves to the contemplation of the cityscape with **Sergej Stoetzer**'s chapter, which offers a semantic analysis of the gaze to illustrate the way in which spaces – specifically urban and tourist spaces – are visually reproduced. Photographs taken as the basis for photoelicitation interviews enabled research participants to build digital representations of their favourite parts of the city. In taking their photographs, the participants moved through various 'identity' phases from resident to tourist and back again. Overall, Stoetzer illustrates how reproductions of space can provide interesting insights into the way in which space is conceived and experienced. The conception and use of space is further explored by **Lisa Power** and **Clive Baker**, in the context of the Gurkha Museum in England. Whilst the museum clearly documents the military history of the Gurkhas and their association with the British armed forces, it also concentrates on the social and cultural heritage of the Gurkhas' homeland, Nepal. Power and Baker discuss how the layout and content of 'museum space' structure the visitor experience, and thereby the way in which the story of the Gurkhas and the Nepalese people is intended to be read. For Power and Baker, a quick glance or a deeper gaze reveals very different aspects of the story, not least of which is the absence of the soldier's voice.

Speaking of absent voices, **Freya Higgins-Desbiolles** offers us the often-absent voice of the researcher. Casting aside the normative necessity for objectivity, she challenges us to listen to her story and how it has affected her research. Her self-appointed role as an 'activist academic' means that she has no intention of being anything other than subjective in investigating the power structures that lie behind local difficulties with tourism and that inform our understanding of the crisis of tourism. Her work draws on visual memory and asks what it means to be an academic in a society with increasing gaps between rich and poor. **Stefania Antonioni, Laura Gemini** and **Lella Mazzoli**'s research into local identity in the Italian town of Levanto employs a combination of photo elicitation and focus group interviews to explore the relationship between the gaze of the tourist and the gaze of the local inhabitants. In so doing, they are able to show how local people 'see' and understand the tourism potential of their own town.

Related to this is the chapter by **Elisabeth Dumont, Mikel Asensio** and **Manuel Mortari**, which explores the process of image construction supporting the development of tourism in two European towns – the Belgium town of Mons and the Spanish city of Ávila. Interviews with key stakeholders are among the methods employed to examine reactions to the promotional logo adopted by the local authorities in each destination. Interesting issues emerge from these interviews concerning the mismatch between local resident perceptions of

place and the views of the tourism authority that has the power to decide what and how to promote the town.

The role of the visual in mediating the encounter between tourist, local resident and site/sight provides the focus for the chapter by **Ketwadee Buddhabhumbhitak**. Buddhabhumbhitak draws on the findings from an empirical study of backpackers in Thailand to highlight the disparity between the ideology of backpacking and the actual behaviour of backpackers. By analysing the data obtained from interviews, Buddhabhumbhitak shows that far from immersing themselves in the host culture backpackers do little more than gaze at the people they encounter. Such superficial immersion is felt to be the cause of negative social impacts for the host society. The negative consequences of the gaze also provide the focus for the next chapter. Here, **Gayathri Wijesinghe** and **Peter Willis** explore the lived experiences of female receptionists working in a luxury hotel in Sri Lanka who find themselves the object of a male tourist gaze. The receptionist's account of seeing, knowing and telling incorporates metaphor and poetry to explore and explain what the tourist gaze feels like. The experience presented highlights issues of power and gender as well as the sexualized nature of reception work.

Taking a social constructivist approach, **James Moir**'s chapter analyses the visuality of tourism through a discourse of travel as sight/site-seeing. For Moir, sight-seeing is a form of visual rhetoric where the inner realm of the imagination and the outer realm of 'reality' combine to structure a tourist's perceptual relationship with the destination visited. Moir concludes by arguing that this inner/outer duality represents an under-researched area within tourist studies. Shopping as a form of sightseeing provides the focus of the next chapter. Here, **Hilary du Cros** offers a fascinating view of Chinese tourists' encounter with and consumption of Western goods and services in shopping malls and markets. Employing observation, interviews, video and digital technologies, du Cros highlights how for some Chinese tourists the shopping experience is as much about a visual consumption of the experience of shopping as it is about the purchase of material goods such as watches, suits and jewellery. The connectivity between visibility and visitability is explored in **Maria Cardeira da Silva**'s anthropological perspective of the Mauritanian desert region of Adrar. 'Spontaneous' museums, guest books, placards and photographs are analysed for what they reveal about the tourists' search for cultural knowledge and meaning.

The cultural knowledge supporting the rise of the culinary travelogue provides the context for **David Dunn**'s chapter illustrating the ways in which television employs visual stimuli to authenticate and validate the gastronomic journey. By drawing upon the work of British Chefs such as Elizabeth David, Jamie Oliver and Rick Stein, Dunn reveals how the lingering gaze of the camera stimulates both taste and tastes, and in so doing inspires the culinary aspirations of the viewer. For the final chapter, television gives way to film as **Les Roberts** explores the cinematic geographies mapped in the British director Alex Cox's 1988 film about the English city of Liverpool entitled *Three Businessmen*. Taking the form of a travelogue or odyssey, Robert's argues that the film reveals the contested geographies of tourism, global capital and culture-led regeneration.

What emerge as important themes in the conceptualization of tourism and visuality are nostalgia, the ways in which photographic images act as a mediating element in prefiguring perceptions, the sentimentality of landscapes, the conception and use of space (i.e. space as a social construct), and the negative consequences of the tourist gaze. As these themes show, the digital, corporeal, virtual and conceptual visual landscapes created through tourism in all its guises have brought profound change to all aspects of the human condition. The importance and versatility of 'reading' tourism through the tourist lens will add significantly to our understanding of tourism as a force in changing both familiar and previously remote and unreachable spaces of what in tourism studies are referred to as 'destinations' (though others may refer to the same spaces as 'home' or even 'away'). Simplistic views of destinations as a collection of attractions, modes of transport and varieties of experience have been swept aside as tourism, tourists and their gaze create the need to rethink the concepts and social frameworks used to observe and narrate human experience and history.

References

Albers, P.C. and James, W.R. (1988) Travel photography: a methodological approach. *Annals of Tourism Research* 15, 134–158.

Appadurai, A. (1996) *Modernity at Large: Cultural Dimensions of Globalisation*. University of Minnesota Press, Minneapolis, MN.

Avgerinou, M. and Ericson, J. (1997) A review of the concept of visual literacy. *British Journal of Education Technology* 28, 280–291.

Bauman, Z. (2000) *Liquid Modernity*. Polity Press, Cambridge.

Bauman, Z. (2005) *Liquid Life*. Polity Press, Cambridge.

Burns, P. (2004) Six postcards from Arabia: a visual discourse of colonial travels in the Orient. *Tourist Studies* 4, 255–275.

Burns, P. and Lester, J. (2003) Using visual evidence in tourism research. *Tourism Recreation Research* 28, 77–81.

Chalfen, R.M. (1979) Photography's role in tourism: some unexplored relationships. *Annals of Tourism Research* 6, 435–447.

Crang, M. (1997) Picturing practices: research through the tourist gaze. *Progress in Human Geography* 21, 359–373.

Dann, G.M.S. (1988) Images of Cyprus projected by tour operators. *Problems of Tourism* 3, 43–70.

Dann, G. (1996) The people of tourist brochures. In: Selwyn, T. (ed.) *The Tourist Image, Myths and Myth Making in Tourism*. John Wiley & Sons, Chichester, pp. 61–82.

de Botton, A. (2002) *The Art of Travel*. Hamish Hamilton, London.

Echtner, C.M. (2002) The content of third world tourism marketing: a 4A approach. *International Journal of Tourism Research* 4, 413–434.

Echtner, C.M. and Prasad, P. (2003) The context of third world tourism marketing. *Annals of Tourism Research* 30, 660–682.

Edwards, E. (1996) Postcards-greetings from another world. In: Selwyn, T. (ed.) *The Tourist Image: Myths and Myth Making in Tourism.* John Wiley & Sons, Chichester, pp. 197–221.

Feighey, W. (2003) Negative image? Developing the visual in tourism research. *Current Issues in Tourism* 6, 76–85.

Franklin, A. (2004) Tourism as an ordering: towards a new ontology of tourism. *Tourist Studies* 4, 277–301.

Franklin, A. and Crang, M. (2001) The trouble with tourism and travel theory? *Tourist Studies* 1, 5–22.

Garlick, S. (2002) Revealing the unseen: tourism, art and photography. *Cultural Studies* 16, 289–305.

Hughes, R. (1980) *The Shock of the New: Art and the Century of Change.* BBC Publications, London.

Kember, S. (2003) The shadow of the object: photography and realism. In: L. Wells (ed.) *The Photography Reader.* Routledge, London, pp. 202–217.

Markwell, K.W. (1997) Dimensions of photography in a nature-based tour. *Annals of Tourism Research* 24, 131–155.

Markwick, M. (2001) Postcards from Malta: image, consumption, context. *Annals of Tourism Research* 28, 417–438.

Mitchell, W. (2003) Benjamin and the political economy of the photograph. In: L. Wells (ed.) *The Photography Reader.* Routledge, London, pp. 53–58.

Morgan, N. and Pritchard, A. (1998) *Tourism, Promotion and Power: Creating Images, Creating Identities.* John Wiley & Sons, Chichester.

Palmer, C. and Lester, J. (2007) Stalking the cannibals: photographic behaviour on the Sepik River. *Tourist Studies* 7, 83–106.

Pink, S. (2007) *Doing Visual Ethnography,* 2nd edn. Sage, London.

Pritchard, A. (2001) Tourism and representation: a scale for measuring gendered portrayals. *Leisure Studies* 20, 79–94.

Scarles, C. (2004) Mediating landscapes, the processes and practices of image construction in tourist brochures of Scotland. *Tourist Studies* 4, 43–67.

Schwartz, J. and Ryan, R. (eds) (2003) *Picturing Place: Photography and the Geographical Imagination.* I.B. Taurus, London.

Sontag, S. (1977) *On Photography.* Penguin, Harmondsworth.

Urry, J. (1990) *The Tourist Gaze.* Sage, London.

Urry, J. (2002) *The Tourist Gaze,* 2nd edn. Sage, London.

Uzzell, D. (1984) An alternative structuralist approach to the psychology of tourism marketing. *Annals of Tourism Research* 11, 79–99.

Wells, L. (2003) Reflections on photography. In: L. Wells (ed.) *The Photography Reader.* Routledge, London, pp. 12–18.

1 The Changing Tourist Gaze in India's Hill Stations: Vignettes from the Early 19th Century to the Present

Kathleen Baker

Department of Geography, King's College London, London, UK

Introduction

The aim of this chapter is to explore the major groups of visitors to India's hill stations during the British era, broadly from the mid-19th century to Indian Independence in 1947, and to compare and contrast the gaze of these earliest recorded visitors with that of more modern domestic tourists. Inevitably, we face problems in doing this. First, the term 'tourist' was rarely applied to the earliest European visitors to hill stations, although that was what they were, so instead, the term 'visitor' is used as an alternative to 'tourist'. Second, representing the past is inevitably an act of the present, and however much we try to empathize with the past, we are, nonetheless, observing it through a contemporary lens (Driver, 1992, p. 36). Third, when discussing historical situations we must consider through whose eyes we are seeing history. In this case, the answer has to be through Western eyes, as much of the literature and imagery from the British colonial era in India is based on reports and evidence generated by the British. A comparatively small amount derives from the work of Indian authors.

Concerning more recent times, our explanation of the modern, predominantly Indian visitor's gaze on India's hill stations is also based on Western perceptions. The problems involved with visualizing events (both past and present) are noted by Gregory (1994), while Wright (1947, p. 15), who considers the role of imagination in geography, forces us to reflect on whether we can justly say that there is any congruence between 'The world outside and the pictures in our heads'. Views of the world are transient, and as the world of the 19th century is not one we knew or experienced, we have to rely on literature and imagery produced by authors and artists from that period. Even though we now live in a globalized world where comparisons are frequently drawn across continents and regions, we still face problems explaining the tourist experiences of other cultures. Inevitably, these must be framed within the cultural context of the observer (Lowenthal, 1972), which, in itself, is a limitation. The justification for a Westerner's attempt to compare the gaze of 19th-century European visitors to Indian hill stations with those of modern Indian tourists is indeed thin; however, it is hoped that a combination of the author's personal experience of hill station life in the wake of the Empire,[1] supplemented by secondary source information – fieldwork in

---

[1] The author lived in Yercaud for ten years and has also visited several other hill stations including Simla, Mussoorie and Dehra Dun in the Himalayas; Munnar, Ponmudi and Thekkady in Kerala, and Ootacamund, Conoor and Yercaud in Tamil Nadu. Fieldwork in Yercaud and Ooty was carried out in December 2006 and December 2007.

© CAB International 2010. *Tourism and Visual Culture*, Volume 1
(eds P. Burns, C. Palmer and J-A. Lester)

Ooty and Yercaud in 2006 and 2007 and visits to several other hill stations, both colonial and post-colonial – will ensure that the pictures and explanations in the author's head, though still remaining personal constructions, might to some extent concur with the reality of the 'world outside'.

Before considering the different visitors to hill stations and the factors that may have influenced the construction of their gaze, I first consider the form, function and evolution of hill resorts. Where possible the aim is to generate a visual image of these settlements in pictures, but where such images are unavailable, we resort to words as a means of creating visuality.

Evolution of India's Hill Stations

Most of India's hill stations were created in the colonial era by the British, for the British (Shaw, 1944; Spencer and Thomas, 1948; Thomas, 1948; Reed, 1979; Kennedy, 1996; Kohli, 2002). As their names suggest, they were confined to the hills and mountains, usually between altitudes of 1200 m and 2250 m (roughly 4000 and 8000 ft) and are to be found in the Himalayas and further south on high land in the peninsula. Figure 1.1 shows the locations of some of the major hill stations. It is not quite certain how many there were, but Kennedy (1996) has identified some 60, around 20 of which have developed since independence in 1947. India's hill environments are believed to have been discovered unofficially, by explorers from the East India Company who wanted to know more about the sub-continent (Price, 1908). Other visitors in the early 19th century were soldiers seeking good health, but very soon a far wider civilian population was 'going to the hills' for the same reason (Spencer and Thomas, 1948). Soldiers would return to the plains refreshed and hill stations, with their cooler air, developed a reputation for possessing curative powers. People with fevers or diarrhoea were said to have been restored to health after visiting the hills. 'Going to the hills' in 19th-century India showed certain parallels with 'taking the waters' in the spa towns back home (Urry, 2002). Secretly, those who made these pilgrimages were hoping for cures, but never was it proven that either the hill environments or the spa

waters had healing properties, and the myth gradually faded.

From the early years of the 19th century, growth of the leading hill stations, Simla, Darjeeling, Mahabaleshwar, Ooty and others, was rapid, and throughout the century the hills became increasingly attractive as summer resorts for the European population in India. However, going to the hills was not all that easy for the earliest European visitors, as access was so difficult (Price, 1908). There were no roads, only paths, and in places, these were steep and difficult. Wildlife abounded, some of it dangerous, and no sooner had tracks been cleared than they were overgrown or washed away by the monsoon rains. When at the hill station, comforts would have been few in those early days. All that would have made the whole journey bearable were the cooler temperatures, the reduction in the flies and biting insects, the spectacular scenery and possible meetings with like-minded British explorers and soldiers (personal communication, former hill station residents).

The early 19th century was a time when the British were considering India as a potential settler colony as the climate of hill stations was ideally suited to a British or European population. A particular virtue of the hills, from the viewpoint of the early visitors was that unlike the plains, they were thinly settled. The majority of Indians considered the cool atmosphere of the hills unhealthy and going out into the 'night air' was, and to some extent still is, perceived the surest way of getting a cold (author's fieldwork). If a future settler colony were to be based on the hills, then these hills had to attract colonizers. Kennedy (1996) argues that the adoption of the term 'hill' station was an attempt to scale down the remoteness, the isolation and the overpowering sensation of 'nature untamed' in what was really a mountain environment. Mountains were popular in works of art, and the Grand Tour had brought an appreciation of the Alps to Britain but these picturesque images in no way compared with the magnitude of India's 'hills', particularly the Himalayas. According to Reynolds-Ball (1907, p. 311) 'Himalayas are to the Alps what these mountains are to the Welsh Hills', and though much smaller, even the Western and Eastern Ghats of southern India presented an image of nature as a major barrier to human existence (Fig. 1.2). It was not just that

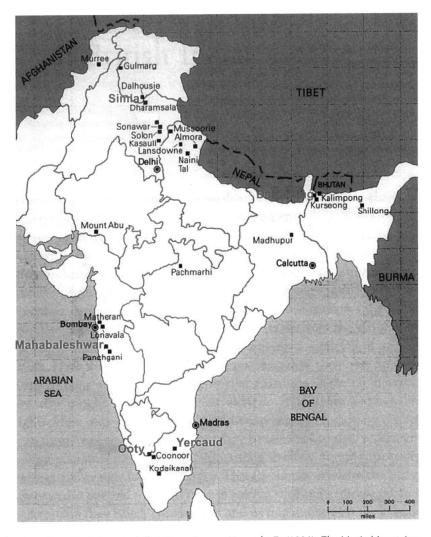

Fig. 1.1. Location of India's major hill stations. Source: Kennedy, D. (1996): *The Magic Mountains: Hill Stations of the British Raj.* University of California Press, Los Angeles, California.

the 'hills' were veritable mountains, clearing the land and keeping it clear was a major problem as the vegetation in this tropical domain grew literally twice as fast as in the temperate zone (Oades, 1988; Kirschbaum, 1995; Six *et al.*, 2002). In an attempt to pacify the environment and to create a sense of the familiar, John Sullivan, the founder of Ooty in 1819, was one of the first Europeans to introduce the seeds and cuttings of trees, flowers and shrubs from Britain and thus to create an illusion of rural Britain in India; an image of Eden.

From the late 1820s, efforts were directed towards making hill stations places that felt safe and familiar. Houses built were of cottage style, with gardens and hedges reminiscent of village England, and familiar seeds and plants from Britain and Europe fortified this image (Figs 1.3a and 1.3b). Darjeeling, Shillong, Ooty, Conoor and other hill stations were the sites of Government Botanical Gardens where saplings of trees, fruit and flowers, garden plants, plants from the wild and from other parts of the Empire were bred and spread through the local hill communities.

Fig. 1.2. The Eastern Ghats, South India, an impediment to human habitation. Source: author (2006).

(a)   (b)

Fig. 1.3. (a) Colonial cottage in Yercaud, recently renovated and extended; (b) virtually derelict cottage in Yercaud. Source: author (2006).

These gardens were used for recreation by European residents and by visitors because of their quiet beauty and because they generated a sense of the familiar through their staged authenticity (MacCannell, 1999). It should be noted that plants that thrived in the Himalayan Botanical Gardens were quite different from those of the south, but there was, nonetheless, some degree of familiarity to be found in gardens of both the north and the south, and the produce of all the gardens contributed to the ordering of the vegetation on the hill stations, and to the taming of nature in these environments. In writings about hill stations, it seems to be taken for granted that the British acquired the land easily, but this was not always the case and Pradhan (2007) reveals considerable tensions in some places between the colonial power and the hill tribes.

When, after the mid-19th century, Simla, Darjeeling, Mahabaleshwar and Ooty received visits from governors and governors-general, the imperial government, which was based on the plains, was persuaded of the benefits of spending at least part of the year in the hills, and subsequently, hill station development became incorporated in state policy (Kennedy, 1996, p. 12). Construction on the hill stations was swift and their physical transformation rapid. Timber was needed for building on the plains and for building on the hills, and this period saw the removal of much of the forest around hill stations. In addition to the need for timber, a more open landscape generated feelings of security in visitors and reassurance that nature was not overtaking human existence. However, within two decades, the folly of heavy felling became apparent: soil erosion became a major problem and landslides increased in number and frequency (Kennedy, 1996). The British response was to re-forest the land using species imported from Australia such as wattle, Australian blackwood and Eucalyptus, species it was believed would further improve the appearance of the hills and encourage settlement. As Table 1.1 shows, hill stations increased significantly from the 1840s to the 1850s and though their numbers grew more slowly after that, the British consolidated their position in the hills (Kennedy, 1996).

Table 1.1. Growth of hill stations in the 19th century.

Date founded	Number of hill stations
1820s and 1830s	12
1840s and 1850s	23
1860s	7
1870s	1
1880s	5
1890s	1

Derived from Kennedy (1996, pp. 12–13).

Several factors came into existence in the mid-19th century, all of which had a bearing on the development of hill stations: first, the colonial administration had become more established by the middle of the 19th century and with thoughts of India becoming a settler colony, the marriage of Crown employees to Indians and Anglo-Indians was restricted. This had been encouraged and became common practice earlier in Britain's presence in India and as a consequence, a significant Anglo-Indian population had grown up (Stoler, 1989; Joseph, 2004; Ghosh, 2006). The restriction on marriage to Indian women saw many more British women coming to India as wives of colonial administrators and soldiers, and travel to India was made infinitely easier by the opening of the Suez Canal in 1869. Unused to the extreme heat of the Indian plains, it was usual for wives and children to spend at least the hottest months of July and August in the hills and this alone contributed to the growth of the hill stations. From the mid-19th century, British women on hill stations outnumbered British men, the only place they did in India, and in their cottage homes and gardens, women reproduced the homeland and its culture. The strict social etiquette that developed on the hills, and that was sustained by women through the home, was perceived as fundamental to the continued survival of the Empire (Kennedy, 1996; Clayton, 2006).

Second, the colonial government's support for spending part of the year in the hills saw hill stations become linked with the administration of the colony. By the turn of the century, hill stations had become the focal points from which the British ruled India. As a consequence, hill stations most closely linked with the colonial administration such as Simla, Darjeeling, Mahabaleshwar and Ooty saw particularly rapid expansion. Simla, which became the seat of the Viceroy and the summer capital for the Raj, developed five satellites, some of which were specifically for the military. Cash crops such as tea, coffee and cinchona had been introduced on hill stations and these too became increasingly important after the mid-19th century. Darjeeling and Ooty benefited economically from tea production, as did Coorg and Yercaud from coffee.

A third reason for the growth of hill stations was that after the Indian Mutiny of 1857, the

British administration became increasingly wary of Indians on the plains. The Mutiny was a major shock to the Raj, which clearly shied away from admitting that perceptions of the Raj by the Raj did not accord with those of the majority of Indians in India. Worlds of perception and reality were thus far apart (Money-Kyrle, 1956), and the insecurity caused by the Mutiny almost certainly fuelled the British retreat to the hills. Here, their comparatively large numbers gave the illusion that they were less of a minority than on the plains. This distancing of the administration from the plains was strongly opposed by government officers remaining in Calcutta and Madras, and also by the growing strength of the Indian Nationalists, who complained that the core of the British Administration was becoming increasingly isolated and out of touch with the pulse of India (Clarke, 1881). In spite of this, the British remained blinkered and pressed ahead with the development of their hill stations, a symbol of their power and domination in India. They left the administration on the plains in the safe hands of Anglo Indians, people trusted because of their close ties with the Europeans and whose very existence according to Said (1979) reflected European possession and mastery of the Orient.

Hill stations declined between the wars and were a shadow of their earlier colonial splendour by independence. Most of the British had gone by then and of those who were still there, most had left by 1960. After a relatively quiet period, hill stations have now been rediscovered as tourist resorts. Predictably, they have quite a different flavour from colonial times. They have grown in importance along with global and domestic tourism, with increasing disposable incomes among India's middle classes (Fernandes, 2000, 2006) and the explicit desire of this group to enjoy their leisure time. Improved technology has enhanced the quality of roads and vehicles, and developments in electronic technology have brought to a wider audience in India and overseas the existence and beauty of hill stations. Bearing in mind all the limitations identified at the start of this chapter, we now return to the visitors to the hills, past and present, and examine how their gaze may have been constructed and how it has changed over time.

The Tourist Gaze

As Urry (2002) observes, 'What makes a particular tourist gaze depends upon what it is contrasted with; what the forms of non-tourist experience happen to be. The gaze therefore, presupposes a system of social activities and signs which locate the particular tourist practices, not in terms of some intrinsic characteristics, but through the contrasts implied with non-tourist social practices, particularly those based within the home and paid work' (Urry, 2002, pp. 1–2). The gaze, however, has its critics: Crouch (2002) argues that major limitations of the gaze are that it is two-dimensional, is limited to the visual and does not speak of engagement with the environment. Crouch (2002) advocates the need to extend the gaze, to include the embodiment of space and the multidimensional experiences of tourists themselves. He observes that the sensing of space by the tourist or visitor is far more complex than the gaze would suggest; however, in our case, proceeding with analysis of the embodiment of space would be extremely difficult in historical settings as access to tourists is impossible. The gaze, however, is arguably a more attractive tool for analysis because it can be based on existing images and cultural stereotypes (Pagenstecher, 2007); thus, unattractive as it may seem to some, the gaze may be constructed by the non-involved bystander. It is this detachment which has made it popular and the tourist industry is arguably one of the worst culprits, as the marketing of destinations is now 'Fordist', according to Pagenstecher (2007), and is based on the constructed gaze of the 'average' tourist who is denied all individuality (Perkins and Thorns, 2001; Coleman and Crang, 2002).

The gaze can also provide the context through which space becomes enlivened by the human conduct, which gives it meaning (Massey, 1994, cited in Crouch, 2002). Using the gaze, as did Foucault (2003, p. ix), for 'the act of seeing' and analysing power relations between medical practitioner and patient, leisure visitors can similarly exert control on the people and environments which are the subjects of their gaze. This is especially relevant to the way in which Europeans gazed upon and saw hill environments, the way they took them for their own and modified them to match their own imported idealized images.

Despite its perceived limitations, the gaze is adopted as the main analytical tool in this chapter and will be used initially to construct the contrasts between the visitor experiences of Europeans to the hills and their daily lives, as we understand them to have been. Where possible, the analysis is extended to include the engagement with space by visitors, or their embodiment of space. In the latter stages of the chapter, the discussion turns to modern India, and here we draw not only on the concept of the gaze, but also on the concept of the tourist glance (Chaney, 2002) to understand better the motivations and experiences of visitors whose access to the hills has been improved significantly by space–time compression (Harvey, 1989), and who experience the environment at a far faster pace than tourists who came before them.

Visitors and their Gaze in the European Era

Some of the earliest visitors to the hills were soldiers, sick or exhausted from the heat of the plains and in need of rest and convalescence (Kennedy, 1996). The gaze of those earliest visitors would have contrasted with their non-tourist experience, which was the work of the colonial government. First, they would have been based in the plains where temperatures were high, frequently over 40°C away from the coastal areas in the heat of the dry season and before the advent of the rains. Other than 'punkas', rudimentary fans, operated manually by an Indian servant, there would have been little to offer the European visitor respite from the Indian heat, which, on the plains, continued oppressively day and night. In the hills, temperatures were much lower and better suited to peoples of European origin. It should be said that Europeans were, for many years, concerned about the tropical climate. The extreme heat was perceived to be the cause of sickness, and diseases such as malaria though the effects of bacteria, extremely active under tropical and humid conditions, were apparently unknown at the time. There was also a strong perception that the hot climate weakened the white man

and that Europeans would die out if they settled in India (Bird, 1863; Kenny, 1995; Arnold, 2004). Stoler (1989) explains this belief more precisely, namely that 'colonial men [were] susceptible to physical, mental and moral degeneration when they remain[ed] in their colonial posts too long', that 'native women [bore] contagions', and that 'white women [became] sterile in the tropics' (Stoler, 1989, p. 636). While there is now evidence to show that such assumptions were erroneous, at the time they were of considerable concern to the Europeans and hence hill stations were perceived as safer environments than the plains. Though the environment might have *appeared* healthy, mountain streams and lakes apparently fresh and clear would have contained bacteria with just as devastating effects as the waters of the plains, especially on the lower hill stations at 1200 m (around 4000 ft) above sea level. Higher stations were undoubtedly safer. Those above 1500 m (approximately 5000 ft) were generally malaria free, but there were never any guarantees. It soon became apparent that the hills did not provide a cure for illness, that people could and did become ill in the hills, but that their rarefied atmosphere was also restorative for European visitors and so the hills remained popular.

In addition to the peaceful environment, there would have been no seething crowds, so typical of major cities on the plains such as Calcutta, Bombay and Madras, where the administration was based. Though the civil lines would have separated the residential areas of the colonial population from the non-colonial, any engagement of colonial officials with the urban areas would have brought them into contact with noise: noise from the sheer numbers of people on the streets; from the shouts of mobile vendors selling their wares; from daily temple rituals where loud clashing of cymbals, ringing of hand bells and discordant music from a range of instruments summoned the holy to gaze on the temple deity; from the processions and noise that accompanied weddings, temple festivals and other celebrations, and from mosques where the Muslim faithful were called to prayer. Most of these sounds were virtually absent in the hills. Neither would there have been the persistent swarms of flies and biting insects, nor the smells of urban life on the plains, just peace and quiet during the day, with the exception of birdsong, and at night, the noisy silence of insects such as crickets, of night birds and the call of prowling animals in search of prey.

In addition to providing a contrast with the plains, the hills would also have been reminiscent of Britain and other parts of Europe, and a substitute for returning home to England (Kennedy, 1996). The vastness of the hills and their untamed appearance was doubtless daunting for some of the earliest visitors, though once at hill stations such as Ooty, Coonoor and Yercaud in Tamil Nadu, the gentle rolling scenery was more evocative of the English Downs. Cool temperatures would have been similar to those of temperate Europe; hills draped in cloud and mist would have reminded visitors of European landscapes (Reynolds-Ball, 1907). When the mists lifted (Fig. 1.4), glorious weather, rarely too hot, would have evoked memories of summer days in Britain and Europe. Facilities and accommodation on the hills were poor, virtually non-existent in the earliest days of settlement but the feelings of being close to nature would have been some compensation. Being people who were clearly adventurous (these early visitors had undoubtedly taken considerable risks

by joining the colonial service or the army), the joys of hiking in the mountains, of watching both birds and animals and of hunting the abundant wildlife would have been exhilarating and a welcome contrast to daily life on the plains.

Another contrast would have been the local inhabitants. In the south, many, though not all the hill tribes were gentle people with well developed subsistence skills, who lived close to nature. British visitors to Ooty were charmed by the Todas with their long hair in ringlets (Fig. 1.5), their quiet pastoralism, and their unusual and attractive beehive-shaped huts. Some thought the Todas were related to peoples of the Bible, inhabitants of an Eden (Kennedy, 1996) and Fig. 1.6 reveals a 19th-century representation of Ooty's hills. Here we see Europeans gazing on a romantically constructed Toda family and their buffaloes – a scene almost biblical in its form, of people in peaceful harmony with nature. Similarly, on the Shevaroys, the elegant manner of the Malayalis, who would stride effortlessly for miles across the hills, appealed to the European visitors, as did the Woddas – stone masons with a gentle demeanour and incredible strength. Both men

Fig. 1.4.   Mist-covered hills of Yercaud, Eastern Ghats. Source: author (2007).

(a) (b)

Fig. 1.5. (a) Toda woman with her hair in ringlets; and (b) Toda temple, the model for traditional Toda dwellings. Source: author, The Botanical Gardens, Ooty (2007).

Fig. 1.6. Romantic image of Toda family with their animals, observed by people in European dress, drawn 1856. Source: Price, F. (1908) *Ootacamund: A History*. Asian Educational Services, New Delhi. Reproduced with permission from Asian Educational Services.

and women carry remarkably heavy stones, and the Woddas' capacity to break and dress stone for any purpose with the simplest of tools was a constant source of amazement to Europeans (personal communication, hill station residents). The hill tribes were thus a major contrast to European visitors' experience both on the plains and in Europe, and they thus provoked considerable interest.

The earliest visitors to hill stations would have taken their time to absorb their new environment. They would have stayed weeks, probably months in recuperation and restoration, and it could be argued that the concept of the gaze (Urry, 2002) could be taken further (Crouch, 2002), as visitors engaged with the environment, participating in the peaceful existence of the hills. Their impressions of the hills, be they a reflection of gaze or embodiment in the environment were recorded in sketches and paintings (Price, 1908; Kennedy, 1996). Images produced were picturesque, focusing on the beauty of the landscape rather than the harshness of life faced by either Indians or Europeans. Scenes such as those from Ooty and Conoor reflected gentle, rolling landscapes, unthreatening and reminiscent of the temperate West (Price, 1908). Figure 1.7 shows St Stephen's church in Ooty, set against a background not dissimilar to the English Downs. Wending their way to church is a small family, more typical of a European than an Indian family, portrayed with a sentimentality that evokes the European's pride in their conversion of Indians to Christianity. As with Fig. 1.6, Fig. 1.7 also exudes paternalism, peace and safety – something that would have attracted visitors. Similarly, images of the Himalayas represented the sublime, awe-inspiring magnificence of the mountains at one extreme

and gentle beauty of the landscape with its animal and bird life at the other (Pradhan, 2007).

The Tourist Gaze at the End of the 19th Century

By the turn of the century, most hill stations were much larger and more established. Visitors intent on work, rest and play included members of the Administration, their wives and families, and inevitably, the army. Access had improved. Unmade roads were now much more than tracks, though they frequently fell into bad repair in the rainy season. To improve the reliability of access, railways (Fig. 1.8) were constructed by the British (using Indian labour) at Darjeeling, Simla and Ooty. For most other hill stations, visitors would begin their journey on horseback or in a horse-drawn cart where the road was not too steep. Once the road became too steep the horses would be taken back to the plains and the journey continued on foot or, for women and children, in a sedan chair, which

Fig. 1.7. Ootacamand St Stephen's Church. Source: Price, F. (1908) *Ootacamund: A History*. Asian Educational Services, New Delhi. Reproduced with permission from Asian Educational Services.

Fig. 1.8. The Nilgiri railway – Udagamandalam to Mettapalayam. Source: author (2007).

put enormous strain on the Indian porters. On the steep road to Yercaud, the porters were frequently bold enough on the steepest parts to refuse to carry the sedan chairs with their occupants unless their wage was increased (personal communication, Yercaud resident). Luggage would have been transported by horse or bullock cart as far up the hills as possible, and beyond that, it would have been head-loaded by porter. The journey to the hills would have been time consuming and exhausting for all involved, but mostly so for the porters, whose interests were little considered. In spite of the exhausting journey, hill stations remained popular as the visitor's gaze was set on the pleasurable experiences that lay ahead and the contrast with the daily grind for men of the administration based on the plains, and for their wives.

Simla had become the summer capital for the administration of all of India, and Ooty was the summer capital for the Madras Presidency, and similarly, Mahabaleshwar for Bombay. By the late 19th century, European visitors were more numerous than in the past: many colonial administrators came on leave for the hottest months of the year, and some of these stayed longer in the hills to continue the business of government. The wives of colonial administrators based on the plains came to the hills with their husbands, or ahead of them to enjoy a longer summer break. Some came with their children to escape the heat, and some came to visit their children in boarding schools on the hills. These were similar to many of today's leisure tourists. Significant numbers of soldiers would also spend their leave in the hills but colonial administrators and their families had comparatively little to do with soldiers in the ranks. Only the officer classes were considered socially acceptable, and only the most senior ones at that. Missionaries were also among the visitors to the hills and all too frequently were excluded from the society of senior officials of the Crown. The social hierarchy was thus clearly structured and in many ways bore a resemblance to India's caste system. Moving from one level to another was extremely difficult.

If we are to understand how the tourist gaze was constructed, we must first have some understanding of what the lives of the visitors were like when they were not in the hills. A high proportion of visitors would have been in the

British Colonial Service, the people who governed India. Graduates from British universities, these men were trained for their work in India. Most eventually rose to be District Officers, responsible for several hundred districts, the basic administrative units in India. They would have had the help of no more than a handful of British and Anglo-Indian officials, who would be concerned with the practical issues of government and communication with the higher echelons of the administration. They would have had to deal with tax collection, labour problems, local conflict, rising Nationalism, local disputes, issues of law including tax disputes, with the education of staff for the administration (Frykenberg, 1986), with local problems such as disease epidemics, famines and attacks on local people by wild animals. They would also have had to coordinate the activities of other branches of the colonial administration within the District, for example, the Forestry Service and the Survey of India. Though life in the Colonial Service is frequently portrayed as one of self-indulgence, of being waited on by servants, and of lavish social activities, and though there is much truth in this, the work of Empire was nonetheless challenging, personally demanding, often difficult and sometimes dangerous. The numbers of administrators were comparatively few and their levels of responsibility substantial. Indians were often treated harshly and with derision, possibly a result of the power bestowed on colonial officials, whose perceptions of their own superiority may well have been reinforced by the negative sentiments expressed about Indians since the late 18th century in Britain, by authors such as Dow (1770) and Macaulay (1907) (cited in Arnold, 2004). Most colonial officers were committed to the success of the Empire, and as a consequence, theirs was often a life of worry, of loneliness through separation from their families, at times of being hated, attacked, and in some cases killed. With this as a background, the desire to get away to the hills for respite is clear.

Besides District Officers, there were many others who assumed significant positions in the administration, including officers in the Forest Service, the Education Service, the Survey of India, the Police and the Political Service, which was made up of officers from the ICS or the Army, and whose principal role was to work with the many princes who ruled large areas of India, overseen by the British. Other officials were involved in the Medical Service and played a role in commercial enterprise such as quality control on produce from India's tea, coffee and jute plantations. For these too, work could be arduous, and although most would probably have had a higher standard of living than they would ever have achieved in Britain, nevertheless, this came at a price as theirs was a working life in relative isolation and trips to the hills would thus assuage their thirst for Western company.

India's Colonial Administration was virtually all male, though some wives did play major roles in their husbands' work and became very involved in Indian life. Some wives went up to the hills for most of the year but the hardier among them would remain with their husbands, keeping a close eye on local conditions and participating in their husbands' work where they were able. As the following quotation indicates, some women made stalwart efforts to learn the local language.

> You had to learn the language even as a woman, or you missed so much . . . I had a munshi to teach me, but he always taught along military lines, because that was what he was used to. He would say, 'Go to the adjutant, and tell him that number 3 company has mutinied.' And all I wanted . . . was how to say, 'The meat is tough.'
>
> (Patricia Edge, whose husband was in the Army and the Survey of India. Source: http://www.lib.lsu.edu/special/exhibits/india/chap2)

The role of the army was to keep the peace throughout India and consequently, soldiers were stationed in remote cantonments with few sources of entertainment, the North West Frontier being one example. Some were already stationed on the hills, such as the satellites around Simla, or at Ooty, but where they were in the heat of the plains, the hills had considerable appeal for periods of leave. They offered a rich social life and a relative abundance of women, Indian, Anglo-Indian and British, many of whom were prepared to enjoy, or endure, the attentions of the soldiers.

The impact of Christian missionaries, like the colonial period, was also at its strongest between the late 19th century and the end of the First World War. However, they were viewed with some degree of suspicion by the higher echelons of society on the hill stations. Christianity in colonial India came from several missionary sources: the Society for the

Propagation of the Gospel, an Anglican mission; the London Missionary Society, where the Anglicans joined forces with the Presbyterians; Baptist, Methodist, Congregationalist and many other missionary societies, from Britain, from Europe and from America (Cox, 2002; Kent, 2004). Despite their best intentions of converting the heathen to Christianity, missionaries were given a wide berth because they were educating Indians, teaching them English, as this was the medium through which conversion could take place. Clearly, a religion that taught that all people were equal was appealing to the oppressed, and missionaries' close involvement with the poor encouraged the conversion of many from the lowest castes and the casteless. This infuriated the higher castes who had much to lose through the liberation of the lowest in the caste system. Some missionaries also used their role to advance the status of women (Sawant, 2000), and predictably, this was not welcomed in Hindu society. The potential for missionary work to cause serious problems for the Colonial Administration was clearly recognized. Since the mid-18th century, the East India Company had become increasingly anxious that the actions of the God-fearing missionary could threaten their commercial activities in India (Kitzan, 1971; Daughrity, 2004), and the murder of three Australian missionaries in China in the late 19th century reinforced this concern (Welch, 2005). A further reason why missionaries were not welcomed by all on hill stations was that their objectives were best met by their close involvement with Indians, especially the poorest and most oppressed, people usually ignored by the majority of the British in India. Missionary work was also a calling for many single women and this too was perceived as suspect by some. Nevertheless, their work of spreading the Christian gospel found favour with Europeans and Fig. 1.7 is testimony to this. Though few missionaries participated in the extravagant social life on the hills, the cool air of the hills and the opportunity for relaxation were welcome relief from their labours of teaching English, preaching Christianity and fortifying the poorest, in particular women on the plains (Sawant, 2000).

The anticipation of getting away from the plains, from India and from Indians by many of the visitors to the hills was, to some extent confounded as the more the hills were transformed to accord to an image of Britain and escape from India, the more labour was needed from the plains in order to make the vision a reality. Labour, permanent and temporary was needed to construct roads, railways, bridges and buildings; labour was needed to maintain public spaces, to service clubs, reading rooms, tennis courts and offices of the administration; to act as house servants, cooks, gardeners, *ayahs* to help look after children, *syces* to look after the horses, and to meet many other British needs. Kennedy (1996) estimated that every visitor required approximately ten Indians to sustain their life on the hills. Rather than getting away from India and Indians, colonial administrators coming to the hills would have been just as close to the colonized as they were on the plains, but although Indians were all around, they, as 'the other' lived quite apart from the British, usually in overcrowded areas poorly provided with services. The picture of Coonoor bazaar (Fig. 1.9) aptly shows the concentration of crowded Indian dwellings at the foot of the hill. The solid, spacious buildings of the colonial administration located nearer the top are not clearly evident on the picture but the contrasting constructions are still visible to visitors.

The gaze of the colonial administrator in the hill stations would thus have consumed on the one hand a model of rural England, and on the other, the very clear contrast with colonial India, which was the context for the idyll. It is highly probable that the sharply contrasting situation of Indians in their dwellings would have been ignored or gone unnoticed by most visitors, though not by missionaries who would have been powerless to change perceptions of the Indian by the British, had they wished to do so. In analysing the gaze of British visitors on the hill stations, it is arguable that 'gaze' is not sufficient to understand the experiences of the visitors who enjoyed not only rest and relaxation but an active sporting and social life as well (Perkins and Thorns, 2001). Perhaps, in regard to this group, Crouch's (2002) appeal for understanding the embodiment of space on the hills and the very different experiences of the visitors, which contrasted with the norms of everyday life, might be more apt.

Idyllic images of Britain, which contrasted with life on the plains, were constructed physically in every hill station, be it Simla, Darjeeling,

Fig. 1.9.   Crowded dwellings around Coonoor bazaar. Source: author, Coonoor (2007).

Ooty, Conoor or somewhere as small as Yercaud. They all had features in common: at the centre of each was the Anglican church, the club which was a particularly British institution (Sinha, 2001), reading rooms, tennis courts and a lake probably created by damming a stream (Price, 1908). In addition, there were opportunities for hunting, shooting and fishing and all such pursuits favoured by the English gentry and widely adopted by Europeans in India (even though they might never have participated in such sports, were they in Britain). Ooty's hunt club, for example, which dated from 1835 was renowned and continues to this day to meet once a month to charge through the Nilgiris, chasing the scent of a jackal rather than a fox (*Independent on Sunday*, 2005). Images of huntsmen in their deep pink uniforms remain – a lingering legacy of Ooty's colonial past. This engagement with the landscape is not peculiar to the European visitor to India and has been noted in Perkins and Thorns' (2001) analysis of current international tourists in settler societies such as New Zealand.

Social life on hill stations also contrasted markedly with the plains: it was more abundant, lively and was taken extremely seriously (Crossette, 1998). The hills were the place where young men and women could meet, as other opportunities were comparatively few. There was a sense of excitement and anticipation at the balls and the dances, which were used as 'coming out' occasions for young women, announcing their readiness for marriage. European society on the hills rippled with frisson as rumour, gossip and scandal abounded (Kennedy, 1996). Social life was all the sweeter because the gender balance was fairly equal, contrasting with the plains where men far outnumbered women. Also, schools in the hills were good and many tried to re-create the British public school in India: institutions such as Bishop Cotton's school in Simla; St. Paul's of Darjeeling; St. George's College, Mussoorie; St. Joseph's of Coonoor; the Lawrence School at Lovedale, near Ooty, and to a lesser extent in the colonial era, Montfort and the Sacred Heart Convent in Yercaud attracted children of the Raj (Fig. 1.10). These and many others had clear religious affiliations and were renowned for their academic quality. Even more importantly, such schools enabled children to be educated

(a)   (b)

Fig. 1.10. Schools from the colonial era: (a) Sacred Heart Convent, Yercaud; (b) Breeks School, Ooty. Source: author, Ooty and Yercaud (2007).

relatively close to their parents, or at least, to their mothers.

In their attempts to re-construct and pre-serve Britishness in India, an increasing ritualistic importance became attached to the perpetuation of social traditions that had their roots in Britain (Kanwar, 1984). In the major hill stations, dinners were formal affairs and Crossette (1998) writes of numerous full-dress balls and costume-party evenings. In places like Simla, Darjeeling and Ooty, the best wines and champagnes were drunk regularly and food not easily available today was made available for officials of the Crown. Women who ran the households for their husbands (Blunt, 1999), especially wives of senior colonial administrators, would have ensured that fine food was served on tables set with fine linens, silver cutlery and crystal. This opulence was all part of the perception that maintaining high standards was key to the continuation of Empire. Standards of etiquette and behaviour were arguably taken to extremes, exceeding those in Britain. They were perceived as strengths by those who upheld them, and were used to emphasize to the Indian one of the strengths upon which Empire was based. Between social events at clubs and summer residences, the British on the hills enjoyed horse races, horse shows and gymkhanas. It was an absolute necessity to be able to ride well where roads were poor and many Crown officials were army-trained horsemen. Shooting (game) was another pastime, mainly

but not exclusively for men. Amateur theatricals, bridge parties, whist drives and mah-jong evenings all provided amusement, and for those hours of rest and relaxation, local libraries provided literature to suit a variety of visitors. Painting and sketching were popular and in the majority of colonial homes, it was possible to find at least one home production of Monarch of the Glen, or similar artistic construction. Crossette (1998) notes that besides the lavish social events and relaxation there were also assignations to enliven long afternoons and dark mountain nights.

Excessive extravagance was confined largely to the major hill stations. The smaller settlements where official functions were limited were much more prudent. Nevertheless, even at these stations visitors from the plains looked forward to a relatively rich and lively social diet for the duration of their stay and the anticipation of all this conditioned the visitors' gaze. The lives of Indians were largely ignored except where they formed a regular part of the workforce or where the 'otherness' of the hill tribes interested European visitors.

The Tourist Gaze in the 1950s and 1960s – the End of an Era

Hill stations had declined significantly after their heyday, which lasted from the late 19th century until the end of the First World War. After this, travel to and from Britain improved, and following the end of the Second World War in 1945 and rising Indian Nationalism, it was clear that the last days of the Empire were looming. Fearful for their future, many British residents returned to Britain. There was also significant migration from the hill stations to Rhodesia, South Africa and Australia, for in spite of their allegiance to Britain, many residents who were second-generation British in India knew no 'home' other than India, and fearful of the British climate, they chose to live nearer the equator than in Britain. With India's independence in 1947, the Administration with its enormous retinue left India, and so did the British army. European visitors to the hills declined significantly; property, including tea and coffee estates, were sold to Indians and comparatively swiftly, the social balance changed. By the 1950s, Indians had taken over the clubs, the estates and other social and economic strongholds of the British, but in spite of this, each hill station retained a relic of European dwellers. Some were planters, and some retired from the army or commercial life.

A significant group of visitors to the hills at this time were missionaries who were no longer predominantly European or American but included many Anglo-Indians and Indians. Another still significant group of visitors included British and other Europeans who had returned to Europe but came back to India perhaps once or at most twice to see those who had stayed on. In this period, visitors to the hills also included academics from Europe and North America who were interested in botany, history, health and social change, and retired members of the British army (author's experience). Returning to the tourist gaze, missionaries continued to come to the hills mainly for a rest, not for a lively social life. The Shevaroy hills in particular grew in importance as a 'stronghold' for religious organizations, and many missionaries came to relax and gain strength from their parent organizations. Even in those days, there was mild cynicism towards missionaries by the remaining Europeans. The tourist gaze of visitors from abroad was focused on keeping in touch with relatives and friends, of glimpsing once again the magnificence of the hills, and experiencing with nostalgia, the remaining

richness of an era past. As Crossette (1998) observes, the hill stations may have languished in the postcolonial years, but they were never completely forgotten.

The Modern Tourist Gaze

Stagnation of the hill stations in the years following independence came to an end when domestic tourism began to flourish in India. Robinson (1972) observed the vigorous growth of recreation movements throughout South Asia while noting that they had attracted little attention in the literature at that time. Visitors to Ooty were already on the increase by the early 1970s, and even in Yercaud, the green shoots were visible with the first 'new' post independence hotels established at about this time. Tourism grew rapidly on the hill stations after 1991 when India's economic liberalization policies saw an increase in both the numbers and prosperity of the middle classes. This, together with Indian Nationalism has generated a new progressive image of India both within India and overseas (Bhardwaj et al. 1999; Mawdsley, 2004; Fernandes, 2006; Foster, 2007; Fuller and Narasimhan, 2007). As part of the growing wealth of the middle classes, a leisure culture has developed and with it, increasing demand for leisure breaks. In 1987, an estimated 34.82 million domestic tourists travelled within India for leisure breaks, to visit family and friends, as pilgrims and for business purposes. By 2006, this figure had risen to 420 million domestic tourists (NCAER 2003; Sreekumar, 2005) – an increase of over 585%. A survey by NCAER (2003) revealed that the proportion of tourism households was highest among the urban, middle-income groups. Owing to their increased disposable income, many middle-class domestic tourists are now taking three to four holidays a year within India, and hill stations are proving to be popular destinations (Sreekumar, 2005; India Core, 2008).

But what is it that prompts India's domestic tourists to visit hill stations; what conditions their gaze? What do they expect of the experience, and are their expectations met. How does the gaze of Indian domestic tourists compare or contrast with that of their European predecessors? Broadly, three main groups of domestic tourists were identified during the period of fieldwork: leisure tourists, business tourists and pilgrims. However, owing to constraints of time, fieldwork was conducted mainly with one group – the leisure tourists, who will be the focus of discussion.

Regarding the gaze of the modern leisure tourist, expectations are to a large extent 'conditioned' by Web descriptions of hill stations as this source of information is widely available in India. Over 70% (51 visitors) of the 72 Indian leisure tourists to the hills interviewed in December 2007 claimed to have used the Web to learn more about Ooty and Yercaud. Although each hill station is different, they still share many similarities, and Web images tend to highlight common features of scenic beauty such as the lake, the Anglican church, cottages with their gardens and hedges, a range of local picnic spots, waterfalls, wildlife, sites with panoramic views from the hills, tours of tea gardens and coffee estates and particular features such as the Botanical Gardens in Ooty, the Nilgiri railway, and above Yercaud, the Shevarayan temple. According to OotyIndia.com (2008), visitors are attracted to hill stations because

> they not only offer respite from the dust and pollution of the city but also give people a chance to see the undefiled beauty of nature. The green hills, the cascading waterfalls and sparkling brooks all make the hill stations a delight for the eyes of the city-weary.
> (Available at http://www.ootyindia.com/tourist-attractions.html)

As many of the leisure tourists to the hills are middle-class Indians (Table 1.2), and as the gaze is constructed partly by the contrast with their non-tourist daily lives, I digress now to consider the nature of the working lives of professional middle-class Indians. The characteristics of employment in corporate industry, including the IT sector and major Indian companies operating call centres, are of particular interest, as these are the types of employers included in the sample of tourists in the hills.

It would seem that growing affluence of the middle classes has come at a price: long hours of work, which increasingly absorb not only men but women too, are bringing about changes in social structures. Women are drawing increasingly on the service of others to look after their children while they work, and respondents, particularly younger women, talked about the problems of balancing the demands of family and work (Radhakrishnan, 2008). Pressure at work and a sedentary lifestyle are trapping many who are succumbing to a range of illnesses, including 'lifestyle diseases', defined as coronary heart disease, cancers and diabetes. In addition, there have been growing reports of weight problems, depression and family breakdown among the middle classes (Mehdi, 2007). Though there may be many who are satisfied with their jobs and especially with their incomes (author's fieldwork), the pressures at work, which are increasingly being documented, provide a good basis from which to construct the perceived tourist gaze (Mahapatra, 2007).

Advertisements for virtually every Indian hill station cited on the Web highlight the serenity, calmness and physical beauty of the environment, and almost every single respondent

Table 1.2. Employment of sample of leisure tourists in Ooty and Yercaud, December 2007.

Nature of employment	Ooty (total)	Ooty (women)	Yercaud (total)	Yercaud (women)
IT industries	8	3	6	3
Managers	4	–	3	–
Business	5	–	4	–
Call centres	3	3	4	2
Doctors	4	2	3	1
Lawyers	4	1	4	1
Retired	5	3	6	2
Housewife	4	4	5	5
Total	37		35	

Source: author's fieldwork, December 2006, 2007.

interviewed said that they had come to the hills for 'rest and relaxation', for a break from work, 'to get away from it all' and/or to 'enjoy the natural environment'. These same words were used again and again. Asked exactly what these terms meant, respondents explained that the hills provided escape from the noise, the rush and the pollution of the city; escape from the long hours of work; time to relax with wives/husbands and families in a beautiful setting, and on the hills they felt close to nature.

Discussion: Comparing and Contrasting the Gaze over Time

Getting away from it all (to peace, quiet and 'undefiled nature') embodies similar sentiments to those of the Europeans who so enjoyed 'going to the hills'. While the desire to experience proximity to nature was as strong among European visitors as among modern Indians, it is noteworthy that the colonials were keen to escape the heat, the flies and the noise of the plains, but Indians rarely referred to escaping the heat. Pollution and congestion are more contemporary concerns in modern urban India (Mohanraj and Azeez, 2005). Almost all the modern visitors enjoyed the scenic beauty of the hills and spent much of their time preoccupied with this aspect of their trip. They were far less interested in constructed monuments, even though these were always advertised. It could thus be argued that the values that India's domestic tourists attribute to space on the hills, and the ways in which they engage with it are significantly different from their European predecessors (Massey, 1994, cited in Crouch, 2002). In colonial times a great deal of energy was devoted to mastering, possessing and even transforming space on the hills so that it conformed to predetermined criteria, which related to Britain and the Empire. It was this obsession with recreating the landscape – this staged authenticity – which attracted many visitors for whom returning to Britain was not an option. Many took the beauty of the environment even further, claiming to have found 'paradise' and 'Eden' on the hills (Price, 1908; Kennedy, 1996), a paradise they tried to possess and from which most Indians were excluded.

Most modern Indian tourists, however, have neither such obsessions nor such pretentions, and space on the hills is now invested with very different meanings (Massey, 1994). They are predominantly places of beauty and escape for Indian tourists, and although Europeans also sought to escape to the hills, it was for different reasons and from different pressures. Because the conditioning of both sets of visitors is so very different, inevitably, the eyes through which they see the hills are markedly different.

One notable difference between European visitors and modern domestic tourists concerns travel and the length of their stay on the hills. In the 19th century, the journey was lengthy and tiring and visitors stayed for weeks and months. Today, travel is much easier. With the development of technology in the form of air travel, good roads and cars, travel has become part of the leisure experience, extending the time couples and families can spend together. There is evidence that more families are travelling together now than ever in the past (Varghese, 2005). This brings to mind Urry's (2002) scapes and flows where travel itself becomes part of the scape, influencing the flows of tourists. Along the routes enterprises develop, small at first, responding to increasing demand by tourists for restaurants, local crafts and many other products, access to which adds to the intensity of consumerism and becomes part of the holiday. Hill station visitors were knowledgeable about a range of destinations and were eager to relate where they had been, and where they were going next. The nature of their engagement with the hills accords with the findings of Chaney (2002) and Larsen (2001), who refers to the 'mobile travel experience' where participants are able to experience a moving landscape as immobile observers, glancing rather than engaging any more closely. Technological improvements have increased time–space compression and Harvey (1989) argues that this has enhanced rather than diminished the significance of space and place. However, much depends on the term 'significance'. In colonial times, cultural capital was undoubtedly obtained from visiting hill stations and experiencing British culture for a period of the year. There was considerable snobbery between the hill stations and the clear hierarchy that existed between them would have conditioned the visitors' gaze. Inevitably, this disappeared with the independence of India but it could be argued that the domestic leisure tourist's capacity to ascend one set of hills, take in the scenery, descend to the plains and move on swiftly to conquer another destination is, in itself, used as a form of cultural capital. There is a hunger for seeing as much as possible, for consuming environments by glimpsing and glancing, capturing them on camera rather than engaging more deeply with them (Chaney, 2002; Larsen, 2001). Bell and Lyall (2002, p. 21) argue that 'today's technologies of movement, from aircraft to video camera, both inspire and facilitate new forms of consumption'.

Perhaps one could argue that with modern leisure tourism still relatively new, the experience of travel or travelling hopefully is just as important to India's domestic tourists as arriving at destinations. Perhaps one could go on to advocate that in much the same way as a destination develops and matures (Butler, 2006), a similar progression can be found in the nature of demand by tourists. Initially, the experience of travel itself is of paramount importance; next, a variety of entertainment at destinations is demanded; then the tourist seeks quality of experience at each; this is followed by an overt desire to appear to be learning, benefiting from the experience of being a tourist. The next stage is where, in this age of environmental and social concern, the self-deluding tourist still wishes to continue to consume the environment and its occupants but in a manner that marks them out as being environmentally friendly, not socially destructive, and of benefit to the destination.

At the moment, though they might dispute it, evidence from the field visit showed little depth of interest of domestic tourists in their destinations but far more interest in where they had been, and their travel plans for the immediate future. Does this perhaps show some similarities with tourists at the time of the Grand Tour? Engagement with space has clearly changed, and as factors such as technology now have a major influence on the gaze, it is no surprise that the nature of the leisure visitor gaze on the hill stations has changed markedly over a century.

Escapism is always important in tourism (Ryan, 2002) and that is common to the motivation of visitors to the hills past and present. However, the above analysis does show that while the gaze of the European visitor to the hills was driven by the obsession to escape to the staged authenticity of a replacement for 'home', that of the modern visitor is driven by the headiness of travel and of escape from the growing pressures associated with India's increased participation in the global economy. Perhaps the greatest difference is that the element of staged authenticity is no longer critical to the modern tourist gaze.

Acknowledgements

Grateful thanks are due to many people who helped me with the preparation of this chapter. My thanks, go to many Europeans formerly residents of the hills for providing me with considerable background information, many of whom are no longer alive; to current officials in the Departments of Tourism and Forestry in Ooty; to coffee planters and residents of Yercaud, in particular, Peter and Caroline Wilson, and Mohan Rajes; and to Mother Bernard of the Sacred Heart Convent, Yercaud. I am also grateful to the many tourists who were kind enough to speak to me in Ooty and Yercaud, and to Derek Gurr whose technical help has been invaluable.

References

Arnold, D. (2004) Race, place and bodily difference in early nineteenth-century India. *Historical Research* 77, 254–273.
Bell, C. and Lyall, J. (2002) The place of nature, Section 1. In: Coleman, S. and Crang, M. (eds) *Tourism: Between Place and Performance*. Berghahn Books, New York.
Bhardwaj, D.S., Kandari, O.P., Chaudhary, M. and Kamra, K.K. (eds) (1999) *Domestic Tourism in India*. Indus Publishing, New Delhi.

Bird, J. (1863) On the vital and sanitary statistics of our European army in India, compared with those of French troops under like conditions of climate and locality. *Journal of the Statistical Society of London* 26, 384–405.

Blunt, A. (1999) Imperial geographies of home: British domesticity in India, 1886–1925. *Transactions of the Institute of British Geographers* 24, 421–456.

Butler, R. (2006) *Aspects of Tourism: The Tourism Area Lifecycle, Vol. 1, Applications and Modifications.* Channel View Publications, Clevedon.

Chaney, D. (2002) The power of metaphors in tourism theory. In: Coleman, S. and Crang, M. (eds) *Tourism: Between Place and Performance.* Berghahn Books, New York, pp. 193–206.

Clarke, H. (1881) The English stations in the hill regions of India: their value and importance with some statistics of their products and trade. *Journal of the Statistical Society of London* 44, 528–573.

Clayton, A. (2006) *The British Officer: Leading the Army from 1660 to the Present.* Pearson Education, London.

Coleman, S. and Crang, M. (eds) (2002) *Tourism: Between Place and Performance.* Berghahn Books, New York.

Cox, J. (2002) *Imperial Fault Lines: Christianity and Colonial Power in India: 1818–1940.* Stanford University Press, Stanford, CA.

Crossette, B. (1998) *The Great Hill Stations of Asia.* Westview (www.nytimes.com/books), Boulder, CO.

Crouch, D. (2002) Surrounded by place: embodied encounters. In: Coleman, S. and Crang, M. (eds) *Tourism: Between Place and Performance.* Berghahn Books, New York, pp. 207–218.

Daughrity, D.B. (2004) Hinduisms, Christian missions, and the Tinnevelly Shamars: a study of colonial missions in 19th century India. http://www.arts.ualberta.ca/axismundi/2004/Hinduisms.pdf

Dow, A. (1770) A dissertation concerning the origin and nature of despotism in Hindostan. In: Dow, A. *The History of Hindostan* (3 vols).

Driver, F. (1992) Geography's empire: histories of geographical knowledge. *Environment and Planning D: Society and Space* 10, 23–40.

Edge, P. (no date) Available at http://www.lib.lsu.edu/special/exhibits/india/chap2 (Accessed 12 June 2007).

Fernandes, L. (2000) Restructuring the new middle class in liberalizing India. *Comparative Studies of South Asia, Africa and the Middle East* 20, 88–112.

Fernandes, L. (2006) *India's New Middle Class: Democratic Politics in an Era of Economic Reform.* Minnesota Press, Minneapolis MN.

Foster, P. (2007) India's domestic tourism takes off, 2 May. Available at http://blogs.telegraph.co.uk/foreign/peterfoster/may2007/indiatourismtakeoff.htms (Accessed 18 June 2008).

Foucault, M. (2003) *The Birth of the Clinic.* Routledge (English translation of original 1989 publication), London.

Frykenberg, R.E. (1986) Modern education in South India, 1784–1854: its roots and its role as a vehicle of integration under Company Raj. *The American Historical Review* 91, 37–65.

Fuller, C.J. and Narasimhan, H. (2007) Information technology professionals and the new-rich middle class in Chennai (Madras). *Modern Asian Studies* 41, 121–150.

Ghosh, D. (2006) *Sex and the Family in Colonial India: the Making of Empire.* Cambridge Studies in Indian History and Society. Cambridge University Press, Cambridge.

Gregory, D. (1994) *Geographical Imaginations.* Blackwell, Oxford.

Harvey, D. (1989) *The Condition of Postmodernity.* Blackwell, Oxford.

Independent on Sunday (2005) Bolly Ho! 30 January.

India Core (2008) Tourism (paragraph on domestic tourism). Available at http://www.indiacore.com/tourism2.html (Accessed 19 June 2008).

Joseph, B. (2004) *Reading the East India Company, 1720–1840: Colonial Currencies of Gender.* University of Chicago Press, Chicago, IL.

Kanwar, P. (1984) The changing profile of the summer capital of British India: Simla 1864–1947. *Modern Asian Studies* 18, 215–236.

Kennedy, D. (1996) *The Magic Mountains: Hill Stations of the British Raj.* University of California Press, Berkeley, CA.

Kenny, J.T. (1995) Climate, race and imperial authority: the symbolic language of the hill station in India. *Annals of the Association of American Geographers* 85, 694–714.

Kent, E.F. (2004) *Converting Women: Gender and Protestant Christianity in Colonial South India.* Oxford University Press, Oxford.

Kirschbaum, M.U.F. (1995) The temperature dependence of soil organic matter decomposition and the effect of global warming on soil organic C storage. *Soil Biology and Biochemistry* 27, 753–760.

Kitzan, L. (1971) The London Missionary Society and the problem of authority in India, 1798–1833. *Church History* 40, 457–473.

Kohli, M.S. (2002) *Mountains of India, Tourism, Adventure and Pilgrimage*. Indus Publishing Company, Delhi.

Larsen, J. (2001) Tourism mobilities and the travel glance; experiences of being on the move. *Scandinavian Journal of Hospitality and Tourism* 1, 80–98.

Lowenthal, D. (1972) Geography, experience and imagination: towards a geographical epistemology. In: Davies, W.K. (ed.) *The Conceptual Revolution in Geography*. UCL Press, London, chapter 4, pp. 77–107.

Macaulay, T.B. (1907) *Critical and historical essays*, 2 vols, II, pp. 502–503.

MacCannell, D. (1999) *The Tourist: A New Theory of the Leisure Class*. University of California Press, Berkeley, CA.

Mahapatra, R. (2007) Poor lifestyle takes toll on India's army of call centre workers. *The Sydney Herald*, 30 December. Available at http://business.smh.com.au/poor-lifestyle-takes-toll-on-indias-army-of-call-centre-workers-20071230-1jk3.html (Accessed 17 June 2008).

Massey, D. (1994) *Space, Place and Gender*. University of Minnesota Press, Minneapolis, MN.

Mawdsley, E. (2004) India's middle classes and the environment. *Development and Change* 35, 79–103.

Mehdi, A. (2007) Impact of Preventive Health Care on Indian Industry and Economy, Report commissioned by the ICRIER (Indian Council for Research on International Economic Relations) September. Available at http://www.ethicsworld.org/ethicsandemployees/PDF%20links/FindingsPolicy.pdf (Accessed 27 June 2008).

Mohanraj, R. and Azeez, P.A. (2005) Urban development and particulate air pollution in Coimbatore city, India. *International Journal of Environmental Studies* 62, 69–78.

Money-Kyrle, R.E. (1956) The world of the unconscious and the world of commonsense. *British Journal for the Philosophy of Science* 7, 86–96.

NCAER (National Council for Applied Economic Research) (2003) Domestic Tourism Survey, 2002–03. Sponsored by the Ministry of Tourism and Culture: Government of India. Available at http://tourism.nic.in/survey/dtsurveypdf (Accessed 20 June 2008).

Oades, J.M. (1988) The retention of organic matter in soils. *Biogeochemistry* 5, 35–70.

OotyIndia.com (2008) Nilgiri hills. Available at http://www.ootyindia.com/nilgiri-hills.html (Accessed 18 July 2008).

Pagenstecher, C. (2007) The construction of the tourist gaze. How industrial was post-war German tourism? Available at http://eh.net/XIIICongress/cd/papers/4Pagenstecher392.pdf (Accessed 2 April 2007).

Perkins, H.C. and Thorns, D.C. (2001) Gazing or performing? Reflections on Urry's tourist gaze in the context of contemporary experience in the Antipodes. *International Sociology* 16, 185–204.

Pradhan, Q. (2007) Empire in the hills: the making of hill stations in colonial India. *Studies in Historical Transformation* 23, 33–91.

Price, F. (1908) *Ootacamund: A History*. Government Press, Madras. Reproduced (2000). Asian Educational Services, New Delhi.

Radhakrishnan, S. (2008) Examining the 'global' Indian middle class: gender and culture in the Silicon Valley/Bangalore Circuit. *Journal of Intercultural Studies* 29, 7–20.

Reed, R.R. (1979) The colonial genesis of hill stations: the Genting exception. *Geographical Review* 69, 463–468.

Reynolds-Ball, E. (1907) *The Tourist's India*. Swann Sonnensdiein and Co., London.

Robinson, G.W.S. (1972) The recreation geography of South Asia. *Geographical Review* 62, 561–572.

Ryan, C. (ed.) (2002) *The Tourist Experience*. Continuum, London.

Said, E. (1989) *Orientalism*. Penguin, Harmondsworth.

Sardar, M. (2000–) Company painting in nineteenth-century India. In: *Timeline of Art History*. The Metropolitan Museum of Art, New York. http://www.metmuseum.org/toah/hd/cpin/hd_cpin.htm (October 2004).

Sawant, S. (2000) Savitibai Phule's role in initiating women's education in Maharashtra. Paper (no. 5) presented at the 16th European Conference on South Asian Studies, University of Edinburgh, 5–9 September 2000 http://www.sociology.ed.ac.uk/sas/conf16/panel46.htm

Shaw, M. (1944) Some South Indian hill stations. *Scottish Geographical Magazine* 59, 81–87.

Sinha, M. (2001) Britishness, clubbability, and the colonial public sphere: the genealogy of an imperial institution in colonial India. *The Journal of British Studies* 40, 489–521.

Six, J., Feller, C., Denef, K., Ogle, S.M., de Moraes Sa, J.C. and Albrechtm, A. (2002) Soil organic matter, biota and aggregation in temperate and tropical soils: effects of no tillage. *Agronomy for Sustainable Development* 22, 755–775.

Spencer, J.E. and Thomas, W.L. (1948) The hill stations and summer resorts of the Orient. *Geographical Review* 38, 637–651.

Sreekumar, K. (2005) Domestic tourism booms. *Times of India*, 19 May.

Stoler, A.L. (1989) Making Empire respectable: the politics of race and sexual morality in 20th-century colonial cultures. *American Ethnologist* 16, 634–660.

Thomas, W.L. (1948) The hill stations and summer resorts of the Orient. *Geographical Review* 38, 637–651.

Urry, J. (2002) *The Tourist Gaze*, 2nd edn. Sage, London.

Varghese, N. (2005) Tourism industry upbeat on domestic, foreign travel. Available at http://www.thehindu businessline.com/2005/06/25/stories/2005062501060400.htm (Accessed 18 June 2008).

Welch, I. (2005) Women's work for women: women missionaries in 19th century China. Paper presented to the Eighth Women in Asia Conference 2005. Women's Caucus of the Asian Studies Association of Australia and The University of Technology, Sydney, 26–28 September.

Wright, J.K. (1947) Terrae incognitae: the place of imagination in geography. *Annals of the Association of American Geographers* 37, 1–15.

2 'Memory Tourism' and Commodification of Nostalgia

Roberta Bartoletti

Facoltà di Sociologia, Università degli Studi di Urbino 'Carlo Bo', Urbino, Italy

Introduction

Memory tourism is a quite heterogeneous phenomenon that represents a new frontier in tourism in contemporary society. The social and cultural context from which this new form of tourism emerges is late modernity, which is characterized by a radical crisis of memories – of both collective and individual memory – that is connected to the process of modernization itself. From this crisis of memory, a sentiment of modern nostalgia arises that can be exploited by the market in different ways. One of these ways is what I call 'memory tourism', which can be understood as a new form of commodification of emotions that is functional for the reproduction of both modern society and of the market.

My analysis begins from several basic hypotheses: first, that nostalgia can be taken as a symptom indicating that individuals are ill at ease with the changes in their way of life produced by modernity, including the dissolution of founding collective memories; second, that, when faced with this dissolution of traditional ties and the loss of a strong sense of 'belonging', modern society must identify new strategies able to motivate individuals to participate in its processes of social reproduction, in particular

by keying in to their emotions. Within this framework the market plays an important role. The commodification of nostalgia can indeed be considered one of these strategies and tourism is one of the most interesting areas where we can observe this process of commodification of emotions.[1]

From this perspective, I'm going to illustrate two cases, which I feel to be emblematic of this new frontier of modern tourism that offers nostalgic experiences to consumers: the case of Heidiland and Heididorf in the Swiss Alps, and the case of 'Ostalgia tourism' in the regions of former East Germany. These cases also illustrate two different examples of memory tourism, with different connections to embodied memories and with the social and media imaginery, that in this framework plays a very important role. Finally, I will construct a tentative definition of memory tourism, identifying its main characteristics.

The Study Background: the Modern Crisis of Memories and Nostalgia as a Modern Illness

Before moving on to illustrate memory tourism, I need to provide a brief premise regarding the

---

[1]This perspective is coherent with a performative approach to tourism as experiential consumption, beyond the traditional paradigm of 'sight' (MacCannel, 1999). About the tourist experience as performance, compare for example Coleman and Crang (2002) and Gemini (2008).

actual status of collective and individual memory in modernity that is connected with the emergence of nostalgia as a typical modern illness.

First and foremost, I need to explain the characteristics of modern society that I intend to focus on (Giddens, 1990; Luhmann, 1997). Modern society is characterized by the high degree of contingency not only of its forms, but also of all of its events, relationships and identities (Luhmann, 1992). Contingency means that each phenomenon in modern society is neither necessary nor impossible: there are no longer profound ties and each selective process in society could well be a different one; the society is open to other possibilities that could be actualized in the future. Individuals who are best suited to a highly contingent society are therefore flexible, adaptable and open to new ideas and circumstances.

The relationship that modern society has with memories is itself in turn highly contingent: what is remembered or forgotten could be otherwise, and the ties to founding narratives upon which identities are grounded are becoming weaker and weaker.[2] As a result, social memory in modernity is characterized by its contingency, as well as by its digital nature, in the sense that everything that modern society remembers or forgets – be it events, meanings, or ideas – is no longer part of an organic whole, of something whole that melds its identity, but is instead something that lends itself to being dismantled, taken apart and separated before being reassembled without any particular limitations. In other words, the relationships between what is remembered and what is forgotten as part of social memory are becoming ever more based on a general sense of their equivalence.

When using the term 'collective memory', we traditionally refer to the typically modern meaning of the word given by Maurice Halbwachs (1980, 1992). The collective memory he described in the early decades of the 20th century was already a form of modern memory in that it was no longer unitary nor prescriptive. Indeed, modern collective memory is multifaceted and fragmented, contingent and weakly rooted in individual living memory. It is, therefore, a weak version of the traditional collective memory, characteristic of a community, which was once binding and had deep and prescriptive significance for the groups and individuals involved. A wider-ranging idea of collective memory is that described for example by Jan Assmann (1992): by collective memory, he intends a set of memories that together meld to create the identity and specificity of a group as 'a community which together remembers' (the *collectivité-mémoire* of Pierre Nora, 2001, is very close to this idea). The past that the community together remembers is a mythical past, in other words a founding narrative.[3] Halbwachs observed the fact that these founding memories were undergoing a clear crisis as early as the dawning of the 20th century.

Herein lies the radical difference between the memory of modern society (the social memory) and both the collective memory, characteristic of the traditional communities, and the memory of individuals themselves, which are instead specific and organic, in other words holistic. The memory of individuals resists contingency, in that it contributes to forming personal narratives and identities that are unique and could not be otherwise, and it is this specificity that gives sense and meaning to individual lives and to the world around them.

Within this framework, I believe that nostalgia can be considered a symptom of the dissociation between the contingent, digital memory of modern society and the individual memory, which has retained its holistic and prescriptive nature. From this perspective, nostalgia appears as a typically modern form of individual feeling.

More precisely, nostalgia appeared for the first time in Europe as an illness. Indeed, the word was coined by a Swiss medical doctor by the name of Johannes Hofer, in 1688, to indicate a new form of malaise, which appeared to be striking ever-greater numbers of his countrymen. Dr Hofer defined nostalgia as 'the sad mood originating from the desire for return to one's native land' (Boym, 2001, p. 3). The word nostalgia derives from two Greek roots: *nostos,*

---

[2]The term memory is used to indicate a selective structure that functions by means of the dual operations of remembering and forgetting.

[3]See also Anderson (1991) and Hobsbawm and Range (1983) in relation to national memory.

which means a return home as well as the song of returning home, and *álgos*, that indicates suffering.

The first sufferers hit by this new ailment were individuals who for various reasons were living far from home: not just soldiers and sailors, but also servants working abroad, as well as the many country folk who had abandoned the countryside to work in cities and towns far from home. Their nostalgia appeared to be not only a problem of mental anguish or heartache, one might say a problem of the soul, but also a lack of bodily well-being, as it appeared to be the cause of physical prostration, with symptoms ranging from nausea to lack of appetite, visual and auditory hallucinations or even cerebral inflammation. This individual sense of feeling poorly was indeed so widespread as to be considered of near-epidemic proportions, and even began to be seen as a public health problem.

Thus, nostalgia had already struck in many European nations as early as the 17th century, but only reached the USA later, around the middle of the 1800s, where it was seen mainly in soldiers from rural areas who as civilians had been farmers, while soldiers coming from other professions or in any case from urban environments seemed to be more immune to it. After having tried in vain to find a medical treatment to cure the problem and found that even sending patients home was not sufficient to guarantee their complete recovery, the medical establishment of the 19th century viewed nostalgia as an incurable ailment.

Nostalgia is thus an individual sense of anguish but of epidemic proportions and with collective roots. And it is for this reason that I believe it can be considered an ailment typical of modernity, in so much as it is a result of the irreversible sense of loss that this world produces, after which no true return home is possible. The object of modern nostalgia is in fact not a real, physical location to which it would be possible to return, and the sense of loss we feel instead regards the organic ties, which bound individuals to their community and to the land, to which also correspond organic ties between individual and collective lives, between individual and collective memory, between *bios* and *logos*. This would explain why those who were found to suffer most from a sense of nostalgia were people from rural areas, particularly farmers, those who still had strong ties to their communities and to the world that modern society was dissolving: one could say, in other words, that those who had undergone less socialization toward modernity suffered the most.

Thus, nostalgia arises from this crisis in collective, prescriptive, organic, pre-modern memory. And yet nostalgia is not simply and not precisely an expression of that sense of loss of the rural pre-modern community, which risks becoming a sort of ideal, utopian moment in modern imaginery. Nostalgia instead reveals both individual and collective sensitivity that can be considered a symptom of the persistence of non-contingent memories, despite the fact that concrete, traditional points of reference for those memories (including ways of life, forms of social relationships, objects and their meaning) have now been lost.

And yet, interestingly, nostalgia can also be a resource, in that it represents a form of wish that can't come true – at least in its former authentic sense. While it is true that one can never truly 'return home', it may instead be possible to simulate the existence of a mythical home through its invention and reconstruction. In reality, this will be not a place of memories but rather a place for consumption and entertainment: if the mythical home has disappeared forever, the marketplace can therefore continually re-invent it, creating new occasions for consumption.

Methodology and Findings of the Research: the Case Studies of Heidiland and of Former East Germany

I intend to present the characteristics of this new frontier of emotional tourism and define 'memory tourism' as a modern phenomenon of commodification of nostalgia through two case histories. The first case is that of *Heidiland* and *Heididorf*, the region and the village of Heidi, which have been recently invented in the Swiss Alps and can be understood as a concrete evidence of exploitation of nostalgia by the tourism industry, primarily caused by the disappearing of pre-modern rural life and of the ancestral contact with nature (Bartoletti, 2007, 2009). The second case is that of former East Germany where a 'way of life' that disappeared after the fall of the Berlin Wall was transformed into a supply of nostalgic touristic experiences.

Data were collected through direct observation and participant observation, and through the analysis of both the scientific literature and media products as indicators of media imaginery (primarily newspaper articles, and the Heidi novel and Japanese animated cartoons as different products of the media industry).

The visual data can be considered 'visual indicators' that in this case were produced by the researcher herself during field observation. Visual indicators are one of the tools used in the methodology of visual sociology (Wagner, 1979; Faccioli and Harper, 1999; Gemini *et al.*, 2006). These visual indicators could be used in a subsequent phase of the research, based on in-depth interviews using photoelicitation with actual or potential tourists. The visual indicators that I will illustrate regard three different variables within the imagery of nostalgia tourism:

- Visual indicators of 'nostalgia experiences' that the tourism system 'promises' to tourists (Figs 2.1–2.3, 2.10–2.12, 2.14 and 2.15).
- Visual indicators of 'nostalgia objects': typical objects of memory tourism that can be

seen, bought, visited and so on (Figs 2.4–2.7 and 2.13–2.15).
- Visual indicators of 'nostalgia tourists' (Figs 2.8, 2.9 and 2.16–2.18).

Case study 1 – Nostalgia of the pre-modern past and of kindness: Heidiland and Heididorf in the Swiss Alps

Heidiland and Heididorf, the region and village of Heidi, can be found in the Swiss Alps, in the northeastern region of Bad Ragaz. The link between Heidi and this alpine region is not casual, despite the fact she is a fictional character. It was indeed in this mountain area that, during the second half of the 19th century, author Johanna Spyri spent her holidays and the region most likely inspired her to use it as a background for the story of Heidi.

The 'credit' for having invented the 'Heidiland' trademark must be given to the director of the local tourism board in Saint Moritz, Switzerland, who registered it in the late 1970s, using the name 'Saint Moritz in Heidiland'. In reality, the figure of a humble little mountain girl was inappropriate in promoting such an elite tourist

Fig. 2.1.   Nostalgia experiences: take a walk along Heidi's path through the Heidi village.

Fig. 2.2. Nostalgia experiences: petting zoos and drinking water from a mountain stream in Heididorf.

destination. As a result, the trademark remained unused until 1997, when the rights to it were sold to a chain of highway restaurants and to the region of Bad Ragaz, which needed to give an identity to its tourism initiatives. In 1997, the official trademark for the 'Heidiland vacation region' was created and launched for the alpine tourism district of Sarganserland-Walensee.

In the same year, the town of Maienfeld, which lies just a few kilometres outside the borders of 'Heidiland', decided to defend its own 'rights' to the story, opening and launching what it called 'Heidi's House – the Original' which was also protected by a registered trademark. Maienfeld is indeed the little city quoted at the beginning of Johanna Spyri's first Heidi novel:[4] from Maienfeld starts a path that leads to Dörfli, the Alpine village where Heidi came to live with her grandfather. In its first year alone, Heidi's House in Maienfeld attracted more than 15,000 visitors, more than a quarter of whom were Japanese. In the year 2000, Maienfeld welcomed more than 60,000 tourists – 50% of them from Japan.

After an initial period of competition between Bad Ragaz (Heidiland) and Maienfeld (Heididorf), both of which revendicated the paternity of the orphan, in 2005 the two areas decided to join together to form a single tourism district with a precise shared identity, integrated services and trademark, and thus to work together despite their considerable cultural, social and economic heterogeneity.

What sights and attractions do Heidiland and Heididorf offer vacationers? Undoubtedly, Heidiland and Heididorf allow visitors to experience days gone by, and a rural, pastoral,

---

[4]This was *Heidis Lehr- und Wanderjahren*, published in 1880. The second Heidi novel is *Heidi kann brauchen, was es gelernt hat*, published a year later.

Fig. 2.3. The petting zoo.

Fig. 2.4. Nostalgia objects: Heidi's House – the Original.

Fig. 2.5. Nostalgia objects: Heidi's room.

Fig. 2.6. Heidi and Peter.

Fig. 2.7. The kitchen in Heidi's House.

Fig. 2.8. Nostalgia tourists: Japanese tourists interpreting Heidi.

typical alpine lifestyle, which no longer exists. This is achieved by offering services ranging from excursions featuring picnics with a drink of fresh milk straight from the milk pail, hiking along mountain paths like those Heidi would have used, hunts for the flowers so loved by Heidi, as well as petting zoos and even the chance to accompany the animals as they are put out to

Fig. 2.9. Japanese tourists interpreting Heidi.

Fig. 2.10. Nostalgia experiences: the Nostalgia tour in Berlin, Checkpoint Charlie.

pasture, as Peter, Heidi's beloved friend, did. Along the same lines, visitors can enjoy a drink of clear, cold spring water from a mountain stream and have the chance to visit a mountain shepherd's hut preserved just as it would have been in Heidi's days, or even to sleep in a straw bed just as Heidi did. Obviously, alongside these experiences, which were created above all for

Fig. 2.11. Ostalgia experiences: once upon a time Checkpoint Charlie; false GDR visa.

children, Heidiland offers the traditional activities found throughout the Alps: trekking, skiing, and so forth, but with the added value of the Heidi myth.

And of course, in the little village of Maienfeld, tourists can visit 'Heidi village' and 'Heidi's House – the Original'. In effect, Heidi's House lies at the heart of the concept of Heidiland, since it is the focal point of a mythical world that has disappeared and for which we can only feel a sense of longing, of nostalgia. Heidi's House is a concrete symbol of the home we have lost, reconstructed to be able to offer it to anyone who feels nostalgia, to anyone who wants to experience it. The Heididorf website (www. heidiland.com) explains that 'The authentic house of Heidi has been turned into a museum that reveals how Heidi lived in these mountains over 100 years ago': which of course glosses over the fact that Heidi's house is a *fictional* place; and yet 'Heidi's House – the

Original' is presented as 'the' mythical home of Heidi, and as such, as authentic, unique, unrepeatable and unsubstitutable.

Heidiland and Heididorf give us a typical example of the way in which tourism can exploit nostalgia, a sentiment that is individual and yet nonetheless has strong collective roots, and is universally present throughout modern societies. More precisely, the success of Heidiland as a tourism region has been fuelled by the nostalgia linked to the disappearance of rural lifestyles, of ancestral ties to the land and nature, and of the organic ties that bind individuals and traditional communities. Because this sense of longing cannot find an 'authentic' satisfaction – in that, as we have seen, the mythical home no longer exists – the market has infinite possibilities to create added value by responding to this unquenchable, endless desire of modern consumers.

In our case study, the invented 'Heidi's House – the Original' is a concrete version of

Fig. 2.12. Frontier house and Allied soldier.

Fig. 2.13. Ostalgia object: the Trabant (as the 'Brandenburgertor').

Fig. 2.14.   Ostalgia experiences and objects: GDR everyday life in the Dresden museum 'GDR Time travel'. Eastproducts in a typical GDR shop.

the mythical home that can be viewed, touched and even entered. Heidi's House offers a 'return home' to tourists willing to travel to Maienfeld and to buy a ticket for a relatively modest fee. This return home involves not only a return to a pre-modern lifestyle, but also a chance to return to childhood. Nonetheless, this experience can only be ephemeral and contingent.

Within this framework, the media and their imagery have played and continue to play an important role: the story of the little orphan is famous thanks not only to the Heidi novels but also to the films, TV series and, last but not least, the Japanese animated cartoons of the 1970s.[5] Thanks to the media, the myth of

Heidi has now undoubtedly spread worldwide, and has been renewed time and time again over the years through different forms of remediation, and using codes suited for different generations.

Heidi is indeed a textbook example of the transformation of an element of collective memory (and more precisely of cultural memory[6]) into a fragment of modern social memory, a process that took place over the space of the century spanning from 1880 when Heidi was 'born' to today, and that has been fuelled by the profound assonance between the fictional story and the sense of loss that characterizes the lives of individuals in modernity. More precisely, the

[5]The original novel has been translated into more than 50 languages and approximately 50 million copies have been published. No less than ten films inspired by the story of Heidi have been made: the first, a silent film made in 1921 in Hollywood, was followed in 1937 by a more well known version starring Shirley Temple (Leimgruber, 2005).

[6]Cultural memory and communicative memory are the two forms of collective memory classified by Jan and Aleida Assman. They define 'cultural memory' as the more institutionalized form of collective memory: it is an objectified memory that conserves and transmits its contents as autonomous from single, individual memories and from concrete interaction. Typical objectifications of cultural memory are rituals, myths, texts or remembrance objects such as temples and monuments (J. Assman, 1992; A. Assmann, 1999).

Fig. 2.15. GDR leisure time.

two novels in which Johanna Spyri narrates Heidi's story can be considered elements of Switzerland's cultural memory, as they are rooted in a specific collective memory, that of the inhabitants of the Alps as observed and narrated by a middle-class woman from Zurich[7] who, through Heidi, was able to express a discomfort with the modern world, which was not only personal but also a malaise shared by many Swiss in the 1800s, as well as in other nations. The times and places in which the novel has been successful are indeed particularly significant: the first Heidi novel appeared in 1880 and was immediately followed by a sequel in German, a French translation (1882) and a translation of the first edition into English, which was published in the USA in 1884. This first wave of enthusiasm for the Heidi story corresponded with modernization and its constituent processes, including industrialization and urbanization. What is more, it occurred in the areas most affected by these changes: the Old Continent of Europe and the new American society. There, the same rapid, violent transformations described implicitly by Johanna Spyri in her novels were underway, and the contradictions emerging were the same: those between city and country life, between the Frankfurt in which Heidi finds herself segregated and the life in the mountains for which she is so deeply and painfully nostalgic. Along the same lines, the more recent success of the Heidi story in Japan in the 1970s, which coincided with an equally rapid and traumatic period of modernization, is, I believe, further evidence that the myth of Heidi is linked profoundly to the modern nostalgia.

Heidi thus is a mythical figure in Swiss identity and history, which, more than any other, is identified with the homeland, the loss of one's

---

[7]More precisely, it is an imagined collective memory. Nations are defined as imagined communities in Anderson (1991).

Fig. 2.16.   GDR museum visitors: souvenir picture with Trabant.

Fig. 2.17.   GDR museum visitors: stopping for a break.

Fig. 2.18. GDR museum visitors: observing their own past.

homeland and with nostalgia.[8] Moreover, the consolation that Heidi feels in the novel when she returns to her mountains is also effective for her friend, Clara, who in the city was trapped in a wheelchair but, upon arriving in Heidi's world, regains her health, her *joie de vivre* and the will-power needed to walk again. It is the very same miraculous, thaumaturgical efficacy of the community and the mythopoiea that saved Clara (convincing her bourgeois family to return each year to the mountains with Heidi) that Heidiland 'promises' its visitors today. Clara and her family were thus, in a certain sense, the first 'pioneers' to visit Heidiland because of a sense of nostalgia, and were the first to witness the power of healing and consolation that can derive from this type of modern pilgrimage.

However, there is a substantial difference between the fictional story and the possibilities that Heidiland offers its visitors: in the Heidi novels, several of the visitors from Frankfurt are able to stay 'forever'; the doctor, for example, abandons the city and moves to live in Heidi's grandfather's old home. The story ends,

therefore, with a return home, which in modernity is instead impossible. The modern pilgrims to Heidiland are indeed condemned to experience this return as ephemeral and contingent, destined to rapidly fade away and be replaced once again by a form of nostalgia that cannot be solved. Modern tourists are obviously destined to leave Heidiland, searching once again for new realms in which to ease their nostalgia temporarily. From the market standpoint, it is absolutely indifferent that the object of this nostalgic experience is the mountains, goats and flowers described in the story of Heidi, which is proposed as a contingent form of 'return home'. Any other experience would suffice, as long as it was able to attract a flow of tourists. Nostalgia can so become a banal 'nostalgia of style' with 'no explicit appeal to return, no acute sense of loss, and no reference to embodied memory to mar the glib evocation of vanished commodity forms' (Ivy, 1995, p. 56). Just as Heidi's home, and the Swiss mountains, paths, animals and nature in general, have become 'nostalgia commodities', we can imagine that the market will

---

[8]In German, the words *Heimat*, *Heimatverlust* and *Heimweh*, respectively, all derive from the same root *Heim*, and mean home, dwelling, hearth.

invent other products in the future. This equivalence of different experiences is not necessarily shared by the nostalgic visitors searching for consolation in Heidiland, be they Swiss, American or Japanese, as they clearly hope to find a realm of memory there that is in assonance with their way of feeling, and not just an occasion for entertainment or amusement. Perhaps they feel they can find it there and nowhere else; and yet, this is precisely the point of view of individuals, not of the market.

Case study 2 – Nostalgia for a disappeared everyday life and material culture: Ostalgia tourism in former East Germany

The second paradigmatic case study is that of former East Germany (German Democratic Republic), where the disappearing of a way of life after 1989 was the occasion to create a market supplying nostalgia experiences and nostalgia objects.

After the fall of the Berlin Wall, there was a general devaluation of East Germany's past in the public narratives of the re-unified Germany. This devaluation is also reflected in the fate that its products at first met: after 1989 most of the typical goods of the GDR went into decline, many companies went bankrupt and factories closed, and the East German goods were replaced with goods from the West. The products of the East were, however, part of a much wider-ranging material culture that dissolved together with the GDR, producing a strong feeling of disorientation in East Germans. However, already as early as the early 1990s, the citizens of the former East Germany began to show signs of resistance, and of going back to cherish their own goods. Perhaps one could even say that they began to love them as they had never loved them before. The reason is clear: East German consumers recognized these goods as symbols in their own biography, whose value was underlined and reinstated through consumption. Products of the East became tools to use in re-affirming their own identity (Behrdal, 2001; Bach, 2002; Bartoletti, 2007, 2008). Consumption goods thus became the tools used to tell a counter-narrative in the field of consumption and tastes in contrast with the traditional one implying an inferiority of the products and citizens of East versus West Germany. Through their consumption, East Germans affirmed an individual and collective memory and an identity that was positive, in which the history of these goods and personal biographies could no longer be separated. In this process of transformation, which is both material and symbolic at the same time, the products of the East have been transformed into 'East brands'. These brands have become effective markers of an identity that is no longer proposed as inferior or as a losing contender against Western goods. Instead, these brands assert their specificity through positive values that range from simplicity to authenticity, unaffectedness, naturalness and solidity. These characteristics are presented as common not only to the products but also to the consumers of the East, and this phenomenon is part of the much vaster phenomenon of 'Ostalgia', that is, a nostalgia for the old East Germany which can be seen, above all, in consumption habits and consumption practices.

Ostalgia is therefore a feeling of nostalgia that appeared soon after German reunification and can be understood as a sense of loss regarding the everyday life led in the former East Germany. I will argue that Ostalgia is not a sense of longing for the socialist past, but rather a sense of loss of a material culture that was relevant in constructing cultural meanings and personal identities (Douglas and Isherwood, 1979).

This nostalgia for embodied memories and consumption experiences of East Germans inspired the construction of an 'Ostalgia market' and in particular of 'Ostalgia tourism' that offer nostalgic experiences to Western tourists, who can experience the consumption practices of a disappeared world. The reconstructed former GDR world proposed to Western tourists is in reality mostly stereotyped and sometimes grotesque. Western tourists may desire to experience it because it represents a way of life and consumption that is alternative or simply different from that of Western capitalistic societies. However, these commodified experiences are at the same time at the disposal of the former citizens of the GDR themselves, who can become tourists in their own land, a particular kind of tourist: tourists in the past – in their own past – and in their own memories. Therefore, in the case of German Ostalgia, memory tourism is based on embodied memories – in this case that of the former GDR citizens – but it offers nostalgic experiences to all tourists that may be interested in travel back in time to a recently disappeared past.

I will illustrate this complex example of tourism of memory through different kinds of experiences and tourist products, illustrating the supply of (n)ostalgia tours in the city of Berlin and the growing phenomenon of GDR-museums.

A tourist in Berlin can experience an Ostalgia tour by bus or by boat on the river. The 'East Berlin Nostalgia Tour' is presented as follows on the Berlin Tourism Office website: 'The 'Ostalgia' tour presents important places of the GDR. In Berlin every district has its own history and identity. In the years of its separation in two parts, two different political and ideological systems were developed and therefore two different historic evolutions took place in Berlin. After the fall of the wall Berlin became one city again, but the past is vivid in various places. The recent history of Berlin has many aspects and different ways of handling. On the one hand there is the difficult historical discussion, on the other hand is the (n)ostalgic mood. The actual wow of the German film 'Good-bye Lenin' made this kind of mood clear to an international public. Our tour shows both sides'.[9] The tour includes, for example: the headquarters of the *Staatssicherheit*, the so-called *Stasi*; the Karl Marx Allee, which is presented as a 'unique open-air museum of Socialist Realist architecture in Germany', where in 1953 the worker's rebellion started, and, of course, the remains of the Berlin Wall.

One of the most relevant Ostalgic sightseeing stops in Berlin is indeed Checkpoint Charlie, the former border crossing point between East and West Berlin where Soviet and American soldiers stood face to face, after the construction of the Wall in 1961. Today it is possible to get a (false) visa in the passport of the former GDR, supplied by a false GDR soldier (Fig. 2.11) and to take a picture in front of the (reconstructed) border house together with (false) Allied or Soviet and GDR soldiers (Fig. 2.12). It is clear that in this case history and a specific past (both historical and political) give sightseeing value to the former east side of the city (when we can

forget the 'difficult historical discussion', which is not just historical but primarily political).

It is also clear that the memories of former GDR citizens are now better understood around the world through the media imaginery, in this case thanks to a film that in 2003 was the most successful film in Germany (both in the western and eastern sides of re-unified Germany). The reference is to a historical past, of course, but the gaze (the observer's perspective) is that of the tourism system and of the media imaginery.

In connection to these Ostalgia tours, both in Berlin and other former GDR cities, there have also been set up travel agencies for tourists which offer 'Trabant Safaris'. The Trabant was the popular autarchic car of the GDR and today it undoubtedly represents a 'realm of memory' of former East Germany and a GDR 'cult object' at the same time (Behrdal, 2001; Bartoletti, 2008). Tourists can get in and drive a Trabant themselves, following the audio-guide, which gives explanations. Two tours are offered: 'Berlin Classic' and 'Berlin Wild East'.

Western Ostalgic tourists sometimes encounter the Ostalgic citizens of the former GDR, who have themselves been transformed into tourists of their own past. This can occur in the many private museums of everyday life in the GDR that have been opened in former East Germany in recent years. The most recent among them was opened in July 2006 in the centre of Berlin: it is the *DDR-Museum der Alltagskultur* – GDR Museum of everyday culture – and it attracted 9000 visitors in the first weekend after its opening alone.[10] I visited one of these museums in 2006: the museum, in the Dresden suburbs, opened in 2005 and is named *Ddr-Zeitreise* (GDR Time Travel). Its visitors are not only tourists, but also inhabitants of the area. During my visit I encountered groups of young students from different East European states (Poland and former Czechoslovakia, both former socialistic States) (Figs 2.16 and 2.17) but also Dresden citizens who were visiting their past through old-fashioned scenes of daily life (Fig. 2.18): work, leisure, play, technology, mobility, the household and so on are the themes of the different rooms

---

of this museum. Seen through the eyes of former East German visitors, banal everyday old-fashioned objects take on a significant symbolic value, occasioned by their sudden disappearance and their connection with specific (and unsubstitutable) biographies. With the elicitation of the visual indicators of these different types of visitors, it could be possible – and it would be significant, I think – to understand how these different tourists feel about their own experience in the museum and how they imagine and perceive the other visitors that are observing and evaluating their past and their biographies.

Conclusions: Towards a Definition of 'Memory Tourism'

Through the emblematic cases of Heidiland/Heididorf and of Ostalgia tourism in East Germany, it is possible to define more precisely the characteristics of memory tourism as a form of marketing of nostalgia, based on commodified memories that are very different and heterogeneous but, in the perspective of the tourism market, absolutely equivalent. Through this commodification, these memories are supplied to a wide public of consumers.

I can precisely define this form of tourism starting from a review of its possible contents. The question is: what kind of memories can be commodified by memory tourism?

First, they can be 'the memories of others', which can be attractive because their meanings or values are close or similar to the embodied memories or desires of the tourists, even if they haven't experienced them directly. This is, for example, the case of the Japanese visitors to Heididorf, who feel a nostalgia caused by modernity, linked to the disappearing of a traditional way of life, or the case of the West German citizens (and not only Germans) that are attracted

by Ostalgic forms of consumption experiences in the former GDR in order to experience a world and a material culture that is alternative to that of capitalist society. In both of these cases, the tourist experience risks becoming a banal 'nostalgia of style', whose contents are equivalent, but it is not necessarily so. In all these cases, the media imaginery plays a very important role.

Second, the tourists can experience a revival of their own memories, which can be living and embodied memories, or of the memories of their ancestors: in this case the tourism of memory lead to 'realms of memory' (*lieux de mémoire*) of the history of the tourist itself. In this case, the value of these experiences is typically linked to a founding narrative, that can be biographical (personal) or collective. This is for example the case of the 'paths of memory' at the sites of the First and Second World Wars,[11] such as the 'Remembrance Trail' along the sites of the battlefields of the Somme in the Great War in France or the '*Sentieri partigiani*' (Partisans' Paths) in the Italian Appennine mountains,[12] if the tourists are the people that lived through these events or are their direct or indirect descendants (by this I mean relatives or symbolic descendants, that feel a sense of belonging to a collective history that has its founding protagonists, a kind of secular 'ancestors'). This is also the case of the Ostalgia tourism in the perspective of the former GDR citizens, where the value of the experienced past is more biographical. These memories are less appealing for the market if they cannot be generalized to a vaster universe of consumers, thanks also to the help of the communication media. As a result, in all these cases the commodification of memories and of nostalgia is more limited.

Memory tourism may also seem similar to heritage tourism, and there are some important connections.[13] In reality, however, there are also some important differences: in heritage tourism, both nostalgia and embodied memories are not

---

[11]Compare http://www.pathsofmemory.net/ (Accessed 25 July 2008) and the D-Day Museum in Portsmouth. This website covers locations in six European countries (UK, France, Germany, Spain, Italy and Belgium) relating to the two World Wars and the Spanish Civil War.
[12]Compare for example http://www.partigiano.net/gt/sentieri.asp, related to the Appennines of Piacenza or http://www.istoreco-re.it/isto/default.asp?id=626& lang=ITA related to the Appennines of Reggio Emilia, both in the Italian Region Emilia-Romagna (both accessed 26 July 2008). See also Bartoletti (2003) about the case study of Brescello (Italy).
[13]See for example Urry (1996).

strictly necessary. Heritage tourism is moreover frequently connected to a concrete, traditional cultural heritage, whose vestiges bear witness to a glorious past; in memory tourism we do not necessarily need such precious cultural objects: this lack is evident in the case of Heidi's House, for example, but also in the Ostalgia tourism.

The great strength of memory tourism as a form of emotional tourism is that it can develop everywhere there are embodied memories that can become universal, that can be generalized: it does not need anything else. In any case, memory tourism offers to tourists a nostalgic experience, a trip back in time: it does not necessarily offer sights worth seeing, but it certainly provides something worth feeling. And this is the most precious commodity in contemporary society.

References

Anderson, B. (1991) *Imagined Communities*. Verso, London.

Assmann, A. (1999) *Erinnerungsräume. Formen und Wandlungen des kulturellen Gedächtnisses*. C. H. Beck, Munich.

Assmann, J. (1992) *Das kulturelle Gedächtnis: Schrift, Erinnerung und politische Identität in frühen Hochkulturen*. C. H. Beck, Munich.

Bach, J.P.G. (2002) 'The taste remains': consumption, (n)ostalgia, and the production of East Germany. *Public Culture* 14, 545–556.

Bartoletti, R. (2003) *Sulle tracce di una invenzione. Viaggi e pellegrinaggi mediatici*. Golem L'indispensabile, no. 8 (August). http://www.golemindispensabile.it/index.php?_idnodo=7432&_idfrm=61 (Accessed 23 July 2008).

Bartoletti, R. (2007) *Memoria e comunicazione. La modernità osservata attraverso le cose*. FrancoAngeli, Milan.

Bartoletti, R. (2008) La fabbrica delle memorie. Oggetti di consumo e biografie nella Germania Orientale post-socialista. *Sociologia del lavoro* 108, 94–110.

Bartoletti, R. (2009) The crisis of collective memory and commodification of nostalgia: the case history of Heidiland in the Swiss Alps. In: Packard, N. (ed.) *Sociology of Memory: Papers from the Spectrum*. Cambridge Scholars Publishing, Cambridge.

Behrdal, D. (2001) 'Go, Trabi, Go!': reflection on a car and its symbolization over time. *Anthropology and Humanism* 25, 131–141.

Boym, S. (2001) *The Future of Nostalgia*. Basic Books, New York.

Coleman S. and Crang, M. (eds) (2002) *Tourism: Between Place and Performance*. Berghahn Books, New York.

Douglas, M. and Isherwood, B. (1979) *The World of Goods. Towards an Anthropology of Consumption*. Routledge, London.

Faccioli, P. and Harper, D. (eds) (1999) *Mondi da vedere. Verso una sociologia più visuale*. FrancoAngeli, Milan.

Gemini, L. (2008) *In viaggio*. FrancoAngeli, Milan.

Gemini, L., Antonioni, S. and Mazzoli, L. (2006) *Turisti per casa. Turismo, comunicazione del territorio e identità locali: il 'caso' Levanto*. FrancoAngeli, Milan.

Giddens, A. (1990) *The Consequences of Modernity*. Polity Press, Cambridge.

Halbwachs, M. (1980) *The Collective Memory*. Harper and Row, New York.

Halbwachs, M. (1992) The social frameworks of memory. In: Coser, L.A. (ed.) *On Collective Memory*. University of Chicago Press [1925], Chicago, IL.

Hobsbawm, E. and Ranger, T. (eds) (1983) *The Invention of Tradition*. Cambridge University Press, Cambridge.

Ivy, M. (1995) *Discourses of the Vanishing*. University of Chicago Press, Chicago, IL.

Leimgruber, W. (2005) 'Heidiland: Vom literarischen Branding einer Landschaft'. In: Mathieu, J. and Boscani Leoni, S. (eds) *Die Alpen! Les Alpes! Zur europäischen Wahrnehmungsgeschichte seit der Renaissance/ Pour une histoire de la perception européenne depuis la Renaissance*. Peter Lang, Bern.

Luhmann, N. (1992) Kontingenz als Eigenwert der modernen Gesellschaft. In: Luhmann, N. *Beobachtungen der Moderne*. Westdeutscher Verlag, Opladen.

Luhmann, N. (1997) *Die Gesellschaft der Gesellschaft*. Suhrkamp, Frankfurt am Main.

MacCannel, D. (1999) *The Tourist: A New Theory of the Leisure Class*. University of California Press (1976), Berkeley, CA.

Nora, P. (ed.) (2001) *Rethinking France: Les Lieux de mémoire, Volume 1: The State.* University of Chicago Press, Chicago, IL.

Urry, J. (1996) How society remembers the past. In: Macdonald, S. and Fyfe, G. (eds) *Theorizing Museums.* Blackwell, Oxford.

Wagner, J. (ed.) (1979) *Images of Information: Still Photography in the Social Sciences.* Sage, Beverly Hills, CA.

3   Edward Hopper: Glancing at Gaze with a Wink at Tourism

Teresa Costa

*ESHTE – Escola Superior de Hotelaria e Turismo do Estoril,
(Estoril Higher Institute for Hotel and Tourism Studies), Portugal*

Vivian: Enjoy Nature! I am glad to say that I have entirely lost that faculty. People tell us that Art makes us love Nature more than we loved her before; that it reveals her secrets to us; and that after a careful study of Corot and Constable we see things in her that had escaped our observation. My own experience is that the more we study Art, the less we care for Nature. What Art really reveals to us is Nature's lack of design, her curious crudities, her extraordinary monotony, her absolutely unfinished condition. Nature has good intentions, of course, but, as Aristotle once said, she cannot carry them out. When I look at a landscape I cannot help seeing all its defects. It is fortunate for us, however, that Nature is so imperfect, as otherwise we should have no art at all. Art is our spirited protest, our gallant attempt to teach Nature her proper place. As for the infinite variety of Nature, that is a pure myth. It is not to be found in Nature herself. It resides in the imagination, or fancy, or cultivated blindness of the man who looks at her.

(Oscar Wilde)

'After a careful study of Corot and Constable'

Vivian's speech in Oscar Wilde's *The Decay of Lying* can be construed as either summarizing directly or at least connoting much of that addressed in visual culture at large and in tourism literature in particular. In fact, replacement of the reference to Corot and Constable by the word 'images' and extension of the mere landscape observation to the surrounding world would enable reading the above quote as a statement advancing Irit Rogoff's assertion that:

> In today's world meanings circulate visually, in addition to orally and textually. Images convey information, afford pleasure and displeasure, influence style, determine consumption and mediate power relations.
>
> (Rogoff, 2002, p. 25)

Such a proposition means, as Rogoff (2002) further implies, that choice (or rejection) of matter, action, mode or agent represented is meaning on its own and that people come to interact with a wide range of either full images or visual scraps (e.g. films, billboards, photos, postcards) that combine and are worked, through experience and unconscious processing, into a meaningful narrative (also discussed by Mirzoeff, 2002).

Because of their own particular natures, tourism and image seem innately linked. One of the traveller's primary purposes is to glimpse and gaze at whatever surrounds him or her – a land, sea or cityscape, a group ethnically differentiated from the subject viewer, a ritual. Since all interacting (within different pictorial codes) images determine perception and consumption, what the tourist thus sees is determined by the pre-visit narratives he/she is able to construct (a process determined by gender, social, economic and educational factors).

Literature in the area of tourism particularly highlights the tourism–photography link. Unarguably photography shapes tourism and there would be no present-day tourism without photography (Human, 1999; Urry, 2002). Photography anticipates and determines many visual experiences, which more often than not linger in the tourist's post-travel memory as 'reality', no matter how remote from the actual visiting experience. Were viewers not previously endowed with an available code of signs/images, they would probably be readier to uncover 'Nature's lack of design' Vivian refers to in the quote above, or even those intrusive elements tourists promptly overlook to warrant calling the travel experience pleasurable – Markwell's account of the efforts undertaken by participants in a nature-based tour to avoid satellite dishes and any other sort of unpleasant sight is illustrative of the gratifying holiday experience tourists seek (Markwell, 1997). A prosaic truth is that in demand–supply-based economies, consumers need to acknowledge a balance of power in the act of commodity acquisition: a fair deal. Uncontrollable factors ranging from climate conditions to social unrest – the unexpected days of heavy rain or a strike at a museum – frustrate anticipated gratification, which should result from the travel purchase and experience. Hence, the selection of positive images is, for most tourists, a way to justify expenditure, in other words, to account for the purposefulness of the tourist experience:

> [. . .] pictorial selectivity serves to reinforce the myth of the perfect holiday in the perfect world, rather than demonstrating the problematics of travelling in the reality of a less-than-perfect world, and thus diminishing the educational value of the photographic collection, and by extension, the educational value of the tour experience as a whole.
>
> (Markwell, 1997, p. 150)

When addressing matters pertaining to the formation of a destination image, the role of images can be more pragmatically understood within the wider surrounding visual semiotic field. Not just photography but images of all kinds conveyed through different media (especially not for profit output such as films, documentaries, news reports, internet sites) dictate – covertly or overtly – the tourist pre and post-visit experience and help reinforce or detract from the destination image (Beerli and Martín, 2004).

For the travelling subject, photography materializes the understanding of the visited place, validates the tourist experience and plays a social role in developing group bonds among the travelling party (Markwell, 1997). Though arguments over a 'power fallacy' may come to the fore, it is hardly disputed that photography may result in a form of neo-colonialism or a statement regulating power and ethnic distinctions and relations, as accounted for in different ways and contexts by Cohen et al. (1992), Human (1999), Mellinger (1994) and Rogoff (2002).

Ubiquitous it may be because of immediacy and undemanding availability brought about by technological progress, photography is not the only representational medium bearing an imprint in tourism. Long before photography, painting (alongside literary writing) played a major role in advancing the fame and fortune of locations by fostering expectation within a restricted elite of educated gallery-goers and art-knowledgeable, well-off people.

There obviously emerges a great divide between photography and painting. Though subjective and carrying the photographer's bias, photography is mimetic and frequently perceived by image consumers as a frozen moment of reality and while painting may be referential, it is not necessarily mimetic. Still, the artist's creativity intervening in the process does not hinder the influence of paintings as mediators of the way people perceive reality. Art influences perception even when the mimetic aspect is eschewed in favour of compositional techniques, where structural factors are more important than matter portrayed: true, for example, of Modernist art where structural issues are part of the message/meaning. Specific such examples might include Léger's cubist painting *The City* (1919): the profusion of angular intersecting shapes and volumes and the contrast of chromatic patches and geometric forms, among which abstract human forms can be spotted. This seems a compressed metaphor of a travelling experience undertaken in any big city – the painting is far more forceful than any single photograph, which can solely portray a splinter of reality or a commensurate shard of a place tourists believe to exist as they comprehend it – the host country and community.

Similarly, just as photographs are not ideologically free (matter included or excluded is the statement), so painting also implies a choice of the matter depicted and of structural qualities and modes of depiction. In fact, painting presses on one step further by allowing full rein to creativity and its very own nature is an admonition to viewers that they are seeing through artistic eyes and perspectives and in accordance with the singular aesthetic–ideological framework adopted by the painter. In that respect, painting may be rendered less deceitful than photography for the viewer is warned by the very substance of this medium as to the subjective imprint left by the artist – his imagination and creativity and thus painting – art at large (Shohat and Stam, 2002) – may also prove to be a perception-mediating device shaping reality visually.

Modernist art was imbued by underpinning how 'medium is message'; it therefore remains an open issue to establish the message construed by painting in its link with travel. This though, is beyond the scope of this chapter. Addressing this argument as to the most suitable academic field is not envisaged within the scope of this essay as it focuses on matter represented rather than on the painterly qualities of the medium even if these might be mentioned, especially when coming into play as part of the message (Mitchell, 2002, provides ample discussion on the art/non-art argument).

Painting has over time, before and alongside photography, contributed to shaping perspectives of the world as working and living environments transformable into alluring spaces of travel and leisure. This is especially true from the 18th and 19th centuries onwards when landscape and rural-related scenes came to figure pre-eminently in Western painting thus fostering a development in the link between art (the aesthetic experience) and landscape/nature. Once regarded as an inferior art form, landscape painting became influential and ownership of landscape painting became associated with affluence and good taste (Aitchison et al., 2002). Along with other less-known painters, Turner and Constable contributed to the crystallization of nature scenes associated with an

English love of nature and fostered an appreciation through art itself. Romanticism through its focus on a healing nature determined the consumption of landscape, which developed into a prized commodity even as its importance as a labour environment steadily declined. There is an evident link between artistic mediation and tourist consumption of place/space which led, for example, to the designing of cultural maps by the British Tourist Authority and to the establishment of a literary mode of tourism (Scotland, Lake District, Hardy country; Aitchison et al., 2002). The unmistakable indebtedness of tourism to the art world is far more reaching than present-day mass consumers of place can acknowledge or even recall:

> In the last quarter of the eighteenth century, the aesthetic of the Picturesque became a fashionable way of contemplating the actuality of scenery, consciously derived from painters' compositions. Hitherto, art could imitate landscape. Now, a landscape could imitate art. The major influences included Claude, Ruisdael and other members of the Dutch school, as well as the quintessentially English landscapes of Thomas Gainsborough, whose rustic scenes such as *The Woodcutter's Return* (1773) and *The Watering Place* (1777) portrayed a deep countryside, untouched by the agricultural improvements and enclosures which were by now changing the face of much of the Midlands and Eastern England.
>
> (Aitchison et al., 2002, p. 35)

The art–tourism link can be found in the habits of travellers embarking on their Grand Tours (sketching, reading literary texts related to certain landscapes, notably Byron's, or even getting portrayed within a classical monument scene by Panini) and modern tourists alike (the latter, and depending upon their pocketbook, driven not so much by art acquisition but by taking delight in art appreciation).

The impressionist involvement with land and seascapes – and with a space described as *pictur*esque, a word stressing the picture-like quality of place – cannot be overlooked for the considerable magnitude of nature-related settings they portray, the leisure moments they reveal or even the means of transport taken as their compositional themes. The ineffable luminous quality of impressionist painting – resulting from outdoor work – is the same as that to be found in many of the commercial images used for tourism promotion. The prominent role of impressionist painters in fostering landscape consumption cannot be overstated as the exhibition 'Impressionists by the Sea', held at the Royal Academy of Arts (London, 2007), illustrates. Bringing together a vast array of paintings by different artists (Courbet, Corot, Boudin, Jongkind, Monet and Manet), this exhibition demonstrated how a grammar of seascapes was devised by artists roaming the seashores of Normandy, notably Trouville, Deauville, Dieppe, Honfleur and Etretat. The exhibition catalogue continually emphasizes the crucial and influential role of artistic representation over time and specifically how paintings produced in Normandy worked as catalysts for tourism when displayed in the Paris Salons and galleries to a town-weary, leisured and affluent society. As the century wore on and as greater numbers of tourists flocked to the painter-discovered and increasingly crowded coastal towns, painters pressed on further in search of solitary, secluded seascapes. However, beaches and seaside pathways populated by tourists, along with villas and hotels can be admired in the luminous seascapes painted by Monet – for example, *The Pointe de la Hève* (1864), *Regatta at Saint Adresse* (1867), three different canvases entitled *The Beach at Trouville* (1870), *The Hôtel des Roches Noires, Trouville* (1870) and *Camille on the Beach at Trouville* (1870) – and Boudin – the latter producing a series of paintings between 1863 and 1865 on the Normandy coast, namely, three different paintings entitled *The Beach at Trouville* (1863 and 1865), *Bathing Time at Deauville* (1865) and *The Empress Eugénie on the Beach at Trouville* (1863). Notably, two of Boudin's paintings, almost like photographic renderings, depict tourists engaging in leisurely pursuits on the beach (Royal Academy of Arts, 2007).

Furthermore, taking ethnicity as a motivator for travel, one might establish how far Gaugin's exotic and intensely coloured paintings contribute to tourist/consumer perceptions of an ethnically and culturally marked territory, given that connection between painting and publicity images is clearly demonstrated by Berger (1972) in his analysis of the similarities between advertisements and paintings. The impact of painting on the gaze is a debatable issue. In the past, the availability of paintings was confined to a relatively restricted elite. Correspondingly, the audience the paintings thus attracted was limited to those who owned them or who were able to see them in museums, galleries or reproduced on paper. This remains true today even though, in recent years, digital and electronic devices have become a major medium for circulating images of paintings, with several museums or web museums displaying works by acknowledged artists online, enabling a more democratic access to images of paintings. This means that the amount of images of paintings available to the audience today has grown immensely. In the past, people travelled to the paintings, today the paintings travel to people's homes – the same way iconographic advertisement travelogues do (Nakamura, 2002). The immediately recognizable issue is that, in this circumstance, image consumers do not see the painting itself but instead a visual reproduction:

> The uniqueness of every painting was once part of the uniqueness of the place where it resided. Sometimes the painting was transportable. But it could never be seen in two places at the same time. When a camera reproduces a painting, it destroys the uniqueness of its image. As a result its meaning changes. Or, more exactly, its meaning multiplies and fragments into many meanings.
>
> (Berger, 1972, p. 19)

What you see then is modified by the visual medium deployed in the reproduction; therefore, painterly qualities (such as brushstroke work, the artistic nature of paint, or even colour) may be affected or lost. Observation of a pointillist painting through the new media may impair a clear-cut assessment of the painting style. Thus, mediated observation of paintings through reproductions results in gazing at a double-mediated image. Such a circumstance does not necessarily hinder the painting's capacity to shape visual perception especially when considering that viewers trained by intense exposure to present day visual semiotic codes are not naive and quite capable of interpreting reproduced painting images as being different from the original (medium-affected). Correspondingly, they are also capable of understanding paintings as a highly subjective mimetic or 'midpoint-mimetic' artefact, which may still entice their curiosity about a certain place.

Hopper: Gazing at Landscape and Making up Mental Photographs

The travel–painting link in Hopper's work can be traced by analysing a selected corpus of images that reveal how a travel/tourism-related narrative can be construed around his paintings. Edward Hopper's love of travel is amply acknowledged in literature and highlighted by his biographers in particular. As with many other fellow artists, Hopper travelled to Europe in 1906–1907, 1909 and 1910. The trips to Europe were prompted by the urge to learn about painting and not so much by any wish to experience travel. He stayed for longer periods in Paris, as was usual for painters at the time, but he also travelled to Madrid and Toledo in his last European trip. While he never left the American continent after 1910, he did go on several car journeys with his wife to California, Texas, South Carolina, Massachusetts and Mexico. From 1912, he spent summers in Gloucester, Massachusetts, but from 1914 onwards the coast of Maine would become a favoured destination for travel and a theme for many oil paintings and watercolours – supported by the construction of a studio house in Truro, where he spent almost all his summers from 1934 onwards (Levin, 1980; Liesbock, 1988; Kranzfelder, 2000; Wynne, 2002). It seems travel and inspiration formed a bond in Hopper's case:

> While Hopper found inspiration in New York City where he resided most of the year, he often grew restless or found himself unable to paint. One of his means of coping with this feeling was to travel with Jo. They went to famous tourist attractions, as well as to extremely ordinary places. In the latter, Hopper was often able to discover visually interesting subject matter despite the commonplace surroundings.
> (Levin, 1980, p. 46)

Love of travel dictated the purchase of Hopper's first car in 1927, one of the few luxuries Hopper indulged in throughout his life. Furthermore, the titles of his paintings clearly identify the places he visited – the titles are a verbal strategy keeping referentiality clear – although they may be more or less realistic renderings of the landscapes he saw. Paintings seem to work for Hopper as photographs do for other travellers;

they are his way of apprehending place and sharing his images of it.

Hopper's paintings are popular for heightening visual perception and for the scarcity of people and/or objects they depict. The less they display, the more interpretive freedom they allow by a process of negative differentiation and the more the viewer's gaze is focused on the few things represented. Many of his canvases recognizably reproduce or induce a somehow voyeuristic feeling through the impression of gaze they elicit (Hughes, 1999). Windows, for example, are a threshold placing the observer out of the scene and inviting an intrusive gaze (Schmied, 2005). Focus on Hopper's oeuvre reveals that many of his paintings underpin a travel narrative induced by his own experience as a traveller.

It comes as no surprise that the last Hopper exhibition at the Whitney Museum, NY (held June–December 2006), was titled 'Holiday in Reality: Edward Hopper'. Even before that, the major 1980 retrospective exhibition held at the Whitney Museum of Modern Art testifies to the importance of the travel theme to Hopper, a fact that led to the organization of a full section around the theme 'travelling man'.

Travel means commoditized place consumption. Many of Hopper's paintings take places and landscapes as their themes and, in particular, New England is widely featured in his land and seascapes. By looking at paintings such as *Prospect Street, Gloucester* (1928), *Blackhead, Monhegan* (1916–1919), or *The Lighthouse at Two Lights* (1929), the viewer observes inviting images of the countryside and secluded places which seem to have been arrested in time. The same way a tourist takes photographs, Hopper rendered his apprehension of place in paint contributing to an on-going inter-pictorial dialogue where, for instance, notions such as solitude, rural setting and the absence of far-fetched modern comforts seem to be implied as positive.

Painting landscapes is obviously not original. As stated above, the same has been done by many painters long before and after Hopper. Besides the aforementioned European painters, in North America, Albert Bierstat produced some of the most awe-inspiring renderings of the American wilderness and the Luminist school did likewise. What seems to distinguish

Hopper is that by looking at his paintings you can remake a travel narrative anchored on a tripartite division, which is at the basis of tourism: place, transport and accommodation. The relation to travel is overtly exposed in his choice of representing lonely roads and even the car as part of the travel experience – a commodity certainly cherished by travellers (Urry, 2002). A significant group of Hopper's paintings, imbedded in his wider artistic production, accrue to become a recognizable tale within the tourism semiotic code.

The secluded, unspoilt landscapes Hopper produced, sometimes watercolours resulting from spur of the moment inspiration, could be promotional invitations aimed at the tourist. As stated above, the allusion to travel is denoted by the inclusion of roads in some paintings as in *Route 6, Eastham* (1941) or *High Road* (1931) where the roads, crossing the canvas diagonally, evoke the travel experience leading the viewer's eyes well away to a final destination beyond the picture: perhaps the untouched countryside, seeming to herald quaint inns, bracing air and vast, deserted landscapes ready for tourist consumption. The same could be stated about *Highland Light* (1930), *Gloucester Beach, Bass Rocks* (1924), *Seawatchers* (1952) or *Jo Sketching on the Beach* (1925–1928), which, together, depict the sunny non-crowded beach that sun and sea lovers yearn for.

Hopper's experience as a commercial illustrator may account for the message implicit in the images. Economic constraints at an early stage of his career forced Hopper to hire out his skills to several business magazines. Commercial illustration must have demanded two things from Hopper: a realistic approach and the capacity adequately to pass on the commercial message inherent to the information he illustrated. Despite abhorring the commercial illustration profession, he continued for about a decade. In this time, Hopper developed skills – a precision in depiction, accuracy in trace and the capacity of conveying a message resorting to little detail – which became assets he subsequently employed in the development of a mature personal style (Levin, 1980; Schmied, 2005). As Kate states '(. . .) it was in the pages of magazines like *System* that he would have observed firsthand the doctrines of selling and display' (1995, p. 170). Among the magazines

that Hopper worked for, up to the mid-1920s, we can name *Sunday Magazine, System, The Magazine of Business, Country Gentleman, Wells Fargo Messenger* and *Dry Dock Deal* (Levin, 1980).

Curiously enough, one of the last magazines he worked for was *Hotel Management* – the cover of the September 1924 issue, for instance, was illustrated by Hopper. In this case, you can unarguably establish a parallel between his commercially oriented work and his rendition of leisure moments in two paintings he dedicated to sailing: *Ground Swell* (1939) and *The Lee Shore* (1941). Comparison of the magazine's cover and the paintings reveals how commercial illustration did become a clear influence.

Hopper's sharp artistic sense did not allow local colour to go unnoticed either. His trips to Mexico furnished the local atmosphere that resulted in paintings like *Adobe Houses* (1925) and *El Palacio* (1946). The former is a rendering of a ramshackle dwelling you might want to preserve as an illustrative memoir of your trip. The latter, by contrasting sharply with Hopper's renderings of New York and New England, stands apart. *El Palacio* shows the diagnosing tourist's eye at work. Though hues have been combined to awaken a positive impression in the viewer, a certain undertone of poverty seems to be conveyed by the plainly drawn and undecorated buildings, where a sense of ruin is denoted through damage in one of the houses. Contrasting with this sense of poverty, the local hotel is ironically called 'Palacio', the word itself an ironic token of the foreignness of the territory. Perhaps hitting out at the 'going global' of major corporations, a Ford sign can be seen in the foreground, among the buildings – almost a post-tourist image.

En route

As stated above, the roads featured in Hopper's paintings can be interpreted as a sign of travel (as indexes, from the semiotic point of view). The same happens to the gas stations he featured, which embody the (independent) traveller's experience. Two paintings, *Gas* (1940) and *Four Lane Road* (1956) expose the theme of travel as gas stations are definitely part of the trip and the roads entice the viewer to follow.

A further example of a captured travel moment is *Jo in Wyoming* (1946), a watercolour illustrating how the Hoppers combined travelling and painting as inseparable activities. Once again, this is almost a photograph Hopper might have taken during the course of the car journey. The same might be said of a particular fleeting moment when a glimpse was caught as if from a train window. *House at Dusk* (1935) resembles a photograph taken from a vehicle in motion. The viewer is looking from a slightly higher standing point to capture solely the upper part of the building but which seems not to have been the camera's objective. Today, the tourist *en route* would most likely delete this 'failed photograph' from the digital camera.

Depictions of other means of transport are also present in his work. Trains and boats are a relatively common topic among Hopper's paintings – his boyhood spent in Nyack, a coastal town, dictated an early interest in seagoing vessels, such as trawlers for instance (Levin, 1980).

Thinking of the travel world, two examples of people 'on the move' are given by depictions of train interiors where lonely characters sit in carriages, seemingly half unaware of the surrounding world and immersed in reading: *Compartment C, Car 293* (1938) and *Chair Car* (1965). These last two canvases are a lot more representative of the estrangement Hopper's solitary figures usually typify. The lighter tone of the naïve gaze at landscape cannot be traced here and no sign shows us that these inward-looking travellers are enjoying their journey.

Staying over

The third motif anchoring Hopper's travel narrative is accommodation. Hopper's representations of hotels are confined to the lobby, lounge and bedroom, that is to say, to the public areas of the hotel, emphasizing the tourist perspective inherent to the paintings. *Rooms for Tourists* (1945) presents viewers with a small well-lit place, possibly a small inn or bed & breakfast. The off-white façade is brightly illuminated and

through the windows a warm yellowish light reaches the street, stressing the inviting character of the place. The same atmosphere cannot be found in *Hotel Room* (1931) or *Hotel by the Railroad* (1952) where a sense of sadness pervades the paintings, especially the latter, the sombre colours underscoring the inexpressive attitude of the elderly couple.

Hopper's *Hotel Lobby* (1943) is also a space eliciting doubtful impressions, while both *Hotel Window* (1956) and *Western Motel* (1957) present the onlooker with solitary, introspective characters. The places are devoid of the movement expectable in hotel public areas. Moreover, the window at *Western Motel* overlooks a dark landscape, which evokes an ominous feeling of barrenness. But the most enigmatic painting dealing with accommodation is *Rooms by the Sea* (1951). The near surrealistic tone of this painting stresses a baffling contradiction. The light hues employed elicit a sense of warmth; nevertheless, the perspective used in the painting leads the onlooker to realize that beyond the door you plunge into the ocean. There seems to lurk a rather sardonic message in this painting. Proximity to the sea is generally valued by tourists, tour operators and hotels alike. But in this case, the vicinity of the sea becomes a revealed and concealed threat to whoever leaves that room and seems to imply many of the negative things in tourism – a too liberally euphemistic description of destinations is just one example. *Rooms by the Sea*, understood within the tourism context, is probably one of the most ironic and incongruous images you can think of and surreptitiously satirizes much of the travel discourse produced both verbally and visually in the tourism field, sustaining a counter-narrative that opposes Hopper's inviting landscapes. We could almost think of this painting as a remark on Echtner's assertions:

> In terms of tourism promotion, Brown (1992) discusses the symbolic nature of the tourism experience. Tourism is presented as a form of symbolic consumption whereby tourists display their identity and social roles through the destinations they choose. Thus, it is argued that tourism destinations represent specific symbolic experiences. The goal of tourism promotion becomes the portrayal of these symbolic experiences using the appropriate sign systems.
> (Echtner, 1999, p. 52)

'Cultivated Blindness'

Hopper was a traveller and painted as a traveller and, thus, incorporated his tourist experiences into his art. The narrative organized here around his paintings, in non-chronological order, is only possible because of an on-going inter-pictorial dialogue that multiplies commonplace perceptions and behaviours associated to tourism. As in the case of his Impressionist forerunners, Hopper's paintings assimilated a travel-related narrative and contribute to the field of tourism through place and moment depiction, as do photographs and promotional images. Moreover, they highlight how far the travel theme grew important over the last century to attract repeated attention by a major artist. Hopper's travel narrative becomes ever clearer if considered against the backdrop of the world of work he portrayed through his paintings of offices.

Hopper seems to have willingly played the role of tourist: his unspoilt land and seascapes fit the tale of happy holiday to perfection. However, they contrast with the less cheerful renderings of inward-looking travellers and sad hotels, which divert their gaze as if the presence of other people alone could mar the travel experience. Hopper's hotel guests are antipathetic to the idea of finding other tourists, so introspective they look and it therefore seems as if Hopper is warning us that travelling is not always the enjoyable experience advertised by operators, travel agents and local tourism boards. Thus far, Hopper's work features a visual narrative that apparently heralds attractive landscapes while at the same time denouncing the less enjoyable aspects of travel, exposing the 'cultivated blindness' inherent to tourists.

Besides forming a core narrative of travel, Hopper's paintings have, to a certain extent, become a measure for reality. When visiting online information linked to places like Cape Cod, Gloucester and Truro the modern traveller will find mention to Hopper's connection to those sites. Hence, you may confirm that pictorial representation through art seems to enhance the interest of the destination while, of course, Hopper's popularity is exploited to expand the market potential.

References

Aitchison, C., Macleod, N.E. and Saw, S.J. (2002) *Leisure and Tourism Landscapes. Social and Cultural Geographies*. Routledge, London.

Beerli, A. and Martín, J.D. (2004) Factors influencing destination image. *Annals of Tourism Research* 31, 657–681.

Berger, J. (1972) *Ways of Seeing*. BBC & Penguin Books, London.

Cohen, E., Nir, Y. and Almogor, U. (1992) Stranger–local interaction in photography. *Annals of Tourism Research* 19, 213–233.

Echtner, C.M. (1999) The semiotic paradigm. *Tourism Management* 20, 47–57.

Hughes, R. (1999) *Visions. The Epic Vision of Art in America*. The Harvil Press, London.

Human, B. (1999) Kodachrome icons. Photography, place and the theft of identity. *International Journal of Contemporary Hospitality Management* 11, 80–84.

Levin, G. (1980) *Edward Hopper. The Art and the Artist*. W.W. Norton & Whitney Museum of American Art, New York.

Liesbock, H. (1988) *Edward Hopper. The Masterpieces* (trans. Anne Heritage). Schirmer Art Books, Munich.

Kate, R. (1995) Edward Hopper and the American imagination. *Antiques* 148, 166–175.

Kranzfelder, I. (2000) *Edward Hopper. Visão da Realidade* (trans. J.L. Luna). Taschen Verlag, Cologne.

Markwell, K.W. (1997) Dimensions of photography in a nature-based tour. *Annals of Tourism Research* 24, 131–155.

Mellinger, W.M. (1994) Toward a critical analysis of tourism representations. *Annals of Tourism Research* 21, 756–779.

Mirzoeff, N. (2002) The subject of visual culture. In: Mirzoeff, N. (ed.) *The Visual Culture Reader*. Routledge, London, pp. 3–23.

Mitchell, W.J.T. (2002) Showing seeing. A critique of visual culture. In: Mirzoeff, N. (ed.) *The Visual Culture Reader*. Routledge, London, pp. 86–101.

Nakamura, L. (2002) 'Where do you want to go today?' Cybernetic tourism, the Internet and transnationality. In: N. Mirzoeff (ed.) *The Visual Culture Reader*. Routledge, London, pp. 255–263.

Rogoff, I. (2002) Studying visual culture. In: N. Mirzoeff (ed.) *The Visual Culture Reader*. Routledge, London, pp. 24–36.

Royal Academy of Arts (2007) *Impressionists by the Sea*. Royal Academy of Arts, London.

Schmied, W. (2005) *Edward Hopper. Portraits of America* (trans. J.W. Gabriel). Prestel Verlag, Munich.

Shohat, E. and Stam, R. (2002) Narrativizing visual culture. In: N. Mirzoeff (ed.) *The Visual Culture Reader*. Routledge, London, pp. 37–59.

Urry, J. (2002) *The Tourist Gaze*. Sage, London.

Wynne, C. (ed.) (2002) *Edward Hopper. Summer at the Seashore*. Prestel Verlag, Munich.

4   A 'Vice Among Tourists'? Trans-national Narratives of the Irish Landscape, 1886–1914

K.J. James

Department of History, University of Guelph, Guelph, Ontario, Canada

Introduction

The guidebook *'Irish Times' Tours in Ireland* (1888, p. 127), describing the tourist's early-morning approach to Ireland from Holyhead, Wales, contrasted the 'dull, ragged, and bare' scenery at the tourist's back with the splendours of the Irish coast at sun-rise: 'The deep purples of the shadier cliffs stand out against that brilliant green of field and cliff, which neither Kent nor Cumberland can outvie.' The juxtaposition of the striking scenery on view to the tourist as Ireland neared, and the 'dawning' of the day as the shore was reached, produced a highly evocative narrative of the tourist's first glimpse of the Irish coastline.

The explicit discussion of Kent and Cumberland, and the contrast between Welsh and Irish coasts, also added an important comparative dimension to the 'image' of the Irish coast, and implicitly relied on the reader's familiarity with those British sites in order to succeed as a rhetorical device. Promoters of the Irish tourist sector hoped that such narratives, and the positive images they sought to implant within the British tourist imagination, would lead tourists to visualize Ireland as a proximate vacation-ground in which they could behold the grandeur of Britain and also sneak glimpses of continental Europe. In turn, the Emerald Isle could outvie not only England and Wales, but also Scotland, Switzerland, and a host of other countries, in attracting British tourists to its shores. The promoters of tourism anticipated that the late 19th century would witness the dawn of a new era in Irish tourism, heralded by increasing numbers of visitors.

In producing images of Ireland to advance this goal, tourism-advocates repeatedly reached across the Irish Sea to find a vocabulary with which to frame Ireland's attractions as a tourist destination. Motivations behind describing landscapes in this way were multi-faceted. Borrowing from a lexicon of continental place-names that signified both striking beauty and modern comfort, place-promoters sometimes aimed to portray Ireland as a tourist destination that was equally scenic and comfortable to tour. By transferring to Ireland positive images associated with the Swiss and Norwegian tourist sectors – and in particular their reputations for cleanliness and comfort – promoters of the Emerald Isle aimed to inscribe Irish 'Alps' and 'fjords' in the tourist imagination.

The instrumentality of employing such a vocabulary was clear: the Earl of Mayo, a proponent of 'tourist development' and leading member of the Irish Tourist Association (ITA), lamented in 1895 that Ireland's proponents laboured under a crippling disadvantage: positive images were more easily conjured of continental countries, thanks to extensive and effective promotional campaigns, so that 'every place they went abroad they would see the most

© CAB International 2010. *Tourism and Visual Culture*, Volume 1
(eds P. Burns, C. Palmer and J-A. Lester)

beautiful posters of scenery in Switzerland, and the water-places in France and Spain'. Could not the people of Ireland find a means of generating and disseminating equalling compelling images of 'their Elysian Field, too'? (*Irish Tourist*, 2['New Series', 1895], p. 21). By deliberately evoking continental destinations in Irish tourist imagery, the sector's proponents produced narratives to prefigure tourists' encounters with the Irish landscape. They hoped that tourists would develop positive predispositions towards Ireland as a touring ground, and would be attracted to her shores.

The tourist's Ireland was organized by many promotional texts drawing on a vocabulary of international tourist destinations to describe Irish landscapes. By deconstructing the language used by the Irish sector's promoters, this chapter focuses on the production of destination images during a period of intensive activity aimed at improving the tourist infrastructure in Ireland and promoting the country to the British tourist market. This chapter views such activities as expressions of wider, contested ideologies in which discussions of continental models for economic and political development were linked to ideas for economic improvement and political pacification in the last decade of the 19th century.

Irish Tourist Development and Trans-national Imagery

Current research into destination-image production and promotion has been nourished by the expansion of the concept of 'tourist consumption' to incorporate 'visual' elements, to explore landscapes as texts, and to theorize systematically the production of tourist-destination images and explore them as narratives that express wider systems and distributions of social, economic and cultural power (Morgan and Pritchard, 1998; Pritchard and Morgan, 2000; Ateljevic and Doorne, 2002). Though the category has been criticized for its diffuse quality, a number of social scientists have proposed multi-dimensional models of the 'tourist-destination image', which encompass 'impressions, beliefs, ideas, expectations, and feelings towards an arena . . . suggesting the involvement of both cognitive and evaluative components' (Dann, 1996).

Affective, as well as perceptual, dimensions of the tourist image have been highlighted in studies of destination-images and place promotion, which treat place as a product that is both marketed and consumed (Nadeau *et al.*, 2008). While the consumption of such images was heavily and critically mediated, their producers often drew on a range of mythic sites ('Eden') and popular holiday-grounds ('Brighton') to develop positive dispositions on the part of tourists to visit Irish places that were otherwise construed as 'virgin' terrain in the popular imagination (Nelson, 2007, p. 11) . Studies of the contemporary production of tourist place-images in Ireland (Tresidder, 1999; Markwick, 2001; Bruhns, 2002; Cronin and O'Connor, 2003; Sheridan and O'Leary, 2005) stress that a broad range of 'texts' contribute to this process. Historically, guidebooks have played a particularly critical role in the prefiguring of Irish landscapes for tourist consumption (Koshar, 1998; Michalski, 2004; Nelson, 2007).

This chapter draws on two genres of travel narrative – the guidebook and the travelogue – whose influence in prefiguring Ireland for public consumption was critical during a formative period for Irish tourism, lasting from the first to the third Home Rule debates. It also examines the trade press to explore ways in which discussions about tourist development within Ireland's 'Tourist Movement' employed continental comparators. By exploring, through historical case studies, how these texts organized images of the country and how such images were structured, this study, building on the work of Zuelow (2006), argues that theories and perspectives drawn from sociology and tourism studies can enrich our understanding of the dynamics of Irish tourism history. In so doing, this chapter contributes new perspectives to a burgeoning field of study, in which the lenses of social and economic organization (Furlong, 2003), and literature and folklore (Ryle, 1999; Hooper, 2005; Williams, 2008) have been employed to illuminate the sector's relationship to late-Victorian Irish culture and politics.

The narration of Irish tourist-destination images usually centred on the production of rural 'sights' that were discussed in guidebooks such as *Black's* and *Murray's*, as well as in railway guides (Mehegan, 2004). Nationalist cultural politics conferred special importance on the Irish West as the repository of the country's soul (Nash, 1993; Cusack, 2002). It also became subject to reconstruction and commodification as a touring-ground – and the focus of intensive promotion as inviting tourist space (Kneafsey, 2002). This campaign was led by prominent figures in the tourist sector, including unionists who hoped to see Ireland's prosperity advance within the framework of the Union. In promoting its charms, they made frequent recourse to comparison. Specific Irish sights were portrayed as parallels of European destinations, to assert that Ireland's beauty was at least on a par with that of other countries, and also that her amenities could be developed along continental lines, so that her landscapes would merit not only the attention of the British tourist, but a place alongside other centres of 'fashion'. In Ireland, therefore, tourists could not only admire comparatively unspoilt scenery, but in beholding it, were promised glimpses of the majesty and amenities found in Germany, Norway and Switzerland, too.

'Equal to the Finest Parts of Wales or of Scotland': Ireland as UK Tourist Ground

Trans-national comparisons of the Irish tourist sector did not always involve continental countries. Indeed, comparisons with other countries within the UK lay at the heart of promoters' efforts to claim resources for infrastructural development and promote the country to the 'domestic' UK tourist market. Assessments of the comparable visual qualities of holiday-grounds in Ireland, Scotland, England and Wales were often employed by tourism promoters in the Emerald Isle to assert Ireland's rightful place alongside more popular tourist destinations in the UK – notably the Scottish Highlands, Snowdonia and the English Lake District. The images of the landscape presented in this framework were thus both 'constructed and constructing' (Morgan and Pritchard, 1998, p. 17). At a deeper level of analysis, they were outgrowths of political strategies in which comparisons of scenery encoded an implicit congruency between districts in 'sister countries' of the UK. This was the premise underlying programmes of tourist development spearheaded by groups such as the ITA – a body comprising leading unionists, including many prominent businessmen and

political figures (Furlong, 2003). Indeed, promoters of Ireland expressed frustration that its attractions were not as widely appreciated as sites in other parts of the UK, and hoped that this could be remedied. The suggestion that Britain offered 'natural' comparators for Ireland was implicit in many guidebook discussions, too. *Hardy's Guide* assessed Connemara as at least the peer of the other small countries in the Union:

> Connemara will appear black with mountains, dotted with lakes, and studded with bogs; its coast will be seen rugged, and indented with fine harbours, while the inland country, though wild, mountainous, and ill-cultivated, and so little known and visited, that its name is a proverb, is yet equal to the finest parts of Wales or of Scotland . . .
>
> (n.d., p. 318)

The triangulation of the Highlands, the English Lake District and Killarney as the pre-eminent domestic touring districts of the UK was a frequent feature in tourist guidebooks, with famous British sites providing an index against which the beauty of the Irish district was assessed – and claims to Ireland's parity, and often its superior status as a touring district, formulated. *The Lakes of Killarney* (Ballantyne, 1869, p. 10), in the Nelson's Hand-Books series, claimed that Ireland's comparatively 'neglected' lakes were 'superior, in many points, to those of England, and to the far-famed Trossachs of Scotland'. The identification of Ireland as a 'domestic' tourist site within the UK – and as a prospective holiday ground for the British tourist – was underpinned by an evaluation of tourism as a performance of patriotism, linking a tour of Britain's 'sister isle' with a broader project of strengthening the commercial, political and sentimental bonds of union across the Irish Sea (*The Times*, 23 August 1898). The audience for such pleas was the British tourist. The leading trade periodical the *Irish Tourist* complained that English tourists ignored their sister island, 'whose natural beauties and architectural features compare most favourably' with European and British sites. 'Why study scenery in Norway, Switzerland, or even in the Highlands of Scotland, when they can find as much beauty in Wicklow, in Wexford, in Connemara or in Down?' it asked (3 [1896], p. 1). Leading patrons of tourist development, not least a succession of Lords Lieutenant from the 1880s to the Great War, regarded deepening links between Britain and Ireland as a critical objective. They hoped that increased traffic from Britain would strengthen personal and political affinities between residents of Ireland, England, Wales and Scotland, demonstrate the fruits of Union, and knit their holiday grounds into a varied but integrated 'domestic' tourist market. Their use of comparison to claim Killarney's place alongside the English Lake District, and western Ireland's place alongside the Scottish Highlands, was embedded within this wider political project.

Places 'More Pretentious in Name': International Comparison and Destination-labelling

In constructing images of Ireland that referenced continental European countries, tourist-development advocates and tourist guidebooks tended to draw regularly and repeatedly on a specific set of continental sites – the Norwegian fjords, the Swiss Alps and the German Rhine. These sites were located in countries whose trajectories of economic development were also being systematically examined as Irish and British political and commercial leaders considered Ireland's prospects for economic and cultural modernization. Evaluating them in tandem, tourism promoters believed that continental countries offered examples for Ireland's tourist sector, too. These countries were presented within discourses that privileged them as models of how Ireland could be modernized within the structures of the UK, rather than through political independence. Norway – especially in the period before 1905, when it remained under a personal union of the crowns with Sweden – and Switzerland, the small independent Alpine state, were common comparators. They were seen as predominantly rural societies that had realized economic prosperity through parallel industrialization and tourist development – which, to some observers, constituted an 'alternative' path of economic development to Britain's gritty, urban factory system (James, 2006).

By producing images of Ireland that referenced these countries, tourist-development advocates hoped both to mobilize positive images of touring in countries such as Switzerland, Norway and Germany, and transfer them to Ireland, drawing tourists who had long neglected the sister isle. The continental countries had achieved success in building an impressive, modern physical infrastructure for the tourist. Ireland's modernizing sector could be signalled to the touring public by borrowing place-identifiers from the international tourist lexicon – 'fjords', 'rivieras' and 'Alpine' labels, for instance – which anticipated the tourist's encounter with Ireland's coasts, mountains and valleys. Such labels conveyed the message that Ireland's terrain was infused with the grandeur of continental Europe, and offered a wide variety of scenery in which key 'beauty sights' on the continent were assembled.

The *Daily News* enthused that 'It is no exaggeration to say that Cork County and her neighbour Kerry are a microcosm of all that is beautiful and grand in natural scenery' (in *How to See the Far-famed Lakes of Killarney*, 1901). The Great Western Railway billed the route from Kenmare to Bantry, for instance, as a path 'Over the Irish Simplon to the Irish San Remo' (*Southern Ireland*, 1906, p. 70). It also pointedly asserted that Ireland offered rivals to these continental sites: 'If Glengariff is Ireland's San Remo, assuredly in Parknasilla she provides a powerful rival to Mentone and Monte Carlo' (*Southern Ireland*, 1906, p. 65). The language of 'rivalry' was widely used in such evaluations, the pre-eminent trade periodical the *Irish Tourist* referring half-jokingly to Switzerland, whose sector was pronounced exemplary, as 'our friends, the enemy' (*Irish Tourist* 5 [July 1898], p. 43).

Irish tourist promoters, such as the ITA (founded in 1895 to advance the sector), and Lords Lieutenant, including Lords Zetland, Houghton and Cadogan, expressed profound ambivalence towards these 'competitors', sometimes viewing them admiringly and even enviously, often claiming that they attracted relatively undue praise while Ireland languished 'unvisited', and repeatedly conjuring them in their discussions of Ireland.

While many tourist publications endorsed the Earl of Zetland's claim that, having travelled 'a great deal in the world', he never looked upon more beautiful scenery than in south-west Ireland (*Cook's Excursionist and Tourist*

Advertiser, 21 April 1900), those who argued for the singular splendour of Irish sea- and land-scapes resorted to an international vocabulary of tourist places to produce images of Ireland. This resulted in an array of monikers, which featured prominently in tourist promotional material. Portrush, Co. Antrim was described as the 'Scarborough of the North', and Newcastle, Co. Down its 'Brighton' (*Irish Tourist* 6 [May 1899], p. 7), while one writer labelled Crolly, Co. Donegal 'The Angler's Brighton of Ireland' (*How to See the Far-famed Lakes of Killarney*, 1901, n.p.). Glengarriff, Co. Cork, Achill, Co. Mayo and Valentia, Co. Kerry were described in various places as the 'Madeiras' of Ireland (*Views of Glengarriff*, n.d., n.p.; Curtis, 1909, p. 353; *Art Journal*, 1907, p. 297; *Tours in the Emerald Isle*, 1895, p. 45). Rostrevor, Co. Down, called Ireland's 'Montpellier', also competed with Buncrana in Co. Donegal to be its 'Mentone' (*The Traveller's Gazette*, November 1914, p. 8; *Irish Tourist* 2 [1897], p. 10; *Irish Tourist* 5 ['Special Horse Show Number', August 1898], p. 106).

The irony may have been apparent to many readers of the *Irish Tourist*: it lamented that although Buncrana's climate was similar to that of Switzerland, English visitors persisted in going to 'Continental water-places more pretentious in name', when they could comfortably avail themselves of 'Mentone in Ireland' (*Irish Tourist* 5 ['Special Horse Show Number', August 1898], p. 106). Such comparisons featured in place-promotions of Europe, Australia and North America. Indeed little 'Brightons' could be found throughout the Old and New Worlds. But some continental comparators were systematically employed not only in place-naming, but also in wider expositions of the Irish landscape and tourist sector. Conflations of the Blackwater and the Rhine, for instance, were widespread in promotional material, though some commentators heaped scorn on the resulting image that was promoted to the tourist market.

'Why Not Come and See it in Ireland?' Constructing and Contesting the 'Irish Rhine'

When William Makepeace Thackeray posed the question: 'What sends picturesque tourists to the Rhine and Saxon Switzerland?', he used the image of a Europe teeming with tourists on well-trodden paths to narrate how Ireland was comparatively – and unjustly – overlooked:

> Within five miles round the pretty inn of Glengariff, there is a country of the magnificence of which no pen can give an idea. Were such a bay lying upon English shores, it would be a world's wonder. Perhaps, if it were on the Mediterranean, or the Baltic, English visitors would flock to it by hundreds. Why not come and see it in Ireland?
>
> (*Irish Tourist* 1 [July 1894], p. 49).

Thackeray's authority was invoked in the last quarter of the 19th century by tourist-development advocates and guidebooks, which produced images of the Blackwater as the 'Irish Rhine'. But the appropriateness of the title was also contested. The *Irish Tourist*, for instance, published a mock conversation between 'An Englishman' and 'An Irishman', in which the former sceptically inquired as to whether the Irish Rhine was 'worthy of that appellation' and in return received a barrage of comments extolling the river (*Irish Tourist* 1 [August 1894], pp. 70–71). The guidebook '*Irish Times*' *Tours in Ireland* (1888, p. 177) disputed putative similarities between the two – 'Both, to begin with, are rivers, and both have banks – and there are castles, some of them ruined, and some of them not – standing upon their craigs or amidst their slopes'; but it contended that 'here the resemblance commences and ends'. The Rhine was portrayed as a 'broad, sweeping stream' on whose banks the sound of industry resounded, where 'Ancient history and modern progress are mingled and confounded together'. In contrast, the Blackwater at its broadest was 'little more than a mile across', and it lacked the Rhine's historic fortifications. In Ireland, such sites had 'crumbled to dust', its castles and lower banks descending from 'stately splendour into mouldering decay'.

This vivid evocation of the Irish river's decline was allied to an assessment of the Blackwater's historic splendour – indeed, it boasted a history so storied and singular, the guidebook pointedly asked, 'what is the use of comparison? What does it gain in dignity by wearing a borrowed name?' Here a theme common to criticisms of comparison found clear expression: to what extent did efforts to construct Irish destination images on the back of 'foreign' places deny the singularity of the Emerald Isle's landscapes and, by extension, her distinctive history and culture? This viewpoint was periodically expressed in travelogues and other sources, although the 'Irish Rhine' remained central to tourist place-promotion.

Even if the appropriateness of the label was disputed, the use of the Rhine as a comparator was part of a strategy by Irish tourism promoters to produce images that tapped its status as a familiar place in the tourist imagination. The tourist-development advocate, publisher and editor of the *Irish Tourist*, F.W. Crossley, contrasted Ireland's hidden splendours with attractions of more established continental destinations: 'we have everything to tempt the tired who love the beautiful, and who long to get away from the conventional run up the Rhine, or the week in Paris, when Paris has gone to the seaside' (*To-day*, in *Irish Tourist 2* ['New Series', 1895], p. 7). Here, the comparison with the famous German river was part of a wider comparative evaluation of tourist traffic, in which Ireland was promoted as an under-visited, yet scenic peer of Germany. Writers argued that British tourists who declined to venture abroad, and instead savoured the hidden delights of Ireland, would enjoy:

> new scenes and new experiences, unalloyed by *désagréments*, which too frequently occur in continental show-place districts. Why not see our own country first and other lands afterwards? The 'wide and winding' Rhine, throughout its course, is but a sodden pool compared with the noble Atlantic loughs and fjords sentinelled by the cliffs of Achill, or the cloud-piercing headlands of Donegal or Antrim, to say nothing of the panorama presented by the western and southern coasts of Munster.
> (Wakeman, 1884, p. 21)

If the appropriateness of labelling the Blackwater as the 'Irish Rhine' was disputed, it illustrates the strategies that aimed to transpose positive associations with European landscapes to comparatively unknown Ireland. Irish tourism promoters argued that Ireland was at least as worthy a vacation-ground to the British tourist – and an alternative to going 'abroad'. Allied to these claims was a clarion call for the

sector's improvement, which also drew heavily on trans-national comparisons.

'Norway in Ireland': Trans-national Imagery and the Tourist Imagination

Like discussions of the 'Irish Rhine', comparisons of Irish and Norwegian landscapes pointed to scenery – the mountainous coasts and wild fjords on Ireland's West coast – but also encoded broader appraisals of the tourist sector in both countries. The Great Southern and Western Railway promoted tours to the 'Lakes and Fjords of Kerry', promising that 'Except in the Swiss valleys and parts of Norway, there is no scenery in Europe to compare with the inland route from Caragh to Parknasilla' (O'Mahony c. 1902, pp. 180–182). Tourists' attention was directed to the Killaries in Connemara, which were said to resemble the fjords of Norway. *Cook's Traveller's Gazette*, for instance, asserted that the district recalled 'the beauty of the fjords of Sogne and Hardanger' (22 April 1911, pp. 15–16). This comparison was endorsed by the travel writer J. Harris Stone (1906, pp. 8–9), who also wrote that the 'longest and most characteristically Norwegian fjord is the Great Killary' – a sea and landscape that 'irresistibly recalls the Sogne and Hardanger Fjords'.

Such descriptions claimed a degree of visual symmetry between Irish and continental sights, but this comparison was embedded within a wider evaluation of the Irish and Norwegian tourist sectors in which the Nordic country's more modern amenities were highlighted and identified as worthy of emulation. In 1893, the Leitrim estate opened a hotel at Rosapenna, Co. Donegal that had been designed in Stockholm and constructed of Norwegian timber. It was to serve as the key marker of a new touring district – 'Norway in Ireland' – in which the Norway label qualified not only the landscape, but the physical amenities on offer to the tourist. This was allied to intensive efforts by the Leitrim estate and Irish railway companies to promote the 'opening up' of the county by constructing a narrative of Donegal's development from wild and inhospitable terrain to inviting sporting-ground. The construction of the 'Norwegian' inn conferred the mark of 'improvement' on the

Irish district, signifying greater accessibility, comfort and a clear break with the traditional standard of Irish hotel accommodation. Indeed, in the narrative of Donegal's improvement, the district's wild and uncivilized reputation was signalled by the fact that before the hotel's erection, the best-known local site was the place where the third Earl of Letrim had been assassinated in 1878.

By displacing this gruesome imagery of the Rosapenna tour, which evoked Ireland's reputation for perennial unrest, the marketing of the district as Ireland's 'Norway' suggested that rugged scenery could now co-exist with luxurious tourist amenities. George Milner (1900, p. 111), writing of travels in Donegal, declared that: 'I have said that Rosapenna Hotel was made in Norway. Its resemblance to the inns of that country is so close that I often thought myself travelling again in 'Gamle Norge.' It is constructed entirely of polished pine wood, and is exquisitely clean.' This hotel and other comfortable, if less luxurious hotels at which he stayed elsewhere in the county, led Milner to declare that 'English people need not now be afraid of travelling in North-western Donegal'. Yet, as with the Irish Rhine, the use of the Norway place-label also attracted criticism. Alfred Yockney, editor of the *Art Journal*, likened the adoption of the 'Norway in Ireland' moniker to cloaking Rosapenna's scenery in disguise:

> There is a vice among tourists which irritates the placid traveller. Looking over his neighbour's territory, the lesser passer-by will deny the singularity of the scenery spread out before him. It suggests some choice spot in his own country, or, worse still, a 'bit' in the landscape of the people next nation but one away. It is sometimes patriotism and pedantry which prompts such observations, but more often it is merely the bad habit of comparison. Thus in Ireland visitors and guide books refer to Palestine, North Wales, Switzerland, Holland, Madeira. Here is Paris, there Bruges, and, of course, Paradise and Arcadia are dragged in . . . The Midland Railway, not to be outdone by the claim for Cornwall by the Great Western, have invented a Northern Riviera in Antrim. Near Carrigart, through which the stranger passes on arrival by land or sea, is the Rosapenna Hotel, well-equipped, commodious and famous as a resort for golfers and anglers. To build it in foreign style, and to emphasize the lack in

> Donegal of the necessary material, a quantity of timber was shipped across the North Sea. Already there was a fjorded coast, and 'Norway in Ireland' was the sequel. There was some excuse for this parallel on other than scenic grounds . . . Still, whoever christened Rosapenna with a Scandinavian attribute was guilty of wasteful and ridiculous excess which, the play tells us, attends the painting of the lily, or the perfuming of the violet. Viking blood may be necessary to animate the fisheries, but splendid natural resources give the Mulroy district a reputation of its own. It needs no imported character, no disguise.
>
> (*Art Journal*, 1907, p. 1)

Although Yockney described this rhetorical strategy of framing scenery with reference to foreign places as a 'vice among tourists', he was no doubt conscious that it was the outgrowth of a programmatic branding campaign by the Leitrim estate. It prefigured the tourist's encounter with Norwegian architecture, and Norwegian hospitality, on offer at Rosapenna, and made the Rosapenna Hotel a key marker for Donegal's fledgling, modern tourist sector. While this was part of an effort to reconstruct the image of 'dark Donegal' for the British tourist market, discussions within tourist-development circles frequently invoked Switzerland as the pre-eminent example of successful 'tourist development'.

'Our Friends, the Enemy': Swiss Tourism through an Irish Lens

Though the *Irish Tourist* and many guidebooks made reference to 'Alpine Ireland', with Wicklow, Donegal, the lakes and fjords of Kerry (1 [June 1894], p. 13), and the area around Glencar (*Irish Tourist* 2 ['New Series', 1895], p. 4), variously described as the 'Switzerland of Ireland', the most frequent reference to Switzerland within tourist discourses did not involve the projection of Swiss tourist-destination imagery onto the imagination of prospective tourists to Ireland, but appraisals of Swiss and Irish tourist infrastructures – with the Alpine country lauded as an example for Ireland. Popular images of Switzerland as a prosperous rural country that had maintained its rustic charms, while developing a modern tourist infrastructure, were nourished by a variety of explicit comparisons – produced by contemporary examinations of its advanced systems of technical education and its rural industry (*Report of the Recess Committee c.* 1906, p. 38). These examinations were part of an ongoing assessment of Ireland's political status and economic prospects as the British state searched for possible avenues for economic modernization and for a related diminution in political unrest. F.W. Crossley, of the *Irish Tourist*, stoked enthusiasm for the tourism sector's modernization under the auspices of syndicates and trades bodies, endeavouring to open up the country as groups in continental Europe had successfully done.

Tourism promoters who referenced Switzerland as a comparator often expressed frustration with the comparatively poor state of Irish tourist amenities. They credited Switzerland's appeal as a tourist destination to the quality of her tourist services. Proponents of the Irish sector regularly calculated the income the sector brought to the small Alpine state. The *Irish Tourist* (3 [June 1896], p. 30) enumerated 7637 Swiss hotels and pensions, with 82,055 beds, representing £20,470,000 in invested capital with a return of 7.5% (see different data in *Irish Tourist* 2 ['New Series', 1895], p. 22). Moreover, these hotels and pensions employed 26,810 servants and paid out £307,000 to them in wages. Mitchell G. Mulhall also described the prosperity that tourism had brought to the country in his report for the Recess Committee: 'The magnificent natural scenery of the country is likewise an unfailing source of income' (Mulhall c. 1906, p. 280).

The extent to which these positive evaluations of amenities lay at the heart of the Irish image of Switzerland is evident in the *Irish Tourist*: 'The Swiss evidently know the value of advertising', it opined (2 ['New Series', 1895], p. 22). Tourist-development proponents concluded that Ireland did not lack scenery that was as breathtaking as the Alpine state, but rather Switzerland had an enviable reputation for cleanliness, comfort and efficiency. They believed that similar standards could be achieved in Ireland, under the aegis of bodies such as the Irish Hotel and Restaurant Proprietors' Association, founded as the Irish Hotel Proprietors' Association in 1890 (Wilson, 1900–1901, p. 59).

Unlike both the 'Irish Rhine' and 'Norway in Ireland', which found their way into the popular tourist lexicon, and which were promoted in guidebooks and on railway posters, comparisons with Switzerland were usually generated and discussed within tourist-development circles, and were part of wider discussions of Ireland's path to 'improvement' in which the Alpine country set high benchmarks for cleanliness and comfort. The focus of such discussions was the quality of Irish hotels, which tourism promoters such as F.W. Crossley hoped to elevate to the highest Swiss standard. 'The trend of opinion amongst even the most fair-minded of 'sympathetic Saxons', the *Irish Tourist* intoned in 1896, 'points to the fact that the 'hotelling' in most parts of Ireland is now sadly lacking in both quantity and quality' (3 ['New Series'], p. 29). Redressing this image, and the lax 'tourist culture' which underlay it, became a cornerstone of campaigns within the tourist-development movement.

To Irish observers, the popularity of Switzerland as a tourist-destination rested on the successful projection of a 'national tourist image' not only linked to positive appraisals of her majestic mountains, but also to her comfortable trains, and above all her clean accommodation and solicitous hotel staff. Lord Houghton (1895, p. 498) wrote that he hoped Irish hotels would soon approach 'the best Swiss or Scottish Standard'. If descriptions of the comfort and cleanliness of Irish hotels referred to the elusive Swiss standard, it was usually to underscore that accommodations in Ireland had a long way to go. In a *Through Guide*, for instance, M.J.B. Baddeley (1892, p. xii) wrote of Irish hotels' 'laxity of management', 'unpunctuality' and of 'the most suicidal habit' of the Irish hotel-keeper: 'carelessness about those sanitary arrangements which are now-a-days essential to the success of any place professing to accommodate tourists'. Indeed, he remarked that the word 'Irish' in tourist parlance conjured unhappy images; it: 'will, for English readers, still sufficiently express the prevailing character' of hotels in many towns.

Improvement could, some believed, be effected by means adopted in Switzerland. Local tourist committees in Ireland, such as the Killarney District Tourist Association, were modelled on similar bodies on the continent 'and especially in Switzerland' (*Irish Tourist* 3 [May 1896], p. 23). It offered Ireland an example of how scenery could be marketed and consumed – to the advantage of rural inhabitants, landlords and the state. Irish tourist-development advocates alluded repeatedly to Switzerland in plotting Ireland's path to improvement, presenting the Alpine country's sector as more advanced, but implicitly asserting that impediments to the Irish sector's development were surmountable, and never citing its political independence as a factor in development.

The assertion that essential differences between the two countries centred not on qualities in the landscapes, but on the quality of tourist amenities, also implied that the Irish sector could be raised to the Swiss standard. This was conveyed in popular images of the professional Swiss waiter and his rustic, untrained Irish counterpart. At an April 1895 meeting at which the ITA was organized, the Lord Lieutenant, Lord Houghton, expressed hope that 'some day a race of waiters and other attendants will be established, such as we see in Germany and Switzerland, who are gifted with a sort of preternatural alertness' (*Irish Tourist* 2 ['New Series', 1895], p. 20). The image of the professional Swiss waiter served as a foil for Ireland's second-rate counterpart – 'Boots', a permanent employee of the hotel who, as a 'native of the district', was portrayed in guidebooks as earnest and well-intentioned, but also a hallmark of the hotel's 'Irish' character – the adjective signifying standards which fell below those that prevailed in England, Scotland and the continent (Cooke, 1896, pp. 12–13; Baddeley, 1892, pp. xii–xiii; *The Times*, 6 September 1884).

The broader comparative evaluation that underlay images of Swiss and Irish hotels, and contrasts between the professional waiter and folksy Boots, was premised on Ireland's prospects for emulating Switzerland and, like that small country, capturing a lucrative share of the British tourist market (Tissot, 1995). *The Times* (14 August 1905) lamented that English tourists possessed a far 'less intimate' acquaintance with Killarney and Connemara than they did with 'Switzerland and the Tyrol'. 'The attractions of scenery are now looked upon as a valuable commercial asset in many countries;' the newspaper contended, 'not only in Switzerland, where the figures representing profit are gigantic, in

Italy, Tyrol, and the South of France, but in the New World, in Australasia, and the East.' Against this array of competitors, the Irish sector's proponents faced the challenge of formulating images of its landscapes that encoded 'continental' comfort. Hence they developed myriad markers which transposed continental European sites in Ireland. In response to the vexing question of why tourists study 'scenery in Norway, Switzerland or even the Highlands of Scotland' when as much beauty was on offer in Ireland, tourist development promoters arrived at one conclusion. As the *Irish Tourist* put it pithily, 'Many have been deterred from travelling, by the evil character borne by Irish hotels' (3 [May 1896], p. 1). Their improvement would betoken the dawn of Ireland as a touring-ground, where British visitors could visit Ireland as comfortably – and as regularly – as they did Switzerland. Indeed, in 1903 the *Irish Tourist* mischievously suggested that, amid recent reports of Alpine tourist deaths, visitors to the Emerald Isle would have their efforts repaid both in comfort and safety:

> The list of Alpine disasters continues its ghastly career. It is nothing short of suicidal for tourists to attempt these mad Swiss excursions, particularly when here in Ireland we have scenery, including mountain and cliff, before which the white Alps seem like a cheap diorama. Why go to Switzerland and get dashed down a fathomless abyss when you can scale the cliffs of Moher and risk little but a broken rib or two? I have nothing to say against Swiss hotels, they are admirable, from the palatial mansions of Geneva to the comfortable hydro of Davoz Platz. But here we have good hotels too, and quite as moderate as those of Switzerland – and besides, we have no glaciers.
> (*Irish Tourist* 1 [August 1903], p. 1)

In comparisons of Irish tourist development, Switzerland was situated as a 'rival' whose singular advantage over Ireland lay in the quality of her services and amenities. To advocates of the Irish sector's 'improvement', she served both as a foil for narratives of Ireland's backwardness, and as a harbinger of Ireland's potential transformation under their stewardship. Rather than developing a wider political interpretation for the economic and commercial backwardness of the Irish sector premised on a critique of the union with Great Britain, tourism advocates believed that infrastructural improvement would provide the necessary foundation for Ireland's prosperity – a widespread view in the 1890s, exemplified by the establishment of voluntary bodies such as the ITA and state-sponsored bodies such as the Congested Districts Board, which were active during the heady era of 'constructive unionism'.

Conclusion

Images of the Irish Rhine, 'Norway in Ireland' and Switzerland were incorporated within wider debates over Ireland's political status, with D.J. Wilson writing in the *Irish Tourist* in 1897 (4 [August 1897], p. 91) that the forthcoming visit of the Duke and Duchess of York might confer on the country that which she most starkly lacked in comparison with Scotland and Switzerland – neither improved hotels, nor scenery, but the mark of 'fashion'. This became a clarion call for a variety of tourist-development initiatives that aimed to insert Ireland within the tourist imagination, draw British tourists to Ireland's shores, and tap a lucrative domestic market. By qualifying Irish landscapes in ways that invited the prospective touring audience to visualize a great German river and breathtaking Norwegian fjords on the Emerald Isle, the sector's proponents planned to confer on Ireland the elusive mark of fashion. But in the promotion of specific destination-images, and in their discussions on the direction of tourist development, leaders of bodies such as the ITA gave expression to a wider ideology of political, economic and cultural development. Through an improved infrastructure and carefully-stewarded, systematic 'improvement' aimed at appealing to the British tourist market, they plotted the path to wider Irish modernization, through which she would claim her place among continental rivals, which were at one and at the same time her 'friends' and 'enemies'.

Acknowledgements

The author wishes to thank the Social Sciences and Humanities Research Council of Canada for supporting this research programme.

References

Primary sources (newspapers, books and articles)

Art Journal

Baddeley, M.J.B. (1892) *Ireland (part I). Northern Counties, including Dublin and Neighbourhood*, 3rd edn. Dulau & Co., London.

Ballantyne, R.M. (1869) *The Lakes of Killarney*. T. Nelson and Sons, London.

Cook's Excursionist and Tourist Advertiser

Cook's Traveller's Gazette

Cooke, J. (1896) *Handbook for Travellers in Ireland*, 5th edn. John Murray, London.

Curtis, W.E. (1909) *One Irish Summer*. Duffield & Co., New York.

Hardy, P.D. (n.d.) *Hardy's Tourist's Guide. Fourth Tour: Galway, Connemara, and the Irish Highlands*. Simpkin and Marshall, London.

Houghton, Lord (1895) Ireland Unvisited. In the *National Review*. Reprinted in *Littell's Living Age* 206 (24 August), 496–503.

How to See the Far-Famed Lakes of Killarney. The Great Southern & Western Railway of Ireland (1901) American Bank Note Co., Ltd, New York.

'Irish Times' Tours in Ireland: A Descriptive Handbook for Tourists (1888) 'Irish Times' Office, Dublin.

Milner, G. (1900) Four 'Vagrom men' in Donegal. *Manchester Quarterly* 19, 103–122.

Mulhall, M.G. (c.1906) *Report on State Aid to Agriculture and Industry in Switzerland', Appendix I, Report of the Recess Committee on the Establishment of a Department of Agriculture and Industries for Ireland. 'A New Edition'*. Browne & Nolan, Dublin.

O'Mahony, J. (c. 1902) *The Sunny Side of Ireland: How to See it by the Great Southern and Western Railway*, 2nd edn. Alex. Thom. & Co., Ltd, Dublin.

Report of the Recess Committee on the Establishment of a Department of Agriculture and Industries for Ireland. 'A New Edition' (c. 1906) Browne & Nolan, Dublin.

Southern Ireland: Its Lakes and Landscapes (1906) Revised edn. Great Western Railway, London.

Stone, J.H. (1906) *Connemara and the Neighbouring Spots of Beauty and Interest*. Health Resort Publishing Co., Ltd, London.

The Irish Tourist

The Times

The Traveller's Gazette

Tours in the Emerald Isle (1895) Thomas Cook & Son, Dublin.

Views of Glengarriff, Killarney, and the South-West Coast (n.d.) Guy and Company, Limited.

Wakeman, W.F. (1884) *The Tourists' Guide to Ireland*. 'Official Guide', Ltd, Dublin.

Wilson, D.J. (1900–1901) The tourist movement in Ireland. *Journal of the Statistical and Social Inquiry Society of Ireland* 11, 56–63.

Secondary sources

Ateljevic, I. and Doorne, S. (2002) Representing New Zealand: tourism imagery and ideology. *Annals of Tourism Research* 29, 648–667.

Bruhns, M. (2002) Irish drinking. *Source* 31, 20–23.

Cronin, M. and O'Connor, B. (2003) *Irish Tourism: Image, Culture and Identity*. Channel View Publications, Clevedon.

Cusask, T. (2002) A 'countryside bright with cosy homesteads': Irish nationalism and the cottage landscape. *National Identities* 3, 221–238.

Dann, G. (1996) The people of tourist brochures. In: Selwyn, T. (ed.) *The Tourist Image: Myths and Myth Making in Tourism*. John Wiley & Sons, Chichester, pp. 61–81.

Furlong, I. (2003) Frederick W. Crossley: Irish turn-of-the-century tourism pioneer. *Irish History: A Research Yearbook* 2, 162–176.

Hooper, G. (2005) *Travel Writing and Ireland, 1760–1860: Culture, History, Politics*. Palgrave Macmillan, Basingstoke.

James, K.J. (2006) Handicraft, mass manufacture and rural female labour: industrial work in north-west Ireland, 1890–1914. *Rural History* 17, 47–63.

Kneafsey, M. (2002) Tourism images and the construction of Celticity in Ireland and Brittany. In: Harvey, D.C., Jones, R., McInroy, N. and Milligan, C. (eds) *Celtic Geographies: Old Culture, New Times*. Routledge, London, pp. 123–138.

Koshar, R. (1998) 'What ought to be seen': tourists' guidebooks and national identities in modern Germany and Europe. *Journal of Contemporary History* 33, 323–340.

Markwick, M. (2004) Marketing myths and the cultural commodification of Ireland: where the grass is always greener. *Geography* 86, 37–49.

Mehegan, A. (2004) The cultural analysis of leisure: tourism and travels in Co. Donegal. *CIRCA* 107, 58–62.

Michalski, D. (2004) Portals to metropolis: 19th-century guidebooks and the assemblage of an urban experience. *Tourist Studies* 12, 187–215.

Morgan, N. and Pritchard, A. (1998) *Tourism Promotion and Power: Creating Images, Creating Identities*. John Wiley & Sons, Chichester.

Nadeau, J., Heslop, L., O'Reilly, N. and Luk, P. (2008) Destination in a country image context. *Annals of Tourism Research* 35, 84–106.

Nash, C. (1993) 'Embodying the nation' – the west of Ireland landscape and Irish identity'. In: O'Connor, B. and Cronin, M. (eds) *Tourism in Ireland: A Critical Analysis*. Cork University Press, Cork, pp. 86–112.

Nelson, V. (2007) Traces of the past: the cycle of expectation in Caribbean tourism representations. *Journal of Tourism and Cultural Change* 5, 1–16.

Pritchard, A. and Morgan, N.J. (2000) Privileging the male gaze: gendered tourism landscapes. *Annals of Tourism Research* 27, 884–905.

Ryle, M. (1999) *Journeys in Ireland: Literary Travellers, Rural Landscapes, Cultural Relations*. Ashgate, Aldershot.

Sheridan, G. and O'Leary, S. (2005) French tourist images of Ireland and *l'imaginaire irlandais*. *Irish Studies Review* 13, 151–162.

Tissot, L. (1995) How did the British conquer Switzerland? Guidebooks, railways, travel agencies, 1850–1914. *Journal of Transport History* 16, 21–54.

Tresidder, R. (1999) 'Tourism and sacred landscapes. In Crouch, D. (ed.) *Leisure/Tourism Geographies: Practices and Geographical Knowledge*. Routledge, London, pp. 137–148.

Williams, W.H.A. (2008) *Tourism, Landscape and the Irish Character: British Travel Writers in Pre-Famine Ireland*. University of Wisconsin Press, Madison, WI.

Zuelow, E.G.E. (2006) 'Ingredients for cooperation': Irish tourism in North-South relations, 1924–1998. *New Hibernia Review* 10, 17–39.

5 Decolonizing the Gaze at Uluru (Ayers Rock)

The Australian Centre, School of Historical Studies,
University of Melbourne, Victoria, Australia

Imagining space as constituted out of difference and interrelations enables the political recognition of the possibility of alternative trajectories.
(Massey, 1999, p. 285)

[T]he very function of fascination is to blind us to the fact that the other is already gazing at us.
(Žižek, 1997, p. 114)

Introduction

With visitor numbers reaching more than half a million each year, Uluru, an international icon of Australia, can truly be called an icon of the tourist gaze. Flocking together at sunrise and sunset, their cameras clicking endlessly to capture the Rock's changing colours, hundreds of tourists each day indulge in the Western 'addiction to gazing' (Oettermann, 1984). Meanwhile, coaches and helicopters disrupt the tranquillity that now is only rarely allowed to descend upon the place. Aboriginal 'country', embodiment of Tjukurpa (Aboriginal sacred law and lore of the creation time), has been commodified into a tourist 'landscape'; Uluru, itself the sacred junction of several Aboriginal creation stories, has been turned into a readily consumable tourist

spectacle. The Rock, it seems, has been carved out of the land and, despite its official Hand-back to traditional owners in 1985, has been torn out of the hands of its people, the Anangu.[1] Yet, this assessment represents only one facet of the site's many contested meanings for Indigenous and non-Indigenous Australians. To Anangu, Uluru has been sacred for thousands of years, providing physical and spiritual shelter for countless of generations. Its significance as natural and national 'heart' of the Australian nation on the other hand, is a recent development that began with the opening of the site for tourism in the 1950s and 60s (McGrath, 1991; Cathcart, 2002). The image of the Rock has since come to symbolize many things: embodying to some a sense of national belonging, it is a symbol of (neo-)colonial cultural appropriation to others (Marcus, 1999). The site continues to resonate with the conflicts and efforts of inter-cultural understanding and the hope for reconciliation in postcolonial Australia (Whittaker, 1994). Divergent narratives and images of Uluru result in different, often conflicting ways of relating to and interacting with the place. The most contested issue in this respect is the climb to the Rock's summit. While for Anangu the climb is of

---

[1] Anangu is the name by which Aboriginal people from the Central and Western desert regions refer to themselves. Originally, it means 'person' or 'people'. The two main language groups at Mutitjulu, the Aboriginal community inside Uluru-Kata Tjuta National Park, are Yankunytjatjara and Pitjantjatjara but Ngaanyatjarra and Luritja are also spoken in this region.

sacred significance and permitted only to initiated men of the Mala group, many visitors to Uluru still consider it a part of their tourist pilgrimage. Recent papers on the issue discuss the importance of representation for tourist decision-making (James, 2007) and the complex ethical questions involved in this decision, particularly for domestic Australian tourists (Waitt *et al.*, 2007). Aboriginal political and cultural agency has an increasingly significant impact on the management of both tourist behaviour and the Uluru-Kata Tjuta National Park itself. Looking at representation and tourist performance at Uluru, this chapter focuses on the kind of experiences tourists can gain through opening up to alternative perspectives as offered by Aboriginal representation. The discussion then shows how Aboriginal management of the tourist gaze can disrupt habitual Western ways of seeing, encouraging tourists to engage instead with 'other' ways of knowing place.

John Urry's metaphor of the tourist gaze (2002) has become synonymous with the tourist consumption of places and cultures, as it conceptualizes the link between image and imaginary. However, its limitations for an analysis of the non-visual aspects of tourist practice have been pointed out (Crang, 1997, 1999; Crouch, 2000; Perkins and Thorns, 2001; Crouch and Lübbren, 2003; Larsen, 2005). The one-directional (tourist) gaze retains a range of power relations at the core of the critical concept itself, not least as it implies the Other as its passive and immobile object. As feminist critique has pointed out, denying the Other's independent subjectivity, the notion of the dichotomous gaze covertly rewrites the power configurations of subject and object, presence and absence (Veijola and Jokinen, 1997; Rose, 2004, 2007). It thus passes over the possibility of a poly-dimensional space of coequal histories and knowledges as the ground for the coexistence of plural identities (Massey, 1994, 2005). Landscapes and people are turned into the blank slates of the Western desire for exotic difference (Mitchell, 1994; Schama, 1995; Urry, 2002). The concept itself thus allows no space for the Other's answering gaze nor for the consciously deviant tourist

resisting the prescriptions of the gaze. Again, in this form of critical cultural enquiry it is 'the 'Us' that is the hero of the story' (Rose, 2004, p. 20); an approach that continues to neglect both the power of Indigenous connection to land as well as the human ability to form new and interactive grounds of shared place production (Edensor, 1998, 2000; Baerenholdt *et al.*, 2004; Larsen, 2005). Therefore, in my examination of Aboriginal knowledge in practice for the tourist setting at Uluru, I not only ask 'How do 'they' see 'us'?' (Evans-Prittchard, 1989) as it would mean little more than the reversal of the gaze from its self-appointed centre, but instead I ask 'How and what do Aboriginal people make 'us' see in their country?' Indigenous ways of seeing are often specifically linked to knowledge of place and country. A multi-layered reading of place acknowledges Indigenous presence and accepts its ontological authority, emphasizing its significant consequences for the management of tourism and tourist behaviour.

The theoretical prioritizing of the 'European gaze' – one habitually adjusted to the passive consumption of culture as imagery – furthermore neglects the gazing body's 'posture' in space and the resulting implications for perception (Veijola and Jokinen, 1994, 1997, 2003; Crang, 1999; Crouch, 2002). In the following case study, I therefore understand the gaze as embodied and spatially situated, working in multiple directions, and breaking up the conventional opposition of observer and observed. Vision informs only fractions of the 'meaning-making' self; knowledge of environment and people enters mind and bodies in many ways. Tourist and place identities, furthermore, are formed in both material and discursive relationships (Massey, 2004). While I consider the discursive involvements that shape the tourist expectations, my emphasis is on the spatial and representational structures that are active in the experiential encounter. In acknowledging the often unrepresented material agency of place, my focus is on knowledges produced through intercultural recognition and interaction in the tourist moment.[2] Through an analysis of the

---

[2] These knowledges in Central Australia have grown from the Indigenous connection to country over millennia. Yet for too long they were considered invalid because they stand outside of the institutionalized knowledge context, i.e. see Foucault (1972, 1973).

different (physical and narrative) postures presented in fieldwork interviews, I discuss variations of the gaze – or rather, as Veijola and Jokinen suggest, different experiential 'sensualities and modalities' – as they can be found in tourist settings in Central Australia.

Study Background – a Word in Favour of the Tourist – and Methodology

> The visual and embodied experience of the tourists does not always follow the linear narrative of entering, seeing and conquering. The one who moves and gazes touches the scenery in different ways, sensualities and modalities: with passion, arrogance, violence – playfulness.
>
> (Veijola and Jokinen, 2003, p. 274)

The tourist has been described as the postmodern successor of Benjamin's voyeuristic flâneur (Bauman, 1998; Urry, 2002),[3] a vagabond who traverses other people's lives and spaces but is incapable of forming responsible human connections and meaningful relationships (Bauman, 1998). The tourist thus widely suffers from the ill reputation of both passing consumer and neo-colonial invader: his or her disembodied and detached 'camera eye', the ultimate tool of visual consumption and imaginative appropriation, disciplines people and places into images that can be cut out of their meaning contexts. Stuck behind the camera and in the hands of profit hunting 'professionals' in the tourist industry (Urry, 2002), the tourist is complicit in the destruction of 'authenticity', as tourist photography, if seen as the continual reproduction of signs,[4] enters and repeats the endless rotations of what Urry calls the 'hermeneutic circle' (Urry, 2002).

The questions and findings of this chapter arise from research into international tourists' experiences of the Australian desert. I read the Western, non-domestic traveller's fascination with the wide open spaces and the harsh climate of the desert as the desire for an authenticity – or an authenticated experience – that to many appears to have been lost in their sensually restricted and densely populated urban home environments. Not only are notions of authenticity disputed (Pearce and Moscardo, 1986; Wang, 1999; Olsen, 2002; Cohen, 2004), the general Western turn away from the material and towards a priority of the experiential suggests that the tourist's quest is increasingly directed towards an authenticity of experience (MacNaghten and Urry, 1998; Steiner and Reisinger, 2006; Kim and Jamal, 2007).[5] Following Wang's (2000) concept of an existential authenticity, I suggest that the tourist interest is directed less toward an authenticity of the *object* but rather toward finding authentic modes of experience. As travel practices and experiences are the expression and continuation of personal narratives (Desforges, 2000; McCabe and Stokoe, 2004; Noy, 2004; White and White, 2004), tourism also involves practices of self-knowing, self-representation and self-actualization (Crang, 1999; Butcher, 2003). In this perspective, tourism becomes a personalized search for an authenticity of the self in which 'the concept [of authenticity] becomes mobilized by different tourists in different locations according to different criteria' (May, 1996, p. 711). The experience of the authentic thus involves the expression of the self in all its relations with the world (Hetherington, 1998; Crouch, 2004; Steiner and Reisinger, 2006). Tourists pitch their subjectivities and their bodies as contact zones between the self and the unknown, collecting, negotiating and testing knowledge as mosaic stones of personal life-stories. Tourism is a 'knowing practice' that happens in the zones of embodied being, feeling and imaginative processes. Knowledge processes are combined and productive – rather than consumptive – processes that simultaneously depend on the tourist's situatedness in both metaphorical and material space.

---

[3]Veijola and Jokinen (1997) discuss the figurations of the male gaze in the flâneur, the tourist and other postmodern figurations from a feminist perspective.

[4]Contrary to this, Crouch (2002) and Larsen (2005) for example suggest the emphasis on tourist photography as social performance and individual meaning making.

[5]The experience of 'togetherness' with non-human bodies, for example has been described for tourists swimming with dolphins in New Zealand by Cloke and Perkins (2005).

The aim of my qualitative field research, conducted during a pilot field trip to Central Australia in November 2006, was hence to investigate how discursively constructed images and received experiences tie in with the tourists' narratives of self. I conducted 20 semi-structured, conversational interviews with tourists at various sites and stages of their travels in Australia. This collection of narrated experience was extended by ethnographic observation of tourist behavioural patterns at tourist locations in Central Australia. The research population consequently ranged from coach tourists with highly organized and tightly scheduled programmes to groups whose interest in local life and Aboriginal culture motivated a longer stay. Another group of interviewees is represented with self-drive tourists, and other independent travellers, such as backpackers and single travellers. These so-called Free Independent Travellers (FITs), because of their autonomous time management, are more likely to spend more time at the Rock, take a walk around its base and seek a closer encounter with Aboriginal culture through the park's Cultural Centre or Aboriginal tour companies (Blamey and Hatch, 1998; NT-Government, 2005). Contrary to the FITs, it is the mass- or coach-tourist, who remains in the 'tourist bubble' of coach and resort (Boorstin, 1964), and who is usually expected to have little interest in a genuine interaction with the destination environment. While different tourist types arguably pursue different experiences (Cohen, 1979), these typologies, however, seem to be less reliable in Australia and amongst visitors to Uluru. According to my findings, in the Australian context these typologies allow no general conclusions concerning the tourists' attitudes. Because of long distances from home and within Australia, international travellers in the majority travel on a restricted budget and schedule. The unfamiliar conditions and the vastness of the country furthermore let it seem advisable to some tourists – who would usually prefer self-organized travel – to entrust themselves to the hands of knowledgeable 'professionals'. As my interest focuses here on the transformational potential of Aboriginal place representations, therefore, I largely neglect the impact of tourist typologies. Ethnographic participant observation captures behavioural patterns of tourists at the Rock.

The affective and haptic dimensions of the tourist experience on the other hand remains elusive. Using the techniques of photo- and audio-elicitation (Duffy et al., 2007; Wood et al., 2007) and asking participants to take photos or find other means of communicating their subjective experience, such as concentrating on physical sensations in interview questions, assisted in the collection of this kind of emotional data.

'Seeing and Doing' – Images and Postures at Uluru

Tourist postures I – The climb

Tourist discourses of 'site sacralization' (MacCannell, 1989) directly utilize Uluru's multilayered appeal as Aboriginal sacred site and national icon, its significance in various esoteric New Age constructions as well as the perceived simplicity of its surrounding 'pristine wilderness' (Hill, 1994). Uluru can be made to appeal to a range of tourist types: from the spiritual and nature-loving tourist to the adventure tourist or those on a quest of the nation's symbolic heart. Pictures of the Rock avoid the depiction of roads, cars or other infrastructure while even single tourists are commonly missing from these images, evoking a remoteness that appears to offer the space for spiritual solitude and silence. Such images address what MacCannell calls the egocentric observer (MacCannell, 2007). Despite the increased marketing of the Aboriginal relationship with Uluru and its promotion as a site where the tourist can experience the 'mystery and spirituality of one of the oldest cultures in the world' (from the film 'Selling Australia', Redwood, 2001), Aboriginal people are similarly missing from most photographs. The guiding desire of many tourists journeying to Central Australia is to see the icon with their own eyes and to be 'touched' by the place in a way that is only possible when they are physically there. Most of my interviewees stated that such a visit to the Rock was their main objective for travelling to Central Australia. At the same time, they were often quite aware that their expectations had been pre-shaped by the already known and endlessly reproduced 'framed image' of Uluru centred in the empty plain. Asked about their expectations prior to their visit, many answered, 'Well, I guess, I expect just what the tourist expects' (Frank, Interview, 2006). My observations illustrate, however, that visitors to Uluru nonetheless search for the personal encounter to experience what Benjamin (1973) describes as the *aura* of the original object, i.e. of the Rock's 'presence in time and space, its unique existence at the place where it happens to be' (Benjamin, 1973, p. 222). Yet, framed by tourist narratives of 'the vast and unspoiled wonders of Australia's interior' (CATIA, 2007), the repeated and recycled image pre-selects what is expected and what is subsequently seen (Urry, 2002). The desire to take visual possession of Uluru's presence, to 'pry [it] from its shell' and to objectify it in the reproducible image, is to "destroy its aura" for the perceiving individual (Benjamin, 1973, p. 225). The tourist thus encounters the "paradox of desire" as described by Žižek:

> The paradox of desire is that it posits retroactively its own cause, i.e., the object a [the object of desire in Lacan's terms] is an object that can be perceived only by a gaze "distorted" by desire, an object that does not exist for an "objective" gaze.
>
> (Žižek, 1997, p. 12)

Excising Uluru out of its context, the framed image creates the empty surface for the projection of desire from which, in reality, the observer only receives what has been projected onto it before. In other words, in looking too intently at the desired object, 'straight-on' and 'matter-of-factly', the observer might lose the 'thing itself' (Žižek, 1997, p.11) and is instead left with nothing more than the generic image. The framed and objectifying gaze thus often causes disappointment and inspires the wish to 'interact' and touch the site in a way that authenticates and intensifies the experience. The kind of knowledge this gaze fails to wrench from the rock must be achieved through physical conquest. The cultural posture corresponding to the centred and vertical image of Uluru then, the 'being and doing' (Veijola and Jokinen, 2003) this constructed landscape seems to prescribe, is the heroically elevated position of the 'monarch-of-all-I-survey' that allows the tourist to assume the

surveillant cartographic gaze and replay the gestures of mapping and occupying a seemingly empty country (Pratt, 1992). Following in the logic of the centring gaze from afar, the rock calls for the climber to master it and the surrounding landscape. This urge to physically bond with the natural giant overcomes both domestic and international tourists. But what drives people to a climb that is both dangerous and culturally contested? 'What kinds of bondings and cravings are at work when [. . .] climbing a mountain with a view?' (Veijola and Jokinen, 2003, p. 260).

Uluru as a topographical symbol of the Australian nation harks back to the foundational myths of the explorers who penetrated and opened the wilderness for the settlers (McGrath, 1991). In recent decades, the climb – the tourist's ritualistically repeated conquest of the interior – has therefore been constructed as an important performance of Australian settler identity. Similarly, Veijola and Jokinen draw a parallel between the topography of the mountain and imaginations of nationhood,

> The view from the top of the mountain, downwards, suggests a posture that is proper when symbolizing an autonomous and brave new nation that has just begun to maintain an upright position, like a mammal or a human child that has learned to walk.
>
> (Veijola and Jokinen, 2003, p. 263)

The spatial logic of the vertical position, allowing the horizontal view over an apparently 'empty land'[6] employs 'the imperialist notion that there is a place of overview from which to analyse and 'objectively' report the world' (Edensor, 1998, p. 16). This perspective is thus aligned with the general – masculine – narratives of exploration, mastery and historical progress (Lefebvre, 1991; Birkeland, 1999). Like the frontal gaze onto the rock surface, eclipsing Indigenous presence from its line of vision, the centred viewpoint reduces meaning in the service of the dominant power and knowledge system. It is in the nature of this monological Western knowledge that it does not tolerate the presence of other, Aboriginal knowledges as they may subvert its own grand gestures by asserting prior occupation. Instead, it inscribes the hegemonic world order into the land and

---

[6]A perspective that formed the backdrop to the legal construction of *terra nullius* from British colonial times used as justification for Aboriginal dispossession of their land.

consequently writes its Indigenous inhabitants out of history. At Uluru, this world ordering has been physically inscribed into the fabric of the place. Iron poles and chains installed along the well-trodden pathway to the summit seemingly authorize the climb as the natural posture of the modern tourist.

Despite Anangu's disapproval, non-Indigenous opposition against a closure of the climb is still strong, naming financial loss for both Anangu and non-Aboriginal operators as the main reason (Digance, 2003). Yet, while the climb remains open, an increasing number of local tour operators inform their passengers of Anangu's request and promote the 'don't climb' message.[7] Anangu representation encourages visitors to stay on the ground and experience a different perspective of the rock that is not in conflict with local culture.[8] While some tourists may continue to pursue the summit, the alternative perspective is spreading, often initiating critical reflection on the issue of the climb as my interviews show.[9]

A meeting place of knowledges

The tourist comes here with the camera taking pictures all over. What has he got? Another photo to take home, keep part of Uluru. He should get another lens – see straight inside. Wouldn't see big rock then. He would see that Kuniya living right inside there as from the beginning . . .
Kunmanara, traditional owner, Uluru.
(UKTNP, 2006, p. 20)[10]

Kunmanara's advice, given in the Uluru-Kata Tjuta visitor guide, suggests a different way of looking at Uluru that discards the tourists'

'objective' and 'straight-on' gaze in favour of a more personal way of seeing, and thus reveals the 'thing itself' (Žižek, 1997), the story and meaning of the place as known to its traditional owners. Aboriginal relationship to country in the Central desert regions of Australia is guided by the Tjukurpa,[11] often inaccurately translated as the 'Dreaming', which refers to the creation time and the presence of the ancestors. During their journeys across country, the ancestors created every land feature through their action and song. Then, they 'went back in', i.e. they transformed into landmarks such as Uluru, but also smaller, seemingly less significant geographical features (Rose, 1996). Tjukurpa records and preserves the ancestors' knowledge of country for future generations. It topographically embodies the law of the country, providing not only the knowledge crucial for the sustainable survival in the harsh desert environment but also containing moral directives for human interaction and responsible behaviour in the country. Children and other uninitiated people, however, can only be told so-called 'surface stories' that omit the secret-sacred content of the complete song or story.

One of Uluru's stories that is shared with tourists tells of the epic battle between two snakes, Kuniya the python and the poisonous Liru, a battle eternalized in the shape and texture of the rock. The story explains a set of instructions that relate to the correct use and management of the Mutitjulu waterhole, located at the site of the battle and guarded by the water snake Wanampi. Knowledge of Uluru's Tjukurpa hence informs a particular way of seeing – and acting – that is often hardly perceivable for

---

[7] Field notes 2006/07 and James (2007).

[8] However, as James (2007) has shown, tourists often feel that information about this cultural sensitivity should be promoted more prominently.

[9] James (2007, p. 399) for example notes a significant 20% decline of people climbing Uluru between 1991 and 2004. In the current climate of tourist education, these numbers can be expected to fall further.

[10] 'Kunmanara: Pitjantjatjara for 'one who's name cannot be mentioned'. This refers to the name of a recently deceased person. As part of Pitjantjatjara mortuary beliefs, all people with the same name, or even a name that sounds similar to the one belonging to a person who has died, take the name 'Kunmanara' [. . .] Kunmanara will remain in place until the grieving family deems it appropriate to bring the name back into use. Occasionally an alternative word with the same meaning but different sound may be used' (Ara-Irititja-Project, 2007).

[11] This is not to be misunderstood as a pan-Aboriginal term, the central desert language of Yankuntjatjara for example uses the term *Wapar* for a similar concept, see http://www.environment.gov.au/parks/uluru/tjukurpa/index.html (Accessed 26 August 2007).

the direct and cognitive Western gaze. A local Anangu man's comment illustrates this different nature of Western and Aboriginal ways of seeing and knowing place.

> Do you know what the difference is between you whitefellas and us blackfellas? You whitefella look at the rock – you are all crazy about the rock – you look at it and you have heard the story of Kuniya and Liru. So you look at it and maybe you can see a shape here that looks a little bit like a snake, a little bit like Kuniya and you think, alright, I can see Kuniya alright. But us blackfella, we look at Uluru and we say, oh yes, Kuniya, she's getting old, she's starting to look a little bit like rock now.
>
> (Field notes, 2006)

While the Western gaze remains in the frontal and subject position, scrutinizing its object for fragments of knowledge and looking for signs of what it perceives as a mythological past – but having found the sign, fails to understand the story's full meaning and applicability – the Aboriginal intimacy with country extends far beyond the visual. The rock in Anangu perspective is a living co-presence, the body of the ancestor, forming the personal and collective link to country and with past and future generations. From this embodied presence of living knowledge and culture derives a sense of kinship and responsibility for country and people. Anangu interpretation, according to Tjukurpa, encourages a dialogic relationship with country as opposed to the one-directional gaze of the habitual Western perspective.

During the 1970s, largely unregulated tourism to the Rock led to severe environmental degradation and cultural disturbances at Uluru (Hill, 1994; Davison and Spearritt, 2000). The protection of their country and cultural identity thus depended on Anangu being able once again to tell the stories of the Tjukurpa. With the Rock's official Handback, Anangu won Freehold Title for the national park, which they are currently leasing back to the Federal Government's Australian Parks and Wildlife Service. Anangu have since been able to control representation and management of the site significantly. The Rocks' colonial name, 'Ayers Rock', was changed back to 'Uluru' in 1993, but the actual scope of Anangu control is summarized in the maxim heading the current Plan of Management for the park (Uluru-Kata Tjuta Board of Management, 2000): 'Tjukurpa above all

else'. Today, Uluru-Kata Tjuta National Park is jointly managed by Anangu and non-Aboriginal rangers, following the principles of Tjukurpa. Workshops and compulsory accreditation for tour operators aim to protect cultural integrity, while emphasizing Anangu interpretation of Uluru (Uluru-Kata Tjuta Board of Management, 2000, p.136). The opening of the Cultural Centre became central to this mission, extending Anangu's ability to simultaneously share and manage knowledge of country. Amongst the cultural display, the visitor is simultaneously introduced to Anangu regulation of the gaze: photography in the Cultural Centre is prohibited, and photo displays of traditional owners will be concealed during mourning periods in the case of a traditional owner's death. Spatial restructuring closer to the Rock itself represents further efforts towards the creation of a culturally and environmentally sensitive infrastructure. Sacred sites are generally fenced off to prevent visitors from entering and signs prohibit photography at these sites. Anangu's request to visitors not to climb the Rock is prominently represented in the visitor guide, at the Cultural Centre and at the foot of the climb.

Tourist postures II – The walk

> That's a really important sacred thing that you are climbing . . . You shouldn't climb. It's not the real thing about this place. The real thing is listening to everything.
>
> And maybe that makes you a bit sad. But anyway that's what we have to say. We are obliged by Tjukurpa to say. And all the tourists will brighten up and say, 'Oh, I see. This is the thing that's right. This is the proper way: no climbing.' Kunmanu, tradtitional owner.
>
> (UKTNP, 2006, p. 6)

As I have outlined above, the distinct and contested 'rituals' of engaging with Uluru involve different postures and ways of seeing. The tourist ritual of climbing the rock claims the ontologically symbolic space of the 'above'. This posture creates and reinforces the detached gaze over an objectified landscape. In opposition to this, the traditional Indigenous relationship to country is fundamentally place-related, personal and dialogic. As Kunmanu says above, these different ways of interacting with place – gazing at it versus listening to it – produce different kinds of knowledge. An important part of this place-related cultural etiquette is that Anangu do not climb Uluru. In fact, traditional owner Barbara Tjikatu, in the visitor guide, makes it very clear that respect for Anangu culture and law is only adequately expressed by not climbing: 'If you worry about Aboriginal law, then leave it, don't climb it' (UKTNP, 2004). Instead, tourists are invited to stop and listen and experience the rock by walking around its base. Tourists are thus encouraged to 'break the frame' of the frontal image as they walk close to the rock, to discover the 'below', 'the rear and the back' of the scenery, and thus see what is habitually excluded from the European vision as childish, 'premodern' and even 'past and profane' (Veijola and Jokinen, 2003, p. 263). The invitation to do the base walk instead of the climb is thus also the invitation to change posture and perspective.

The course of the walk is directed by the sequence of the stories told by the various sites around the Rock. Retracing the story in its proper sequence, the visitor is thus led into the Anangu story of place. The inscribed mythology of the Tjukurpa is culturally encoded knowledge that answers to the tourist's desire to 'know' the place, or more importantly, the 'desire to know what cannot be seen' (Game in Crouch, 2002, p. 215). On the 3–4-h walk around the Rock, visitors can experience the unique habitat that has formed here for humans, flora and fauna. They learn to experience the place as a living entity rather than seeing it as a static image. Walkers frequently express their surprise about the 'multi-dimensionality' of the Rock when its many folds and layers, waterholes and caves become visible in the proximate gaze, contradicting the framed surface image of the solid rock. One walker explicitly said that he did not give much attention to the mythological story but reported from his experience:

> First, I wasn't very impressed by the sight of the Rock, you know, when you see it from the lookout. It just looks like what you expect it to look like. But when you walk around it, you begin to see it differently; you realize how big it is. When you look at it from so close you can see its history, the erosions, washed into the surface. It almost looks like the skin of an animal.
> (Daniel, Interview, 2006)

As this quote demonstrates, in many accounts of their experience at Uluru, tourists seem to invest an animate quality into the Rock when they talk about its 'skin' or personalize it otherwise, speaking of it as 'he'. It is not uncommon to observe them waving a farewell to Uluru. Once the observer is taken out of his or her masterly detached position of the straightforward, seemingly all-comprehending gaze, the framed image gives way to a closer look, allowing a more personal, embodied knowledge of place. Knowledge of Anangu interpretation opens entry-points to Aboriginal ontology on an intellectual level. Yet, being encouraged to take the posture 'below', which in European culture is associated with the childlike and inferior, visitors have to abandon their habitual surveying posture and instead enter a face-to-face-level with the rock. Martin and Gisela, a couple from Franconia, said they had decided against climbing the Rock after learning of its cultural significance for Anangu. For them, they said, this decision was a matter of 'mutual respect'. They experienced quite strongly the contradiction between the tranquillity of their walk and the noisy spectacle of the climb. Both agreed that their experience of the place was significantly enriched by the decision not to climb. When I asked Martin about his experience, he seemed lost for the right word to describe the experience from this different perspective, replying: 'I found the sight oppressive but in a positive kind of way . . .' 'Impressive, maybe?' Gisela seconded – 'Well, impressive!' Martin agreed, thereby resuming the rational posture of the aesthetically detached sightseer (Martin and Gisela, Interview, 2006).

Through knowledge of Uluru's mythology visitors learn to see Uluru as a cultural site – rather than a natural landscape – that has been inscribed with a much older knowledge and sense of belonging. Uluru's aura derives from its embeddedness in the 'fabric of tradition' (Benjamin, 1973, p. 225) so that Anangu's cultural presence becomes inseparable from the tourists' experience of the place. Expressing awe at Anangu survival skills and spiritual richness, several participants of an adult study group expressed sentiments such as:

> I now realize how arrogant I have been. I used to think that these people were somehow backward, primitive. But they have a lot of knowledge. It is just different to our knowledge. [It is] the kind of knowledge you need in this land.
> (Group A, notes and Interview, 2006)

In the encounter with the 'other' knowledge, these tourists thus reconsidered the presumed universality of Western knowledge productions. The re- or displacement of the gaze similarly contributes to a shift in perspective. Contrary to its first impression as a readily available sight, Uluru does not open easily to the direct and frontal gaze. On their walk, tourists often find signs that prohibit photography at sacred sites. It is here that they encounter another paradox of the tourist moment at Uluru: the authentic experience lies in the disruption of the most 'natural' of tourist impulses, to capture their experience of a place on photo or film and in the absence of the desired object. But tourists cannot know or comprehend what exactly is being withdrawn from their gaze. In this absence, the cultural site of Uluru retains its auratic existence in the fabric of tradition. Aboriginal politics of representation, as Palmer states, 'meets the Western desire to 'know' [. . .] not with 'naturalized' objectivity, but through a process of personalized and overt inter-subjectivity that returns the non-Aboriginal gaze' (Palmer, 2007, p. 267). Cultural markers – by marking an absence or limitation to the gaze – thus function as entry points into deeper levels of place meaning and, by extension, a shared understanding of place and culture of the sort that the tourist – in her search for an 'authentic' or 'authenticated' experience – is looking for. The prohibited and dispersed gaze can thus open the senses for the 'real thing':

> [I]f we look at a thing straight on, i.e.,
> matter-of-factly, disinterestedly, objectively, we
> see nothing but a formless spot; the object
> assumes clear and distinctive features only if we
> look at it 'at an angle', i.e. with an 'interested'
> view, supported, permeated, and 'distorted' by
> desire.
>
> (Žižek, 1997, pp. 11–12)

As other ways of seeing open up other possible ways of knowing, they create an ethical moment for the recognition of difference. The space at Uluru can thus be experienced as a ground for an ethical encounter with place and across cultures, that does not force the Other under the possessive gestures of the gaze. Encountering limits to their visual consumption changes the tourist's self-perception as passing consumer and raises the awareness of their being guests in an Aboriginal space. It is an encounter across difference that respects – and enjoys – the fundamental distance, the unavailability of the Other as the core of its inalienable integrity. It is this realization that the tourist may learn from Anangu's direction of the gaze: the moment of the encounter, of touching and being touched, is irreproducible and unique.

Conclusion

Perspectives on landscape – and hence the postures of the body they seem to prescribe – are culturally produced. Yet my analysis of perspectives and performances – Aboriginal and non-Aboriginal 'rituals of place' – at Uluru shows how conventional postures and habitual ways of seeing can be disrupted and reconfigured in the interplay of representation and embodied experience. In my discussion, I worked with the premise of an embodied visuality, arguing that what is seen and how it is seen depends on the tourist body's posture in space. Indigenous knowledge management at Uluru invites visitors to change posture, both physically and ontologically. In diverting and interrupting the subject–object divide of the gaze, Anangu representation offers the possibility to enter a personal, dialogic and therefore ethically responsible relationship with place and culture. Anangu do not simply return the outsider's gaze. Their regulation and prohibition of the tourist gaze turns (a perceived) absence into the presence of difference. Most of my interviewees, having learned about Anangu's cultural sensitivities and quite contrary to the image of the tourist as pleasure seeking consumer, perceived themselves as guests on Anangu land and were prepared to conduct their visit accordingly. The tourists' search for the authentic(-ated) experience, as I have shown, can strengthen the motivation to subscribe to a cultural etiquette of place. In the case of the climb at Uluru, this observation may help to disperse some tourist operators' concerns that a closure of the climb would lead to a decline in visitor numbers. On the contrary, if taken out of their habitual postures and being 'displaced' onto the embodied scale of the face-to-face, tourists can no longer sustain their self-perception as unattached consumers. Their willingness to suspend their Western perspective on the land and to consider Aboriginal viewpoints results from a complex interplay of realizations: their own vulnerability in the harsh desert climate is experienced in stark contrast to Aboriginal resilience and skilful survival for thousands of years. In some of my interviewees, this led to the realization of the local embeddedness and relevance of knowledge. Reclaiming place at Uluru, Anangu's active politics of (non-) representation overturn the conceptual absence of the Other as it is prescribed by the Western gaze. Rewriting it instead as the evocative presence of their living culture, Anangu's strong voice asserts cultural integrity by defying the role of the invariably silenced and invisible Other.

Acknowledgements

For their advice on the draft manuscript of this article, I would like to thank Dr Michelle Duffy and Dr Rachel Hughes, as well as Dr Jacqueline Dutton and Dr Michael Cathcart at Melbourne University. My fieldwork in Central Australia in November 2006 was supported by the University of Melbourne's PhD programme. I would like to thank Martin and Cheryl Ludgate for their advice and hospitality as well as tour operators and tourists in Alice Springs and at Ayers Rock Resort, for their participation and contribution to my research. Thanks to Anita Meyer, On-Tours, Alice Springs, for making it possible for me to talk to her tour groups and finally, Ben Van Vranken.

References

Primary sources

CATIA (2007) Central Australian Tourism Association http://www.centralaustraliantourism.com/main.php.

Interview (2006) Field/interview notes. In: Paschen, J.-A. (ed.) Central Australia & Melbourne.

NT-Government (2005) Northern Territory Government media release. German backpackers targeted in travel promotion. www.tourismnt.com.au/nt/nttc/news/mdeia_releases/mr/2005/mr_Feb03_germanpromo.html.

Redwood, J. (2001) The Red Heart. *Selling Australia*. ABC, Australia.

UKTNP (2004) *Uluru-KataTjuta National Park Visitor Guide*.

UKTNP (2006) *Uluru-Kata Tjuta National Park Visitor Guide*.

Secondary sources

Ara-Irititja-Project (2007) Sharing knowledge/glossary. http://www.irititja.com/sharing_knowledge/glossary. html (Accessed 18 March 2009).

Baerenholdt, J., Haldrup, M., Larsen, J. and Urry, J. (eds) (2004) *Performing Tourist Places*. Ashgate Publishing, Aldershot.

Bauman, Z. (1998) Tourists and vagabonds. In Bauman, Z. (ed.) *Globalization: The Human Consequences*. Polity Press, Cambridge.

Benjamin, W. (1973) The work of art in the age of mechanical reproduction. In: Arendt, H., trans. Zohn, H. (ed.) *Illuminations*. New Left, London.

Birkeland, I. (1999) The mytho-poetic in northern travel. In: Crouch, D. (ed.) *Leisure/Tourism*. Routledge, London.

Blamey, R. and Hatch, D. (1998) *Profiles and Motivations of Nature-Based Tourists Visiting Australia*. Bureau of Tourism Research, Canberra.

Boorstin, D.J. (1964) *The Image: a Guide to Pseudo-events in America*. Harper & Row, New York.

Butcher, J. (2003) *The Moralisation of Tourism. Sun, sand . . . and saving the world?* Routledge, London.

Cathcart, M. (2002) Uluru. In: Bonyhady, T. and Griffiths, T. (eds) *Words for Country. Landscape and Language in Australia*. University of New South Wales Press, Sydney.

Cloke, P. and Perkins, H.C. (2005) Cetacean performance and tourism in Kaikoura, New Zealand. *Environment and Planning D: Society and Space* 23, 903–924.

Cohen, E. (1979) A phenomenology of tourist experiences. *Sociology* 13, 179–201.

Cohen, E. (2004) *Contemporary Tourism. Diversity and Change*, Elsevier, Amsterdam.

Crang, M. (1997) Picturing practices: research through the tourist gaze. *Progress in Human Geography* 21, 359–373.

Crang, M. (1999) Knowing, tourism and practices of vision. In Crouch, D. (ed.) *Leisure/Tourism Geographies. Practices and Geographical Knowledge*. Routledge, London.

Crouch, D. (2000) Places around us: embodied lay geographies in leisure and tourism. *Leisure Studies* 19, 63–76.

Crouch, D. (2002) Surrounded by place: embodied encounters. In: Coleman, S. and Crang, M. (eds) *Tourism. Between Place and Performance*. Berghahn Books, New York.

Crouch, D. (2004) Tourist practices and performances. In: Lew, A.A., Hall, C.M. and Williams, A.M. (eds) *A Companion to Tourism*. Blackwell, Oxford.

Crouch, D. and Lübbren, N. (eds) (2003) *Visual Culture and Tourism*. Berg, Oxford.

Davison, J. and Spearritt, P. (2000) The rediscovery of the centre and Aboriginal tourism. In Davison, J. and Spearritt, P. (eds) *Holiday Business: Tourism in Australia since 1870*. Melbourne University Press, Melbourne.

Desforges, L. (2000) Travelling the world. Identity and travel biography. *Annals of Tourism Research* 27, 926–945.

Digance, J. (2003) Pilgrimage at contested sites. *Annals of Tourism Research* 30, 143–159.

Duffy, M., Waitt, G. and Gibson, C. (2007) Get into the groove: the role of sound in creating a sense of belonging in street parades. *Altitude* 8, 1–22.

Edensor, T. (1998) *Tourists at the Taj: Performance and Meaning at a Symbolic Site*, London, Routledge.

Edensor, T. (2000) Staging tourism. Tourists as performers. *Annals of Tourism Research* 27, 322–344.

Evans-Prittchard, D. (1989) How do 'they' see 'us'? Native American images of tourists. *Annals of Tourism Research* 16, 89–105.

Foucault, M. (1972) *The Archaeology of Knowledge*. Tavistock Publications, London.

Foucault, M. (1973) *The Order of Things: an Archaeology of the Human Sciences*. Vintage Books, New York.

Hetherington, K. (1998) *Expressions of Identity: Space, Performance, Politics*. Sage, London.

Hill, B. (1994) *The Rock. Travelling to Uluru*. Allen & Unwin, St Leonards, NSW.

James, S. (2007) Constructing the climb: visitor decision-making at Uluru. *Geographical Research. Journal of the Institute of Australian Geographers* 45, 398–407.

Kim, H. and Jamal, T. (2007) Touristic quest for existential authenticity. *Annals of Tourism Research* 34, 181–201.

Larsen, J. (2005) Families seen sightseeing: performativity of tourist photography. *Space and Culture* 8, 416–434.

Lefebvre, H. (1991) *The Production of Space*. Blackwell, Oxford.

MacCannell, D. (1989) *The Tourist: a New Theory of the Leisure Class*. Macmillan, London.

MacCannell, D. (2007) Keynote. *6th International Symposium on Aspects of Tourism*. Eastbourne Campus, University of Brighton, 13–15 June 2007.

MacNaghten, P. and Urry, J. (1998) *Contested Natures*. Sage, London.

Marcus, J. (1999) The journey out to the centre. The cultural appropriation of Ayers Rock. In: Marcus, J. (ed.) *A Dark Smudge Upon the Sand. Essays on Race, Guilt and the National Consciousness*. LhR Press, Canada Bay, NSW.

Massey, D. (1994) *Space, Place and Gender*. Polity Press, Cambridge.

Massey, D. (1999) Space of politics. In: Massey, D., Allen, J. and Sarre, P. (eds) *Human Geography Today*. Polity Press, Cambridge.

Massey, D. (2004) Geographies of responsibility. *Geografiska Annaler* 86B, 5–18.

Massey, D. (2005) *For Space*. Sage, London.

May, J. (1996) In search of authenticity off and on the beaten track. *Environment and Planning D: Society and Space* 14, 709–736.

McCabe, S. and Stokoe, E. (2004) Place and identity in tourists' accounts. *Annals of Tourism Research* 31, 601–622.

McGrath, A. (1991) Travels to a distant past: the mythology of the outback. *Australian Cultural History* 10, 113–124.

Mitchell, W.J.T. (ed.) (1994) *Landscape and Power. Introduction*. The University of Chicago Press, Chicago, IL.

Noy, C. (2004) This trip really changed me. Backpackers' narratives of self-change. *Annals of Tourism Research* 31, 78–102.

Oettermann, S. (1984) Die Entdeckung des Horizonts [The discovery of the horizon]. In: Bergmann, K. and Ockenfuss, S. (eds) *Neue Horizonte. Eine Reise durch die Reisen*. Rowohlt, Reinbek bei Hamburg.

Olsen, K. (2002) Authenticity as a concept in tourism research. *Tourist Studies* 2, 159–182.

Palmer, L. (2007) Interpreting 'nature': the politics of engaging with Kakadu as an Aboriginal place. *Cultural Geographies* 14, 255–273.

Pearce, P. and Moscardo, G. (1986) The concept of authenticity in tourist experiences. *Journal of Sociology* 22, 121–132.

Perkins, H.C. and Thorns, D.C. (2001) Gazing or performing? Reflections on Urry's tourist gaze in the context of contemporary experiences in the Antipodes. *International Sociology* 16, 185–204.

Pratt, M.L. (1992) *Imperial Eyes. Travel Writing and Transculturation*. Routledge, London.

Rose, D.B. (1996) *Nourishing Terrains. Australian Aboriginal Views of Landscape and Wilderness*. Australian Heritage Commission, Canberra.

Rose, D.B. (2004) *Reports from a Wild Country. Ethics for Decolonization*. UNSW Press, Sydney.

Rose, G. (2007) *Visual Methodologies*. Sage, London.

Schama, S. (1995) *Landscape and Memory*. Random House, New York.

Steiner, C.J. and Reisinger, Y. (2006) Understanding existential authenticity. *Annals of Tourism Research* 33, 299–318.

Urry, J. (2002) *The Tourist Gaze*. Sage, London.

Veijola, S. and Jokinen, E. (1994) The body in tourism. *Theory, Culture, Society* 11, 125–151.

Veijola, S. and Jokinen, E. (1997) The disoriented tourist: the figuration of the tourists in contemporary cultural critique. In: Rojek, C. and Urry, J. (eds) *Touring Cultures. Transformations of Travel and Theory*. Routledge, London.

Veijola, S. and Jokinen, E. (2003) Mountains and landscapes: towards embodied visualities. In: Crouch, D. and Lübbren, N. (eds) *Visual Culture and Tourism*. Berg, Oxford.

Waitt, G., Figueroa, R. and McGee, L. (2007) Fissures in the Rock: rethinking pride and shame in the moral terrains of Uluru. *Transactions of the Institute of British Geographers* 32, 248–263.

Wang, N. (1999) Rethinking authenticity in tourism experience. *Annals of Tourism Research* 26, 349–370.

Wang, N. (2000) *Tourism and Modernity: A Sociological Analysis*. Pergamon, Kidlington, Oxon.

White, N.R. and White, P.B. (2004) Travel as transition. Identity and place. *Annals of Tourism Research* 31, 200–218.

Whittaker, E. (1994) Public discourse on sacredness: the transfer of Ayers Rock to Aboriginal ownership. *American Ethnologist* 21, 310–334.

Wood, N., Duffy, M. and Smith, S.J. (2007) The art of doing (geographies of) music. *Environment and Planning D: Society and Space* 25, 867–889.

Žižek, S. (1997) *Looking Awry. An Introduction to Jacques Lacan through Popular Culture*. Massachussetts Institute of Technology, Cambridge, MA.

6 Tracking the (Tourists') Gaze: Using Technology in Visual Analysis of Identificational Strategies

Sergej Stoetzer

Institute for Sociology, Technical University, Darmstadt, Germany

Introduction

Visual representations of cities are becoming more and more relevant for tourism industries as well as for the tourists themselves. Generated on different layers of professionalism they intend to give the visual impression of a specific place, integrating atmospheric components and shaping the gaze – according to what was anticipated by the professionals in media industries who created the visual representations in the first place (Mercille, 2005). Professional images are oriented towards media distribution in campaigns used to convey a precise picture of what should be regarded as specific to the city in the eyes of the beholder.

Besides these intended images, subjective ones arise from the perception of urban space, experiences, memories and ideas, building tension between the individual constitution of urban space and the adoption of a pre-arranged mixture of symbols, historical issues, visual artefacts and narratives produced intentionally. The individual actor's mental image of the city is formed from this tension along with visitors and tourists, who have usually less time to develop a detailed image. Mapping these mental representations along with their specific meanings using visual methods – photoelicitation interview, photo-collage and interactive digital model of urban space – is the scope of this chapter. Methodically, this research was inspired

by Kevin Lynch's 'Image of the city' (1960), but uses a different empirical design (for a review about Lynch's impact on tourism studies, see Pearce and Fagence, 1996). The underlying theoretical concept of space as socially produced, the research design and empirical data will also be addressed here.

Place-marketing, Tourism and Visual Strategies

Place-marketing as a metaphor describes a promotional strategy that arises from the quest for locational competitiveness with the shift from the managerialist mode of urban governance to the entrepreneurial one caused by the decline of the Fordist model of mass production.

Place-marketing is aimed at the projection of intentionally produced images to external audiences and local populations, bringing together two not always compatible objectives: next to the attraction of capital investment, consumer spending, tourism development and highly skilled migrants, it is also addressed to the internal audience, the citizens, seeking to legitimize regeneration and development policies and increasing social cohesion in times of an increasingly divided and segregated city (Griffith, 1989).

In a globalized world, place-marketing becomes difficult, with communication technologies making the functional differences between

© CAB International 2010. *Tourism and Visual Culture,* Volume 1
(eds P. Burns, C. Palmer and J-A. Lester)

places less important, while reducing the 'quality of authentic places' to simple location factors (Hassenpflug, 1999), so greater effort is spent on differentiating them by increasing their symbolic value: the fear of not being noticed drives the quest for achieving symbolic advantage over other competing cities. This is done by creating city-myths, reimaging or visionary strategies, or referring to the city's great narratives (Griffith, 1989). In particular, visual strategies are chosen for symbolic advantage; the competition for reputation of cities is nowadays carried out iconographically (Löw, 2006). Iconographic strategies in tourism stress the constitution of the Other or the design of effective tourist experiences (Mellinger, 1994; Sternberg, 1997).

Publicity and advertising have been important factors in place-marketing, though the budget used for them seems to be very small compared to other forms of commercial advertising, and local authorities seem to be the main actors here, not international advertising agencies. They tend to communicate less information about functional qualities and emphasize material artefacts (or the materiality of the city) for its symbolic loading. The logic behind this idea is that 'rooted' materiality gives competitive advantages in a 'space of flows' (images of cities, information about them) because of its (relative) immobility.

A strong tendency towards homogenization and convergence in the advertising strategies can be observed, both in what is included and excluded from the imaginary created for these purposes – downplaying or silencing problems and portraying only highly selective versions of a place's history.

The creation of new urban landscapes by flagship buildings and expensive consumer zones supports this tendency, as the services of very few superstar-architects are used to create the symbolic and material atmospheres desired for creating upscale lifestyle enclaves. The gap between anticipated and preferred living conditions, however, has been revealed in different studies, e.g. by Noller and Ronneberger (1995). Next to the architecture of superlatives, more subtle ways can be found by renaming places, or by theming urban landscape from a selection of 'premixed design packages that reproduce pre-existing urban forms', as Boyer (1992) describes it (p. 184; cit. from Griffith, 1998). A

description of these phenomena by urban sociology applying the concept of relational space as a social product (see below) would define them as (re)arrangements of people and social goods found in architectural drawings showing the intended 'users' and trying to locate the virtual building in its later environment. This development may lead to homogenizing pictorial representations of buildings not even built yet by the use of templates provided within the software used during the design process (Löw, 2003). This thesis can be extended to visual representations of an actual built environment, the city, in electronic media in the context of professional production of images for place-promotion purposes.

Visual imagery of cities, as important tourist spaces, differs by the mode of production (professional/amateur), the technology used and the social acceptance, i.e. the level of trust and estimation of authenticity accredited to the images by the observer. Professional photography in glossy brochures may look attractive, but the uncertainty remains if the perception *in situ* will match the picture professionally produced – this is one major motive in (urban) tourism, seeking images that have been picked up from guides, books or media generally (Jenkins, 1999) or that have already become part of a globalized and collective archive of iconographic references and a quest for re-producing its perspective as a kind of self-insurance about an authentic reliving of a framed (tourist's) experience as a desired experience. With the advent of social networking Internet sites, new actors appear on the scene: the users and tourists themselves. Non-professional images of tourist spaces are far less suspected to direct the observer's gaze and perception (see Dann, 1996a, for a methodical discussion and Dann, 1988, 1996b, 1996c, about the extent to which images can control and determine tourists' behaviour). Their level of authenticity is far higher at first glance, driven by the idea that images produced as a kind of grass-roots or bottom-up visualization are more likely to match one's own experience visiting the place in question. The next steps in this development are Web-based social networking sites directed to tourism: photo-sharing sites with the possibility to comment on the places visited and evaluate the accommodations and historic sites.

This quest for the perfect match between an (idealized and even mental) image of a place and its experience *in situ* (the quest for authenticity: MacCannell, 1976) can be illustrated by the use of postcards as touristic icons (Chalfen, 1979; Sontag, 1979; Edwards, 1992) on the one hand (not using own photography to show the visual 'essence' of the tourists' experience) and by geolocating photos as a technical approach to match physical space with the imagined on the other. Postcards (Markwick, 2001; Albers and James, 1988) have a quite long history in showing the traveller's intended visual experience to the ones staying at home – this social and visual construction permits a very high level of accordance between the intended and observed visual image, since for the recipient both only exist as visual projections (in one's mind/on paper: postcard). Social networking communities offering geolocated pictures are a new phenomenon that is spreading quickly.[1] Here satellite navigation is used to capture the position from where a photo was taken, sometimes even the direction of the lens while taking the photo (see Smith *et al.*, 2000, p. 330, for a novel approach to history of urban space and famous places by images). Some of today's navigation devices like mobile phones have cameras that record the GPS co-ordinates into the photo, allowing a 'navigation by pictures' (e.g. 'take me back to where I took this picture').

The recipient can explore places of interest remotely over the net from the (visual) perspective of street level (unlike Google Earth, which uses a bird's-eye view applying aerial and satellite photography) or go directly to the locations coded into the pictures to relive the visual experience.

Visual Encounter of Urban Space

Taking the quest for matching one's own expectations, mental images and professional images with the real-life experiences of visiting a place seriously,

visual essence of urban space can be encountered remotely using sophisticated rendering approaches (3D-Laserscans of city space[2]) to immerse photography (360° panoramic scenes), grass-roots visualizations and DIY projects. Introduced in 2007, Google's new feature *Street View* adds 360° panoramic view from street level to the mapping of roads and hybrid satellite views.

Analysis of the gaze is typically done in a technical way using eyetracker, for example, in marketing studies and psychology. There is a full range of these devices from desktop systems, stereo-trackers for depth analysis of the gaze to lightweight models that can be used in a real environment, like urban space or shopping malls (Fig. 6.1).

In particular, psychologists have used computer-aided methods of tracking the individual gaze by looking at the eye's movements – a technique not used in social sciences so far.

Using this technique, cameras track the oculomotor behaviour (using reflection from the eye's lens artificially illuminated by IR light), while a scene-camera shows what the participant is looking at. Calibrating both, it is possible to watch the eye movement in real-time and capture which elements of a scene were gazed at in temporal order and for how long. Eyetracking can be classified as a technical pictorial analysis by following the gaze. The statistical analysis about fixation period, speed of movement and division of visual attention only helps to interpret what and probably why some elements were gazed upon and others were not.

In this analytical framework, the observer's eye movement is in the centre of interest and serves as a repository for new findings – inside the brain the process of image interpretation is taking place, metaphorically operating as a black box. The semantic importance of visual fragments can only be estimated from the time they were looked at. With different methods the gaze itself comes into focus, allowing us to raise knowledge by qualitative approaches about the interchange of gazes between locals and tourists (Maoz, 2006) or the gendered background of

---

[1]See e.g. EveryTrail, Locr, Mappr (Beta), Panoramio (owned by Google), Plazez-known-where, Triptracker.
[2]This is done for administrative and security issues (training simulations; Löw *et al.*, 2007), but for purposes of tourism industries as well. Here 3D flights through city space and virtual walks are visualized, e.g. regarding Berlin the run of the famous wall can be displayed, even 'through' buildings placed there in the meantime.

Fig. 6.1. Eyetracker used in a shopping mall for evaluation purposes. Copyright eyesquare.

language and imagery used in tourism promotion to prefer the male, heterosexual gaze (Pritchard and Morgan, 2000).

This short overview opens up the field of visual interactive representations of urban and tourist spaces and locates the technique used for 'tracking a semantic gaze' (in methodical and technical terms) within this field of visual (remote) encounter of urban space and perception analysis. This approach visualizes selected parts of the city and lets the observer explore the visual fragments by photos, which are linked by visual content (spatial links). Following these links, the photos will be morphed and cross-faded to evoke the impression of a continuous stream of pictures, like a movie (walkthrough). The technical background comes from an approach that tries to enable people with the least requirements possible to build 3D models of their urban space, working just by linking low-resolution pictures (Tanaka *et al.*, 2002).

The idea of building one's own digital city by linking pictures has some striking similarities with the theoretical conception of relative space in urban sociology. It was therefore chosen for methodological reasons to capture empirically the complex process of the production of space for identificational strategies.

Tourism, Visuality and the Production of Space as a Social Product

The theoretical background of this is a new concept of space in sociology, a relational approach that abandons ideas of time and space as absolutes and rather focuses on the circumstances of space being produced.

A relational model of space does not treat phenomena like famous sites or the circulation or float of pictures of places outside everyday life as given, but enables us to focus upon the processes of production and reception – even from multiple perspectives simultaneously: the professional production of narratives specific to one place and the imaginary created to promote it as a tourist sight, the perspective of people visiting these places and the perspective of local residents constitute different spaces, which can overlap each other at the same place – which now can be analysed, e.g. for their potential to structure social interaction. Furthermore a relative concept of space allows looking at globalization as a two-sided process: The flow of images might support stereotypes (the single house, the Brandenburg Gate, Checkpoint Charlie etc.; Löw, 2003, 2006) that can be viewed from anywhere, but the sensual, aesthetic reception cannot be 'globalized' the same way. Through images, the local can become global, but the basic processes of production and reception cannot.

The practices of sight-seeing, of taking pictures are framed by the logic of reproduction – a capitalistic mode of the production of space, as Henry Lefèbvre (1991) would probably argue: sites and places are valued for their adequacy to pictures that become part of the globalized construction of the tourist icon, the exotic other. This specific logic applies to places '. . . because of the universalization of the tourist gaze, all sorts of places (. . .) have come to construct themselves as objects of the tourist gaze' (Urry, 1990, p. 125) – and to people acting as one would expect from tourists, picturing everything to capture the 'essence' or authenticity of being at one place. The images then serve as a proof of the authentic reliving and recognizing of the places, leading to 'a kind of alienation which has become a prototypical hallmark of photographic 'seeing' in tourism' (Albers and James, 1988, p. 136). Furthermore, people visiting these staged places are even expected to behave like tourists, trying to picture what was created to be extraordinary. If someone would act in contrast to these expectations by continually taking photos of everyday situations and places, irritation can occur.

A physical–scientific understanding of space as relational (Einstein: Theory of relativity) has had a significant influence on the concept of space prevalent in the social sciences. A decade before, space was not a matter of sociology, since it was conceptualized to act as a container, containing social action with no interaction between agency and structure. The explanatory potential of a (social) spatial relativity is far higher, since many social process can be better explained using a theoretical system that treats motion, dynamics, continuous processes and transformations as being the normal state of affairs.

Space in this regard is conceptualized by Martina Löw (2001, 2005) as a relational (re) arrangement of human beings (animals) and objects located at places, consisting of the two interwoven processes of perception/construction and action. She classifies her spatial theory as relational, and differentiates between two processes that constitute space: first, 'the positioning of social objects and people and of primarily symbolic markings in order to denote as such ensembles of objects and people' (Löw, 2001, p. 158). She calls this process spacing. Second, a synthesis effect is necessary in the structuring of space: people and objects are combined producing spaces through processes of perception, imagination and remembering. These two processes do not operate in an arbitrary fashion, and instead observe predefined conditions.

Spaces are created by the arrangement of bodies – both living beings and social objects – which are the products of current and of past (symbolic and material) action:

'Space is the relational arrangement of social objects and people (living beings) in locations' (Löw, 2001, p. 224). Spacing and the synthesis process are both subject to predefined conditions and depend on the nature of actions: societal notions of space, and class-specific, gender-specific and culturally specific habitus all influence these processes; they are also affected by the location of the synthesis process and the external influence of the social objects and people already present. In addition, one can only 'place' that which is available in a given action situation – in other words, spacing processes are negotiation processes based on the symbolic and material goods (and beings) present in a given location; these processes do not take place in a power vacuum (Fig. 6.2; see also Löw, 2001, p. 228).

Spatial arrangements thus have a forming influence on actions and are simultaneously (re)produced by these. This happens in the case of routines in repetitive, everyday life. In describing the constitution of spaces, Löw (2001) refers back to the differentiation made by Giddens (1984) between practical and discursive consciousness: the latter allows us to put our own actions and behaviour into words when we reflect on and consider these – for example, in interviews where residents talk about their neighbourhoods, about their perception of the city or town where they live or about the layout and decoration of their homes. Depending on habitus, these reflective examinations of the one's own spatial behaviour will exhibit varying degrees of sophistication. In order to 'create' such a situation, both time and trust are necessary; visual material can often be an effective aid. For example, residents might describe their neighbourhood with the help of photos that they have made themselves, or might comment on a selection of images or newspaper cuttings.

Practical consciousness is concerned with the knowledge that is updated in everyday behaviour, but is not directly accessible. In repetitive, everyday life, spaces are generally formed from the practical consciousness – people rarely talk about how they generate spaces. However, when this subject is brought up, for example in reflexive contexts, a part of knowledge from the

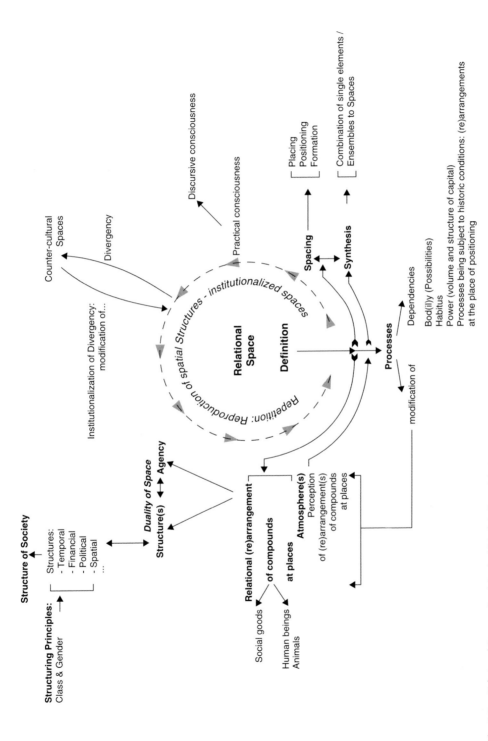

Fig. 6.2. Relational Space – Sociological Model. Copyright Sergej Stoetzer.

practical consciousness is transferred over to discursive consciousness and can thus be communicated: the constitution of space can then be described in words.

Routine, everyday actions that are not consciously reflected upon give form to space – i.e. certain positioning (actions) and synthesis processes are repeated, and societal structures are reproduced by habitual actions. The resulting spaces in turn influence the actions (perception of a generalized arrangement, e.g. normalized synthesis process). 'Appropriate' behaviour in museums, visiting religious sites etc. is based on the production of space from practical consciousness.

This duality of space is termed spatial structure if the production of the space is formed independently of point in time and location according to rules and resources, and is embedded in institutions. Structures are thus anchored in institutions, in 'routines of social action which become permanent' (social entity, organizational form: authorities, etc., and societally pre-ordained patterns of action; Löw, 2001, p. 169).

Spatial structures, alongside legal and economic structures and the structural principles of class and gender, which are rooted in these structures, make up the overall structure of a given society – the spatial is thus not separate from the societal, the former is in fact a part of the latter.

Institutionalized spaces are created when spacing and the process of synthesis continue to function regardless of *individual* actions – normalized synthesis processes and spacings are the consequences. For example, class-specific arrangements of furniture in homes may be identified – Fächergruppe Designwissenschaft (1988) has pointed out that the layouts of living rooms in furniture catalogues are often similar (Löw, 2001, p. 169). The institutionalized arrangement that practical consciousness treats as something self-evident leads to space being perceived in terms of objects (and generally in three dimensions). The everyday notion of space as a container can thus be included in a relational spatial model.

Because of experiences of being an outsider (alienation effects), insight into necessity, bodily desires or the behaviour of others, changes in institutionalized spatial production can take place on two levels: they can cause deviations, which, when they deliberately oppose institutionalized arrangements, can be termed countercultural, and can give rise to once-off or permanent countercultural spaces. These can also lead to changes if the deviations are ongoing and are not just individual deviations – modifications to institutionalized spaces are thus possible, and can go so far as modifications to the spatial structure.

Places are the target of positioning processes, which always act relative to other positionings. People participate in this spatial production in two ways: they can be grouped with other beings or social objects to make up spaces; they also take an active role themselves in the positioning processes. The presence of an academic observer can often systematically distort the spatial situations at a location.

The possibility of creating overlapping, plural spaces on a theoretical level is a significant aspect of this extended notion of space. It is therefore important to state, that the constitution of space cannot be read and analysed easily, it has to be reconstructed from empirical evidence collected carefully – with the possibilities of overlapping and interchanging spaces considered.

Analysis of the Semantic Gaze

The new approach developed for analysing the gaze semantically uses photos taken from urban space, identifying the importance of depicted elements of complex spatial arrangements for guiding social action and identificational strategies. Simple photos from urban space in a low resolution for Web display are used, taken by participants, found online, in an old photo album – the source and time the photos are from only matters regarding the thematic task given. This is done deliberately not to exclude people by highly sophisticated requirements for the technical equipment.

Crucial is the idea to establish links between the pictures. To create a visual impression of a public space, walking down a street or gazing at a well-known historical site, photos should encompass elements of the picture taken beforehand. This often requires a kind of serial photography, taking a picture every 20–50 steps, when turning left or right and so on.

Normal links in hypertext documents link to different parts of text, files, images or new Web pages. The links used 'within' the photos serve another purpose too; apart from their function as a guide through the collected photos, they represent rectangle parts of different pictures belonging to each other because of the pictorial elements both have in common. According to the change of perspective between the two photos (and then of course between the rectangles), the transitions between these two pictures are rendered on the spot. This approach is therefore based on a network of photos derived from the actual town or historic site. It is an interactive collage with links between the pictorial representations of actual places, which was intended for the creation of digital cities by individual actors, allowing them to share their own experiences visually moderated or show memorable sights to other people publicly on the Net.

The software enabling this mapping is called 'Photowalker' and was developed by Hiroya Tanaka as free software. It was intended for building digital models of cities with very few preconditions (Tanaka *et al.*, 2002). Because of its striking similarity of spatial links with the concept of relational space (Löw) in urban sociology, it was chosen for the author's PhD project to trace the significance and semantic importance of the constitution of space for identificational strategies in urban space.

The digital still camera operates as the person's gaze, taking pictures every 20–50 steps. The links between elements of the photos relate to their importance for the creator of the collage. This method works analogously to an eyetracker: the links can be compared with the division of visual attention. At this stage, we still have no insight with which meaning certain relations between elements (of pictures, of real space) are attributed.

To analyse subjective representations of the individual actors' image of the city along with the identificational strategies, students were asked to take photos of their town, Darmstadt, and to link them with this software to create an interactive collage.

So digital still cameras were handed out to students, and they were asked to take photos of what is important to them, regarding the city where they attend their study. The high-resolution images were kept for later analysis and reduced to an image resolution to fit the needs of being displayed within this visualization-technique online (quarter VGA size) (Fig. 6.3).

Linking the pictures is done by identifying persons, objects or even parts of the picture itself on at least another one: the corresponding areas of the photo are chosen by the participant (not the computer!) and then linked according to the persons or objects they both have in common – or that should be considered belonging to each other (symbolic loading). These links between the pictures refer to spatial relations in urban space, carrying a specific meaning – mediated by their pictorial representations and attached with meaning 'inside' virtual space by the actors' selection (of what to link and in which ways).

Following the links, the photos will be cross-faded and morphed allowing the impression of walking through the collage just by choosing the next among the linked pictures. The possibilities of navigating and exploring this

Fig. 6.3. Spatial links. Copyright Sergej Stoetzer.

digital, pictorial representation of the actual city are framed by the structure of the collage itself, by the shape of the network emerging from the links between the pictures.

Assuring that the chosen topic was anticipated while the serial photography took place, the range of choices – which elements between different pictures could be chosen for the collage later to fit the topic – is narrowed down while being at the specific place taking pictures. This instant selection at the 'place of action' is a methodical trick to keep influences (e.g. of atmospheres, conflicting or overlapping spaces) to this process place- and time-specific, meaning that the linking later on reproduces the selection processes that took place in the city's realm, adding no further complexity to the production of space.

Another main aspect of this preparation before the field trip is an alienation, a break with everyday life, routines and institutionalized behaviour. In a specific sense the participants acted as tourists: Regarding John Urry's (1990) definition, they fulfil the requirements of a 'notion of 'departure', of a limited breaking with established routines and practices of every day life and allowing one's senses to engage with a set of stimuli that contrast with the everyday and the mundane' (Urry, 1990, p. 2).

With regard to relational space, the production of and reception of space by the participants collecting visual data in urban space took a shift from institutionalized, practical space to a more reflective one.

Even deviant behaviour compared to the 'normal' and accepted ways visitors and locals take photos of urban space was shown: not every 20–50 steps, picturing assumed nothingness. The participants indeed reported about incidents where they were asked whom or what they were taking pictures of. This approach utilizes the break in accepted and 'normal' ways to take photos as a methodical advantage to distract the participants from their routines and in some regard let them become a tourist in their own city – discovering new details even in paths walked in a daily routine, or at the workplace, known for a decade or more. Several findings support this thesis, starting with evidence found in the study itself and analysis of a detachment

of inhabitants from their town by taking photos like tourists, as Stefania Antonioni, Laura Gemini and Lella Mazzoli have provided (this volume).

In order to be able to compare the levels of analysis between the *reconstruction* of the actor's image of the city based on the visual data (photos, collage) – this is the semantic gaze reconstructed from third point of view – and the actor's own description of that visual representation and its intended effects (the self-description of that semantic gaze), a photoelicitation interview was conducted after the photos were taken. Triangulating the pictures taken by the students with the collage created later on and the interview itself is now possible. The semantic structure of the photo-linked network representing the participant's semantic gaze is now available for analysis.

Examples from the Empirical Basis of the Study

In the following two portraits of Darmstadt from an empirical basis of 15 are discussed[3], presenting provisional findings. Both have in common that at first Darmstadt was attributed with negative imaginations, like 'ugly city' or the buildings described as 'architectonic sins', but as time went by, this attitude changed and interest in the city's history rose, leading to a deeper understanding of what caused the disapproval of the city's visual impression in the first place. Social networks are another mechanism of that change of attitude, mediating the identification with this place by arrangements of people becoming more and more important for the participant.

In order to shorten the time for presenting the collages, an overview of them will be shown instead, generated by extracting the linkage information from the interactive collage itself. The way the photos are presented now is static and from a bird's-eye view, giving significant insight to the structural conceptualization of the city's representation and semantic gaze from the actor's point of view. The networked overview generated from the linkage-structure is energy-minimized by an iterative algorithm

---

[3]Seven female students, eight male.

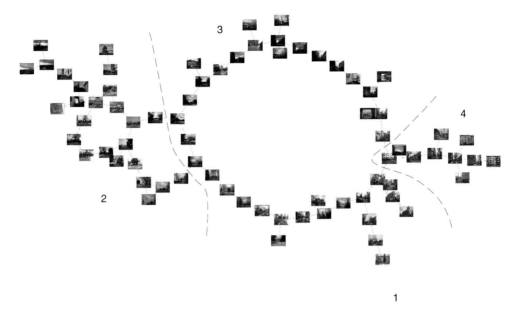

Fig. 6.4. 'Contrasts' between 'ways' and dwelling. Collage from empirical basis; generated overview. Copyright Sergej Stoetzer.

that – metaphorically – replaces the links between the photos with a virtual physical spring (Kamada–Kawai algorithm[4]). During the initial state, the linkage information is interpreted as linear, which means that each photo is added to the existing spatial model without considering the arrangement so far – resulting in different (virtual) spring tensions between the linked pictures. Iterating the algorithm, the overlaps are reduced and the tension in each spring is minimized until the spatial model stagnates.

Starting with the first collage (Fig. 6.4), two major walks with two important additions can be found that are linking the different poles of dwelling, architecture, leisure and tourism-centred activities within a very limited area of the city's surface:

1. The way to the Mathildenhöhe (bottom part of the circular path);
2. Addition I: 'whereabouts Mathildenhöhe';
3. The way back (top part of the circular path);
4. Addition II: serial dwelling.

The starting point is located at the bottom of the overall perspective, showing the view outside the inhabitant's courtyard. Following the links between the pictures (left side of the static overview), the way leads through an exclusive residential district of Darmstadt – old fabric and big front gardens symbolizing exclusive power over space. The villas are inhabited by widows of famous artists or by student leagues. These student dwelling societies offer luxurious accommodations with everything one needs to begin a university study in Darmstadt: a furnished room with IT infrastructure and TV, a community to affiliate oneself with in an environment that no student alone can afford, a villa with garden and rooms for assembly in one of the best residential areas the town has to offer.

Darmstadt has a very high rent index in Germany, so winter-term students beginning their study in Darmstadt have the problem of finding proper accommodation. This has become so bad that the university was thinking about a container settlement for the worst cases.

The student duelling societies therefore offer a generous living potential – the price for this is paid by subordination to mostly rightwing ideology, obeying the group's orders and discussions held at the residence about politics in general and their own efficiency in studying.

---

[4]Kamada and Kawai (1989).

The destination of the first loop walk is located on a small hill above the city centre. The whereabouts is located at the top of the overview, too, in two additional loops showing a famous side of Darmstadt, the Mathildenhöhe. Jugendstil-Buildings and art-exhibitions, concerts take place there – this was and still is the place where fine arts are located.

In the interview, the participant stressed the importance this place had for him: the ability to spend time there in the summer by naming it a recreation area. Benches, lawn, nice avenues and people meeting there to play or listen to music, to watch a game of boules or play chess with giant figures are quite compelling.

The Mathildenhöhe is one of the most famous sides of Darmstadt with a great history in art (known especially for its colony of artists); the 'Hochzeitsturm' ('wedding tower') showing the five fingers of one hand can be found again in a schematic abstraction in the city's logo. In order to make sure that the side remains attractive to visitors, tourists and mostly elderly people, the town decided to tighten security laws there. Surveillance cameras were put up and security personnel patrols with dogs to ensure everything looks nice and no one sits on the grass. Even slight deviant behaviour – far *below* social disorder like public drunkenness or urinating – is punished by being ordered off the park. The city's attempts to ensure a so-called safe and nice-looking environment that can be used for place-marketing emphasizing the city's potential in fine art, leisure and recreation and as a good host for tourists have created an atmosphere of unease; the quality of the place has decreased to those staying there longer than a guided tour would take.

The way back on the right-hand side contrasts sharply with the first one – it shows a different kind of dwelling, namely a formerly workers' housing estate in a close neighbourhood. The problems of increased density of dwellings, like rubbish, social disorder or dilapidation, are mainly mentioned in the interview, but the serial character of dwellings is depicted.

In the second collage,[5] five segments can be identified, representing different themes and paths, connected to each other by one picture in the middle, a photomontage looking like a postcard. The starting pictures of each of these five walks through Darmstadt's imaginary space are situated here (Fig. 6.5).

1. Labour and internment camp;
2. Kavalleriesand-Kasernen;
3. Formerly private bank ('Bank für Handel und Industrie');
4. Houses and courtyards at the Magdalenenstraße;
5. Residential castle.

The labour and internment camp was located on the property of the Telekom's research centre directly after the Second World War (by allied forces) and fragments of it, like the old gatehouse with the main entrance, are still existing, but usually don't get noticed, even by people working there for 10 or more years, like the student taking these pictures.

The second theme shows a view of a barrack square on the same area as the internment camp, the Kavalleriesand-Kasernen. The original picture was taken after the war and the participant tried to find the exact position again from which the old photo was taken, trying to show the relationship of tension between similarities and changes that occurred over the decades.

This basic idea determines the entire collage – the quest for authenticity in finding the exact spot the 'old' photos were taken from, even if this involves barely legal activities (trespassing on private property, climbing out of the garrets to take some of the pictures needed etc.).

The first two motives have a very close relationship to the biographical background of the student, working at these locations for about a decade before studying again. They represent the main idea of this collage, identifying places that the old pictures were taken from and trying to show what remained, what was altered, vanished or which new elements appeared on the scene – inspired by a publication doing just that and evoking a first interest in the rest of the city, not just the place of work.

The third tour shows a former private bank (until 1932; built 1873–1875), the Bank für Handel und Industrie. It is located quite close to

---

[5]This collage is analysed in Stoetzer (2006) too, and contrasted with another, inviting the observer to follow traces other people have left behind.

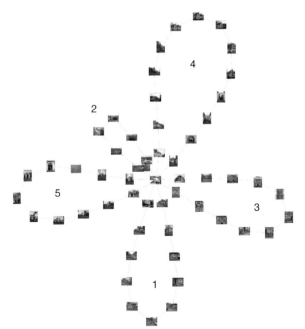

Fig. 6.5. Collage 'postcard' from empirical basis; generated overview. Copyright Sergej Stoetzer.

the inner city next to a former railway station that was relocated to its present location in 1912. The roof was damaged during the Second World War and two storeys were added afterwards, with very little architectural sensitivity – so the student commented: the building is protected as an architectural monument, but the reconstruction of at least the façade could have been made better to be fair to the building's architectural and aesthetic roots.

The houses and courtyards at the Magdalenenstraße were chosen for their old fabric being still intact. The old half-timbered houses created a specific flair that could be (at least partly) preserved.

The residential castle with the university constitutes the second main biographical reference: the place of study. Similarly to the motive before, the castle's courtyard is also shown, as well as references to the underlying theme of similarity/change and references to destruction caused by war (and buildings in the post-war period): close to the university, a single house was discovered that still shows signs of another building that must have been next to it, but was destroyed by the bombing of the city in September 1944.

In engaging with pictures of pre-war Darmstadt, the city's history showed great potential, explaining what was perceived as 'architectural sins', leading to a more forgiving judgement of the city's present appearance: the formerly nice-looking city with a lot of Jugendstil buildings was nearly completely destroyed on 11–12 September 1944, making rapid rebuilding after the war necessary. The buildings of the post-war period were perceived as sterile, but knowing the city's history lead to a reinterpretation of Darmstadt's outer appearance, victimizing the city of historic circumstances beyond its influence, in times of global conflict. Identity as belonging to certain groups and places is inscribed this way by institutionalizing the process of production of space, specific to places.

Summary and Future Prospects

Inscribing meaning to certain places by repeated action becomes visible – either directly in materiality (rearrangement or new forms of distribution of persons or objects to change the meaning associated with places, modifications of material artefacts themselves) or by addressing social and personal networks: traces of persons 'belonging' here inscribed in a (more or less) collective memory – making sure that the person in mind is added to the institutionalized construction of space and meaning for a specific place, even if he/she is not or will never be present there. A relational concept of space helps understanding these phenomena. Analytically, the meaning of what is constituted as space is brought up by the semantic gaze – the linking of photos attached with a certain meaning.

There are quite a few areas of application for this way to create virtual cities from photos using the semantic gaze: from an artistic, collage-like approach, it can be used in education to work with digital media (informatics or art) in combination with a subject like history or social studies to present interactive pieces of art (or of social research) at the schools festival.

It could be used in tourism to show the (short) way to the beach from the intended accommodation, the way from the nearest train station to a hotel or different walks around a historical or religious site to become acquainted with before going there (or even as part of a virtual pilgrimage – MacWilliams, 2002 – for handicapped people).

The imaginary provided supports the impression of the non-professional background and therefore has more credibility in terms of authenticity than photos in glossy brochures or otherwise professionally generated and distributed images.

Moreover, there are fascinating possibilities for visualization and research as this 3D model for virtual cities offers a low-budget and grass-roots approach to building digital cities without any need for programming. This can be taken up again by local interest groups or individuals to show their neighbourhood, their community – this has happened in the Asian region so far, but references to Europe are very rare. In fact, this software is nearly unknown here.

Building a collage as a network of photos with semantic links between pictures and places, the students participating were able to build their subjective image of the city as a digital city existing in a medial space – like the official image production using ordinary Web pages. Showing fragments of the city's space with a specific importance, these iconographs (a semantic network of photographic essences of places) can be analysed following a 'semantic gaze' in order to examine the processes by which identity is bound to places by repetition, memory or imagination and social networks.

References

Albers, P. and James, W.R. (1988) Travel photography: a methodological approach. *Annals of Tourism Research* 15, 134–158.
Chalfen, R.M. (1979) Photography's role in tourism: some unexplored relationships. *Annals of Tourism Research* 6, 435–447.
Dann, G.M.S. (1988) Images of Cyprus. *Problems of Tourism* 11, 43–70.
Dann, G.M.S. (1996a) Tourists' images of a destination – an alternative analysis. *Journal of Travel and Tourism Marketing* 5, 41–55.
Dann, G.M.S. (1996b) The people of tourist brochures. In: T. Selwyn (ed.) *The Tourist Image: Myths and Myth Making in Tourism*. John Wiley & Sons, Chichester, pp. 61–81.
Dann, G.M.S. (1996c) *The Language of Tourism*. CAB International, Wallingford.
Edwards, E. (1992) The tourist icon: four Australian postcards. *Tourism in Focus* 6, 4–5.
Fächergruppe Designwissenschaft (ed.) (1988) *Objektalltag, Alltagsobjekte: Bekleidung u. Möbel d. Familie K.* Schriftenreihe der Hochschule der Künste, Berlin, 1/1988.
Giddens, A. (1984) *The Constitution of Society: Outline of the Theory of Structuration*. Polity Press, Cambridge.
Griffith, R. (1998) *Making Sameness: Place Marketing and the New Urban Entrepreneurialism. Cities, Economic Competition and Urban Policy*. N. Oatley, London, pp. 41–57.
Hassenpflug, D. (1999) Citytainment. Die Neuerfindung der Stadt im Zeichen des Imagineering. In: *Praxisreport Industriebau. Kreative Beweglichkeit – Offene Grenzen. Neue Partner*. D. Sommer, Vienna, pp. 86–105.
Jenkins, O.H. (1999) Understanding and measuring tourist destination images. *International Journal of Tourism Research* 1, 1–15.
Kamada, T. and Kawai, S. (1989) An algorithm for drawing general undirected graphs. *Information Processing Letters* 31, 7–15.

Lefèbvre, H. (1991) *The Production of Space*. Blackwell, Oxford.

Löw, M. (2001) *Raumsoziologie*. Suhrkamp, Frankfurt.

Löw, M. (2003) Inaugural lecture: Prinz Charles, Hollywood und Hongkong. Raumsoziologische Annäherung an Architektur und ihre Bilder. [http://raumsoz.ifs.tu-darmstadt.de/pdf-dokumente/loew_ant.pdf].

Löw, M. (2005) The constitution of space. The double existence of space as structural ordering and performative act. Lecture at Paris I/Sorbonne, 14 March 2005. [http://raumsoz.ifs.tu-darmstadt.de/pdf-dokumente/loew-constitution-of-space.pdf]

Löw, M. (2006) Immer einzig und überall gleich. Chancen und Risiken moderner Städte. 33. Römerberggespräch. Frankfurt [http://raumsoz.ifs.tu-darmstadt.de/pdf-dokumente/Loew-Roemerberg.pdf]

Löw, M., Steets, S. and Stoetzer, S. (2007) *Einführung in die Stadt- und Raumsoziologie*. Opladen, Frankfurt.

Lynch, K. (1960) *The Image of the City*. MIT Press, Cambridge, MA.

MacCannell, D. (1976) *The Tourist: A New Theory of the New Leisure Class*. Macmillan, New York.

MacWilliams, M.W. (2002) Virtual pilgrimages on the Internet. *Religion* 32, 315–335.

Maoz, D. (2006) The mutual gaze. *Annals of Tourism Research* 33, 221–239.

Markwick, M. (2001) Postcards From Malta. Image, consumption, context. *Annals of Tourism Research* 28, 417–438.

Mellinger, W.M. (1994) Toward a critical analysis of tourism representations. *Annals of Tourism Research* 21, 756–779.

Mercille, J. (2005) Media effects on image. *Annals of Tourism Research* 32, 1039–1055.

Noller, P. and Ronneberger, K. (1995) *Die neue Dienstleistungsgesellschaft: Berufsmilieus in Frankfurt Am Main*. Campus Frankfurt.

Pearce, P.L. and Fagence, M. (1996) The legacy of Kevin Lynch. Research implications. *Annals of Tourism Research* 23, 576–598.

Pritchard, A.M. and Morgan, N.J. (2000) Privileging the male gaze. Gendered tourism landscapes. *Annals of Tourism Research* 27, 884–905.

Smith, B.K., Blankinship, E., Ashford III, A., Baker, M. and Hirzel, T. (2000) Image maps: exploring urban history through digital photography. In: Ishida, T. and Isbister, K. (eds) *Digital Cities. Lecture Notes in Computer Science* 1765, 326–337. Springer, Berlin.

Sontag, S. (1979) *On Photography*. Penguin, Harmondsworth.

Sternberg, E. (1997) The iconography of the tourism experience. *Annals of Tourism Research* 24, 951–969.

Stoetzer, S. (2006) Picturing urban identities. In: Berking, H., Frank, S., Frers, L., Löw, M., Meier, L., Steets, S., Stoetzer, S. (eds) *Negotiating Urban Conflicts. Interaction, Space and Control*. Bielefeld, Piscataway, NJ, pp. 177–194.

Tanaka, H., Arikawa, M. and Shibasaki, R. (2001) Technologies for digital cities – A 3-D photo collage system for spatial navigations. In Tanabe, M., d. Besselaar, P.V. and Ishida, T. (eds) *Digital Cities II. Computational and Sociological Approaches, Second Kyoto Workshop on Digital Cities*, Kyoto, 18–20 October 2001, revised papers, pp. 305–316.

Urry, J. (1990) *The Tourist Gaze*. Sage, London.

7 Gazing at the Gallant Gurkha: Glimpsing Nepalese Society

Lisa Power and Clive Baker

*Faculty of Business, Sport and Enterprise,
Southampton Solent University, Southampton, UK*

Introduction

One of the most comprehensive collections of military heritage outside of London is to be found in Winchester, where regimental and corps traditions live on through six military museums. One of these, the Gurkha Museum, commemorates the services of the elite Nepalese Gurkhas and their British officers who have served the crown since 1815. The historic Brigade of Gurkhas is unlike other British regiments, for whilst it is a fully integrated part of the British Armed Forces with Gurkhas performing the same duties as other units at home and abroad in defence of the UK, all Gurkhas are recruited, serve and are discharged as Nepalese citizens with recruitment and selection taking place once a year in Nepal. The focus of the Gurkha Museum is, however, not solely on the Gurkha's military achievements, as emphasis is also placed on the social and cultural heritage of their homeland Nepal. This chapter explores the way in which the museum displays on the one hand the harsh realities of military life for the 'bravest of the brave, most generous of the generous' Gurkha, whilst on the other hand presents a socio-cultural dimension of wider Nepalese life including the interrelationship between dress, food and religion. It explores how the visitor's glance presents a soldier, whereas the deeper gaze reveals the gallant Gurkha.

Background to Regimental and Corps Museums

A report from the London School of Economics (2006), commissioned by the Museum, Libraries and Archives Council (MLA) and the National Museums Directors' Conference, shows that museums and galleries are a vital ingredient of Britain's cultural sector, attracting over 42 million visits per year. This popularity is reflected by the fact that at least 43% of the population visited a museum or gallery at least once during 2005 (LSE, 2006), a higher attendance than at the Premiership plus the whole of the rest of league football for 2004–2005. Museums are clearly an integral part of the cultural life of the nation and are typified by their diversity and extensive collections.

Whilst there are some 1984 museums in England (MLA, 2005), 234 have weapons and war as the broad subject matter of their collection. Around 152 (Children, 2000) of these are regiment and corps museums ranging from the Royal Scots Dragoon Guards Museum in Edinburgh to the Duke of Cornwall's Light Infantry Museum in Bodmin, Cornwall. The first objective of this type of museum articulated in the Ministry of Defence's Policy Towards Regimental and Corps Museums (MOD, 1998, p. 10) is to 'make the public aware of the regiments and corps, their roles and achievements thereby contributing to the projection of a

© CAB International 2010. *Tourism and Visual Culture*, Volume 1
(eds P. Burns, C. Palmer and J-A. Lester)

positive image of the Army'. This is particularly important in an era when the total strength of those serving in the British Armed Forces is declining (MOD, 2008). Whilst a recent Mori poll (Ipsos MORI, 2008) places familiarity with the British army as 'fairly high' with those with serving friends or relatives tending to be more informed, this knowledge is perhaps unsurprisingly, less pronounced in the young. MOD policy is trying to overcome this by broadening access to military museums to a younger generation by providing educational resources 'with particular reference to the national curriculum' (MOD, 1998, p. 10). This is in keeping with the Department of Culture, Media and Sports (DCMS) current priorities for museums (DCMS, 2006, p. 10), whereby museums will 'fulfil their potential as learning resources'. Nevertheless, despite this ambition to reach out to a wider public, the MOD acknowledges that the interpretation of military history is a sensitive area and recognizes the potential diversity of its audience which can include 'the specialist and partisan, the general and the uninformed, as well as the hostile and anti-military' (MOD, 1998, p. 2).

The specialist visitor may indeed relate to the second of the MOD's objectives for these types of museums, namely to 'contribute to the esprit de corps of the regiments and corps' (MOD, 1998, p. 10). As corps museums tell the history of the regiment, new recruits are traditionally taken there as part of their induction and basic training to be shown the regimental artefacts and material history of the regiment (Stephens, 2006). They serve therefore as expressions of the continuity of the past whilst educating recruits and creating a sense of pride and comradeship, which may as Jones (1996, p. 152) suggests 'enable it to fight more effectively'. Regimental and corps museums have both military and social significance and as such also form part of the range of leisure and tourism activities available to both domestic and overseas visitors.

Although it is difficult to put an exact figure on visitor numbers to military museums, tourism associated with battlefields and war is a vibrant sector of the market both domestically and internationally. Britain's military past has even given rise to specialist tour operators who provide battlefield and history tours where

tourists can go 'Walking with Wellington' in Portugal or Spain or on a more personal note on the Somme, France, they can 'visit a particular battlefield area, cemetery or memorial, because of its importance in your family's history' (Holts Tours, 2008, p. 5). The wide assortment of military associated attractions includes war memorials and cenotaphs, mausoleums, historical re-enactments and museums displaying medals, weapons, uniforms and dioramas of battlefields. Smith (1996, p. 248) goes as far as to suggest that, 'memorabilia of warfare and allied products . . . probably constitutes the largest single category of tourist attractions in the world'.

Alongside attractions such as the Cathedral and King Arthur's Round Table, Winchester's six military museums are listed on the city's Tourist Information section of its website (Winchester City Council, 2008). One of these, the Gurkha Museum, is the focus of this chapter.

Background to the Gurkha

Today the Gurkhas have a unique place within the armed forces and their cultural heritage. Their connection with the British Army who regarded the Gurkha as a 'martial race' (Streets, 2004), thought to be naturally warlike and aggressive in battle, dates back to when after suffering from heavy casualties in the invasion of Nepal in 1815, the Treaty of Segauli was signed which gave the British army the right to recruit Nepalese subjects (Parker, 1999). Following the partition of India in 1947, an agreement between India, Nepal and Britain meant that four Gurkha regiments from the Indian army were transferred to the British army eventually becoming the Gurkha Brigade, whose famous motto is: 'Kaathar hunnu bhanda marnu ramro – It is better to die than be a coward'. The Royal Gurkha Rifles today consists of the Brigade of Gurkhas, which comprises of two battalions including support from its own signal, logistic and engineer troops. Whilst the brigade has affiliations with the King's Royal Hussars and the Royal Scots, its origin as a Rifle Regiment began with an association dating back to the days of the Indian Mutiny with the 60th Rifles known as the Royal Green Jackets who now form part of the newly formed Rifles. The characteristic rifle-green uniform and black buttons on the uniform collars of their ceremonial tunics and the Rifle Regiments marching pace of 140 paces to the minute refers back to this era (British Army, 2007a). The Gurkhas have subsequently fought for the British in both world wars and served all over the world including Hong Kong, Malaysia, Borneo, Cyprus, the Falklands, Kosovo, East Timor, Sierra Leone, and currently in both Iraq and Afghanistan. Their bravery on the battlefield has been acknowledged by their award of 13 Victoria Crosses with a further 13 being awarded to Gurkha officers. Whilst the Brigade could have completely disappeared as part of any of the recent reviews, it has been retained for practical as well as more emotional reasons. In fact, with the British Army deployed all over the world, culturally the Gurkhas' gaze may be more acceptable to some than that of other British soldiers.

The Gurkha Museum, Winchester

The first established Gurkha museum started life as a Nissan Hut inside the Queen Elizabeth's Barracks, Church Crookham, which opened on 21 June 1974 (Davis, personal correspondence). Increased security following terrorist activity targeting military establishments on mainland Britain affected civilian visits to the camp, as in order to reach the museum visitors had to book in and out of the camp itself and had to submit to car searches, which implies that prospective visitors needed to make a real effort to visit the museum. It might therefore not be unreasonable to assume that the 'non-army' visitor to the museum must have had some military connection or specific interest in the Gurkhas to go to that much trouble; in other words, the museum was not chanced upon by visitors or tourists. The modernization of the British army and its subsequent regimental amalgamation made the closure of Church Crookham inevitable and the move to historic Peninsula Barracks, Winchester, a reality. The new Gurkha museum opened in Winchester in July 1990 providing more space and unrestricted access for the general public, effectively opening up the life of the Gurkha to a new public, namely the tourist.

The origins of the artefacts in the Gurkha museum (Asquith, 2000a, 2000b) are much the same as those found in many other regimental museums starting as a collection of items taken as souvenirs or as trophies together with equipment that had become outdated and which had found its way into storage, not unlike the attics of most family homes. For many the regiment and its material artefacts is home and these objects represent not only the family history but its cultural origins, which in the case of the Gurkha Museum is Nepal for the soldiers and the UK for its officers. The museum therefore clearly provides benefit to the regiment although unlike other regimental and corps museums it does not serve to encourage recruitment, as only Nepalese serve as soldiers although it may serve to persuade potential British officers to enlist.

The aim of the museum is to commemorate the service to the crown of the Gurkha and the British officer from 1815 to the present day. The museum faces the challenge of not only representing the rich history of the corps but also needs to remind a post-empire Britain of who these soldiers are and where they come from, and explain why these Nepalese men hold their place at the heart of the British army. Whilst many of the early visitors to the museum may have been ex-soldiers or people directly related to someone involved in the last war with a working knowledge of the British army, today's visitor by contrast may not know any members of the armed service because of the smaller number of people involved. In addition, knowledge of the Gurkha let alone Nepal may be limited, although the publicity surrounding the recent (February 2007) review of Gurkha Terms and Conditions of Service may have served to heighten awareness. In this respect army museums may have to cater for a wider range of needs than most museums, as they clearly have a responsibility to their regiment as well as the Ministry of Defence and the general public (Stephens, 2006). The test for the Gurkha museum is to stay true to its aim whilst providing a context that is both informative and presented in an interesting manner to the visitor who may not possess a military background. As Jones (1996, p. 154) suggests, 'The challenge facing the curator of regimental collections is to locate meanings for them which render them relevant to broad audiences.'

At first glance, the Gurkha Museum in Winchester may appear to be similar to many if not all regimental and corps museums but the very name of the museum as well as the unique symbol of the Gurkha, the kukri, displayed on the entry sign suggests something rather unique. What follows is an overview of the artefacts on display at the museum and an examination of how depth of gaze can reveal what may not be seen at first glimpse.

Dicks (2003, p. 146) suggests that museums are 'powerful agencies for defining culture to the public' and what makes the Gurkha museum unique is that it is not just military culture that is on display but that of Nepal. At the start of the museum the perspective is 'pitched straight at the Himalayan foothills' (Gurkha Museum, 2009), as large photomurals engulf the visitor in a riot of bright colours depicting not the expected soldiers but ordinary Nepalese men, women and children. The illustrated market scenes are timeless and it is only on closer inspection that amongst traditional clothing the leather jacket and jeans worn by one of the market goers reveals that these are contemporary pictures. The photographs present Nepalese people at work and at play in what would not be out of place in a promotional travelogue or brochure. The visitor's gaze is drawn to the 'otherness' and 'exoticness' of Nepal.

This section of the museum differs from all subsequent areas and stands out because of: (i) the vibrancy of the colours, which are in stark contrast to the rifle green and black that predominate in the rest of the museum; (ii) the smiles; and (iii) the frequent appearance of women. No similar images appear again in the museum. This area serves almost as a separate information room (Alpers, 1991), designed to provide a glimpse into Nepal and its culture in order to contextualizes the Gurkha and his homeland. A touch-screen computer provides further background on history, religion and customs; the caste systems is explained and it is made clear that Gurkhas in the regiments ignore caste divisions and whilst the Gurkha will follow his own customs and traditions, this will not be allowed to interrupt his military way of life. As traditional music plays in the background, the mountain terrain and terraced hillsides where Nepalese hill people live and work are clearly depicted. The evoked message is that it is the harshness of this geographical setting that provides the Gurkha with his physical strength, resilience and

self-sufficiency. Photographs of Nepalese hill tribesmen and women bent forwards carrying heavily weighted wicker baskets of firewood and other goods up precipitous inclines is subsequently mirrored in the hill selection stage of becoming a Ghurka soldier. This involves prospective new recruits in the 'doko', running up a 4.2-km-long steep course carrying 35 kg of rocks in baskets on their backs (Webb, 2007a). A familiar part of the hardship of daily life is thus adapted into part of the recruitment process.

Vitrines contain a variety of everyday objects from sickles for gathering crops to blankets used by shepherds and carvings that would surround the doorframes of houses. Traditional dress is displayed, and bridal hair ornaments and precious-stone-encrusted gold bracelets and necklaces are presented. This serves once again to create the cultural environment, which enables the visitor to understand why the hill tribesman leaves his homeland to become a Ghurka. Commentary explains that Gurkha soldier's wives wear heavy gold as a symbol of their wealth. The potential earnings during both service and retirement and subsequent escape from poverty are pertinent reasons for the young Nepalese youth to enlist. What is not explained and should be regarded as an omission is an indication of the economic situation in Nepal, as it is its position as one of the poorest countries in the world with 37.7% of the population living on below $1 a day (UNDP, 2005) that is likely to provide the impetus to enlist in the British army in the first place. The reality is that in 2005 15,000 Nepalese men (Hansard, 2006) applied for 370 (British Army, 2007c) places.

The knives on display introduce the visitor to the infamous renowned national weapon, the kukri, which symbolizes the duality of this museum representing not only the regiment but to some the Gurkha himself and even Nepal. It is therefore a very appropriate image for both the regimental cap badge and the museum. The knife's scabbard has two pockets on the back holding blunt steel for sharpening the blade or striking sparks from flint (the chakmak) and a little skinning knife (the karda) that visitors might recognize as a penknife. It is primarily a tool, much like the Leatherman carried by hill walkers and climbers. The kukri, which also has cultural and religious significance, can be very ornate and there are a number of highly decorated kukris on display throughout the museum. In addition to its spiritual resonance, the kukri is a weapon therefore symbolizing both peace and war, attack and defence. The kukri carried by officers and soldiers alike becomes for the Ghurka 'a chopping extension of his dominant arm' (British Army, 2007b) with all that this implies for a soldier. Caplan (1995, p. 133) suggests that the kukri appears in much of the fictional and military literature written about the Gurkhas and is inevitably linked to 'Gurkha Tales' portraying their 'tenacity, strength and courage' and as such is one of the dominant images that serves to stereotype these particular soldiers.

These ethnographic objects are placed in a combination of what Kirshenblatt-Gimblett (1998, p. 20) refers to as 'in-context', namely traditional wall displays and glass cases, and *in situ* displays such as dioramas and tableaux. She argues that the second category tends to 'appeal to those who argue that cultures are coherent wholes in their own right, that environment plays a significant role in cultural formation, and that displays should present process and not just products'. The combination of the two in this section of the museum shows that the Ghurka is a product of his environment and becoming a soldier is a result of processes within that environment. There is a clear duality here between the military and civilian life of the Gurkha. The emphasis on women in the initial display reflects an interest in the human image of not only the soldier but also his family. It suggests a world outside of the army with his other 'family' his blood kin. The artefacts and touch screen displays can assist the visitor to construct meanings of Nepalese national identity and help to place the Gurkha in his homeland and provides a socio-cultural context especially for the non-expert visitor. This first gallery presents a visually stimulating and inviting introduction to Nepal although some of the deeper meanings and significance are lost if the visitor chooses to glimpse rather than gaze.

This part of the museum also provides an illuminated relief map of Nepal and the surrounding area, which assumes geographical prior knowledge on the part of the British visitor, as the map shows the position of Nepal in relation to India and Asia rather than to the UK. The display therefore lacks an orientation map possibly because of the nature of the museum's

original military visitor base who may have been familiar with the subcontinent and its geography, something that is not necessarily the case today. Tension may therefore be created between the museum's expectation of visitor knowledge and actual knowledge. A more 'in-context' (Kirstenblatt-Gimblett, 1998, p. 21) approach that establishes a relationship between the UK and Nepal may be useful.

Leaving this section of the museum, what follows is very different, as future displays concentrate on the military role of the Gurkha. Through a directed approach (Dean, 1994), one choice of pathway facilitates a chronological order, and the displays themselves are organized by date from the original fighting of the Nepal war, through Gallipoli and the Malay Emergency through to the Brunei Revolt, the Indonesian Confrontation and the Falklands, to the present day. Interpretive methods include tableaux, dioramas, models, panel displays and pictures. Displayed overhead is a timeline that provides orientation through the use of historically familiar figures such as Florence Nightingale, Napoleon Bonaparte and the Duke of Wellington.

Dicks (2003) suggests that experiences play a key role in museums and the visit does indeed become an experience, as turning a corner triggers a soundtrack, and a loud cry from a life-size model of a charging Gurkha armed to the teeth soon turns a glance into a gaze that is further held by a short commentary. The realities of warfare are not shirked away from. Further graphic dioramas show the Gurkha in action, the kukri as a tool of war. One tableau features the bloodbath of machine gun and barbed wire of the First World War whilst another a jungle camp with sentries awaiting the enemy. This type of display shows some of the violence of war in a seemly realistic and gruesome manner but at the same time manages to sanitize the horror.

Like many military museums, there is a great deal of attention shown to uniforms (Uzzell, 1989), which reflect the official institution of the regiment (Jones, 1996, p. 155). Uniforms are a powerful representation of cohesiveness and conformity, and symbolic of the armed forces. Pearce (1994, pp. 19–20) uses the example of an infantry officer's red jacket on display at the National Army Museum, London, to assess how such an object can 'accumulate meanings as time passes' and that this type of object through its 'power of the real thing' has the ability to excite the viewer. The uniforms usually displayed on models illustrate how the soldier or officer would have appeared as they took part in major events in regimental history and are predominantly green in colour, reflecting the Gurkhas long association with the 60th Rifles and its successors. The presence of Scottish tartans including MacDuff Tartan worn by the pipers of the Gurkha Transport Regiment, the MacLeod tartan worn by the pipers of the Queen's Gurkha Engineers and the Grant Tartan worn by pipers of the Queen's Gurkha Signals reflects the association of various Highland regiments with the men of Nepal. Tartan also appears in the women's dress that forms part of the cultural display at the start of the museum but it is not clear whether this is a traditional Nepalese weave or if it is a consequence of these military links; what it does do, however, is reflect the duality of the images displayed.

Unsurprisingly for a military museum, medals are also exhibited but these are frequently placed alongside works of art and items of cultural significance. The background to each display case is an enlarged section from a painting or photograph, or image of the event portrayed. The artwork provides not only a pleasing aesthetic background to the artefacts but may also serve to remind those with a deeper background knowledge of military history that before the development of photography the armed services placed emphasis on training British officers to produce visual images of the terrain and battlefields. A brass role of honour may at first appear to be a work of art but on deeper inspection clearly honours those who were killed in battle. The recovery of the plate reflects the modern change in the British army tradition and values, for the role of honour refers to combatants who were buried where they fell, in comparison to current conflicts when fallen soldiers are brought home.

A large wall map centres on the North West Frontier of India and to the student of military history the visual message may be obvious, as it is the location of many historic events. For those visitors less familiar, more than a glimpse at the display would reveal familiar locations such as Helmand, Kabul and Kandarhar, names of destinations frequently in the news today. Another life-size but static figure portrays an Afghan fighter pointing a Jezzel. All that needs to change

is the weapon and a tableau presenting a scene from yesterday's history becomes a representation of today.

The museum's mission also puts the focus on the British officer and his relationship with the Gurkha soldier. Photographs of Queen's Gurkha Officers reflect a peculiarity of the late Indian Army of the Empire period. For example, in a photograph labelled 'Kajar 1906 4th Gurkha Rifles a group of British Officers and their ladies at camp', the visitor gets a glimpse of informal military life with the officers in civilian clothes taking what appears to be afternoon tea with the 'memsahib'. The women would not be out of place in Brighton let alone India. Everything is ordered, with senior officers (recognizable even in everyday clothes) to the forefront of the picture with junior officers to the side. A closer gaze reveals the pet dogs, possibly more associated with younger single officers, and a blur that on closer inspection is clearly an Indian servant moving through the background. The life and indeed death of the British officer is largely confined to the museum stairwell and is reflected in a limited number of period photographs. In most similar museums, it seems that the history on display is often that of the officer who is in the main responsible for recording it but not here. It is the officer that comes second. The individual Gurkha is represented by photographs with citations of those awarded the Victoria Cross. These pictures bring an additional poignancy that the medal alone fails to do.

As the visitor progresses through the upper floors of the museum, more familiar scenes, which have been played out on our television screens, appear. In events from the Falklands to the streets of Northern Ireland and the spectre of terrorism, the Gurkha soldier is seen representing the British army. By now, the displays are easily recognizable but minor items stand out if the visitor's attention is drawn beyond field uniforms often worn today as fashion items. The Falklands display for example contains ration packs containing common items such as branded cigarettes, although one ration pack contains more luxurious items. If the visitor chooses to read the text provided, they will discover that the Argentinean Officers have better ration packs than their men, unlike in the British army.

Moving to the exit, evidence of the peacetime role of the Gurkha soldier is presented, which almost brings the visitor full circle to where they started with the life of the soldier and his family in the hills of Nepal. This is reflected in the contents of the shop at the exit, which sells not only the expected cap badges and military history books but also brightly coloured textile items and Nepalese silver jewellery as well as recipe books on Nepalese cuisine and tea, a juxtaposition of the military and the civilian.

Conclusion

There are a number of omissions from the museum. For example, the visitor does not see anything on the political history of Nepal. This is perhaps understandable as the British Army traditionally separates itself from this aspect of life, but nevertheless an oversight. No mention is made of the pensions issue with the differentiation in pay levels not just between officers and men but British soldiers and Gurkhas, which has only just been partially resolved. This is extremely important when the total contribution of the Gurkha to the Nepali economy is its fourth largest foreign currency earner. Relatively little mention is currently made of the methods of recruitment and selection that really illustrate how tough the Gurkha has to be and how hard it is to get in to the brigade. Webb (2007b) also reflects upon a change in the make-up of the Gurkha force itself, for the need for fewer recruits has led to higher standards of education being set as entry requirements, which in turn has resulted in more townspeople rather than the traditional hill people being accepted. This in itself is creating a duality within the makeup of the Gurkha as a military unit.

The museum sets out not only to commemorate the service to the crown of the Gurkha and the British officer from 1815 to the present day but also to provide an enjoyable and educational experience. It is possible that the nature of some of the exhibits in military museums may lead to some unease on the part of the educator in particular. The very nature of being a soldier implies the legal right and duty to fight and if necessary kill according to orders and to make the ultimate commitment to give their own lives in doing so. Some might make accusations that regimental museums showcase military triumphs and glorify war and killing, and it is true to suggest that at the Gurkha Museum some of the representations are quite graphic in their presentation of the combat experience. However, at no time are these representations inappropriate or gratuitous and the dioramas that feature some of the harsher realities of soldiering contribute greatly to the overall visitor experience. Whilst the reality of war is not avoided the dual role of today's soldier in policing and peace-keeping is also represented, reflecting the reality of soldiering in the modern world.

The Gurkha museum is evolving primarily because of external pressures. It is no longer just about the culture and traditions of a military unit. Whilst the background to the Gurkhas' homeland explicitly sets out to inform the visitor about the cultural significance of religion, customs and tradition, the other galleries do so but on occasion by default. The links between the military and civilian cultures are there throughout the museum if the visitor knows where to look, although at first glance they are not always clearly defined and there may, however, be too great an assumption of prior knowledge. It is nevertheless correct to suggest that, as the visitor progresses around the museum, a greater understanding of what it means to be a Gurkha who is both a British soldier and a Nepalese citizen develops, what may not be heard loudly enough is the voice of the Gurkha soldier himself.

Acknowledgements

Thanks to Major Gerald Davis, Curator, the Gurkha Museum, Peninsula Barracks, Romsey Road, Winchester, www.thegurkhamuseum.co.uk.

References

Alpers, S. (1991) The museum as a way of seeing. In: Karp, I. and Lavin, S.D. (eds) *Exhibiting Cultures. The Poetics and Politics of Museum Design*. Smithsonian Institution Press, Washington.
Asquith, S. (2000a) The Gurkha Rifles 1815–1918. *Regiment Magazine*, October, 26–28.

Asquith, S. (2000b) The Gurkha Rifles 1918–2000. *Regiment Magazine*, November, 64.

British Army (2007a) History of the Royal Gurkha Rifles http://www.army.dod.uk/brigade_of_gurkhas/rgr/index.htm (Accessed 27 March 2007).

British Army (2007b) News and Views from Gurkha Company http://www.army.mod.uk/linkedfiles/brigade_of_gurkhas/g_coy_s_news.doc (Accessed 27 March 2007).

British Army (2007c) The origin of the kukri. http://www.army.mod.uk/brigade_of_gurkhas/history/kukri_history.htm (Accessed 27 March 2007).

Caplan, L. (1995) *Warrior Gentlemen. 'Gurkhas in Western Imagination'.* Berghahn Books, Providence, RI.

Children, G. (2000) What is it good for? *Museums Journal*, May, 21–23.

Dean, D. (1994) *Museum Exhibition Theory and Practice.* Routledge, London.

Department of Culture, Media and Sports (2006) *Understanding the Future: Priorities for England's Museums.* October. DCMS, London.

Dicks, B. (2003) *Culture on Display. The Production of Contemporary Visitability.* Open University Press, Milton Keynes.

Gurkha Museum (2009) www.thegurkhamuseum.co.uk (Accessed 5 February 2009).

Holts Tours (2008) Holts Tourism Battlefields and History. www.holts.co.uk (Accessed 6 June 2008).

Ipsos MORI (2008) British Army Reputation Tracking. August.

Jones, S. (1996) Making histories of war. In: Kavanagh, G. (ed.) *Making Histories.* Leicester University Press, Leicester.

Kirshenblatt-Gimblett, B. (1998) *Destination Culture.* University of California Press, Berkeley, CA.

London School of Economics and Political Science (2006) Museums and Galleries in Britain Economic, Social and Creative Impacts. www.mla.gov.uk/resources/assets//M/museums_galleries_in_britain_10528.pdf (Accessed 20 February 20007).

Ministry of Defence (1998) Executive Committee of the Army Board MOD(A) Policy Towards Regimental and Corps Museums. MOD, London.

Ministry of Defence (2008) UK Defence Statistics 2008. www.dasa.mod.uk/ukas (Accessed 6 August 2008).

Museum, Libraries and Archives Council (2005) Museums Statistics in England www.mla.gov.uk/resources/assets//E/egmus2005_doc_9460.doc (Accessed 20 February 2007).

Parker, J. (1999) *The Gurkhas.* Headline, London.

Pearce, S.M. (1994) Objects as meaning; or narrating the past. In: Pearce, S.M. (ed.) *Interpreting Objects and Collections.* Routledge, London, pp. 19–29.

Smith, V. (1996) War and its tourist attractions. In: Pizam, A. and Mansfield, Y. (eds) *Tourism, Crime and International Security Issues.* John Wiley & Sons, Chichester, pp. 247–264.

Stephens, S. (2006) *National Service Museums Journal*, July, 26–29.

Streets, H. (2004) *Martial Races: The Military, Race and Masculinity in British Imperial Culture 1857–1914.* Manchester University Press, Manchester.

United Nation Development Programme Human Development Report (2005) www.undp.org (accessed 6 March 2007).

Uzzell, D. (1989) The hot interpretation of war and conflict. In: Uzzell, D. (ed.) *Heritage Interpretation: Volume 1: The Natural and Built Environment.* Belhaven Press, London, pp. 33–47.

Webb, A. (2007a) The cream of the crop. *Soldier Magazine*, January, 21.

Webb A. (2007b) From the cradle to the grave. *Soldier Magazine*, February, 33.

Winchester City Council (2008) www.visitwinchester.co.uk/site/things-to-do/p_41 (Accessed 6 August 2008).

8   In the Eye of the Beholder? Tourism and the Activist Academic

Freya Higgins-Desbiolles
School of Management, University of South Australia, Adelaide, Australia

Introduction

The one path that still leads in the direction of scholarly objectivity, detachment, and neutrality is exactly the one originally thought to lead away from these classic virtues: that is an openly autobiographical style in which the subjective position of the author, especially on political matters, is presented in a clear and straightforward fashion. At least this enables the reader to review his or her own position to make the adjustments necessary for dialogue.
(MacCannell, 1992, pp. 9–10)

In the interests of scholarly objectivity, some analysts of tourism are at pains to put aside any personal predilections and experiences that might colour their perspectives.

In the new millennium, tourism has offered a few rare works of exception that demonstrate that scholarly understanding can develop from material which is both personal and scholarly (Botterill, 2003; Hall, 2004; Nash, 2007). The analysis contained within this chapter suggests the image of tourism held in the mind of the researcher can shape and influence their engagement with the study and analysis of tourism and that an exploration of such images is worthy of investigation. Here, I offer an auto-ethnographic narrative, which reveals the source of my vision of tourism as a societal phenomenon as well as insights to my approach as an 'activist academic'.

Image and Representation in Tourism

Image and representation have long been fruitful lines of enquiry for tourism analysis. According to Gartner (2000, p. 295), images are the:

> perceptions, beliefs, impressions, ideas and understanding one holds of objects, people, events or places. An image is a simplified, condensed version of which the holder assumes to be reality. Held and stored images are the means humans use to organise the various stimuli received and processed on a daily basis, and help to make sense of the surroundings and the world in which one lives.

Image analysis in tourism has usually concerned the images held of people, products, experiences and/or the destination. The encounter between the tourist and the host of the tourist destination is mediated in effect by the images held in the mind's eye of each of these key players leading to complex and nuanced interactions that defy simple description and analysis. Dennis O'Rourke's classic film *Cannibal Tours* (1988) illustrates this beautifully as he 'documents' the encounter between western tourists and the toured 'Other', embodied in this case by locals of the Sepik River region of Papua New Guinea. A startling feature of the film is the lack of any real contact and understanding between the interviewed western tourists and the local Papuans, as each group responds to

© CAB International 2010. *Tourism and Visual Culture,* Volume 1
(eds P. Burns, C. Palmer and J-A. Lester)

images they hold of each other rather than to the actual opportunity for encounters.

Related to this imagery is the 'tourist gaze' described by Urry (2002), which is not only about the visual exploration of the objects of the tourism encounter, but is also about a social organization and systematization mediated by 'professional experts who help to construct and develop our gaze as tourists' (Urry, 2002, p. 1). As Morgan and Pritchard's (1998) work argues, tourism images and representations are about power and should be analysed for their significance.

> At the dawn of the third millennium, images are the currency of cultures, reflecting and thereby reinforcing particular shared meanings and beliefs and particular value systems. Tourism marketers through their marketing images create identities which represent certain ways of seeing reality, images which both reflect and reinforce particular relationships in societies. These are relations which are grounded in relations of power, dominance and subordination which characterise the global system.
> (Morgan and Pritchard, 1998, p. 3)

It is important to remember that images have consequences in this way and should be critically examined within this context. What has been little examined to date is the image/s of tourism that tourism researchers hold in their mind's eye, whether consciously or subconsciously. It is likely that we all hold such images and their significance may not be inconsequential.

There is, however, tourism literature that moves us in such a direction and opens up the possibility for such an investigation. For instance, Nash commissioned some of the longest serving and most renowned analysts of tourism to recount their professional histories and thereby shed light on the development of the tourism discipline (2007). Using social action theory, Nash suggests social action '. . . considers socially situated actors to be thinking, and perhaps feeling about their own actions as they pursue their subjectively informed course of action' (2007, p. 22). What we find in these stories of some of the most renowned thinkers in the tourism discipline, such as Dean MacCannell, Malcolm Crick and Graham Dann, is that their personal life journeys profoundly influenced the way they thought about and then researched tourism.

Additionally, Hall made a recent contribution to a text on qualitative tourism research which examined reflexivity in terms of 'situating myself and/with others' (2004). Contextualizing his discussion of academic reflexivity in the changing environment presented by the postmodern turn and within the crisis of capitalism, Hall argues that we in the tourism discipline need to engage with the personal perspectives and stories that we hold and reflect on how they shape our research. Hall (2004, pp. 139–140) states:

> Accounts of any discipline and of research within that field of study are *situated*. That is, 'they depend on the point of view of the author, which in turn reflects how he/she is positioned intellectually, politically and socially' (Barnes and Sheppard, 2000, p. 6). However, how often does one read research which explicitly recognises its situatedness in tourism? Despite the postmodern recognition of the absence of absolutes, this does not seem to have been widely translated into the representation and reading of tourism research and scholarship. Why?

A powerful example of the scholarly impact such work can have is provided by David Botterill in a journal article which provides an 'autoethnographic narrative on tourism research epistemologies' (2003). This work will be discussed further later in this analysis.

These new avenues in tourism research open up ways for us to rethink our positions on tourism by examining our personal views and experiences and reflecting on the tourism research agendas that germinate from such seeds. However, before proceeding to my own autoethnographic narrative, which models this, it is first useful to explore the dichotomy of views evident in the early years of tourism academic analysis, which greatly influenced the development of tourism scholarship towards a social scientific approach characterized as objective and value-free.

Historical Views of Tourism and the Rise of the 'Scientification' of Tourism Scholarship

Dichotomous and opposing perspectives of tourism have been a long-standing feature of tourism discourse since Graburn described tourism as a 'sacred journey' in the same text Nash noted its neo-imperialistic nature (in Smith, 1977 as noted by Crick, 2007, p. 68). Two key contradictory perspectives impacting the image of tourism and its study are the pro-tourism and the anti-tourism rhetoric featured in the late 20th century.

Pro-tourism rhetoric has been around since the development of the modern industrial tourism system in the wake of the Second World War. This pro-tourism stance has been labelled 'boosterism' because of its intended effect of promoting and advancing the spread of tourism development. Hall defines boosterism as a 'simplistic attitude that tourism development is inherently good and of automatic benefit to the host' (2000, p. 21). Proponents of boosterism are typically economists within government departments who are pro-growth and industry professionals who stand to financially gain from the spread of tourism. In his analysis of the different paradigms operating in thinking on tourism called the 'platform theory', Jafar Jafari called this the 'advocacy platform' and suggested its adherents promoted the 'contributions of the "industry" to growth and development' (2005, p. 1). As part of this effort, tourism businesses began to champion the notion of tourism as an 'industry' in order to gain the respect and support of economists, economic developers and governments for tourism as a tool for economic development (Davidson, 1994, pp. 20–21). Leiper (1995, pp. 103–105) argues that the 'tourist industry' image was created to:

- Secure broad public relations goals for organizations such as the Pacific Asia Travel Association, the UN World Tourism Organization and the World Travel and Tourism Council;
- Create pride and professionalism among employees;
- Establish clout wieldable in politics.

Davidson and Leiper convincingly reveal that the effort to gain widespread acceptance of the notion of tourism as 'industry' was in part an attempt to gain considerable political advantage, which is pursued to obtain economic benefits.

Despite the predominance of the boosterism perspective in the tourism arena (Hall, 2000, p. 21), the limitations and damages of tourism became apparent as early as the 1970s with the degradation of Mediterranean coastal resorts and the overdevelopment of destinations like Waikiki. As a result, mass tourism was called into question. Some of the negative impacts observed included crowding, environmental degradation, pollution, economic leakages, tourism-induced inflation, commodification of culture, cultural change induced by the demonstration effect, population displacement and vulnerable, tourism dependent economies. As a result of the proliferation of such problems with the expansion of tourism since the 1970s, a clear 'anti-tourism' stance has developed. Key to this critique of tourism were: tourism non-governmental organizations (NGOs) such as the Ecumenical Coalition on Third World Tourism who in particular advocated for the needs of 'host' communities; local people's organizations in local places confronting tourism's negative impacts in such places as Goa, India; and key segments of academia investigating the social impacts of tourism (Crick, 1989; Burns, 2005). Seaton states 'anti-tourism factions include social scientists who have often been caustic about the tourism industry and its impacts, and who have advocated a conservationist, protection-from-tourists attitude to "traditional" cultures and environments abroad' (2000, p. 27). Jafari noted that the adherents of the 'cautionary platform' pointed to these negative impacts of tourism and called for caution in the use of tourism for development and thereby challenging the rosy picture of tourism painted by the advocates following the boosterism tradition (2005, p. 1).

Following these oppositionary perspectives, tourism analysis expanded to include: the more synthesizing approach of the 'adaptancy platform', which explored alternatives forms of tourism development that maximized the benefits of tourism while minimizing the negative impacts (Jafari, 2005, p. 2), and the more holistic and systems-oriented analysis of tourism under the 'knowledge-based platform', which, according to Jafari, is leading to the 'scientification of tourism' (Jafari, 2001, pp. 31–32). Jafari (2001, p. 2) contends:

> While these four platforms, generalizing the tendency of their eras, appeared in the foregoing order, they did not replace one another. Indeed, they are all present today, echoing the voices by which they are characterized, with the last one being responsible for enhancing the academic position of tourism worldwide.

In his work reviewing the scientification process of tourism, Jafari lauds this process and asserts 'tourism now has almost all properties and tools typically associated with the more established field of investigations' (2001, p. 32). However, Macbeth has challenged Jafari's position as well as the value and desirability of these developments in tourism research. In a comment on Jafari's 2001 version of his analysis of tourism scholarship, Macbeth (2005, p. 965) asserts that:

> rather than showing maturity, tourism scholarship, by becoming overly 'scientific' in its epistemology, would be more limited and restrictive in its understanding of the world . . . [However] understanding values and the role they play is an important aspect of the maturation of tourism scholarship.
> Objectivity, as a key aspect of scientification, is too often a mask that restricts the ability to see underlying values and philosophy of knowledge that restrict the interrogation of ethical positions.

Macbeth's analysis leads him to add not only a sustainable development platform but also an ethics platform to Jafari's previous four platforms, which he argues 'is needed to interrogate the morality of the positions taken in policy, planning, development and management' (2005, p. 962). What is of relevance to this analysis, however, is the insight that the tourism discipline is hampered by this reverence for objectivity and scientification.

Critical, Emancipatory Research and Autoethnography

Personal perspectives are irrevocably shaped by experiences and insights that are gained in one's formative years. However, as academics of tourism, significant pressure is subtly exerted to adhere to modes of scientific inquiry that are characterized as dispassionate, rational, objective and value-free. As a self-proclaimed activist academic, I knew that such a model would not accommodate the vision I hold for my work. In my research, I draw on postcolonial, indigenist and feminist literatures in order to develop a critical and emancipatory research agenda.

Velazquez (1998, pp. 65–66) describes critical, transformative research:

> Transformative research is not a methodology. It is an orientation toward research that is defined by its intended outcome: producing a more just and equitable world . . . Transformative research stimulates critical awareness of power relationships and empowers researcher and participants with the knowledge to change power relationships.

In particular, postcolonial theory has usefully forced 'a radical rethinking of forms of knowledge and social identities authored and authorized by colonialism and Western domination' (Prakash, 1994, p. 87). This has liberated regimes of knowledge in numerous profound ways, including an acknowledgement of the legitimacy of drawing on personal, self-reflexive and qualitative enquiries to arrive at understanding.

Denzin (2000) has stated 'The next moment in qualitative inquiry will be one at which the practices of qualitative research finally move, without hesitation or encumbrance, from the personal to the political' (cited in Holman Jones, 2005, p. 763). Within this sphere, autoethnography has emerged as a leading methodology, which can profoundly link the personal and the political (Holman Jones, 2005). Ellis and Bochner describe it as a form of writing that 'make[s] the researcher's own experience a topic of investigation in its own right' (2000, p. 733) and '. . . displays multiple layers of consciousness, connecting the personal to the cultural' (2000, p. 739). Holman Jones offers 'the personal text as critical intervention in social, political and cultural life' (2005, p. 763), which can transform our understandings. Her work suggests:

> Looking at the world from a specific, perspectival, and limited vantage point can tell, teach, and put people in motion. It is about autoethnography as a radical democratic politics – a politics committed to creating space for dialogue and debate that instigates and shapes social change.
> (Holman Jones, 2005, p. 763)

My work here is inspired by the example of David Botterill, who offered an 'autoethnographic narrative on tourism research epistemologies' (2003). Concerned that the tourism discipline needed a stronger engagement with ontological and epistemological arguments,

Botterill provides a narrative account, which describes his research career but in conjunction with a 'metaphor of a journey of getting to know tourism through social scientific inquiry' (2003, p. 97). Botterill states '. . . when choices are made about 'the research' by an individual researcher: what topic to research? How to research the topic? And the interpretation of the results, they are shaped by the totality of experience surrounding the researcher' (2003, p. 98). Botterill's personal and research journeys led him to join a new area of 'critical realist tourism research', which delves into the way power works in tourism and in particular to focus on topics of 'social inclusion' and 'crisis'. I will now offer a brief autoethnographic narrative, rich in visual references to animate objects and inanimate emotions, about my experience of tourism development in order to uncover some of the sources for my perspectives on tourism as well as briefly suggest how it has influenced and will continue to influence my research agenda.

My Autoethnographic Narrative

My perspective has been shaped by an almost idyllic childhood growing up in a small, visually stimulating rural coastal community: a small island just off the coast of North Carolina in the USA. In my heart, this is *my island*. When my mother moved to this island in the mid-1960s, it had a permanent population of some 500 souls, but these would be joined in summer by (wealthier) people from upstate and interstate who had holiday homes on our island. At that time, we still had the swamps and the marshes that were a feature of many southern coastal areas. We saw alligators and freshwater turtles, as well as egrets and other marsh birds, which thrived on the mud and marsh that sat between our island and the mainland. We also saw foxes, bears and even the odd mountain lion in addition to numerous possums, raccoons and squirrels that featured in this area. On the seashore, loggerhead sea turtles would bury their eggs in summer and after nearly 2 months their hatchlings would then try to make the precarious journey from the shore to the sea. Seashells abounded in these prolific waters. This is how my family made a living – collecting and trading

seashells and selling them to the tourists in the summer season. Locals complained about the impacts of outsiders (among which my family was included!), but still built their businesses and jobs on the economic opportunities that these outsiders offered to their small, poor and out-of-the-way community. Life had a rhythm to it: summer brought the tourists and second-home owners, higher prices in our shops and increased traffic on our one road and bridge off the island; but winter followed when life returned to a more sedate pace, prices lowered, we had the island to ourselves and the shells washed up on the shore from the winter storms.

The peak would always be the week of the 4th of July as nearby Southport held one of the country's oldest and visually dramatic celebrations. Over the years, visitation for this event escalated from a few thousand visitors, to 1972 when the Fourth of July Festival was declared as the official North Carolina Fourth of July Festival and visitation skyrocketed to tens of thousands more tourists. Today more than 50,000 people are attracted to this small community during this time. It was in my teenage years that I observed that many locals would choose to stay at home rather than join the long queue of cars that would take hours to reach the highlight of the festival, the annual parade. Most were working long hours during this time in order to make the money that would tide them over in the off-season.

Things changed dramatically during these years. A permanent bridge replaced the floating, pontoon bridge that a drunken barge boat captain knocked out in 1971. Numerous facilities were built to service the tourists that the locals grew to appreciate, including cafes, restaurants, bars, large retail chains, a cinema and entertainment complexes featuring arcade games, water slides and miniature golf. This ameliorated the boredom for youth and mitigated the need for adults to travel some 75 miles to access such facilities on the mainland.

As the ranks of second-home owners increased and were joined by other types of tourists, more facilities were developed including golf courses, marinas, hotels and up-market residential developments, some of which attracted the more wealthy locals as clients, but more often provided much needed employment in this rather poor area of the state.

I do not know when it was that I realized that the island I loved no longer existed. Perhaps it was the secret joy that hurricanes brought as potential sources of cleansing the coastline that made me aware that my relationship to this place had altered as dramatically as the place itself.

What is this Island (no longer my Island) like now? The marshes have given way to elite coastal properties vying for that elusive 'water view'. What place is there now for the alligators and egrets whose habitat no longer exists? Bears and mountain lions have long since gone. Possums still turn up on people's doorsteps, rummaging through rubbish or pet food, or feature as road kill on ever-busy streets. Loggerhead turtles are endangered, but some tourist facilities have fostered conservation projects to protect their nests *for* the numerous tourists who wish to view them in the egg-laying and hatching periods. What peace can laying mothers or hatchlings find on a beach where most of the coastline is now privatized and developed, where human activity has increased dramatically and safe habitat has receded? Seashells can no longer be seen in much of these coastal waters because of habitat destruction through repeated dredging to deepen boating channels, and the over-exploitation of shell-collectors, both tourists and professionals. And what about the locals with whom I grew up? They are moving away, inland, leaving the Island to the newcomers. There are a multitude of reasons, including: the loss of social amenity as noise and congestion disrupt well-being; increased costs of living, which come from inflation, higher taxes and more costly insurance rates; and perhaps most ironically, a loss of 'place attachment' as what they had loved about their island no longer exists and is unlikely to return.

This true, anecdotal story of my childhood is iconic of the tourism phenomenon. There is an inherent tendency for tourism to lay the 'seeds of its own destruction' (Crick, 1989, p. 338). As it seeks to capitalize on the attractions of place, people and lifestyle, it inevitably changes the assets that were the original attraction. Numerous reactions can flow from a realization of such dynamics. Developers attuned to a globalized world know that replacement destinations for their investments abound. Local government and others interested in maintaining

the place realize that sound planning and management are needed to retain the essence of the attraction and will try to manage and mitigate the impacts of change. Some locals and visitors will embrace the changes as a more upmarket and entertaining place is developed, and the unpleasant features of the past (such as smelly swamps, poor infrastructure and dangerous wildlife) disappear. Those who choose to abandon the locality perhaps move on to more amenable places as change brings opportunities to access jobs, education and experiences not available in their former locality.

But my reaction is to ask: what is lost? My place, my culture and my habitat no longer exist. Like the alligator and the loggerhead sea turtle, I must adjust myself to changes beyond my control and to my detriment. But it is not just the three of us who are out of kilter with the profound changes upon us. Nor is this simply a personal lament, but possibly an inexorable outcome of present circumstances, for my Island is only one among a multitude of places experiencing the same dynamics around the globe. At the time that my swamp was being slowly stifled by encroaching development, the swamps and mangroves of Cancun, Mexico, were being filled in to create a resort destination in a formerly pristine area.

I must emphasize that I am not a 'knee-jerk' anti-tourist of the mould described earlier. As stated, my family were originally tourist encroachers on my Island and we made our enjoyable living from selling shells to the tourists. Members of my family, including myself, have also been frequent tourists over the years, enjoying the habitats of others and perhaps contributing unwittingly to similar profound changes in other places. It was, in fact, a volunteer tourism experience with the US Peace Corps in my early twenties that set me on my activist trajectory.

The intuition seeded in my youth has sparked my interest in visualizing contemporary tourism in the context of globalization. The research agenda I plan to follow moves beyond this personal narrative to examine the dynamics of contemporary tourism under the dominant capitalist system driven by the economic imperatives of unrestrained economic growth and development. It is becoming increasingly evident that such dynamics hold grave implications for our collective well-being. It is for this reason that I have decided to pursue the iconoclastic path of the activist tourism academic, looking, seeing and getting my hands dirty in the real world, taking sides and struggling for the attainment of justice, equity and sustainability through, within, and despite tourism.

Tourism as a Prism: Seeing the World through the Lens of Tourism

The 'looking and seeing' at tourism described above adds emphasis to Mowforth and Munt claim that tourism 'is an activity which helps us to understand the world and ways in which humans interact with the planet and with each other in a range of senses' (Mowforth and Munt, 1998, pp. 2–3). They also contend that tourism 'is a "prism" for understanding broader global issues and relations' (2003, p. 271). Morgan and Pritchard contend, 'Despite its presentation as free time, framed by choice, flexibility, spontaneity and self-determination, the study of tourism leads the researcher not to the periphery but to the core of global power structures' (1998, p. 5).

Such analyses make it clear and irrefutable that tourism is about power and its practices. I have focused my work on using political frameworks to investigate the interstices between contemporary tourism, globalization, sustainability and equity. For instance, in my work analysing tourism as a social force, I have argued that tourism industry discourse serves the needs and interests of a small elite promoting the tourism industry and overshadows the more public-minded, multicultural and equitable forms of tourism that remain evident around the world (Higgins-Desbiolles, 2006). More recently I have analysed how particular forms of tourism, such as justice tourism, might contribute to a more equitable and sustainable globalization (Higgins-Desbiolles, 2008). This work is derived from experiences of working with Indigenous Australian communities, tourism non-governmental organizations and community groups facing a rapacious tourism industry and yet seeking at the same time to harness the potential of tourism for their own humanistic ends. Activism has informed my theorizing and theorizing has informed my activism.

It is clear that tourism presents a site of study that is ripe for the interventions of activist academics, perhaps more palatably called 'public intellectuals'; but few have made their presence known in the field to date. And yet the role of the intellectual in progressive social change has been theorized by such thinkers as Marx and Engels (1970), Gramsci (1992) and Foucault (1980) and modelled by Jean-Paul Sartre (1967) and Edward Said among numerous others. These are thinkers whose work has been utilized in tourism analysis. Should the critical strands of the tourism discipline actively encourage the development of activist academics and public intellectuals in order to see the discipline advance beyond the straightjacket of objective, scientific approaches?

Wearing et al., in their championing of a 'decommodified research paradigm' in tourism, make one foray into this arena with their discussion of the vital roles NGOs can play in moving tourism away from 'the almost exclusive pursuit of industry profits and place social, cultural and ecological value on local environments and economics' (2005, p. 424). This work by NGOs should inspire researchers to pursue a decommodified research agenda according to Wearing et al. (2005). But far more fulfilling would be an exploration of how activism for a more ecological and equitable tourism can be married to academic endeavours through developing a reflective practice of activist academia.

I offer questions posed recently in the field of international relations for tourism colleagues to consider:

- What do we mean by 'activism' – both outside and within academic contexts?
- What does it mean to be an 'academic' and what is our proper role in society? Is the notion of the 'public intellectual' a helpful category?
- What, if any, are the connections between 'public intellectuals' and so-called 'political activists' (Maigushca and Thornton, 2006, p. 101)?

Tourism is changing our world in numerous and profound ways and yet many in the tourism arena treat it as if it is marginal to the grand issues we confront. Such issues include human-induced climate change, political instability and conflict, overuse of finite resources, competing demands for development and population growth and mobility. It is for these reasons that tourism is on the agenda of activists. The question posed here is, should academics be crossing the activism threshold in order to make their work more relevant and meaningful for people and places?

Conclusion

This chapter started with the idea that image and representation are at the centre of many fruitful lines of enquiry for tourism. But 'seeing' does not always bring a recognizable truth. Tourism has been hampered by a reification of the scientific approaches to research and analysis, which has restricted the types of inquiries undertaken and the sources of data heeded. It is clear that respect for visual, qualitative, reflexive and personal perspectives are valued outside of the tourism studies (think, for example of the rise in popularity of visual sociology) and that certain researchers within the discipline are open to embracing these as opportunities to open up new ways of knowing tourism.

I have offered an autoethnographic narrative of my experience of tourism development, framed as they are, by familiar and not so familiar iconographies of place and space, in order to reveal the image, my active construction, of tourism held in my mind's eye that has shaped my engagement with tourism and inspired me to be an activist academic. Perhaps gazing on (or simply seeing) my narrative will allow others to reflect on themselves, their values and practices as citizens, tourists, and for some, tourism academics and open up questions on new possibilities in knowing, doing and seeing tourism.

References

Botterill, D. (2003) An autoethnographic narrative on tourism research epistemologies. *Loisir et société/Society and Leisure* 26, 97–110.

Burns, P.M. (2005) Social identities, globalisation, and the cultural politics of tourism. In: Theobold, W.F. (ed.) *Global Tourism*, 3rd edn. Elsevier, Amsterdam, pp. 391–405.

Crick, M. (1989) Representations of international tourism in the social sciences: sun, sex, sights, savings, and servility. *Annual Review of Anthropology* 18, 307–344.

Crick, M. (2007) A difficult passage, largely unassisted. In: Nash, D. (ed.) *The Study of Tourism: Anthropological and Sociological Beginnings*. Elsevier, Amsterdam, pp. 60–75.

Davidson, T.L. (1994) What are travel and tourism: are they really an industry? In: Theobold, W. (ed.) *Global Tourism: The Next Decade*. Butterworth-Heinemann, Oxford, pp. 20–26.

Denzin, N. (2000) Aesthetics and the practices of qualitative inquiry. *Qualitative Inquiry* 6, 256–265.

Ellis, C. and Bochner, A.P. (2000) Autoethnography, personal narrative, reflexivity: researcher as subject. In: Denzin, N. and Lincoln, Y. (eds) *The Handbook of Qualitative Research*, 2nd edn. Sage, Thousand Oaks, CA, pp. 733–768.

Foucault, M. (1980) *Power/Knowledge: Selected Interviews and Other Writings, 1972–1977*. Pantheon Books, New York.

Gartner, W.C. (2000) Image. In: Jafari, J. (ed.) *Encyclopedia of Tourism*. Routledge, London.

Gramsci, A. (1992) *Selections from the Prison Notebooks*. Columbia University Press, New York.

Hall, C.M. (2000) *Tourism Planning: Policies, Processes and Relationships*. Prentice-Hall, Harlow.

Hall, M. (2004) Reflexivity and tourism research: situating myself and/with others. In: Phillimore, J. and Goodson, L. (eds) *Qualitative Research in Tourism: Ontologies, Epistemologies and Methodologies*. Routledge, London, pp. 137–155.

Higgins-Desbiolles, F. (2006) More than an industry: tourism as a social force. *Tourism Management* 27, 1192–1208.

Higgins-Desbiolles, F. (2008) Justice tourism: a pathway to alternative globalisation. *Journal of Sustainable Tourism* 16, 345–364.

Holman Jones, S. (2005) Autoethnography: making the personal political. In: Denzin, N. and Lincoln, Y.S. (eds) *Sage Handbook of Qualitative Research*, 3rd edn. Sage, Thousand Oaks, CA, pp. 763–791.

Jafari, J. (2001) The scientification of tourism. In: Smith, V.L. and Brent, M. (eds) *Hosts and Guests Revisited: Tourism Issues in the 21st Century*. Cognizant Communication Corporation, New York, pp. 28–41.

Jafari, J. (2005) Bridging out, nesting afield: powering a new platform. *Journal of Tourism Studies* 16, 1–5.

Leiper, N. (1995) *Tourism Management*. RMIT Press, Melbourne.

Macbeth, J. (2005) Towards an ethics platform for tourism. *Annals of Tourism Research* 32, 962, 984.

MacCannell, D. (1992) *Empty Meeting Grounds*. Routledge, London.

Maigushca, B. and Thornton, M. (2006) Activism, academia and education. *Millennium – Journal of International Studies* 35, 101–104.

Marx, K, and Engels, F. (1970) *The German Ideology*. Lawrence & Wishart, London.

Morgan, N. and Pritchard, A. (1998) *Tourism Promotion and Power: Creating Images, Creating Identities*. John Wiley & Sons, Chichester.

Mowforth, M. and Munt, I. (1998) *Tourism and Sustainability: New Tourism in the Third World*. Routledge, London.

Mowforth, M. and Munt, I. (2003) *Tourism and Sustainability: Development and New Tourism in the Third World,* 2nd edn. Routledge, London.

Nash, D. (ed.) (2007) *The Study of Tourism: Anthropological and Sociological Beginnings*. Elsevier, Amsterdam.

O'Rourke, D. (1988) *Cannibal Tours*. CameraWork films. Directed and produced by Dennis O'Rourke.

Prakash, G. (1994) Postcolonial criticism and Indian historiography. In: Nicholson, L. and Seidman, S. (eds) *Social Postmodernism: Beyond Identity Politics*. Cambridge University Press, Cambridge, pp. 87–100.

Sartre, J.P. (1967) Preface. In: Fanon, F. *The Wretched of the Earth*. Penguin Books, London.

Seaton, A.V. (2000) Anti-tourism. In: Jafari, J. (ed.) *Encyclopedia of Tourism*. Routledge, London.

Smith, V. (1977) *Hosts and Guests: The Anthropology of Tourism*. University of Pennsylvania Press, Philadelphia, PA.

Urry, J. (2002) *The Tourist Gaze,* 2nd edn. Sage, London.

Wearing, S., McDonald, M. and Ponting, J. (2005) Building a decommodified research paradigm in tourism: the contribution of NGOs. *Journal of Sustainable Tourism* 13, 424–439.

Velazquez, L.C. (1998) Personal reflections on the process: the role of the researcher and transformative research. In: De Marrais, K.B. (ed.) *Inside Stories: Qualitative Research Reflections*. Lawrence Erlbaum Associates, Mahwah, NJ, pp. 59–66.

9 Gazes on Levanto: a Case Study on How Local Identity Could Become Part of the Touristic Supply

Stefania Antonioni, Laura Gemini and Lella Mazzoli
University of Urbino 'Carlo Bo', Department of Communication Studies, Urbino, Italy

Introduction

This work is founded on the idea that the identity of a territory is an important resource for its inhabitants, their lives in the sense of the diltheyian 'Erlebnis' (Dilthey, 1982) and also for its tourist development.

From this point of view the small town of Levanto represents the case examined because it is a paradigmatic example of the most suitable logic for tourist development in the Italian context. As we will see, we started from the grassroots, i.e. from the inhabitants and from the definition of identity as communicative life-experience of the territory, to check in which way the development process carried out from the local administration is shared by the inhabitants.

We will proceed in our work following the theoretical trends characterized by 'place marketing' strategies and destination management, but also the considerations that the sociology of tourism causes us to reflect upon.

Levanto is a small town near one of the best-known Italian tourist destination, the Cinque Terre. Its territory extends from the hills to the sea and its economy has always been based on fishery, agriculture and, by the 1920s, tourism. Levanto is an interesting case study because it has a particular character that stands up well against the more famous Cinque Terre, a character that gives it an attractive image, like

something to discover and to develop. It is the character that we called 'slowliness', according to its belonging to the international network of towns of 'good living' – *CittàSlow*. This is an association promoting the harmonic relationship between tradition and innovation, taking care of urban design and environment, and looking for a lifestyle less frenzied, all elements recognized as having great intrinsic social value as well as benefits for tourism.

On these bases, sociological research finds in local communities its subject of analysis and in the domestic gaze the assumptions to talk about identity and touristic supply.

Territorial Identity and Tourist Gaze in Levanto. Theoretical Background of the Research

Contemporary society seems to be based, more and more evidently, on an important and interesting paradox: the more we talk about and describe society as world-society – i.e. connected with globalization processes produced by flows of communication and interwoven territorial connections – the more territories, i.e. anthropological places (Augè, 1992), physical and concrete, that we label as 'local', claim their identity, uniqueness, specificity and difference. So the global logic itself is linked to the local, to the dynamics of cultural hybridization and also to the dialectics between agreement and differentiation that society, at different levels, has to manage (Featherstone, 1990; Anderson, 1991; Appadurai, 1996; Luhmann, 1998; Beck, 1999).

This work can be placed in a theoretical framework that, having a clear image of world-society, adopts a perspective of observation starting on one hand from the local reality and from its capability of being (a knot of the global communication net) and on the other hand, of showing itself as a specific identity core.

This theoretical framework is a particularly useful approach to the topic of this analysis that focuses on the local side of a process – tourism – increasingly characterized by the logic of global communication. In other words, tourism is a form of consumption connected to spare time (Dumazedier, 1974; Corbin, 1995; Mothé, 1997), even more crucial for the construction of identity of the modern individual.

It is not by chance that the most advanced reflections on contemporary consumption, which obviously includes tourism, uses the term 'vocation', meaning the process with which the modern consumer, increasingly demanding and conscious, 'chooses' from a range of equivalent and contingent possibilities, those that have sense for him or her, for their needs, for the definition of himself (Gemini, 2006). In a word: their identity.

In this sense, the research of authenticity of a place, its tradition, the local population and its habits of life seems to be one of the most effective elements from which contemporary marketing of tourism draws (Di Nallo, 1998). This may be interpreted as a demand of tourist consumption oriented both to the possibility of meeting habits, historical, cultural and environmental heritage and humanity that produces it all.

On this basis, the research starts with the theoretical and empirical assumption that place identity cannot be separated from its inhabitants and their communication.

Within the context of globalization, recalling the paradox mentioned above, this aspect seems to be more true than the local/stranger duality (Simmel, 1989), a leading distinction in tourism analysis, that becomes an even more reversible relationship, changing according to

the perspective of observation adopted. Local residents also represent its most demanding 'inner customer', both when demanding services and when carrying on activities connected with the tourist supply chain.

This means that anyone can activate their own tourist gaze (Urry, 1995), the capability – or better to say the vocation – of observing a place with 'new eyes', of seizing the 'elsewhere' in a well known location knowing how to give value to beauties, specificities and richness without taking them for granted.

In this way, consuming a place is no more connectable and reducible to the simplistic supply/demand relationship understood by visitors. The active, interactive and creative participation of the locals is an indispensable dimension for giving value to a place and its performances. Consequently, it is necessary to consider the different needs that the same place could satisfy but at the same time could express.

Although most advanced marketing research (including that undertaken for destinations), recognizes the weakness of the target approaches (as a category even more indefinable and undistinguished), conversely it is possible, thinking from a inner point of view that a territory may count not as much on a simple typology of tourist (constructed on social and personal criteria, for example) but on the idea of a vocational tourist, oriented to a particular touristic experience (Pine II and Gilmore, 1999; Schmitt 1999) and to a way of experimenting a kind of 'somewhere else' that has its specificity and its uniqueness.

Therefore, starting from the circularity of the tourist gazes, from the 'real' meeting between visitors and inhabitants, place identity becomes its main resource as well as the element experienced vocationally. All this can be translated – in a more strategic and effective manner – as giving importance to the fact that tourism, in its different aspects and facets, is a crucial economic sector precisely because it is based on desiderata, seemingly embedded in our society.

The case of Levanto is a particularly well fitting example of the dynamics described above. The possibility of verifying empirically the territorial identity seen as communicative life-experience[1] means for this research trying to

---

[1]The idea of communicative life-experience – as conceptualized in Boccia Artieri *et al.* (2004) – has to be seen as the process of definition of the subject's identity, as the observation of the self in the world and as a

measure – with qualitative variables – the level of consciousness of those who express the terms and details of this life-experience, connected with personal identity, of being part of a development plan and touristic promotion. It is not useful to think about a top-down, imposed way of growing, without involving those who will benefit by this process.

So Levanto could be seen as a challenge, shared with many other Italian tourist realities, with the notion of connecting a stay with an idea of local identity. In this sense, local identity is a resource that starts from processes of individualization and differentiation influenced by history and tradition but also by a character or lifestyle. This invokes the necessity of keeping up with the times, of promoting the territory in an open manner, of welcoming the stranger as a keeper of varieties and economic development in a logic of sustainability.[2]

Methodology

Research aims

The research tries to explore the concrete dimensions of Levanto's identity, starting with a first and necessary general hypothesis: the identity of the territory is defined as communicative life-experience, i.e. a series of images and representations made by Levanto's inhabitants themselves, or by those who in different ways live and know this territory (Boccia Artieri *et al.*, 2004).

Identifying the elements of Levanto's identity means for this research using conversations and images necessary for Levanto's inhabitants to construct narrations about themselves and the place identity itself, seen as an indispensable benefit used in tourist promotional material (Boorstin, 1961).

So identity is the framework by which it is possible to find the qualitative measure of the inhabitants' consciousness being a strategic resource for the tourist development of the territory.

In the framework of identity as communicative life-experience, the research divides into a series of operative hypotheses, observing not only the local community but also the following dimensions:

1. Levanto as the place of memories and roots: the sense of belonging and the quality of lives of its inhabitants are used as elements activating the domestic tourist gaze, i.e. oriented towards the inner space, as the capability of giving value to oneself's belonging and promoting it as a benefit attracting tourists.

2. Levanto as a territory vocationally touristic: active dimension of the domestic tourist gaze that can be translated in the knowledge and sharing of realized and ongoing projects, of participation to initiatives, of the private entrepreneur sustained by institutions, etc.

3. Inhabitants' consciousness according to quality and amount of territory's resources: evolution of the relation between tourist demand and supply, diversification and empowerment of strategies for a sustainable development fit for the territorial identity and its specific vocation.

Research methodology

For this specific case study, qualitative methods were used because it allowed researchers to gain insights from Levanto's community, drawing from their knowledge, their life experiences and their own prejudices, to grant to the observed subjects an autonomous construction of the narration.

For this reason, and related to the research target, visual sociology was applied that, thanks to its flexible structure, diminished the risk of too much control by researchers (Cipolla and Faccioli, 1993; Faccioli and Harper, 1999; Faccioli, 2001).

The process of describing Levanto's social reality is grounded in Levanto's community

---

reporting of this observation. Here it is extended to the territorial identity as a dimension constructed in relationship with those who – Levanto's inhabitants – actually live in the territory and contribute to the definition of its specificity.

[2]Sustainability and compatibility of tourist development are absolutely relevant themes, here intended as leading values in the policy and programming processes on territories, using the logic of co-ordination with environment (social and environmental). This logic leads many activities of Levanto's town council and in particular the Service for Environment, Productive Activities and Territorial Promotion and are also the leading principles of the association *CittàSlow*.

observing itself, their own and other's behaviour and defining what they observe by starting with themselves.

They were also invited to express their opinions and expectations about the tourist reality of the territory, to measure their consciousness about their being a tourist resource.

In particular, visual sociology is characterized by the use of images in the research process and enables activation of the relational circle between researchers and interviewees with the richness of human communication (verbal and non-verbal), and in the efficient integration between images and words (Watzlawick et al., 1967).

In this particular case, the fundamental assumption that let the researchers chose visual sociology was the visually remarkable quality of the phenomenon studied (Curry and Clark, 1981) – Levanto and its identity as a tourist resource.

Native image making and interviews with photoelicitation with the first group of inhabitants

The research involved a first group of interviewees composed of six Levanto inhabitants, chosen by the research clients and who had agreed to be part of the research.

According to our theoretical assumptions, the researchers chose two of the most important procedures of visual sociology (Cipolla and Faccioli, 1993; Faccioli, 2001): native image making and interview with photoelicitation.

The interviewees were asked to take some shots representing their way of seeing and living Levanto on the basis of a precise request: trying to be in the shoes of a tourist describing 1 week's holiday in Levanto, taking photos of it and giving them a title.

In this manner, it was possible to construct a common framework for all interviewees and, more importantly, it made possible the construction of their own visual narrative to share with the researchers. These images were then used as the key prompts during photoelicitation interviews. Starting with images and their autobiographic sense, the interviews elicited some generalizations defining the most remarkable themes of Levanto's life-experience to plan the second step of the research.

After the first set of interviews and the analysis of native images made, the researchers chose 16 photos representing the thematic areas that came out during interviews. Those images were treated as visual indicators and were used during a focus group as a photoelicitation technique in the second step. The thematic areas – visualized through photo-indicators – coincide with the research hypothesis in which the research aims were divided. So, to grant the correct course of the following step, visual indicators were associated to a scheme of interview constructed by the thematic areas.

Focus groups

The empirical sample group was composed of six different groups of interviewees chosen by our client according to socio-personal and residence heterogeneity criteria. Focus groups were realized using the photoelicitation technique, i.e. showing images chosen by researchers – as visual indicators of the previous step – associated with the same scheme of interview for every group.

The interviewees' sample comprised a representative sample of 39. This aspect is also accorded by the heterogeneity (of age, socio-economic status, place of residence) of the focus group members that made it possible to treat the research themes following the different observation perspectives of interviewees.

The verbal narratives collected during interviews were linked back to what was said by interviewees regarding the thematic areas that came out from the single interviews and were associated with visual indicators. Thematic areas and corresponding visual indicators were used as outline interview during the focus groups to construct 'Levanto's gaze', as shown in the following paragraphs.

Principal Findings

The complex life-experience of Levanto's inhabitants follows a very rich and varied series of reasoning. So it is not possible to give unique answers to the questions asked at the beginning of the research, even if the articulation of discourses and narratives collected and analysed shows us a way of reasoning to be particularly interesting and useful. Treating life-experience means treating human beings that – using a brilliant definition by the German scientist and philosopher Heinz von

Fig. 9.1. A beach 'arch'.

Foerster (1984) – are not banal machines but unforeseeable (Mazzoli, 2001) and unpredictable.

Using the auto-descriptions made by Levanto's inhabitants, how could we understand the level of commitment to the tourism policy of their territory?

As we said, qualitative methodology, based on the use of images as photoelicitation for the emerging themes and in interviews, takes side with subjects observed and their reflexive capability: the communicative life-experience spreads out thanks to what interviewees wanted to say about themselves, about the others and about their ideas and opinions.

That is why the analysis of the life-experience of the territory and its economic and tourist aspects starts only from the idea of identity.

Interviewees understood the researchers' input, stepping into the tourists' shoes, or rather playing the role of the domestic tourist, the one able to watch with ever-fresh eyes a well-known place, as if it were 'elsewhere'.

Identity[3]

The first area coming out is the one describing Levanto as a place connected with identity, having an ancient and proud history to which all the citizens interviewed, without gender and age distinctions, feel they belonged. The sense of belonging to this land is shared also with those who have settled in Levanto, choosing it for its quality of life. The morphological quality of the territory, the mild weather, the openness to the sea, the strength of the mountains and the richness of the countryside make nature the Great Mother, to whom everybody is bound. But also the town with its lanes, the streets, the monuments and nearby hamlets form Levanto's cultural heritage that has to be watched over and saved, a heritage to be handed on: so first of all identity forms the memory of the natives (Herbert, 1995).

But those are also elements that can be considered particularly with the slow Levanto's character, which can be recognized as a specific

---

[3]This area is visualized by Figs 9.1–9.4.

Fig. 9.2.   A look at history.

Fig. 9.3.   Environmental disaster.

Fig. 9.4. Loss of memory.

dimension of its identity, and not as a simple label put on for promotional purposes.

So the sense of belonging to that land is very deeply rooted and difficult to extinguish. Also, those who go away for study or work not only tend to return but carry a sense of being a Levanto inhabitant, according to a process that we can call being dynamically deeply rooted (Maffesoli, 1997).

Certainly this sense of belonging and of being strongly tied with one's own anthropological place shows certain negative connotations, and may emerge such as the extreme 'stillness' that makes it difficult for young people to think of a future settled in Levanto.

One interviewee talked about an 'environmental disaster',[4] that could run the risk of losing memory and consequently those elements framing territorial identity: a contrast – noticed in different occasions – between what is seen by Levanto's

inhabitants as strong points (such as the seaside, the landscape, the paths, the cultivations, the monumental heritage, the past tourist style, etc.) and the insufficient attention towards their protection. A critical look turned not only to the administration and to past political choices, but also inwards to themselves. From this first step, we can understand why the possibility of feeling themselves as part of the economic development produces some difficulties to be resolved. The following area is strictly connected with this one, and deals more precisely with the relationship with tourists.

Identity and relationship with tourist[5]

The character of this land, and its double nature, depends on the relation between the sea and the mountains, and is reflected is the anthropological character of Levanto's inhabitants and in their

[4]See Fig. 9.3.
[5]This area is visualized by Figs 9.5–9.9.

Fig. 9.5. The little beach preferred by Levanto's inhabitants.

Fig. 9.6. There's no pollution here.

relationship with those that are not by chance still called *foresti*, a word in the local language that almost defies translation.

Levanto's history as told by our interviewees is not only the story of socio-economic changes in the past but also takes into account the fisherman-farmer who lived cheek-by-jowl with these tourist resources before they were seen as such. These steps mirrored the evolutionary process, characterizing the whole history of tourism, Italian and European (Urry, 1995; Löfgren, 2001). The particular evolution of relevance here

Fig. 9.7.   Forms of quarrelling between Levanto's inhabitants.

Fig. 9.8.   Do not disturb, please.

Fig. 9.9.   Come on foot!

is the one regarding elite tourism, dominating until the 1930s, which counted on the presence of important persons, in the style of vacationers enjoying sun, sea, villas, grand hotels, casinos and the atmosphere recalled with nostalgia by Levanto's inhabitants. But at the same time, they remember the enmity felt (and demonstrated) towards those persons who were a concrete sign of richness and affluence coming from elsewhere and flaunting their wealth. The advent of mass tourism obviously required changes, not only in the whole touristic supply but also in the relationships between locals and outside visitors.

Through Levanto's case study, we can empirically observe – through the communicative life-experience of the interviewees – the historic, cultural and structural passages that led to the coming out of the social system of tourism, and to the subsequent openness of this community to strangers (McCannell, 1989). In other

words, through Levanto's experience we can see the constitution of a reversible relation between local and stranger explaining the birth of an ad hoc social system, framed by touristic communication (Gemini, 2008).

If in the past the foreigner was an individual never establishing a real relation with the community, real and proper semantics on tourists developed as an evolutionary step, fixing the principle of reversibility in the local/stranger couple, and producing the 'host', i.e. a subject interested in establishing a relation with natives (Merton, 1986; Schutz, 1986; Simmel, 1995).

Obviously, those changes show an evolutionary course that (in Levanto but not only there) seems not be taken for granted. In fact, knowing that the enmity towards foreigners could turn into quarrels, as we were told by Levanto's inhabitants, we can also understand why the interviewees told us that carrying out an effective

Fig. 9.10.   A vision.

policy of tourist development continues to be problematic. But toughness, a characteristic recognized to be part of their character by Levanto's inhabitants, can be melted by those who show a sincere interest towards this land that, with its inhabitants, knows how to be very generous.

That is why also this peculiar character can be interpreted as a resource, as a possibility, for the modern tourist, to satisfy that authenticity demand that nowadays seems to fill the columns of the promotional brochures.

The concrete and clear admission of the importance of tourism, the most important income of the territory, promotes a sense of welcoming, also testing it. The visitor is required to understand that the self-restraint, shown by Levanto's inhabitants, is the typical style of touristic communication qualifying Levanto, playing with a relation of mutual faith built across time and that can be seen as a richness (i.e. an aspect of authenticity), because Levanto's inhabitants do not want to show themselves as different from what they really are.

The touristic dimension[6]

According to the first two thematic areas, interviewees applied the tourist gaze first to the 'thing that has to be seen' (Burgelin, 1967) – for Levanto, that means to recognize its beauties, but not only this. Levanto offers experiences – the ones that let it enter in the *CittàSlow* organization – things to be done, to be guided through by a special guide, which could be a Levanto inhabitant himself.

This can be a clear example of the crossing from imagery regarding travel that can be described as a representation – i.e. linking an image of a given reality with its authenticity, that in Levanto is represented mostly by its visual quality of the territory – to transfer into the logic of performing imagery (Gemini, 2008). This one has to be seen as the whole collective representation that gives value to experience, and that doing so becomes the privileged object of the territorial communication.

The series of events linked with the effort of exploiting Levanto's inland, such as for example the one called Mangialunga,[7] are

[6]Area visualized by Figs 9.10–9.13.
[7]Mangialunga, that can be unworthily translated as "eating along", is a trekking path between villages settled in Levanto's inland; each village offers a typical dish so that one can walk on the hillside paths connecting different villages and have different and various moments of restoration.

Fig. 9.11. Villages surrounded by olive trees.

Fig. 9.12. The little market square.

useful occasions to demonstrate the openness towards the stranger, to promote a tourism spread in all seasons, not only connected with the seaside resource, but linked with wine and food tourism.

Certainly, according to interviewees, tourists may be divided into a typology of weekenders, vacationers staying for a longer period,

and second-home owners. Four points may synthesize the interviewees' opinions on this typology:

1.   The weekender is recognized as important but is not the ideal target for Levanto, even if it is necessary to offer him the necessary services, thinking about the construction of loyalty.

Fig. 9.13. The Roman bridge with Saint Frances climb.

2. The vacationer is regarded as a kind of tourist looking for what Levanto's inhabitants like, becoming fond of it and enjoying studying history, culture and traditions regarding this place; this type of tourist grants not only more income, but is also the one that could establish a faithful relationship with locals.

3. The non-resident but owner of a second home is not felt to be a real tourist, nor a useful economic resource. Nevertheless, it is a category that could be part of the tourist promotion, e.g. helping in the territory's maintenance and participating in cultural initiatives, environment protection and so on.

4. Lastly, there are also outsider hosts who by following local traditions in style and tourist taste are very close to Levanto's supply and style.

Also in this thematic area, we find the relation local/stranger that according to the tourist typology marks the ways with which Levanto's community learns first to imagine itself (Anderson, 1991) and then to communicate itself in constructive relationships. In fact, the tourist could be thought of as that barbaric element (Morin, 1977) who on one hand presents himself as carrying variety and novelty, and yet on the other hand (and consequently) could be the cause of the strengthening sense of community, the sharing of projects and development plans that have not to underline the closure and the defence against the 'stranger' but on the contrary make stronger the culture of welcoming in harmony with the community itself and its communication style.

But what does tourism offer Levanto? There is another side shown by Levanto's inhabitants that feel it unpleasantly. Negligence and carelessness towards the environmental and monumental resources, as we have already seen in the first area, seems to invalidate real and concrete development, together with the lack of some services and the expensive costs that could cut off a great portion of potential visitors.

It is not simply finding 'the' responsible for this state: the administration takes its part, it is also harshly criticized, but at the same time citizens recognize that they don't feel responsible themselves. In other words, Levanto's inhabitants realize that they always judge others as being responsible for everything but never themselves.

Fig. 9.14. Citrus and olive trees on Montale's hills.

On the whole, the interviewees seem to be sufficiently conscious of activating a reflexive process that tends to distinguish one's own attitude and one's own behaviour from those of the others, but they are also capable of applying a critical look to themselves.

From this point it is possible to synthesize the main results of the last area.

Citizens as resources[8]

Being a resource for our interviewees means gaining and developing an entrepreneurial way of thinking that probably is only at its beginning and needs to be supported. Private investment could initiate a series of different activities, more or less directly linked to tourism: from agriculture (typical products, wine/food) to house repair in the inland hamlet (diffused receptivity).[9]

All aspects connected with the dimension of joining associations that could get over difficulties that a single subject may meet. But things are not as simple as they seem and do not always go according to wishes; not everybody feels that they can rely on a diffused sense of collaboration, based on shared projects and indeed, to tell the truth, it seems that many interviewees have difficulty in understanding the trends of development in the town council's mind.

At the same time, however, they recognize the work of the recent administrations and the

[8]Area visualized by Figs 9.14–9.16.
[9]See in particular Fig. 9.15.

Fig. 9.15. A view of a house at Ceola, the ancient Levanto.

attempt to promote the territory earns general praise, even if interviews were also taken as an important opportunity to comment, criticize and give suggestions.

Also, the initiative of touristic promotion brings out what we have already seen: Mangialunga,[10] traditional feasts and other events are all possibilities of constructing anew the relationship with tourists, with other citizens, with the administration, but at the same time are also the places in which a different level of participation and the real commitment come out. If everybody seems to agree, as a matter of fact, things are different, even if it is important to continue in this direction, towards a larger supply with which the majority of Levanto's inhabitants agree and contribute, especially in the voluntary forms. This form of social capital can be seen as an indispensable resource in

many spheres. A last quote, coming from a part of the interviewees but interesting for this reason, relates to the advertising and promotional dimension. They wish a more intensive activity of promotion that they would like to share and contribute to manage, connecting it with their role of real testimonial that some of them want to play.

There remains the need for defining a development plan that Levanto's inhabitants wish to know more deeply. It could be the first step towards strengthening and promoting the social capital available in a more coherent and co-ordinated way. Levanto's inhabitants seem to be sufficiently ready to play their part, more so and better than they did in the past. The citizen, to feel himself or herself and to act like a real resource, has to share the project of growth and feel well supported.

---

[10]See footnote 7.

Fig. 9.16. The B&B boom.

Conclusions

This research enabled us to construct Levanto's image through its inhabitants' images and narratives and especially recognize a style and a character of this territory that we can call 'slow'. Images and stories produced by inhabitants – i.e. the memory of a place and its cultural heritage, its authentic character but also its generosity, the need for thinking about economic development without leaving its own nature – make us understand that the word 'slow' is not a label, an advertising slogan but an important element of Levanto's identity.

'Slow' is a way of attracting the kind of tourist expressing this type of vocation: a tourist style connected to good living, to trekking, to the sight of the sunset on the sea, to good dishes, to good wine. All elements that the inhabitants, through their tourist gaze on Levanto, recognize and suggest to strangers. Regarding this theme, we can quote an interviewee when saying: 'tourists like the same things I like'.

Another result of this work could be the usefulness of the visual method applied to research on territorial identity and tourism. In fact, places and their representation are images – iconic but also narrative – evoking concrete experiences lived by those who live every day in that place but also by those who discover it for the first time. Images, especially in the photographic form, let us reconstruct a story, an experience, a memory. They make it possible to share ideas, visions, to communicate the life-experience of that place.

Then in this sense, the visual research could be a model particularly suitable for a visually remarkable phenomenon as the tourist experience of a place.

References

Anderson, B. (1991) *Imagined Communities: Reflections on the Origin and Spread of Nationalism*. Verso, London.

Appadurai, A. (1996) *Modernity at Large: Cultural Dimension of Globalization*. University of Minnesota Press, Minneapolis, MN.

Augè, M. (1992) *Non-lieux*. Seuil, Paris.

Beck, U. (1997) *Was ist globalisiergung?* Suhrkamp, Frankfurt.

Boccia Artieri, G., Antonioni, S. and Gemini, L. (2004) *Comunicazione e Luoghi del Vissuto. Osservare un Territorio al Femminile*. FrancoAngeli, Milano.

Boorstin, D.J. (1961) *The Image. A Guide to Pseudoevents in America*. Atheneum, New York.

Burgelin, O. (1967) Le tourisme jugé. *Communications* 10, 65–96.

Cipolla, C. and Faccioli, P. (eds) (1993) *Introduzione alla sociologia visuale*. FrancoAngeli, Milano.

Corbin, A. (ed.) (1995) *L'Avenement des Loisirs, 1850–1960*. Aubier, Paris.

Curry, T.J. and Clark, A.C. (1981) *Introducing Visual Sociology*. Kendall Hunt Publishing Company, Dubuque, IA.

Dilthey, W. (1982) *Critica della Ragione Storica*. Einaudi, Torino.

Di Nallo, E. (1998) *Quale Marketing per la Società Complessa?* FrancoAngeli, Milano.

Dumazedier, J. (1974) *Sociologie Empirique du Loisir: Critique et Contre-critique de la Civilisation du Loisir*. Edition du Soleil, Paris.

Faccioli, P. (2001) *In Altre Parole. Idee per una Sociologia della Comunicazione Visuale*. FrancoAngeli, Milano.

Faccioli, P. and Harper, D. (1999) *Mondi da Vedere. Verso una Sociologia più Visuale*. FrancoAngeli, Milano.

Featherstone, M. (ed.) (1990) *Global Culture. Nationalism, Globalization and Modernity: A Theory*. Sage, London.

Foerster, H. von (1984) *Observing Systems*. Intersystem, Seaside, CA.

Gemini, L. (2006) L'immaginario turistico e le forme performative del consumo vocazionale. In: Di Nallo, E. and Paltrinieri, R. (eds) *Cum Sumo. Prospettive di Analisi del Consumo nella Società Globale*. FrancoAngeli, Milano.

Gemini, L. (2008) *In Viaggio. Immaginario, Comunicazione e Pratiche del Turismo Contemporaneo*. FrancoAngeli, Milano.

Herbert, D.T. (ed.) (1995) *Heritage, Tourism and Society*. Mansell, London.

Löfgren, O. (2001) *On Holiday: a History of Vacationing*. University of California Press, Berkeley, CA.

Luhmann, N. (1998) Globalizzazione o società-mondo: come pensare la società moderna? *Contratto* a. VI [1997].

MacCannel, D. (1989) *The Tourist: a New Theory of the Leisure Class*. Schocken Books, New York.

Maffesoli, M. (1997) *Du Nomadisme: Vagabondage Initiatiques*. Librairie générale française, Paris.

Mazzoli, L. (2001) *L'Impronta del Sociale. La Comunicazione fra Teorie e Tecnologie*. FrancoAngeli, Milano.

Merton, R.K. (1986) Insiders e Outsiders: un capitolo di sociologia della conoscenza. In: Tabboni, S. (ed.) *Vicinanza e Lontananza, Modelli e Figure dello Straniero come Categoria Sociologica*. FrancoAngeli, Milano.

Morin, E. (1977) *La methode I. La Nature de la Nature*. Le Seuil, Paris.

Mothé, D. (1997) *L'Utopie du Temps Libre*. Editions Esprit, Paris.

Pine, II J.B. and Gilmore, J.H. (1999) *The Experience Economy: Work is Theatre and Every Business a Stage*. Harvard Business School, Boston, MA.

Schmitt, B.H. (1999) *Experiental Marketing. How To Get Customers to Sense, Feel, Think, Act and Relate to your Company and Brands*. The Free Press, New York.

Schutz, A. (1986) Lo straniero: saggio di psicologia sociale. In: Tabboni, S. (ed.) *Vicinanza e Lontananza, Modelli e Figure dello Straniero come Categoria Sociologica*. FrancoAngeli, Milano.

Simmel, G. (1989) *Sociologia*. Edizioni di Comunità, Milano [1908].

Simmel, G. (1995) *La Metropoli e la Vita dello Spirito*. Armando, Roma [1903].

Urry, J. (1995) *The Tourist Gaze: Leisure and Travel in Contemporary Societies*. Sage, London.

Watzlawick, P., Beavin, J.H. and Jackson, D.D. (1967) *Pragmatics of Human Communication: a Study of Interactional Patterns, Pathologies and Paradoxes*. Norton & Company, New York.

10 Image, Construction and Representation in Tourism Promotion and Heritage Management

Elisabeth Dumont, Mikel Asensio and Manuel Mortari

Université de Liège, Liège, Belgium

Introduction

Over the past few decades, many European towns have considered tourism a major source of income and a potential means of alleviating the crises suffered by many urban centres (Law, 2000). Tourism indeed brings with it an aura of economic benefits, allied with improved quality of life for residents. In fact cultural tourism is hailed as a solution to urban growth and a factor of development, since new cultural and leisure activities may serve both tourists and local residents in search of a 'richer and denser life' (Ashworth, 2001). Towns now face increasing pressure to market themselves as attractive tourist destinations. Small cities, of 10,000–50,000 inhabitants, and medium-sized cities, of 50,000–250,000 inhabitants, accommodate more than 60% of the European population (Cavallier, 1998). Decentralization offers them great opportunities to develop tourism but they often lack the means or resources to do so. In this marketing enterprise, visuality plays a major role, as town attempts to create an image that will prove attractive to tourists. As such, the tourist gaze is said to play a major role in shaping tourism policies. Taking different examples across Europe, this chapter shows the intricacy of construction and presents some factors that play a role. It foregrounds the phenomenon of image construction that towns go through, when starting to engage in tourism and develop policies. It focuses on the crossing, sometimes conflicting, or even internalized gazes of citizens, tourists and authorities in charge of tourism. They all cast a light on parts of heritage, leave out others and in some cases even create shadows and shapes that would not be there without the light.

Study Context/Background

Research was carried out in the context of the PICTURE project, which aimed to develop a strategic urban governance framework for the sustainable management of cultural tourism within small and medium-sized European cities. This framework is meant to help establish, evaluate and benchmark integrated tourism policies at the local level with a view to maximizing the benefits of tourism upon the conservation and enhancement of built heritage diversity and urban quality of life. This framework was based on an evaluation of the dynamics of the effects of tourism at large, upon the social, environmental and economic wealth of European small and medium-sized towns, as well as an identification of innovative urban governance strategies for sustainable development of cultural tourism within these towns. Special attention was given to strategies and means of increasing the attractiveness of cultural sites to visitors and extending tourists' stay in specific destinations, through for instance audience management and cultural quality monitoring.

Methodology Used

The results presented in the course of this chapter result from two different sources. On the one hand, the first group of tasks was developed by the University of Liège and Queen's University Belfast for monitoring of a resident's quality of life. These tasks used different methodologies, both qualitative and quantitative. In qualitative terms there was:

1. Participative observation, meaning a frequent presence in the area and a high participation in the local activities and interactions with locals.
2. Semi-directive interviews with different categories of person living in the area (long term residents of different ages, shop owners, people holding hotels or bed & breakfast, local associations, etc.).
3. Interviews with local politicians, administrative officers, urban planners.
4. Rapid appraisal of the perception of the tourists in the area, meaning observation and occasional fast and 'dirty' interviews with tourists visiting the district.
5. Focus groups with local residents after the participant observation and the individual interviews.
6. Visual ethnography, meaning documentation and analysis by pictures and small video clips of what is going on in the area.
7. Analysis of the tourist offerings and deconstruction of the content of tourist brochures. In quantitative terms, a questionnaire was used that allowed an examination of residents' views on a city-wide basis, and was designed in order to be easily adapted by Local Authorities.

On the other hand, we have a second group of tasks that are parts of a tool developed by the Universidad Autonoma de Madrid to monitor the cultural offering of a small/medium town. These tasks were carried out using the following techniques:

1. Self-administrated questionnaires.
2. Semi-structured in-depth interviews.
3. Focus groups.
4. Meaning maps.

Concerning the sample, it was divided into real tourists (i.e. tourists visiting the city), potential tourists (i.e. any person interviewed in a big city different from the destination city) and residents (including local authorities and stakeholders). The issues studied were: (i) previous knowledge of the city (addressed to potential and real tourists); (ii) mental representations of the city (potential tourists); (iii) prototypicity of the offerings (real tourists); (iv) subjective perception of the offering's quality (real tourists); (v) integration of the specific offerings in the whole culture of the city (real tourists); (vi) cultural identity (residents); and (vii) correspondence heritage–identity (residents).

Findings/Analysis/Discussion

Mons offers us a good example of image construction. It is a medium-sized town of about 93,000 inhabitants located in the eastern corner of Belgium, close to the French border and Dutch-speaking Belgium. It also hosts about 15,000 students in its numerous universities and higher education facilities, as well as about 10,000 people residing in the Supreme Headquarters of Allied Powers in Europe (SHAPE). In the 7th century, a pious woman and good wife named Waudru founded a monastery on a hill that had been called Montes by the Romans; with time, this place of cult becomes a powerful institution. She was soon joined by the counts of Hainaut (still the name of the region), who fortified the town and turned it into their capital. The town prospered in the Middle Ages and became very rich under Charles the Great thanks to sheet manufacturing. Prosperity continued when the town became part of the empire of Burgundy or Austria, but religious wars and bombings ordered by Louis XIV in 1691 had a strong negative impact. The town was won by France a couple of times between then and the independence of Belgium (1830), when it was reclaimed and turned into a commercial and mining centre for the whole region called 'Borinage'.

After grandeur comes decadence, as reconversion from the industrial and mining era proved difficult in Mons and its surroundings. The town suffered economically, as well as in terms of image. Mons is the capital of the province of Hainault, the poorest province in Belgium and one that benefited from large investments from the Objective C programme of the UE (in order to raise the 'standards of living'). Its unemployment rate rose to 28%, compared with an overall rate of 12.3% for Belgium on the whole and 17.6% for the Walloon region. Sixty per cent of the population there did not finish their higher education. The rate of liberal professions and enterprises within the cities is very low and little creation of new activities can be found.

As a reaction, Mons has decided to establish 'a new town project to reencounter the way to prosperity'.[1] It suggests a strategic repositioning based on 'consolidating Mons, the creative and affective, through a reinforcing of its cultural and heritage dimensions'.[2] Culture and tourism lie at the centre of this strategy, with the aim of bringing innovation and business to the town. In February 2005, the main axes were identified as: culture, heritage, formation and education, business, trade and retail.

The above-mentioned priorities have been chosen by a team of decision-makers. For the 'culture' priority, Mons was officially declared Cultural Capital of the Walloon Region by the government of the French community in December 2002, and in March 2004 it officially applied to become the European capital of culture for 2015.[3] The town is also very proud of having hosted the European multimedia council where the text that was used to defend the law of cultural exception against the GATS negotiations originated. Town officials have received the support of former Belgian Prime Minister Guy Verhofsdtadt and the mayor of Bruges (former European Capital of Culture) in their bid for Mons to be European Capital of Culture. They also worked together with Lille and are regularly in contact with the town, as well as other towns in Northern France (Valenciennes, Maubeuge). They underline their good infrastructure (existence of three theatres, important museums, chamber orchestra facilities, different festivals, etc.), as well as the creation of new festivals and street activities. For heritage, they highlight the renovation of the town centre, especially the built heritage. The focus is always to aim for quality, elite tourists and visitors. In this context, cultural tourism proves very attractive. It is seen as a sustainable form of tourism attracting people interested in high quality and is therefore especially targeted.

An accent is therefore put on the exceptional, the magnificent, 'high culture' in all cases, partly because 'coming to see the environment as something exceptional, while you always live in it, rather gives one a sense of value'.[4] The two museums that deserve to have their own prospectus in the visitor centre are the Duesberg Museum and that of the Treasures of Saint Waudru's collegiate; the former mainly because of its 'collection of clocks with exotic topics . . . unique in the world' given to the town by two former patrons and the latter because of, among others, 'unique silver reliquaries', a 'superb polychromatic Saint Jacques' and 'some of Jacques du Broeucq's exceptional alabaster works'. Now there is a museum of ethnology, where customs and traditions of everyday life can be found. The history of the people seems of no interest in this construction of Mons.[5] Significantly too, there are markers all over town to give information on 'places of interest'. Many elite buildings receive an explanatory board, sometimes just to say it used to be an auction room, but Mons's little monkey, the one you have to stroke the head of while making a wish to see it come true, does not receive one. Is it because it is too well known, or because a monkey and superstition are not important enough to deserve attention?

---

[1]From 'Vers un projet de ville, ensemble' pdf explaining Mons's strategy found on the town's official Website. http://www.mons.be. Original text in French, author's translation.
[2]From 'Vers un projet de ville, ensemble' pdf explaining Mons's strategy found on the town's official Website. http://www.mons.be. Original text in French, author's translation.
[3]After Antwerp, Bruges and Brussels, and because of quotas 2015 is the first year Belgium can apply again to the status of European capital of culture.
[4]From an interview with an elected high political official. Original text in French, author's translation.
[5]Only unavoidable intangible heritage that has been there for a long time, cannot be avoided and, quite conveniently, attracts a lot of tourists deserves its own prospectuses (Doudou, golden carriage procession). But they are strikingly not mentioned in general brochures like 'the land of Mons welcomes you'.

Everything takes place as if everything was done to forget the working-class past and turn the town from a difficult area into a 'posh' one, an even elitist place or bastion, something that is facilitated by the structure of the town that kept its old walled design, with boulevards having replaced old city walls. The industrial and coal extracting past rarely comes to the fore, to such an extent that on the town's official Website, mines are not mentioned in the quick history section, even though it is an industry that largely contributed to turning Belgium into the third richest country at the beginning of the 20th century. The idea behind Mons' strategy is that the increased care for heritage and the new cultural activities will create a new, positive image of the place and will tempt investors into investing in the area that is centrally located and easily accessible. A new logo was created (Fig. 10.1). It encapsulates this desire summarized in 'ideas and heart' and appears everywhere in the town, including on the working areas.

This logo is a major tool in the construction of Mons. When asked if the concepts it presents relate to inclusion of the inhabitants, the locals, or is it rather relating to the 'welcoming of the tourists', the answer leaves absolutely no doubt: 'it is above all a question of welcoming, obviously, so that people outside know Mons is a pleasant, warm place to be.'[6]

In this construction of Mons and the attempt to create a specific atmosphere, one should be aware of the dangers of concentrating on one single period for built heritage diversity. Indeed, the focus on 18th-century building should not make one forget that Mons also holds other treasures such as high-quality facades of the 19th and 20th century. Contemporary work of

Fig. 10.1. Mons's logo – on ideas and heart (meaning warmth).

shopfronts by Barthelemy and his team offer us a good example of this.

The same risk of diversity exists with the focus on the unique and the 'grand'. At the moment, there seems to exist a tension between a rather bourgeois town (Mons) and the surroundings where the average income lies significantly lower than in the rest of Belgium. The professed aim of the cultural and tourist strategy is to 'pull the region forwards and upwards',[7] thus turning the surroundings into wealthier places as well as distributing the benefits of tourism, partly through longer stays. The rationale is to develop in the region different attractions or cultural activities, especially with the help of State or EU finances. The danger, however, is to alienate locals from their surroundings if they are not integrated into the development and if their history or diversity is not taken into account.

Mons is clearly constructed as a European tourist destination. Because it is applying for the status of European capital of culture, Europe has turned into the main, if not only, point of reference. Mons's Website boasts that the town lies at the crossroads of Europe, only 50 min away from Lille (Capital of Culture 2004), 54 from Bruxelles, 80 from Paris, 150 from London, 202 from Cologne and 208 from Amsterdam (train times). In the brochure explaining why it thinks it deserves to become European capital of Europe, the names of different artists are given who 'have brought a stone to European culture',[8] 'Mons 2015, an eminently European project' or 'the project puts forwards cultural currents common to all Europeans' or 'the project establishes long term cultural co-operations and favours circulation within the Union'. Clearly, the type of tourist expected and the possibilities of funding influence the choices made in the (re)presentation of the town.

Only at one point does the official prospectus mentions that 'the project favours dialogue between cultures of Europe and other cultures of the world', but this takes the form of music

[6]All quotations from an interview with an elected high political official closely involved in culture, tourism and economy.
[7]Interview with a local authority member, April 2004.
[8]From *Mons: capitale européenne de la culture en 2015*. All quotations in this paragraph come from this brochure unless otherwise mentioned. Original text in French, author's translation.

festivals 'pretexts to discover culture, gastronomy or the communities of these countries implanted here', thus reducing these to the other, setting them on display as the exotic to be watched, tasted and discovered but never close enough to be really part of the project and shaping it.

As a summary, is not exactly the tourist gaze that plays a role in image construction here but a solipsistic integrated gaze on the part of the decision makers, combined with attempts to make the right moves to receive funding. Mons' 'requalification', seems to rely mainly on the tastes of the higher people, something that reflects the composition of the people responsible for its strategy, their vision of heritage, their tourist expectations and sources of funding but not really the diversity, history and reality of a socio-economic position of a region that has received European structural funds to recover from a decline of industry.[9] The taking up of the expected tourists' views by the authorities 'selling culture' produces a 'reification of the urban space according to strictly defined lines'. This reification consists in creating a superficial link between a signifier (appearance of space) and a signified (a history, a people, a culture) (Massart, 2004). This imposition of a dominant history works as a form of acculturation and colonization of the subject (Croal and Darou, 2002).

Moreover, since this link is presented as the authentic, true expression of cultural identity while it in fact results 'from complex social interactions and power relations' (Massart, 2004) or 'determined instances of production and control',[10] erasing some aspects and highlighting some others can lead to a dangerous obliteration of other cultures and alternative histories. Moreover, one non-elected official in Mons points out that some choices might prove good in the long term but are not implemented for fear of losing voters or not bringing enough money. One way to avoid this would be to develop more audience surveys, thus surveying tourists but also locals and decision makers regarding heritage values and buildings, and make sure they fit and conflicts do not arise. This has for instance been done in Ávila.

The city of Ávila is located in the central part of Spain, about 100 km west of Madrid. It is the capital of its province, and belongs to the 'Castilla y León' region. According to the population services, the town counts 52,000 residents. The economies of the city have been traditionally based on the primary sector, though in the last half century Ávila has known some industrial and tourism development. The origins of the city date to the first Vetton and Celtic settlements in the area, between the 4th and 2nd centuries BC. The current urban setting is the result of Roman occupation; the Romans were also probably the builders of the first defensive perimeter that, centuries later, would be modified and improved as the Medieval Walls. Ávila lived its period of splendour as a border city, between Christian and Muslim territory, in the 11th century, when the current walls were built. As the re-conquest of the territory pushed the Muslims further south, the city gradually lost its strategic importance and declined, abandoned to a poor primary-sector economy and to a conservative church-administration. The situation essentially remained the same until the 1950s when immigration from the countryside started to revitalize the city and to shift its economy to the third sector. In 1985, following a gradual growth of tourism, attracted by its rich built heritage, Ávila was included in the list of World Heritage Cities. Nowadays the tourism sector is mature, and especially focuses on cultural issues.

The actual tourism strategy was adopted in 1999, as a part of a *Plan de Excelencia* (development plan) designed, managed and financed in partnership by the Ministry of Economy, the Region of Castilla y León, the Municipality of Ávila and the representatives of the private sector of the city (Chamber of Commerce and Federation of businessmen of Ávila). Its planned length was of 3 years, and the total budget amounted to €4.06 million. The generic goals of the Plan were the creation of tourism management structures to complete the existing ones, and the consolidation of the city as an important Cultural–Religious Tourism destination. From the first moment, it appeared that the success of the

---

[9]The whole area, called Borinage, suffered such a bad reputation that the term 'borain' (coming from Borinage) has actually turned into an insult in French.
[10]From Delgado Ruiz (2000). Original text in Spanish, author's translation.

Plan was subject to some conditions: the first was the need for detailed strategic planning, to avoid improvisation and waste of resources. The second condition was that the local population had to be involved in the plan, and had to share its benefits. Another prerequisite was the creation of an agile and dynamic management tool, the Plan Management Office. Finally, there was the obvious requisite that any tourist product issued from the Plan had to be extremely innovative in order to make Ávila's tourism offerings competitive with those of other nearby cities. A series of objectives were defined, in order to achieve the generic goals: (i) increase of overnight stays; (ii) the improvement of the tourist urban offerings; and (iii) positioning of Ávila as a competitive inland cultural tourism destination.

The pursuit of the objectives of the development plan generated a series of actions, some of which are strongly related with the image and the mental representation of the city from the tourist's point of view: (i) restoration of built heritage and design of a logo (Fig. 10.2) inspired by the fortified wall of the city; (ii) reinforcement of the religious tourism offerings; (iii) diversification of the offerings; and (iv) creation of a tourism observatory.

The first action was the restoration and enhancement of the built heritage of the city, focusing particularly on the city wall, in order to open it to visitors. Ávila's wall is the longest and best preserved medieval fortification in Spain, and together with the Cathedral represents the most remarkable built heritage attractor of the city. The purpose of the restoration was to provide Ávila with a monument that could work as a 'logo', as the flagship of the built heritage of the city.

Subsequently, other kinds of cultural offering were associated with the wall (story-telling, theatre on the walls and dramatized visits), enlarging the attraction but also risking to crystallize it around a 'Middle Ages'-related array of activities.

On the other hand, Ávila is frequently associated with Saint Therese, a historical character

famous for her religious mystical experiences, reflected on the poems she wrote. Many films, books and exhibitions have been dedicated to this character, keeping alive this relationship between her and the city. For this reason, Ávila has always been an important destination of religious tourism, interested mainly in the monastery founded by Therese and on the beautiful gothic cathedral. On the basis of these facts, supported by a specific, unreferenced survey, the local authorities took a courageous choice and decided to take advantage of this specific appeal of the city, organizing an important religious art exhibition in the cathedral (in 2004), and creating a museum devoted to the mysticism phenomenon from a multi-religious point of view.

In the last 5 years the local authorities decided to further diversify Ávila's tourist offerings, following three directions: (i) knowing that the city is renowned for its regional cuisine, they organized in co-operation with bars and restaurants a fair of 'tapas' (appetizers) that is held once a year with good results in terms of audience; (ii) Ávila lies only 100 km away from Salamanca, the university of which is one of the main destinations for people interested in studying the Spanish language; the local authorities have decided to make the most of this proximity, and engaged in a partnership to offer language courses and lodgings; and (iii) Ávila is strategically located at about 1 h by car from Madrid, Salamanca, Valladolid and 1.5 h from Toledo; local authorities have decided to take advantage of this to offer a new product, a congress and municipal centre, to enter the market of business tourism.

Finally, the last initiative issued from the Plan de Excelencia and related with Ávila's image and tourist's gaze, is the 'Tourism Observatory'. This platform, devoted to the monitoring of tourism flows and visitor studies, was created thanks to a convention with the Universidad de Salamanca. Actually, the convention is between the Municipality and the Universidad Complutense de Madrid. The Observatory started work in late 2001 with the purpose of collecting and analysing on a real-time basis any information about the situation of tourism in the city, in order to provide updated reports to the Municipality staff and to other stakeholders. The information collected is of quantitative kind, and aims to identify the profiles of the

Fig. 10.2. Ávila's logo, inspired by the city Wall.

visitors, and their consumption and travelling habits. The specific tasks of the Observatory are the following: (i) creation and maintenance of databases with tourism-related information; (ii) periodical reports offering a basic analysis of the situation of the tourism, in general terms and in relative terms (comparing with past years or similar contexts); (iii) specific reports about the effects on the tourism sector of special events (i.e. exhibitions, enhancement of built heritage, etc.); and (iv) writing of the 'Tourism Observatory Bulletin'.

All these are efforts made by the administration to promote tourism in the city, to create and develop a diversified offering, to build and transmit an appealing image of the city. Some of these efforts, issued from a realistic reflection on the main features of the city, reinforce its most evident assets (restoration of the wall and creation of the Museum of Mysticism) and do not add new elements to the image of the city; some others are focused on 'new' tourism products (the fair Ávila en tapas, the language courses, the congress and municipal centre) and try to enlarge the offerings of the city, eventually trying to modify and renew its image. The questions that remain are: what are the results of these efforts? Have they succeeded in shaping the desired image in the mind of potential visitors? And, on the other hand, have they paid any attention to the tourist's gaze for the design of the tourism attraction? Do we have any study that provides feedback about these issues?

Unfortunately, the tourism observatory is devoted to collect information of quantitative kind about the visitor's profile and habits, so its bulletins cannot help answer these questions. The only information available (beside the mentioned unreferenced survey about the Saint Therese character) comes from the studies carried out by the UAM team in the context of the PICTURE project, specifically oriented towards the exploration of the tourist's gaze of the city's offering. Visitors' profiles and meaning map surveys were developed and tested to investigate the image that potential tourists have of Ávila. This study, conducted in Madrid between the months of February and September of 2005, with a sample of 204 potential tourists, provided the information necessary to elaborate on some visualization tools that describe in a very intuitive way the tourist's gaze on the city.

Figure 10.3 represents the share of some elements in the whole image of the city. The identification and cataloguing of all the concepts counted 77 elements that were clustered for the sake of this report (i.e. we have regrouped 'specific monument' and 'monuments in general' into a category comprehensive of both elements: 'built heritage'). The final categories are: Generic geographic notions, Nature and landscape, Culture and history, Built heritage, Folklore, Regional cuisine, Religion, Primary sector, Backwardness, Good economy and Other.

The first column corresponds to the first category ('Generic Geographic Notions'), and represents some generic answers of little interest, dealing with the geographical position of the city, and its belonging to the respective province and region. This category has a share of 13% of the whole representation of Ávila. The second column/category represents all the answers related to nature, landscape, wildlife, climate aspects and outskirts of the city (21% share). The third column/category refers to any element related with culture, history, art, ancient cultures and inhabitants, and the Middle Ages (12% share). The next column synthesizes all answers related to built heritage, architecture, ruins and sites, including Ávila's wall and cathedral (22% share). The fifth column refers to all elements that have to do with folklore issues, such as traditions, fairs, country life, music, theatre (5%

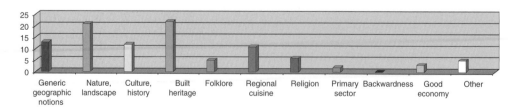

Fig. 10.3.   Share of different elements in the image of Ávila. Copyright UAM, PICTURE.

share). The next category contains answers related to regional cuisine, food and beverages (11% share). The sixth column gathers all elements related to religion, such as Saint Therese, monasteries, churches, catholic religion etc. (6% share). The following four columns have less interest in the context of the current research because they refer to answers not really related to tourism issues such as agriculture, cattle farming, backwardness, progress, good economy and others, with a total share of 10%.

Figure 10.4 represents the main results of the analysis of Ávila's meaning maps. The same previously mentioned categories appear again, plus two more variables: Depth and Links. In the representation of the meaning map, each element is linked to the city with a variable depth level, which is measured by the number of other

elements placed between them. If the depth is minimal, or in other words, if the element analysed is close to the centre of the meaning map, it means that the depth is 1. If there is an element between them, it means that the depth is 2, and so on. The nearer an element is to the centre of the meaning map, the more relevant it is for the subject who answered the survey. In general, the maximum depth reached by the elements of a meaning map suggests a higher complexity in the mental representations. Meaning maps in towns are usually very complex and deep.

Because of depth and complexity, the attraction and the marketing strategies should be more elaborate than in the cases where the average meaning maps prove simple and not too deep. An analysis of the potential tourists of Ávila brings up the following remarks. First, the

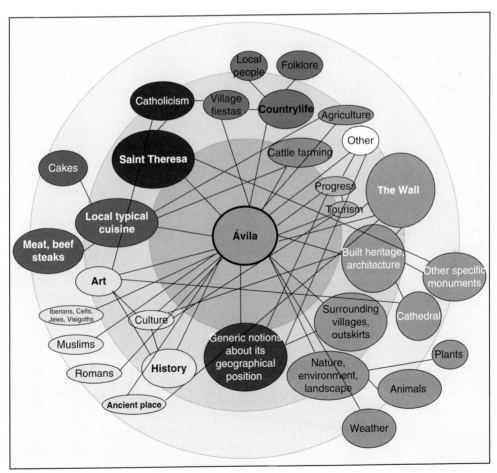

Fig. 10.4. Graphic representation of Ávila's meaning maps analysis. Copyright UAM, PICTURE.

elements that can be considered as more specific are usually found around some general element to which they are related, and they are usually rather far away from the centre (i.e. consider the depth of such specific elements as 'Literature', 'History' or 'Art', with an average depth comprised between 1.72 and 1.78, and compare it with the more general category 'Culture', placed at an average depth of 1.46). There is an interesting exception in the case of the wall, which has to be considered a very specific element, but is placed at an average depth of 1.58, almost the same depth of such a generic element as 'Built Heritage'. Concerning the other variable of this graphic, the average of links, it turns out that each element is related to one or more other elements. If an element is represented with many links, it means that respondents attribute to this element a structural role in the offerings of a city. As in the case of depth, the more generic elements have a higher number of links than the more specific concepts (i.e. 'economy in general' has an average of 2.73 links, while 'cattle farming' has an average of only 1.16 links). For the average visitor, the elements with higher structural relevance are (beside the previously mentioned 'economy in general'): the fact of being 'capital of its province' (2.4 links), the 'built heritage', monuments in general (2.24), 'art' (2.19), 'regional cuisine' (2.18), tourism (2.09), 'traditions and folklore' (2.08) and 'culture' (2).

These data allow checking whether the internalized tourist gaze of local authorities corresponds to tourists' image of Ávila, and whether they are applying their efforts to the right aims. The answer is mixed: in part yes and in part no. Ávila's image is indeed strongly linked to built heritage, to Saint Therese and other religious issues, as well as to local cuisine. However, the rest of the tourism strategy does not show all the expected results in terms of image: Ávila does not appear as a birthplace of Spanish language, nor as an important congress centre. This could change in the future, as strategies need several years before having any effect, but the meaning maps suggest a more serious issue: a lack of adequate and integrated eco-tourism offerings. In fact, an important share (21%) of the mental representation of Ávila is held by nature, wildlife, landscapes and country life, all elements that are neglected or considered of secondary importance by the tourism strategy of the city.

Another tool was developed to diversify the angles of approach. This time the sample is composed of real tourists, i.e. visitors interviewed in Ávila, at the Tourist Information Office. In this case, the survey was a questionnaire with several questions, the last of which regarded specifically the perception of Ávila's cultural offering. Subjects were asked to quote the three elements of any kind that best represented Ávila. Figure 10.5 shows that the most representative specific elements are the wall, Saint Theresa, the Cathedral, the churches and monasteries of the city and, to some extent, local cuisine. Generally speaking, it turns out that visitors view tangible heritage assets as more representative than intangible ones.

Questions arise when these results are compared to those of the meaning maps, for instance: why are 'Nature', 'Local cuisine' and 'Culture and history' almost non-represented in this graphic, while they had a certain weight in the other? The reason lies in the nature of the sample, (real tourists vs potential visitors). For some reason related to the communication and attraction-design strategies, the mental representation of Ávila differs depending on whether one is a potential or real tourist. In other words, the people who go to Ávila are specifically interested in built heritage and religion, and no efforts are made to attract people interested in nature, wildlife, outskirts and country life.

These results indicate that local authorities are partially succeeding in creating the image they want (Ávila, city of built heritage, religion, local cuisine, language courses and congresses), but are wasting an important tourist resource: nature, wildlife and parks. There exist tourism attractions devoted to this resource, but these are not integrated within the offerings of the city: there are dozens of packages to come to Ávila to see a theatre play or a concert on the walls, and spend the night in a hotel, but there are almost no packages to come to Ávila to visit the wall and have a walk in a nearby Natural Park, and sleep in a country B&B.

Conclusions

The two examples examined demonstrate how difficult it is to find tourism strategies planned

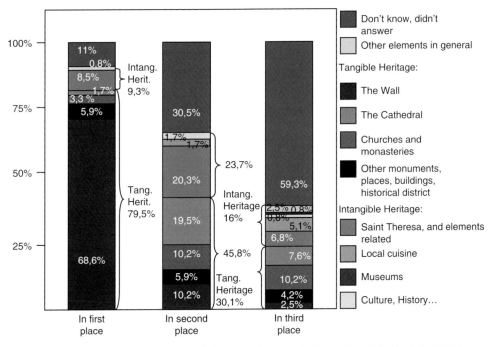

Fig. 10.5. Most representative elements of Ávila, according to real visitors. Copyright UAM, PICTURE.

and developed professionally according to principles that are fully applied in other sectors, such as business administration and marketing. The points of view of the customer, i.e. the tourist, and the residents, i.e. the final beneficiaries of tourism, are often imagined rather than properly surveyed. Despite millions in the budget assigned to ambitious development plans, visitors' and residents' studies are often neglected, or oriented towards quantitative or purely financial issues. Mons' new town project is rich and forward thinking. It nonetheless highlights a phenomenon of image construction based on personal values, political interests and the expected sources of funding with tourism as a tool. The example also points towards some possible dangers of disagreement between the projected image and the internalized image of residents. If some parts of history are erased, and diversity endangered, it can create some alienation and conflicts. The case of Ávila similarly foregrounds on the one hand how studies on tourist expectations and representations can suggest new tourism products. On the other hand, it shows how conservative or uncoordinated development strategies, oriented to consolidated

markets or fashionable objectives, often jeopardize these opportunities.

The two examples underline that it is not so much the tourist gaze that plays a role in image construction but the idea authorities in charge of tourism have of it. Many cities pay attention to the cultural offering, without given adequate consideration the actual or potential demand, nor to the reception of the offering by residents and tourists. Considering the estimations about the tourism market's growth in the next few years (WTO, 2001), this imbalance between supply and demand, if not corrected on time, may have negative and irreversible impacts on the tangible and non-tangible heritage, particularly in small and medium European cities. A more systematic study of the gaze of tourists and residents alike, compared with that of local authorities, would allow more integrated policies and sustainable development. Indeed, it would prevent alienation of locals or destruction of valued sites, while opening the doors for new sources of revenue through different marketing options. Speaking of visuality, it would allow kaleidoscopic images integrating different point of views rather than imposing a specific looking-glass.

Acknowledgements

The PICTURE project is financed by the European Commission, Sixth Framework Programme of Research Specific Programme: Integrating and strengthening the European Research Area Activity: Specific activity covering policy-orientated research under 'Policy support and anticipating scientific and technological needs' – Priority 3. Underpinning the economic potential and cohesion of a larger and more integrated European Union – Topic 3.6. The protection of cultural heritage and associated conservation strategies – Task 5: Cultural heritage and tourism. Contract no. SSP1-CT-2003-502491.

References

Cavallier, G. (1998) *Défis pour la Gouvernance Urbaine dans l'Union Européenne, Fondation Européenne pour l'Amélioration des Conditions de Vie et de Travail.* Office des publications officielles des Communautés européennes, Luxembourg.
Croal, P. and Darou, W. (2002) Canadian First Nation's experiences with international development. In Sillitoe, P., Bicker, A. and Pottier, J. (eds) *Participating in Development, Approaches to Indigenous Knowledge.* Routledge, London, pp. 82–107.
Law, C.L. (2000) Regenerating the city centre through leisure and tourism. *Built Environment* 26, 117–129.
Massart, G. (2004) Commentaries on D3: multidimensional matrix gathering of impacts, methods and policy measures. Unpublished commentaries.
World Tourism Organization (2001) *Tourism 2020 Vision – Europe.* Organización Mundial del Turismo, Madrid.

Further Reading

Alderson, P. and Morrow, V. (2004) *Ethics, Social Research and Consulting with Children and Young People.* Barnardo's, Ilford.
Archibald, R.R. (2004) *The New Town Square. Museums and Communities in Transition.* Altamira, Walnut Creek, CA.
Asensio, M. and Pol, E. (eds) (2002a) *Nuevos Escenarios en Educación. Aprendizaje informal sobre el patrimonio, los museos y la ciudad.* Aique, Buenos Aires.
Asensio, M. and Pol, E. (2002b) Para qué sirven hoy los estudios de público. *Revista de Museología* 24–25, 11–20.
Asensio, M. and Pol, E. (2003a) Aprender en el museo. *IBER, Revista de Didáctica de las Ciencias Sociales, Geografía e Historia* 36, 62–77.
Asensio, M. and Pol, E. (2003b) Educar a través del patrimonio: Cancho Roano el edificio más antiguo de la península. *Aula* 126, 12–15.
Asensio, M. and Pol, E. (2003c) Los cambios recientes en la consideración de los estudios de público: la evaluación del Museu d'Històri de la Ciutat de Barcelona. In: *Actas del II Congreso de Musealización de Yacimientos Arqueológicos.* Instituto de Cultura de Barcelona (ICUB), Barcelona , pp. 310–322.
Asensio, M. and Pol, E. (2005a) Evaluación de exposiciones. In: Santacana, J. and Serrat, N. (eds) *Museografía Didáctica.* ARIEL, Barcelona, pp. 527–633.
Asensio, M. and Pol, E. (2005b) Presentación del Proyecto del Museo Nacional de la Salud. *Revista Quark* 35, 25–36.
Asensio, M. and Pol, E. (2006) Diseñando fractales o de cómo se debería planificar un Museo de Ciencia. *Conferencia de apertura del Año académico en la Academia de Ciencias de Málaga. Memoria anual.* Academia de Ciencias, Málaga.
Asensio, M., Pol, E. and Gomis, M. (2001a) Planificación en Museología: el caso del Museu Marítim. Museu Marítim, Barcelona.
Asensio, M., Pol, E. and Gomis, M. (2001b) Estudios de Público, Evaluación de Exposiciones y Programas y diseño de Áreas Expositivas en el Museu Marítim. *Drassana* 9, 18–31.

Asensio, M., Colomer, L., Ruiz, J. and Sanz, N. (2005a) El proyecto APPEAR: la ciudad y la puesta en valor del patrimonio arqueológico europeo. In: Erice, R. and de Francia, Ch. (eds) *Actas del III Congreso de Musealización de Yacimientos Arqueológicos*. Ayuntamiento de Zaragoza, Zaragoza.

Asensio, M., Ruiz, J., Asenjo, E. and Pol, E. (2005b) El impacto de los yacimientos arqueológicos urbanos: un viaje de ida y vuelta. In: *Urban Pasts and Urban Futures: Bringing Urban Archaeology to Life Enhancing Urban Archaeological Remains*. Comité Europeo de las Regiones, Bruselas.

Asensio, M., Colomer, L., Díaz, P., Fohn, M., Hachimi, T., Hupet, P., Lefert, S., León, C., Léotard, J.M., Luxen, J.L., Le Bouëtte, S., Nicolau, A., Martinet, F., Miles, D., Páll, L., Ruiz, J., Sanz, N., Sarkadi, E., Teller, J., Tinant, M., Zidda, G., Zwetkoff, C., Warnotte, A. and Wilson, V. (2006) The APPEAR Method: A practical guide for the management of enhancement projects on urban archaeological sites. European Commission. Research Report no. 30/4. www.in-situ.be.

Ashworth, G. (1992) Is there an urban tourism? *Tourism Recreation Research* 17, 3–8.

Ayuntamiento de Ávila (1999) Plan de Excelencia turística. http://www.avilaturismo.com/utes/pet_futuro.asp?ute=6001.

Ayuntamiento de Cáceres (2003) *Plan de Excelencia Turística, 1*. Ayuntamiento de Cáceres, Cáceres.

Ayuntamiento de Cáceres (2004) *Plan de Excelencia Turística, 2*. Ayuntamiento de Cáceres, Cáceres.

Bachleitner, R. and Zins, A. (1999) Cultural tourism in rural communities: The residents' perspective. *Journal of Business Research* 44, 199–209.

Bedate, A., Herrero, L.C. and Sanz, J.A. (2004) Economic valuation of the cultural heritage. *Journal of Cultural Heritage* 5, 101–111.

Blondé, A. (ed.) (2000) *Jeunes et Sauvegarde du Patrimoine*. ICCROM, Roma.

Borun, M. and Korn, R. (eds) (1999) *Introduction to Museum Evaluation*. American Association of Museums, Washington, DC.

Butler, R. (1980) The concept of tourist area cycle of evolution: implications for management of resources. *Canadian Geographer* 24, 5–12.

Campbell, A., Converse, P. and Rodgers, W. (1976) *The Quality of American Life: Perceptions, Evaluations and Satisfaction*. Russell, New York.

Chinchilla, M., Izquierdo, I. and Azor, A. (eds) (2005) *Criterios para la Elaboración del Plan Museológico*. Ministerio de Cultura, Madrid.

Conservation of the Built Environment in the Netherlands. In: Phelps, A., Ashworth, G.J. and Johannson, B.O.H. (eds) *The Construction of Built Heritage: a North European Perspective on Policies, Practices and Outcomes*. Ashgate, London.

Crouch, G. and Ritchie, J. (1999) Tourism, competitiveness and societal prosperity. *Journal of Business Research* 44, 137–152.

Cummins, R. (1996) Assessing quality of life. In: Brown, R.I. (ed.) *Assessing Quality of Life for Handicapped People*. Chapman and Hall, London.

Day, R. (1987) Relationship between life satisfaction and consumer satisfaction. In Samli, A. (ed.) *Marketing and the Quality of Life Interface*. Quorum Books, New York, pp. 289–311.

Delgado Ruiz, M. (2000) Usos sociales y politicos del turismo cultural. In Larossa, J. and Skliar, C. (eds) *Habitantes de Babel. Politica y Poéticas de la Diferencia*. Laertes, Barcelona, pp. 245–276.

Diamond, J. (1999) *Practical Evaluation Guide: Tools for Museums & Other Informal Educational Settings*. Altamira Press, Walnut Creek, CA.

Dierking, L. and Pollok, W. (1998) *Questioning Assumptions. An Introduction to Front End Studies in Museums*. Association of Science Technology Centers, Washington, DC.

Dierking, L., Ellenbogen, K. and Falk, J. (2004) In principle, in practice: perspectives on a decade of museum learning research (1994–2004). *Science Education. Supplemental Issue* 88, 48–58.

Dong-Wan, K. and Stewart, W (2002) A structural equation model of residents' attitudes for tourism development. *Tourism Management* 23, 521–530.

Doxey, G. (1975) A Causation Theory of visitor–resident irritants' methodology and research inferences. *Proceedings of the Sixth Annual Conference of the Travel Association*, San Diego, Travel and Tourism Research Association, pp. 195–198.

Dumont, E. (2006) Corporate culture of tourism and sustainability. *International Journal of Environmental, Cultural, Economic and Social Sustainability*, December 2006.

Dumont, E. (2007a) *Richtung Nachhaltigkeit des städtischem Kulturtourismus*. EU Publication, June.

Dumont, E. (2007b) *Sostenibilidad y turismo cultural urbano*. EU Publication, June.

Dumont, E. (2007c) *Towards Sustainability in Urban Cultural Tourism*. EU Publication, June.

Dumont, E. (2007d) *Vers une durabilité pour le tourisme culturel urbain*. EU Publication, June.

Dumont, E. (2007e) *Verso la sostenabilità del turismo culturale urbano*. EU Publication, June.

Dumont, E. (ed.) (2007f) *Strategic Urban Governance Framework for the Management of Cultural Tourism*. EU Publication & Editions du CEFAL, June.

Dumont, E. and Teller, J. (2006) Cultural diversity and subsidiarity: the case of cultural tourism in the European Union. In: *European Studies: An interdisciplinary series in European Culture, History and Politics*, no. 23, March 2007.

Dumont, E., Ruelle, C. and Teller, J. (2004) Multidimensional matrix gathering of impacts, methods and policy measures. Deliverable 3 of Picture project, http://www.picture-project.com/.

Dumont, E., Teller, J. and Origet du Clouzeau, C. (2005). Pour une définition européenne du tourisme culturel. *Espaces* 231, 14–17.

Elvestad, S., Takvam, T. and Heimark, S. (2006) Interaction between cultural tourism and the World Heritage Site of Bryggen in Bergen, Norway. D34 produced as part of the EU PICTURE project (www.picture-project.com).

Falk, J. and Adelman, L. (2003) Investigating the impact of prior knowledge and interest on aquarium visitor learning. *Journal of Research in Science Teaching* 40, 163–176.

Falk, J.H. and Dierking, L.D. (2000) *Learning from Museums. Visitor Experiences and the Making of Meaning*. Altamira Press, Walnut Creek, CA.

Falk, J. and Dierking, L. (2002) *Lessons without Limit. How Free Choice Learning is Transforming Education*. Altamira Press, Walnut Creek, CA.

Fernández-Ballesteros, R. (ed.) (1996) *Evaluación de programas*. Síntesis, Madrid.

Fink, A. (1995) *The Survey Kit*. Sage, London.

Font Sentias, J. (ed.) (2004) *Casos de Turismo Cultural: de la Planificación Estratégica a la Gestión del Producto*. Ariel, Barcelona.

Foo, T.S. (2000) Subjective assessment of urban quality of life in Singapore (1997–1998). *Habitat International* 24, 31–49.

García, M. (2004) Ávila: planificación y gestión turística local en una Ciudad Patrimonio de la Humanidad. In: M. García. *Casos de Turismo Cultural: de la Planificación Estratégica a la Gestión del Producto*. Ariel, Barcelona, pp. 413–441.

Giannias, D. (1997) Quality of life structural analysis. *Journal of Environmental Management* 49, 157–166.

Gilbert, D. and Clark, M. (1997) An exploratory examination of urban tourism impact, with reference to residents attitudes, in the cities of Canterbury and Guildford. *Cities* 14, 323–352.

Haralamboulos, N. and Pizam, A. (1996) Perceived impacts of tourism: the case of Samos. *Annals of Tourism Research* 23, 503–526.

Haywood, K. (1986) Can tourist life cycle be made operational? *Tourism Management* 7, 154–167.

http://www.ayto-caceres.es (Accessed 31 March 2007).

http://www.dinabadajoz.com/presentacion.htm (plan de Dinamización) (Accessed 31 March 2007).

http://www.mons.be (Accessed 1 December 2004).

ICOMOS (1999) International Cultural Tourism Charter. (http://www.international.icomos.org/charters/tourism_e.htm).

Jafari, J. (1997) Scientification of Tourism: Keynote Speech delivered at the Asia Pacific Tourism Association Annual Conference, Taipei, Taiwan, 16 August.

Khawajkie, E., Pavlic, B. and Titchen, S. (2002) *Le Patrimoine mondial entre les Mains des Jeunes*. UNESCO, Turin.

Kim, K. (2002) The effects of tourism impacts upon quality of life of residents in the community. PhD thesis, Virginia Polytechnic Institute and State University.

Korça, P. (1996) Research attitudes toward tourism impacts. Research notes and reports. *Annals of Tourism Research* 23, 695–726.

Krueger, R.A. (1994) *Focus Group, A Practical Guide for Applied Research*. Sage, Thousand Oaks, CA.

Lankford, S. and Howard, D. (1994) Developing a tourism attitude scale. *Annals of Tourism Research* 21, 121–139.

Lask, T. and Dumont, E. (2006) Liege: betting on Tourism for increased economic benefits and reconversion from industry to services. Case Study produced as part of the EU PICTURE project (www.picture-project.com).

MacNaught, T. (1982) Mass tourism and the dilemmas of modernisation in Pacific Islands communities. *Annals of Tourism Research* 9, 359–381.

Maison du tourisme de la region de Mons (2002) Le pays de Mons vous accueille (Tourist prospectus).

Marans, R. (2003) Understanding environmental quality through quality of life studies: the 2001 DAS and its use of subjective and objective indicators. *Landscape and Urban Planning* 65, 73–83.

Massam, B. (2002) Quality of life; public planning and private living. *Progress in Planning* 58, 141–227.

McKercher, B. and du Cros, H. (2002) *Cultural Tourism: The Partnership between Tourism and Cultural Heritage Management*. Haworth Hospitality, Oxford.

Ministerio de Industria, Turismo y Comercio (2001) Plan de Dinamización Turística Tierra de Caballeros Tablas de Daimiel. (http://www.tierradecaballeros.com).

Ministerio de Industria, Turismo y Comercio (2002) Plan de Dinamización Turística de Badajoz. (http://www.dinabadajoz.com).

Mons: Capitale européenne de la culture en 2015. Brochure.

Mosquera, G (1999) Robando el pastel global. Globalización, diferencia y apropiación cultural. In: F. Castro and J. Jiménez (eds) *Horizontes del Arte Latinoamericano*. Tecnos, Madrid.

Murphy, P (1985) *Tourism: A Community Approach*. Routledge, London.

Musée François Duesberg (tourist prospectus).

Nichols, S.K. (1999) *Visitor Surveys: A User's Manual*. American Association of Museums, Washington, DC.

Nogués, A.M. (ed.) (2003) *Cultura y Turismo*. Signatura, Sevilla.

Oñate, J.J., Pereira, D., Suarez, F., Rodríguez, J.J. and Cachón, J. (2002) *Evaluación Ambiental Estratégica*. Ediciones Mundi Prensa, Madrid.

OoP&A (2004) *The Evaluation of Museum Educational Programs: a National Perspective*. Smithsonian Institution, Washington, DC.

Origet du Clouzeau, C. (1998) *Le tourisme culturel*. Presses Universitaires de France, Paris.

Pearce, L. (1996) From culture shock and culture arrogance to culture exchange: ideas towards sustainable socio-cultural tourism. *Journal of Sustainable Tourism* 3, 143–154.

Pearson, M. and Sullivan, S. (2003) *Looking after Heritage Places*. Melbourne University Press, Melbourne.

Peckham, R.S. (2003) *Rethinking Heritage, Cultures and Politics in Europe*. Tauris, London.

Perdue, R., Long, P. and Allen, L. (1987) Rural resident perceptions and attitudes. *Annals of Tourism Research* 14, 420–429.

Perdue, R., Long, P. and Kang, Y.S. (1999) Boomtown tourism and resident quality of life: the marketing of gaming to host community residents. *Journal of Business Research* 44, 165–167.

Pérez, M.L. (1997) El Turismo de la ciudad de Cáceres: otras opciones al turismo histórico-artístico. In: M. Valenzuela (ed.) *Los Turismos de Interior: el Retorno a la Tradición Viajera*. Ediciones UAM, Madrid, pp. 233–247.

Périer-D'leteren, C. (ed.) (1999) *Public et Sauvegarde du Patrimoine*. ICCROM, Roma.

Pizam, A. (1978) Tourism's impacts: the social costs to the destination community as perceived by its residents. *Journal of Travel Research* 16, 8–12.

Plan de Dinamización de Tierra de Caballeros – Tablas de Daimiel. Home page (http://www.tierradecaballeros.com/indexfla.php).

Plog, S. (2001) Why destination areas rise and fall in popularity: an update of a Cornell Quarterly Classic. *Cornell Hotel and Restaurant Administration Quarterly* 42, 13–24.

Pol, E. (2001) 'Vivir en las ciudades históricas': un programa actitudinal. IBER Didáctica de las Ciencias Sociales. *Geografía e Historia* 27, 49–65.

Pol, E. (2006) La recepción de la obra de arte. IBER Didáctica de las Ciencias Sociales. *Geografía e Historia* 49, 7–25.

Pol, E. and Asensio, M. (2001) Así es si así os parece. Un crisol de opiniones que valoran el programa Vivir en las Ciudades Históricas. *Iber Didáctica de las Ciencias Sociales, Geografía e Historia* 27, 67–87.

Pol, E. and Asensio, M. (2006) La historia interminable: una visión crítica sobre la gestión de audiencias infantiles en los museos. MUS-A. *Revista de los museos de Andalucía* IV, 11–19.

Prentice, R. (1993) Community driven tourism planning and residents' preferences. *Tourism Management* 14, 218–227.

Roehl, W. (1999) Quality of life issues in a casino destination. *Journal of Business Research* 44, 223–229.

Russo, A. (2002) The vicious circle of tourism development in heritage cities. *Annals of Tourism Research* 29, 165–182.

Santamaría, J. and Asensio, M. (2003) Paradigmas utilizados por el profesorado de bachillerato en historia del arte. IBER, Didáctica de las Ciencias Sociales, *Geografía e Historia* 37, 18–29.

Screven, C.G. (1990) Uses of evaluation before, during and after exhibit design. *ILVS Review* 1, 2.

Sethi, V. and King, W. (1994) Development of measures to assess the extent to which an information technology application provides competitive advantage. *Management Science* 40, 1601–1624.

Simón, C., Sandoval, M. and Asensio, M. (2006) Promover una investigación que permita dar voz a las personas con discapacidad: sentido, desafío y dificultades para una investigación participativa. In: Echeita, G.

and Verdugo, M.A. (eds) *Actas del II Congreso Nacional sobre Universidad y Discapacidad.* Universidad Complutense, Madrid.

Smith, M.K. (2003) *Issues in Cultural Tourism Studies.* Mansell, New York.

Stovel, H. (1998) *Preparación Ante el Riesgo: un Manual para el Manejo del Patrimonio Cultural Mundial.* ICCROM, Roma.

Teutonico, J.M. and Palumbo, G (2000) Management planning for archaeological sites. The Getty Conservation Institute, Los Angeles, CA.

Toh, R.S., Khan, H. and Koh, A. (2001) A travel balance approach for examining tourism area life cycles: the case of Singapore. *Journal of Travel Research* 39, 426–432.

Tójar, J.C. (2006) *Investigación Cualitativa. Comprender y actuar.* La Muralla, Madrid.

Tosun, C. (2001) Host perceptions of impacts: a comparative tourism study. *Annals of Tourism Research* 29, 231–253.

Travis, A. (1984) Social and cultural aspects of tourism. *UNEP Industry and Environment* 7, 22–24.

Trésor de la collégiale Sainte-Waudru (Tourist prospectus).

Troitiño, M.A. (1998a) *Ávila, Turismo y Realidad Urbana.* Fundación Cultural Santa Teresa, Ávila.

Troitiño, M.A. (1998b) Turismo y ciudades históricas: la experiencia española. In: Marchena, M.J. (ed.) *Turismo Urbano y Patrimonio Cultural: una Perspectiva Europea.* Patronato Provincial de Turismo, Sevilla, pp. 89–105.

Troitiño, M.A. (2000) El Turismo Cultural en las ciudades españolas Patrimonio de la Humanidad. In: Herrero, L.C. (ed.) *Turismo Cultural: El Patrimonio Histórico como Fuente de Riqueza.* Fundación de Patrimonio Histórico, Valladolid.

Troitiño, M.A., García, M., De la Calle, M. and Troitiño, L. (2006) Boletín Informativo del Observatorio Turístico de la ciudad de Ávila, no. 10 (also available in http://www.avilaturismo.com/utes/genericos/agenda.asp?ute=8006).

Ulengin, B., Ulengin, F. and Guvenç, U. (2001) A multidimensional approach to urban quality of life: The case of Istanbul. *European Journal of Operational Research* 130, 361–374.

UNESCO (2003) Text of the Convention for the Safeguarding of Intangible Cultural Heritage. (http://www.unesco.org/culture/ich_convention/index.php?pg=00022&art=art2#art2).

Van der Borg, J., Costa, P. and Gotti, G. (1996) Tourism in European heritage cities. *Annals of Tourism Research* 23, 306–321.

VVAA (1999) Museums for the new millennium. A symposium for the museum community. Washington, DC: American Association of Museums.

VVAA (2001a) *Actas del primer Congreso de Turismo de Extremadura: Badajoz, 7, 8 y 9 de Junio de 2001.* Junta de Extremadura, Consejería de Obras Públicas y Turismo, Dirección General de Turismo, Badajoz.

VVAA (2001b) *Managing Change: the Museum Facing Economic and Social Challenges. Papers of the ICMAH General Meeting.* Museo de Historia de la Ciudad, Barcelona.

VVAA (2002a) *Mastering Civic Engagement: a Challenge to Museums.* American Association of Museums, Washington, DC.

VVAA (2002b) Touriste, Autochtone: qui est l'etranger? *Ethnologie française* 32, 389–566.

Weil, S. (1990) *Rethinking the Museum and Other Meditations.* The Smithsonian Institution Press, Washington, DC.

Weil, S. (2002) *Making Museums Matter.* The Smithsonian Institution Press, Washington, DC.

World Heritage Centre (2005) The criteria for selection. (http://whc.unesco.org/en/criteria/).

World Tourism Organization (2004) *Indicators of Sustainable Development for Tourism Destinations: A Guidebook.* WTO, Madrid.

11 Tourist Immersion or Tourist Gaze: the Backpacker Experience

Ketwadee Buddhabhumbhitak

Naresuan University, Phitsanulok, Thailand

Introduction

The backpacker market has been gaining interest as a niche worthy of research since the 1980s. The typology of a backpacker that is often cited is one of a non-institutionalized tourist who avoids package tours, travels independently and seeks to engage with the host society and culture (Jarvis, 1994; Welk, 2004). However, recent research suggests that backpacker tourism has become another form of conventional mass tourism (Richards and Wilson, 2004b). Cohen (2004) believes a conventional mass tourist is different from an independent traveller, such as a backpacker, because of his degree of 'strangeness'. While a backpacker desires to get rid of his status of strangeness in a host society, a mass tourist is not interested in doing so. It is this change in thinking within the literature that was explored in this chapter. This was achieved by investigating backpackers' ideologies and actions in relation to the concepts of 'tourist immersion' and 'tourist gaze'. These two concepts represent two extremes of a continuum, with 'tourist immersion' being more aligned with independent (backpacker) travel and 'tourist gaze' being more aligned with mass tourism.

Tourist Immersion

When the term 'immersion' is used in the context of tourism, it refers to the degree to which the tourist desires to understand the local society and culture (Jansson, 2006). The degree of socio-cultural immersion that a tourist desires from a host society is varied. It could be said the socio-cultural immersion of the tourist within a host society is determined by how the tourist perceives himself, the meaning of tourism and his attitude to the social world. Cohen (1973) argued that the degree of tourist socio-cultural immersion could be placed on a continuum. He viewed travel as a social activity that varies for each individual. At one extreme of the continuum 'modern man' seeks novelty and shuns familiarity when he travels, while at the other end of the continuum 'traditional man' relies on the familiar 'bubble environment' during his travel. Cohen's (1973) modern man is the conceptual representation of what he called the 'non-institutionalized tourist', who can further be categorized into two main types: the explorer and the drifter. Explorers have an independent travel pattern and avoid mainstream tourist sites. However, despite novelty being sought during his trip, the explorer still looks for familiar conveniences in his travel choices. The drifter also seeks independent experiences and a high degree of novelty, but differs in his degree of immersion in a host society. While the explorer tries to immerse himself in a host society, he cannot abandon his comforts and native way of life. This differs from the drifter who endeavours to immerse himself wholly in a host society by 'living like a local'.

© CAB International 2010. *Tourism and Visual Culture*, Volume 1 (eds P. Burns, C. Palmer and J-A. Lester)

Cohen's (1973) drifter is placed at the end of the continuum with the highest degree of socio-cultural immersion, and is the polar opposite of the mass tourist who has the least involvement in the host environment they visit. However, Cohen accepted that each type of tourist is heterogeneous because of the incessant diversity of the global phenomena. In addition, it is very difficult to maintain the original drifter's characteristics fully. Therefore, Cohen (1973) further categorized drifters. Outward-oriented drifters seek significant interaction with the local people, while inward-oriented drifters seek an enclave of their own kind. It is feasible that a similar distinction exists with today's youth tourists, of which backpackers are a subset. Loker-Murphy and Pearce (1995) suggested that there is one group of youth tourist that seeks only superficial contact with locals and a second group that seeks profound contact with locals.

The backpacker and tourist immersion

It has been widely recognized that backpackers tend towards the non-institutionalized end of the continuum (Murphy, 1997; Cohen, 2004; Richards and Wilson, 2004a), with the drifter remaining the major precursor for the modern-day backpacker. Backpackers desire to be immersed in a host society, to have a significant interaction with a host population, to change their normal structured life and to adopt the host society's social values.

The backpacker's desire to interact with the local population is evident in a number of studies. Adler (1985, p. 321) noted that 'Today's budget traveller is very likely to state that a prime motivation for travelling is 'to meet people' and seek invitations to share meals or stay with locals'. Ross (1993) found that when backpackers were asked what the major positive image of both the ideal and actual destination was, they frequently replied 'friendliness of local residents'. Loker-Murphy (1996, p. 23) found that backpackers are primarily motivated by 'the need for excitement or adventure' and 'meeting local people'. Similarly, Murphy (1997, p. 229) found that amongst their ten highest-ranking motivations, backpackers wanted to 'learn about/experience another culture' and to

'meet with the locals'. Kininmont (2000) surveyed backpackers travelling in Australia and found that more than half claimed they came to Australia to meet the local people. Newlands (2004) found from his survey of backpackers in New Zealand that the main motivation was to explore other cultures and to interact with local people. Jarvis (2004) found that 84% of backpackers travelling through South-east Asia travelled for the cultural experience.

It is often interaction with the local people that backpackers claim distinguishes them from 'tourists' (Desforges, 1998). Noy (2004, p. 86) noted that backpackers draw a distinct line between tourists and themselves by claiming that '. . . they [backpackers] can truly 'reach' and experience "fascinating" people and landscapes'. Similarly, Westerhausen (2002, p. 59) found that backpackers claim they '. . . have closer contact with locals' than mass tourists do. Elsrud (1998, p. 311) concluded that 'Most of them [backpackers] emphasized their desire to be 'participants' rather than 'observers' while travelling. Unlike the charter tourists on a week long trip, who can not expect to be living in close relation to their hosts . . .'. Moscardo (2006) noted that the 'adoption of a counter culture' is still dominating the backpacker experience.

Within a host destination, backpackers make an effort to interact with the local residents. Huxley (2004) found that backpackers used various forms of activity to engage in local cultures, including attending festivals, wearing local clothes, tasting the local cuisine, experiencing local music and films, interacting with local children, and attempting to go to more remote areas around the destination. Similarly, Muzaini (2006) showed that backpackers attempt to acquire cultural immersion in a host society by adopting the personality, outlook and appearance of local residents.

Despite these desires, constraints to immersion have been identified. These constraints include time, the foreign community and language barriers. Despite the fact that backpackers try to immerse in the host society, both Huxley (2004) and Muzaini (2006) feel that they are often unsuccessful due to the institutionalized backpacker 'bubble' within the tourist hub. This supports Cohen's (2006) argument relating to the transitional backpacker enclave and its influence on modern-day backpackers.

Nevertheless, studies indicate that a backpacker's attempt to be immersed in a host society provides potential positive impacts for a host destination (Firth and Hing, 1999; Moran, 2000; Scheyvens, 2002; Westerhausen and Macbeth, 2003).

Despite the suggestion thus far that backpackers are non-institutionalized tourists, some researchers argue that backpacker tourism is now a subset of mass tourism (O'Reilly, 2006). This shift in the backpacker market is argued both in terms of the expansion of the backpacker tourism 'industry' and changes to backpackers' travel patterns and characteristics. This concern was also voiced by Cohen (1973) within his concept of the 'mass drifter'. While it is clear that backpackers have a desire to interact with the host population, it is feasible that backpackers will adopt the behaviour of 'mass drifters' by interacting with '. . . those members of the lower social classes who cater to the mass drifters and associate with them' (Cohen, 1973, p. 99). Murphy (2001) argues that backpackers perceive locals as being the friendly staff who wait and serve them in tourism businesses. Elsrud (1998, p. 319) expressed concerns about the underlying attitudes of backpackers towards the local people when one backpacker commented that the locals in remote Indonesia are 'jungle people'. The suggestion is that while backpackers want to visit these cultures they see them as belonging to a 'lesser world'. Concerns about the nature of backpacker interaction with the host population have also been raised by other researchers. Adler (1985) expressed concerns that backpackers use locals for economic gain by aggressively bargaining for cheaper prices. Mowforth and Munt (1998) were concerned that backpackers seek an 'authentic' experience without having a real local interaction. Additionally, there has been concern that backpackers have little regard for the host destination (Wilson and Richards, 2004). More recently, Teo and Leong (2006) argued that the relationship between host and guest, particularly in the context of Western backpackers and less developed countries, could be compared to the unequal power relations between these two groups. The question raised in this chapter is – are backpackers moving away from tourist immersion and more towards Urry's (1990) tourist gaze?

The tourist gaze

The concept of the tourist gaze as proposed by Urry (1990) compares the visual 'gaze' of tourists with the 'medical gaze' performed in a clinical environment. The main focus of 'gaze' is the power of judgment when one visually 'sees'. Urry noted the power of gaze occurs in accordance with one's existing discourse or, in other words, one's perception of the social world. For example, the medical gaze relates to the discourse of treatment and medicine, while the tourist gaze refers to the way a tourist perceives the tourist experience, which has been socially created by tourists themselves. Simply, tourist gaze is what is in a tourist's mindset. It is about what they see, are aware of, expect and are conscious of.

Urry also discusses tourist gaze in relation to mass tourism and sight-seeing. He argues that if the 'mere sight' or 'mere gaze' occurs, it is likely to be at Boorstin's (1963) 'superficial level'. Effectively, when a mass tourist 'gazes' he cannot connect to the real meaning of what he has seen because he is influenced by the discourse of others. This, therefore, leads to the lack of a deep understanding of a host society.

As the concept of tourist gaze has been revisited by various researchers through time, the definition of tourist gaze has been reconsidered and reviewed. Urry's (1990) tourist gaze was criticized by Leiper (1992) as an approach to view tourism as a homogeneous phenomenon performed solely as a one-way process (Maoz, 2006). Perkins and Thorns (2001) also noted that the idea of gazing is not the best method with which to analyse an adventure tourist, who tends to 'perform' rather than to 'gaze'.

However, Urry (1992) defended his concept by noting that a tourist gaze is not only simple, visually seen process. The gaze represents the metaphor of those who perform 'gazing' towards anything with distinctive characteristics, not only towards a building or object. Urry (1992) further explained that 'tourist gaze' is dynamic and socially constructed, and is affected by certain conditions, such as dynamics within a host society or tourist's length of stay.

Applied to backpacker tourism, it is apparent that there are some factors that could impact on the 'backpacker gaze'. The relationship between tourist gaze and the backpacker has not been widely discussed. It is felt to some extent that a backpacker's reason to immerse in a host society is to avoid the experience of a mere tourist gaze (Jansson, 2006) and become involved in the local society as much as they can.

This chapter tends to agree that the tourist gaze is socially constructed by one's interpretation of one's surroundings. Arguably, the tourist gaze is an illustration of visual process and self-central discourse either with or without the gaze. The subjectivity of tourist gaze is similar to the subjectivity of the backpacker's authentic experience to some extent. Shaffer (2004) argued that the authentic experience was socially performed and constructed by each backpacker and the tourist gaze has emerged in the constructed authentic experience when backpackers have encountered other cultures and societies. Shaffer (2004) also discussed the reproduction of authenticity and the tourist gaze. According to MacCannell (1973), authenticity is the semiotic system, which is socially produced during the touristic experience. Hence, authenticity via 'visual gazing' could be indicative of the backpacker experience. For instance, in order to seek authenticity and localize themselves in a host society, backpackers are most likely to develop a constructed understanding of the locals 'through their eyes'. Whilst backpackers claim that they have immersed in a host society, how can backpackers' perceived immersion be distinguished from truly acquired immersion? Arguably, the tourist gaze could have applied to the backpacker even if he or she had tried to have localized immersion, particularly if the backpacker interpreted local experience from the perception of their own native society.

Method

In 2006, an in-depth semi-structured interview was conducted with 30 international backpackers in Pai, Thailand. Pai is situated in the northern region of Thailand, 135 km north of Chiang Mai province and 111 km east of Mae Hong Son province (Rueprayoachsilp, 2006). In the early 1980s, Western backpackers played a role in the pioneering of Pai as a tourist destination (Gampell, 2003) and European backpackers still dominate the Pai backpacker market (Sooksawasdi, 1998). Although backpackers are not the only types of tourists who visit Pai (Cohen, 2006), they are considered the dominant tourist group. Pai has been considered a 'backpacker enclave' for more than 20 years because of its inaccessibility (Cohen, 2006).

Convenience sampling was used to survey a cross-section of international backpackers visiting Pai. Backpackers were identified by the type of accommodation they were staying in, their independent travel and their long-term travel (i.e. the characteristics of backpackers consistent with Pearce's (1990) definition of a backpacker). All interviews were audio-recorded to ensure the accuracy of data and transcription. The transcribed interviews were analysed using content analysis.

Backpackers' Ideologies

The first topic explored in the in-depth interviews was backpackers' ideologies in relation to travel. This was divided into five areas: backpacker travel motivation, expectation of authenticity, perception of a host destination, perception of host population, and the backpacker self-perception.

Backpacker travel motivation

The results showed that backpacker motivation is a mix of seven themes – novelty (53%), escape (50%), self-growth (40%), host-oriented (27%), self-enjoyment (20%), self-healing (13%) and seeking job opportunities (13%). Among these themes, learning about a host destination ranked fourth. Eight participants (27%) mentioned a desire to interact and learn about the host destination. They wanted to learn and explore local culture and also associate with local people during their time in a host destination. This is consistent with previous literature stating backpackers rated 'meeting local people' highly or within the first five most common motivations for travel (Loker, 1993; Richards and Wilson, 2004c).

Motivations?. . . to learn, to learn as well . . . to experience other cultures, because I think that a lot of people are very closed minded, and they only live in their own little circular community in Australia.

[BP16]

Expectation of authenticity

From the 30 interviews, there were seven themes that emerged in relation to backpackers' expectations of authenticity – non-touristic (40%), primitiveness (40%), relaxation (30%), small-scale (13%), slow pace of life (13%), hippy atmosphere (10%) and no expectation of authenticity (13%). Within the theme of primitiveness, local people are a key factor in creating the authenticity of a destination. A primitive host population refers to those who lack knowledge of the English language, shun Western values, and live simply and modestly. In addition, the presence of the local population rather than foreign tourists was discussed as an indicator of authenticity.

I think local people . . . I mean, first I come for people, you know . . . and after for the cities, for nature, but more for people . . . Yes, a lot of time I try to find different tribe in Thailand, because there are a lot of them and the . . . for that it was attracted me when I was travelling . . .

[BP23]

Noy (2004), proposed that seeking authenticity relates to the backpacker's self-identity and also creates an 'authenticist backpacker'. It is clear that seeking authenticity is a core theme of the backpackers' ideology and that a host society and its population are very important to a backpacker's desired experience. Hence, it is most likely that the host–guest relationship remains the main component of a backpacker's experience.

Backpackers' perception of the destination, host population and self

According to Passer and Smith (2001), perception is the mental process, which suggests one's constructed interpretation or understanding of the surrounding environment. Applied to this study, perception of a backpacker could relate to how much a backpacker's mind was influenced

Table 11.1. The comparison between backpacker's perceptions of a host destination and the host population.

Perception: one word to describe 'Pai' (words used by backpackers)	Perception: one word to describe 'Pai people' (words used by backpackers)
Relaxed (laid back, relaxing, chilled out)	Friendly (friendly, open hearted, accommodating, helpful, approachable, accepting, nice)
Beauty (beauty, beautiful, heaven, paradise, nice, magical)	Quiet (quiet, calm, peaceful, discreet)
Peaceful (quiet, peaceful, quaint)	Attractive (engaging, special, colourful, shining bright, amazing)
Escape (escape from reality, timelessness)	Relaxed (relaxed, laid back)
Friendliness (friendly, inviting)	Happy (happy, smiley, love)
Bohemian/hippy (Bohemian, funky, hippy)	Primitive (genuine, simple, timeless)
Change (changing, expanding)	Change (earn money from tourist, jaded)
Others statements (traveller city, worth)	

by the host society and the local residents. Backpackers were asked to give a word to describe Pai and its inhabitants. As detailed in Table 11.1, it was found that backpackers have a positive perception towards the host society and its residents. In addition, it was found that the image of local people, as perceived by the backpackers, is similar to how they would describe a primitive person, for example, calm and peaceful, simple, genuine and friendly. Additionally, the image of the host destination and society, as reported by backpackers, is often contrary to the image of the people and the modern western society from which backpackers are trying to escape.

In terms of backpacker's self-perception, there were ten themes that emerged from the content analysis of this study. These were independent (27%), relaxed (20%), self-growth (17%), inquisitive (13%), closer to a host society (10%), not a tourist (10%), peacefulness (10%), happiness (7%), fulfilment (3%) and cultural ambassador (3%). Among the most used expressions to describe the backpacker's self-image were themes that related to a host population. Three participants perceived that they were people who liked to get closer to a host society and believed they have had significant interaction with local residents. One participant noted that he had more opportunities to meet local people because he tends to travel cheaply. The idea of being closer to a host society is supported by backpackers' belief that they are not tourists. Another three participants perceived that they are different from normal tourists because they are seeking the meaning of life. These participants also proposed that a backpacker is a traveller, as one participant noted, 'You could say traveller. I travel the world, and I also travel my inner thoughts' [BP27]. Participants believed that, as backpackers, they have a more benign impact on a host destination than tourists do because 'normal tourists come [to the destination] with their rules' [BP23]. In other words, they criticized normal tourists who retain their modern identity and perceive a host destination from a static point of view. It is clear that a number of participants perceived being a backpacker in relation to how they interact with and contribute to the host society.

These results clearly show that backpackers do have a desire to immerse themselves in the host society. However, it is noted that the host society and culture is only one of a number of travel motivations for backpackers. Findings indicate that motivations such as relaxation are also important to backpackers.

Backpackers' Actions

The second topic explored in the in-depth interviews was backpackers' level of interaction with the host society. These are discussed under the headings of: interaction with host population, activities undertaken at the host destination, degree of socio-cultural learning, degree of participation in local events and degree of immersion overall.

Interaction with host population

All backpackers experienced some kind of interaction with the local population (daily or frequent interaction). The most common interaction

environment was commercial places, specifically restaurants (40%), guesthouses (37%), bars (30%), retail shops (17%) and Internet cafés (7%). Massage parlours, neighbouring areas, local markets and public areas were each mentioned by one backpacker (3%). Consequently, the type of interaction could be described as relations between tourism-related service providers and tourists. It could be said that most of the backpackers in this study had limited interactions and with only a select group of local residents. Most of the interactions were quite superficial including, greeting, asking for directions, and having a short conversation. Arguably, such a limited interaction does not provide a real view of a local resident's life, as it is typically from a commercial, tourist-based perspective. In addition, backpackers experienced language barriers and were most likely to communicate in English. This is consistent with Cohen's (1973) and Murphy's (2001) argument that backpackers engage with local people in the tourism sector rather than with the 'typical' local person.

Activities undertaken at the host destination

Whilst claiming to seek authenticity, backpackers' day-to-day activities show that the most common types of activities were relaxing (53%), seeking a good restaurant to eat at each day (43%), reading books (43%), going to hot springs (33%) and riding a motorbike around (33%). However, there were only a few activities mentioned that directly help a backpacker learn about the host society, including, hanging out with local people (3%), learning the Thai language (7%), and learning Thai cooking (3%). Clearly, relaxation dominated as the number one backpacker activity in Pai. Many activities could be classified as 'relaxation', such as 'to do nothing' and 'to relax'. One participant stated that 'We try to . . . but some days you just relax . . . but you know, it's nice to get out about, especially when it's sunny . . .' [BP20].

Degree of socio-cultural learning

In terms of social and cultural learning in Pai, backpackers stated they have learnt certain characteristics of local residents (53%). According to backpackers, these characteristics have a positive influence on their self-identity. The most influential local characteristics are 'learning to be patient', 'learning to trust other people' and 'learning how to view life optimistically'. Other characteristics that are typical of Pai people, including enduring the harshness of life, relationships within the community, and the variety of ethics and tribes, were not identified by backpackers. Eight backpackers (27%) mentioned that they had generally learnt the local way of life, although the context in which the participant viewed the local way of life was different depending on the individual's point of view. It seems that backpackers generalized that the major difference between their own society and Pai society was the typical local way of life. Besides learning local traits, ten backpackers (30%) stated that they had learnt the Thai language from the host society in order to overcome language barrier problems and to fulfil a personal lifelong dream. Participants (13%) also noted that they had learnt local wisdoms such as local herbal remedy, Thai massage and Buddhism. No backpackers acknowledged the Pai traditional craft works like woodcraft techniques, domestic utensils, local tobacco made from banana leaves and hand-made textiles (Manonaya, 2000).

Degree of participation in local festivals

Since the 1900s, Pai has hosted a variety of local annual events (Pai District Office, 2005). Almost every month, Pai offers a variety of local festivals and still maintains the long-standing Tai Yai and Thai Lanna festivals. The results of this study suggested that backpackers only 'gaze' at the local events. Many backpackers (47%) used the terms to 'see' or to 'watch' when describing the nature of their participation. Backpackers could not provide detailed information about the festival that they had attended. For example, backpackers could not remember the name of the festival. No backpackers could recall a Pai-based cultural element, as distinct from typical Thai culture. Arguably, the increased number of international cultural events in Pai confuses backpackers' perception of local events.

One participant considered a non-Thai cultural experience in Pai as their participation in the culture, 'I am going to do the drumming on Wednesday . . . like a drumming session . . .' (which is African culture).

This raises a question that requires examination in the future: should the international cultural experience be the new type of backpacker-oriented service? It has generally been assumed that backpackers travel to new destinations to experience and learn about local culture originating from that area. It is ironic that the number of international activities is rapidly increasing in backpacker destinations. This supports Cohen's (2006) assertion that backpackers are always catered for with backpacker-oriented services. This is a consequence of what Cohen (2006) has called 'the backpacker boom'.

Eight backpackers (27%) stated that they had never participated in events, particularly cultural and religious events. Of the 30 backpackers, only one believed he had an excellent level of participation in local traditions and ceremonies. He was also one of the three backpackers who claimed to have experienced socio-cultural immersion in Pai. The high level of participation by this backpacker could be the consequence of two factors. First, this backpacker's father was married to a Lisu woman. Second, this backpacker had been staying in Pai a long time and decided to reside in a rental house, rather than a guesthouse. Because of these factors, he may have had greater opportunities to attend local events and to have a deeper level of understanding.

Degree of immersion overall

Lastly, backpackers were requested to evaluate their degree of social and cultural immersion in Pai. They were asked directly, 'Do you consider yourself immersed in Pai society and culture?' There were three groups of answers – 'yes, I have immersed in Pai society already', 'no, not immersed yet', and 'I don't know'. Of the 30 backpackers, there were only three backpackers who identified themselves as immersed in Pai society and culture. These backpackers believed that immersion comprises of a familiarity with the community and being accepted as a community member. A large number of backpackers (23 or 77%) indicated that no matter how interested they were in a host society, they could not immerse themselves in the host society for a number of reasons. An additional four backpackers (13%) stated that they were not immersed in the host society at the time they were interviewed but they may become immersed if they could improve some aspects of their travel characteristics.

Largely consistent with Huxley (2004) and Muzaini's (2006) findings, the three main constraints to immersion given by backpackers were dependence on a foreign community, time limitation and a sense of otherness. The dependence on a foreign community in Pai was discussed by backpackers regarding the familiarity and convenience when meeting foreign people, particularly from their own country of origin. For example, a German backpacker stated that he was engaging with German travellers in Pai, exchanging travel stories. Backpackers also mentioned that the opportunity to meet local people is rare compared to the opportunity to meet foreign travellers due to the increased popularity of Pai as a tourist destination. This is consistent with the idea of backpacker communities overseas or what Cohen (2006) called 'the backpacker enclave'. This refers to the communities of backpackers that are loosely constructed by the social interaction amongst themselves. The backpacker enclave offers backpacker-oriented services and also conveniences or activities to enhance backpackers' enjoyment. It is well known that backpacker enclaves have developed at Khao Sarn Road in Bangkok as well as several islands in southern Thailand (Cohen, 2006). Pai is increasingly considered as the backpacker enclave of the north.

Besides the foreign community, backpackers claimed that the limited length of stay meant that they had less time to 'get to know' the local people, saying 'It will take a little bit more time. There are things that are different . . . but . . . maybe if I live here . . .' [BP15], and, 'Yeah, I think it took some time to have the feeling that you belong to here' [BP07]. Furthermore, when backpackers who had identified time limitations were asked, 'how much time do you think you need to immerse into Pai society?', the replies ranged from a couple of weeks, to one month,

several months, a year, and to be a permanent Pai resident. As one participant noted, 'Yeah, the more time, the better' [BP16].

According to Shipway (2000), Slaughter (2004), Speed and Harrison (2004) and Visser (2004), international backpacker's length of stay in one destination ranges from 3 weeks to more than 6 months. Logically, the longer period of time a backpacker spends in any one destination should increase the level of immersion in that destination. Some backpackers who had stayed a long time, for instance 18 months, still did not feel they had immersed in Pai society. However, the relationship between duration of stay and greater immersion should not be neglected as several participants noted they have noticed that fellow backpackers who permanently live in Pai have become immersed in Pai culture.

Another reason backpackers felt they could not immerse in Pai society was their perception of 'strangeness'. Some backpackers sensed 'alienation' during their stay in Pai. There are two types of alienation: being alienated by race and being alienated by host–guest relationship. In terms of racial differences, three backpackers (10%) noted that they felt like a foreigner within the host society. Ironically, one backpacker suggested that a solution for this would be that backpackers have to be born Thai to have a greater level of immersion in this society. Another source of backpacker alienation that exists in Pai society is the host–guest relationship. One backpacker argued that he could not immerse himself in Pai society because he was a traveller living in a host destination – hence the relationship of host and guest creates a social barrier. Cultural and language barriers were also discussed in the interviews. A number of backpackers (10%) experienced difficulties communicating, in terms of both language and cultural background. One backpacker explained that he had to maintain a distance between himself and Pai society because, as a backpacker, it would be hard for him to have a significant relationship and then have to leave.

These findings suggest that backpackers' actions within a host society do not correlate with their expressed desire to immerse themselves in the host society. While some backpackers felt that immersion may eventuate with time, they were quick to give excuses as to why immersion would be a problem. This supports previous claims (Cohen, 2004; Richards and Wilson, 2004b) that there are discrepancies between backpacker ideologies and practices.

Conclusion

It could be said that the backpacker experience in a host society is more akin to 'gazing', despite the desire to gain 'immersion'. However, the gazing performed by backpackers is not the same as the gazing that is performed by mass tourists because of the different social setting in which it takes place. Backpackers have a desire and motivation to learn about a host society and they seek an authentic experience. In contrast, mass tourists do not make the same level of effort to understand a host society. Mass tourists prefer to stay within their 'environmental bubble' and enjoy travel without gaining a deep understanding of what they 'gaze' at.

While backpackers do share similarities with mass tourists, their motivations go beyond recreation and relaxation. They also desire to learn about, and immerse themselves in, the host society. Therefore, it could be argued that the 'the backpacker gaze' is a mix of their socio-cultural immersive desire, the recreation activities provided for backpackers, and the yet-to-be-completed socio-cultural immersion.

References

Adler, J. (1985) Youth on the road: reflections on the history of tramping. *Annals of Tourism Research* 12, 335–354.

Boorstin, D.J. (1963) *The Image, or, What Happened to the American Dream*. Penguin Books, Harmondsworth.

Cohen, E. (1973) Nomad from affluence: notes on the phenomenon of drifter tourism. *International Journal of Comparative Sociology* 14, 89–103.

Cohen, E. (2004) Backpacking: diversity and change. In: Richards, G. and Wilson, J. (eds) *The Global Nomad: Backpacker Travel in Theory and Practice*. Channel View Publications, Clevedon, pp. 43–59.

Cohen, E. (2006) Pai – A backpacker enclave in transition. *Tourism Recreation Research* 31, 11–27.

Desforges, L. (1998) Checking out the planet: Global representations/local identities and youth travel. In: Skelton, A.G.V.T. (ed.) *Cool Places: Geographies of Youth Culture*. Routledge, London, pp. 175–192.

Elsrud, T. (1998) Time creation in travelling: the taking and making of time among women backpackers. *Time and Society* 7, 309–334.

Firth, T. and Hing, N. (1999) Backpacker hostels and their guests: attitudes and behaviours relating to sustainable tourism. *Tourism Management* 20, 251–254.

Gampell, J. (2003) *Pai in the Thai Sky*, http://www.theglobeandmail.com/servlet/ArticleNews/TPStory/LAC/20030208/TRPAII/TPTravel/ (Accessed 15 July 2005).

Huxley, L. (2004) Western backpackers and the global experience: an exploration of young people's interaction with local cultures. *Tourism, Culture & Communication* 5, 37–44.

Jansson, A. (2006) *Specialized Spaces: Touristic Communication in the Age of Hyper-Space Biased Media*. Centre for Cultural Studies, Aarhus University, pp. 1–38.

Jarvis, J. (1994) *'The Billion Dollar Backpackers': the Ultimate Fully Independent Tourists*. National Centre for Australian Studies, Clayton, Victoria.

Jarvis, J. (2004) Yellow bible tourism: backpackers in South East Asia. In: West, B. (ed.) *Down the Road: Exploring Backpackers and Independent Travel*. API Network, Perth.

Kininmont, L.J. (2000) *The Right Mix: Facilities for International Backpackers in Australia*. St Lucia, Queensland.

Leiper, N. (1992) Book review: *The Tourist Gaze* by John Urry (London, Sage Publications, 1990). *Annals of Tourism Research* 19, 604–607.

Loker, L. (1993) *The Backpacker Phenomenon II: More Answers to Further Questions*. Department of Tourism, James Cook University, Townsville, Queensland.

Loker-Murphy, L. (1996) Backpackers in Australia: a motivation-based segmentation study. *Journal of Travel and Tourism Marketing* 5, 23–45.

Loker-Murphy, L. and Pearce, P.L. (1995) Young budget travellers: backpackers in Australia. *Annals of Tourism Research* 22, 819–843.

MacCannell, D. (1973) Staged authenticity: arrangements of social space in tourist settings. *American Journal of Society* 79, 689–703.

Manonaya, P. (2000) *Pai Native*. Pai Primary Education, Mae Hong Son.

Maoz, D. (2006) The mutual gaze. *Annals of Tourism Research* 33, 221–239.

Moran, D. (2000) Interpreting tour experiences: the case of structured backpacker tour in New Zealand. *Pacific Tourism Review* 4, 35–43.

Moscardo, G. (2006) Backpackers and other younger travellers to the Great Barrier Reef: an exploration of changes in characteristics and behaviours over time. *Tourism Recreation Research* 31, 29–37.

Mowforth, M. and Munt, I. (1998) *Tourism and Sustainability: New Tourism in the Third World*. Routledge, London.

Murphy, L. (1997) Young budget travellers: a marketing and decision making analysis. Unpublished PhD thesis, James Cook University, Australia.

Murphy, L. (2001) Exploring social interactions of backpackers. *Annals of Tourism Research* 28, 50–67.

Muzaini, H. (2006) Backpacking Southeast Asia: strategies of 'looking local'. *Annals of Tourism Research* 33, 144–161.

Newlands, K. (2004) Setting out on the road less travelled: a study of backpacker travel in New Zealand. In: Richards, G. and Wilson, J. (eds) *The Global Nomad: Backpacker Travel in Theory and Practice*. Channel View Publication, Clevedon, pp. 217–236.

Noy, C. (2004) This trip really changed me: backpackers' narratives of self-change. *Annals of Tourism Research* 31, 78–102.

O'Reilly, C.C. (2006) From drifter to gap year tourist: mainstreaming backpacker travel. *Annals of Tourism Research* 33, 998–1017.

Pai District Office. (2005) *Smiling District*. Pai District Office, Mae Hong Son.

Passer, M.W. and Smith, R.E. (2001) *Psychology – Frontiers and Applications*. McGraw-Hill, Boston.

Pearce, P.L. (1990) *The Backpacker Phenomenon: Preliminary Answers to Basic Questions*. Department of Tourism, James Cook University, Townsville, Queensland.

Perkins, H.C. and Thorns, D.C. (2001) Gazing or performing? Reflections on Urry's tourist gaze in the context of contemporary experience in the Antipodes. *International Sociology* 16, 185–204.

Richards, G. and Wilson, J. (2004a) Drifting towards the global nomad. In: Richards, G. and Wilson, J. (eds) *The Global Nomad: Backpacker Travel in Theory and Practice*. Channel View Publications, Clevedon, pp. 3–13.

Richards, G. and Wilson, J. (2004b) *The Global Nomad: Backpacker Travel in Theory and Practice*. Channel View Publications, Clevedon.

Richards, G. and Wilson, J. (2004c) The global nomad: motivation and behaviour of independent travellers worldwide. In: Richards, G. and Wilson, J. (eds) *The Global Nomad: Backpacker Travel in Theory and Practice*. Channel View Publications, Clevedon, pp. 14–39.

Ross, G.F. (1993) Ideal and actual images of backpacker visitors to Northern Australia. *Journal of Travel Research* 32, 54–57.

Rueprayoachsilp, M. (2006) *Vieng Tai Community Report*. Pai Elementary Education, Mae Hong Son.

Scheyvens, R. (2002) Backpacker tourism and third world development. *Annals of Tourism Research* 29, 144–164.

Shaffer, T. (2004) Performing backpacking: constructing 'authenticity' every step of the way. *Text and Performance Quarterly* 24, 139–160.

Shipway, R. (2000) The international backpacker market in Britain: a market waiting to happen. In: Robinson, M., Long, P. and Evans, N. (eds) *Reflections on International Tourism: Motivations, Behaviour, and Tourist Types*. Centre for Tourism in Association with Business Education Publishers, Sunderland, pp. 393–416.

Slaughter, L. (2004) Profiling the international backpacker market in Australia. In: Richards, G. and Wilson, J. (eds) *The Global Nomad: Backpacker Travel in Theory and Practice*. Channel View Publications, Clevedon, pp. 168–179.

Sooksawasdi, P. (1998) *Abstract: Expenditures Pattern of Foreign Tourists in Pai District of Mae Hong Son Province*, http://www.grad.cmu.ac.th/abstract/1998/eco/abstract/eco980450.html (Accessed 15 July 2005).

Speed, C. and Harrison, T. (2004) Backpacking in Scotland: formal public sector responses to an informal phenomenon. In: Richards, G. and Wilson, J. (eds) *The Global Nomad: Backpacker Travel in Theory and Practice*. Channel View Publication, Clevedon, pp. 149–167.

Teo, P. and Leong, S. (2006) A postcolonial analysis of backpacking. *Annals of Tourism Research* 33, 109–131.

Urry, J. (1990) *The Tourist Gaze: Leisure and Travel in Contemporary Societies*. Sage, London.

Urry, J. (1992) The tourist gaze 'Revisited'. *The American Behavioral Scientist* 36, 172–186.

Visser, G. (2004) The developmental impacts of backpacker tourism in South Africa. *GeoJournal* 60, 283–299.

Welk, P. (2004) The beaten track: anti-tourism as an element of backpacker identity. In: Richards, G. and Wilson, J. (eds) *The Global Nomad: Backpacker Travel in Theory and Practice*. Channel View Publications, Clevedon, pp. 77–79.

Westerhausen, K. (2002) *Beyond the Beach: an Ethnography of Modern Travellers in Asia*. White Lotus, Bangkok.

Westerhausen, K. and Macbeth, J. (2003) Backpackers and empowered local communities: natural allies in the struggle for sustainability and local control? *Tourism Geographies* 5, 71–86.

Wilson, J. and Richards, G. (2004) Backpacker icons: influential literary 'nomads' in the formation of backpacker identities. In: Richards, G. and Wilson, J. (eds) *The Global Nomad: Backpacker Travel in Theory and Practice*. Channel View Publications, Clevedon, pp. 123–145.

12 Receiving and Shaping the Tourist Appraising Gaze: the Lived Experience of Reception Work in the Tourism and Hospitality Industry

Gayathri (Gee) Wijesinghe[1] and Peter Willis[2]
[1]School of Management, University of South Australia, Adelaide,
[2]School of Education, University of South Australia, Adelaide

Introduction

The *enchantment-seeking* gaze of the attentive tourist as he or she contemplates the offerings of a significant tourist venue has usually been accompanied or preceded by the more transactional *appraising* gaze of an arriving traveller arranging accommodation and food with a hotel receptionist – at one and the same time being careful about his or her budget whilst needing to get a feel for the place and what might be on offer.

This encounter between the receptionist and the traveller as he or she arrives at a venue for the first time is often the first moments in the traveller's actual holiday, and can make a considerable difference to the rest of the stay. In the increasingly elaborated role requirements of the tourism industry the receptionist, who is often young, female and well-presented, has the implicit task to accept (even 'measure up' to) the appraising gaze of the 'stranger' and subsequently through a mixture of friendliness, kindness and some strategic distance seek to convert the visitor's cautious gaze to the more contented gaze of a compliant and generous guest. This 'diplomatic' work, which can be risky and challenging, rewarding and painful, provides the focus for this chapter, the overall

aim of which is to provide a vivid portrayal of the lived experience of such 'diplomatic' receptionist work.

In spite of the centrality of the receptionist role to the functioning of the tourism and hospitality industry, the nature of reception practice is rarely a focus of scholarly writings on the workplace. There appear to be no 'real life stories' from the front desk that portray the experience of reception work generally and in particular the experiences of female receptionists. As a relatively under-researched area, it is not therefore fully appreciated within the broader profession. This discussion, written in the voice of the first author, is based upon the findings of doctoral research designed to address this research gap by investigating the lived experiences of four female receptionists (Wijesinghe, 2007). The research focused on *seeing, knowing and telling* using visual text such as narrative, metaphor and poetry to explore *what it is like* 'to be the object of the tourist gaze'; the intention being to generate an in-depth understanding of their experiences rather than generalizable propositions. The experiences of the female receptionists were presented as ten vignettes portraying and interpreting the lived experience of each receptionist situated within different social, cultural, personal and occupational settings. The significant themes to emerge from the research were analysed within the discourses of culture, feminist theory, power and labour relations, consumerism and notions about the home environment. The implications for practice and professional development were then discussed.

For the purposes of this discussion, we will draw upon one vignette to illustrate what it is like to be the 'object' of the tourist gaze. Here, we extend my original study to examine specifically the elements of the 'gaze' in this one vignette, and its embodiment in a specific social, cultural and temporal setting with strong undercurrents of hierarchal power-relations. To elaborate further – this chapter explores what it is 'really' like for a young attractive non-white female trainee receptionist from a third-world country – in a labour position of subservience – to be the object of the predatory gaze of a middle-aged affluent white heterosexual male guest of VIP standing in the hotel.

The gaze is defined here as an intense look that lingers on the object of the gaze. Jonathan Schroeder notes, 'to gaze implies more than to look at – it signifies a psychological relationship of power, in which the gazer is superior to the object of the gaze' (1998, p. 208). I argue here that the gaze of the guest is one of 'appraisal' as to the 'possibilities' of what is on offer; the host/receptionist has to 'measure-up to' this appraising gaze for the service encounter to be successful. However, in the encounter explored herein the gaze is shown to be mutual; that is, the host also 'appraises' the guest to see whether the guest will 'comply' with the rules of conduct expected in a service transaction.

In seeking to study the lived experience of female receptionists in the hospitality industry, I sought to find a methodological approach capable of revealing the richness of the work to the mind's eye of the reader, so that he/she would be able to experience some of its spirit and colour. The methodology employed, interpretative-hermeneutics, phenomenology and an expressive arts-based textual genre enabled me to bring alive the lived quality of the experience of a hotel receptionist as if the work was a dramatic scene played out on a stage. An arts-based textual approach seeks to take an alternative (and complementary) path to arts-based visual inquiry by bringing aesthetic attention to a portrayal of the experience to *show* the typical

nature of this work and the challenges faced by receptionists in carrying out the work. For example, Springgay and Wilson have shown through their approach of 'A/r/tography' that art provides an alternative way of *knowing*, 'living inquiry is an embodied encounter constituted through visual and textual understandings and experiences rather than mere visual and textual representations. One cannot separate, through abstract means, visual and textual interpretations of lived experience' (2005, p. 902).

In their work on '*Contextualising leisure research to encompass complexity in lived leisure experience: the need for creative analytic practice*', Parry and Johnson (2007, p. 121) argue that:

> . . . the leisure studies community is exploring ways to get closer to understanding the lived experiences of leisure and is also concerned about the way leisure is represented. Rather than simplifying and reducing leisure experiences, leisure studies schools seem to want to contextualise leisure experiences and treat them as a complex phenomenon.

In relation to the above, Parry and Johnson call for the creation and use of more imaginative and creative representations such as autoethnography, fiction stories, visual images, poetry, experimental media and performance. Hence, this study uses autoethnography, narrative, visual images in the form of metaphor, and poetry to study the embodied experience of the gaze in hospitality settings. The findings from the research will be of use to hospitality workers, educators, managers, policy makers and other parties interested in gaining an understanding of hospitality reception practice.

The Hospitality Work Context

Working as a hospitality receptionist lends itself to interaction, as it is foremost a relational activity that involves being linked to others through the duty to provide for people – guests, co-workers and managers – who are at different status levels. An essential part of this job is managing these dynamic relationships, especially interactions with guests. In reception work, guests must be served in such a way that their expectations are met. Some guests can be very demanding and even unreasonable. Expecta-tions can also vary from one guest to another. Guests may have expectations of receptionists ranging from a 'sympathetic ear' to a casual 'fling'. Receptionists must increasingly function within the strict dictates of service that require a high level of performance yet as Mars and Nicod (1984) argue the provision of hospitality has various idealized expectations built into it, some of which are fairly unclear. Furthermore, the quality of the guests' experience is a major part of the service that is purchased:

> The social composition of the producers, at least those who are serving in the front line, may be part of what is in fact 'sold' to the customer. In other words, the 'service' partly consists of a process of production infused with particular social characteristics, of gender, age, race, educational background and so on.
>
> (Urry, 2002, p. 61)

This can create a situation where the boundary between a server's personal and work self become fluid as management who direct the 'gaze' of the guest sometimes try to manipulate a server's appearance, speech and even emotions to satisfy the guests (Mars and Nicod, 1984; Wijesinghe, 2001). In providing hospitality in the contemporary hospitality industry, many pre-scribed service standards have been introduced which contemporary hospitality accommodation establishments – hotels and the like – are seeking to adopt. The hospitality industry continues to investigate its practices and to develop guidelines for good practice, which tourism and hospitality workers are expected to follow. In their marketing campaign, the industry highlights hospitality workers' caring and welcoming activities, appeal-ing to the desire of travellers to be welcomed, cared for and restored. The receptionists play a crucial role in instructing guests on how to make best use of their holiday. They have the peda-gogic role of educating the guests on what to consume and what to expect when on holiday. They are the orchestrators of directing the 'gaze' of the guests towards the kind of pursuits that the industry has made available for purchase. For reception workers, who are at the front line of this industry, meeting these elaborate and idealized requirements within the practicalities of the work-place and their personal circumstances can be a considerable challenge.

The extent of this challenge is highlighted by definitions of 'hospitality'. The *Concise Oxford Dictionary* defines 'hospitality' as 'the friendly and generous reception and entertain-ment of guests or strangers' (Youell, 1998, p. 3). *The Oxford Thesaurus* lists several words that have similar descriptions to 'hospitality', such as, 'graciousness', 'courtesy', 'friendliness', 'cor-diality', 'sociability' and 'generosity' (Urdang, 1991, p. 201). Other definitions of hospitality focus on commercial aspects for example 'a ser-vice relationship that involves supplying the amenities, comforts, conveniences, social inter-actions, and experiences of shelter and enter-tainment that a guest or customer values' (Youell, 1998). In hospitality practice, there is also a requirement to display specific emotions, gestures and discourses that the organization desires for the benefit of customers. As can be seen from these definitions, hospitality is a form of service that involves many intangible aspects. As Mars and Nicod (1984) have argued, speci-fying the boundary of a service is difficult. It is precisely from this inability to define the limits that complications arise in terms of how much service is good service, and when it is all right to say it is enough. This is especially relevant for understanding the 'tourist gaze' portrayed in this chapter. The context in which the tourist gaze takes place, the underlying qualities of hospitality reception work are presented in five conceptual themes. These are hospitality recep-tion work as: a service practice, feminized prac-tice, pleasing practice, ambiguous practice and culturalized practice. These conceptual catego-ries are described in detail below.

Service practice

First, hospitality reception work involves the provision of a service to a guest. From the ser-vice quality model and definitions of hospitality (Parasuraman, 1995), it can be seen that hospi-tality reception practice has a number of tan-gible and intangible components. The term 'service' denotes both the tangible element of providing food, accommodation and beverages as well as the intangible quality of the industry personnel to be hospitable hosts (Metelka, 1990). The intangible human element in the service interaction can be the deciding factor as to whether the service is judged to be good quality by the guest, e.g. '[e]ven if the hamburger is succulent, if the employee is surly, the customer will probably not return' (Sasser and Arbeit, 1976, p. 63, as cited in Urry, 1990, p. 68). It is often this human element that can make or break the experience for the guest. At every point of contact between frontline staff and a guest, there is an opening to make or break the experience. Jan Carlzton (1987), past president of Scandinavian Airline Systems (SAS) referred to this opening as a 'moment of truth'. A moment of truth is the point at which a server and customer interact to produce the service by the former and consume the service by the latter (Carlzton, 1987, p. 2).

As such, hospitality reception work can be referred to as a *service practice*, and can be shown to have a number of elements that typically characterize services. In providing good quality service there is a set of expectations, rules, roles and etiquette to consider. Perceptions of service by guests start with a set of expectations (Czepiel *et al.*, 1985). The expectations relate to the specific setting, server and type of service as well as to the prevailing ethos of the time. Derek Picot (1993) a former hotelier during wartime, writes that it is the server's responsibility to be genuinely concerned with the welfare of guests, especially the guests' safety, e.g. in his book on hoteliers he provides a heroic account of an Austrian hotel manager, who during the time of the war in Iraq in 1990 took the personal responsibility of delivering all his foreign guests to safety through the war zone. Picot's book describes hotel work as being exotic, amusing, bizarre, glamorous and sometimes even requiring real bravery (Guerrier and Adib, 2000, p. 256). Similarly, Telfer (2000) writes that 'Good Samaritan' hospitality depends on whether the service provider is able to identify with the guests' expectations and needs and is able to be compassionate and concerned.

Feminized practice

Second, to be hospitable hosts, receptionists are expected to be kind, warm, generous, nurturing and attractive (Novarra, 1980; Adib and Guerrier, 2003). These are qualities that are considered to be typically feminine (Leidner, 1993). The term receptionist in itself is a feminized noun. It is shown that the nature of receptionist work is highly gendered as it mirrors domestic labour provided by females in the home setting. Therefore, hospitality reception work can be conceptualized as a *feminized practice*. Being a receptionist not only requires displaying female qualities and taking on a female role, but also looking typically feminine especially in a way that attracts male attention, e.g. Adib and Guerrier point out that 'reception work may be constructed as women's work in that it requires a substantial amount of emotional labour. The physical appearance and presentation of a woman receptionist is important; she should be friendly, helpful and sexually attractive' (2003, p. 420). Employers also promote femininity as an asset of the company. For example, the Sri Lankan airlines used to run an advertisement which stated '[w]hen your business is business . . . our business is pleasure' (Joseph Treaster, as cited in Enloe, 1983, p. 33). Hall discusses how these qualities are implicitly incorporated into the procedures for recruiting, training and rewarding servers. She writes 'servers are required to present themselves as sex objects. Hiring young attractive women and dressing them in uniforms to highlight their "sexy" looks is commonplace' (1993, p. 456).

Pleasing practice

Third, the literature on hospitality frequently refers to the requirement to 'wow!' the guests; receptionists are expected to enchant, captivate, charm, magnetize, delight and enthral the guest in a number of ways, e.g. receptionists attempt to delight the guest by inducing positive emotions, or try to 'bring-around' the guest by transforming their negative emotions through the performance of emotional labour. Receptionists also provide a magnification of attentiveness to guests through the performance of recognition labour, which serves to pamper and spoil the guest. Furthermore, receptionists use their looks and speech to attract and charm the guests through the performance of aesthetic labour (Warhurst and Nickson, 2007), which is the projection of a professional image of well-presentedness and stylized communication. As all of these forms of labour serve to please the guest, reception work can be theorized as a *pleasing practice*. Telfer (2000) believes that not all who enter the hospitality profession think of it as just a job. She contends that making people happy by entertaining them could be a strong motive for entering the profession. Those who genuinely want to please the guests will do more than what they are expected to do, or they may ascribe some values to hospitality, to which they aspire (Telfer, 2000, p. 45). She states that 'if a commercial host looks after his guests well out of a genuine concern for their happiness and charges them reasonably, rather than extortionately, for what he does, his activities can be called hospitable' (Telfer, 2000, p. 45).

Ambiguous practice

Fourthly, hospitality reception work is an *ambiguous practice* as it involves both uncertainty and predictability. That is, on the one hand, hospitality servers are expected to follow management directions and provide a highly scripted, prescribed and standardized form of service; on the other hand, servers are expected to be self-directed and provide a highly flexible, unique and customized form of service. On one level, there is much uncertainty as to what actions are appropriate, especially when the exact nature of the service cannot be pre-determined. Examples include situations where guests need to be compensated in an appropriate way (immediately in real time) or idiosyncratic requests have to be met. Guests dictate the nature of the service, as in most other services. However, with hospitality, the dictates of guests are given greater priority because it is a high-contact system. That is, frontline workers have a high degree of contact with guests and as a result have to accommodate more personal requests and customize their interactions, as demonstrated above in the section on *Pleasing Practice*. As a result it is difficult to standardize or rationalize the service as the paying customer may provoke a change in the system of operation that may not have been anticipated (Urry, 1990, p. 68). What is required is for frontline

staff to be flexible in service delivery. As the organization's 'foot soldiers', they have to be given the responsibility to 'respond effectively, quickly, and courteously to the particular needs of the customer' (Urry, 1990, p. 71). Urry contends that the 'variability in demand for many services means that a considerable premium is placed on the flexible use of labour' (1990, p. 68). On the other hand, there are routine tasks that take place in the organization, which can be standardized and regulated to increase productivity and profit for the organization; this standardization can also benefit the guests as they may expect services that are familiar, efficient and competitive. This is where organizations such as McDonald's have been successful. Ritzer has shown that calculability, predictability, efficiency and control (1996) are the four most important factors that have generated success for organizations such as McDonald's.

Culturalized practice

Finally, hospitality reception work can be theorized as a form of *culturalized practice*, as it involves facilitating cultural relations. The study of cultural relations is important to understanding the role of receptionist. As Urry states '. . . work in tourist industries cannot be understood separately from the cultural expectations that surround the complex delivery of such services. Work relationships in tourist industries are significantly culturally defined' (1990, p. 41). As noted previously, meeting guest expectations is very important in hospitality reception work. Travellers from different cultures have different preferences and expectations, which hospitality reception workers need to understand and satisfy, e.g. those who come from a power distance society (Hofstede, 1979) expect the server to communicate respect and take a subordinate role. Reception work also has an American cultural bias in terms of the way in which service standards are set and behaviour is prescribed, and receptionists need to be able to choose between the cultural values inculcated during childhood from the new cultural values that they have learnt at their place of work. Sometimes the organizational culture, which has been adopted from American practices with little or no modification to suit the local culture, can lead to cross-cultural conflict, especially in situations where there are opposing points of view about how to behave in particular situations.

Having explored the underlying attributes of hospitality work, I now turn to discuss the 'tourist gaze' explored in this chapter.

Introduction to the Gaze

The 'gaze', which is a particular form of looking, functions within certain social codes of practice such as: what is the acceptable cultural norm of looking in the communication context? When is it appropriate to look? Whom could one look at? At what and where exactly should the eyes focus? What is the appropriate duration to hold a look? There are many ways of looking (e.g. see the poem *The Eyes Have It*; Baden-Semper, 2002), some looks can be unobtrusive while others may cause people to feel vulnerable, violated and/or sexualized as will be shown in the portrayal to follow.

In his seminal work *Ways of Seeing*, a book based on a popular British television series, John Berger observed that 'according to usage and conventions which are at last being questioned but have by no means been overcome – *men act* and *women appear*. Men look at women. Women watch themselves being looked at' (1972, pp. 45, 47) and women are depicted very differently to men precisely because '. . . the 'ideal' spectator is always assumed to be male and the image of the woman is designed to flatter him' (1972, p. 64). In advertising and in the presentation of females in service work, 'women . . . are being invited to identify both with the person being viewed and with an implicit, opposite-sex viewer', legitimizing the view that women should identify with men and make themselves pleasing for men (Messaris, 1997, p. 44).

Under the Tourist 'Gaze': the Receptionist Experience

In leisure studies, John Urry's work on *The Tourist Gaze* has been a major contribution.

Urry states that '. . . much tourism study is concerned with the consequences of being gazed upon, with for example working within a 'tourist honeypot' and being subject to a gaze is somewhat similar to that within a panopticon' (2002, p. 151). It is challenging for hospitality service providers to work under the tourist gaze. Urry observes that those in high contact areas such as hotel receptionists for example, have to work directly under the gaze of guests with no room to correct a mistake while striving to exceed or at least measure up to the expectations that the hospitality industry has set out for guests. For example, travellers typically arriving at their hotel from the airport or bus have learnt through advertising and word of mouth that they can expect to be greeted by a friendly and attractive receptionist who would make them feel welcome, arrange for their bags to be collected and escort them to their room. They expect the receptionist to converse with them in a concerned and attentive manner, sympathize with their difficulties and suggest interesting pursuits they might enjoy (and pay for) during their stay. As would-be guests on holiday approach the receptionist, their gaze can have multiple elements. One is an enchantment-seeking gaze as the guest contemplates the offering of the venue and its diversionary possibilities. This can be accompanied by a more transactional, appraising gaze getting a feel for the place and what might be on offer. The receptionist is effectively the recipient of the visitor's gaze and with it considerable tacit expectations and challenges are embedded in it. At the same time, the receptionist in her opening encounter meets the enchantment-seeking, appraising tourist gaze with her welcoming smile. Her gaze tacitly carries the welcoming work of hospitality. The receptionist practice manifested in her gaze has elements of caring, feminized, pleasuring, ambiguous and culturalized service. At the same time, her gaze needs to carry prudent appraisal questioning: will this person be a compliant, pleasant and generous guest? Are there signs of trouble to be noted? The receptionist's gaze needs to be alert as well as welcoming.

All the above aspects are illustrated in the stories the receptionists told of the tourist gaze and their response to the gaze (Wijesinghe, 2007). To be *gazed at* in certain ways and to *gaze back* in return was an intrinsic element of the receptionist's experience. This chapter explores a narrative of practice to uncover the ways in which 'the gaze' as a lived experience might be revealed. The narrative is produced by the receptionist herself and reflects the physical, spatial, temporal and cultural relations influencing her experience of receptionist work.

Methodology and Method

The research discussed here was developed within a phenomenological epistemology. Phenomenological research concerns the study of phenomena – what appears to a person in his/ her direct experience. As Carel writes:

> Phenomenology focuses on an in depth exploration of the lived experience or on things as they appear to us (rather than how they might be in themselves). This can be contrasted with a scientific, or objective, description of the world . . . phenomenology suggests focusing on what is easily accessible to us, namely, the different acts of consciousness (such as thinking and believing) and our experiences and perceptions (things as they appear to us).
>
> (Carel, 2008, p. 10)

Thus 'phenomenology must describe what is given to us in immediate experience without being obstructed by pre-conceptions and theoretical notions' (van Manen, 1990, p. 184). It is concerned with intuitively grasping and portraying presences, which are a pre-analytic primordial form of knowing. The qualitative approach adopted here begins with an exploration of a significant and typical event in reception work. This event illustrates *what it is like* to be the recipient of the tourist/guest gaze with its various overtones. The episode herein is chosen by the researcher receptionist involved in the study to typify significant acts of receiving the tourist/ guest gaze. Although, the word 'receive' is chosen here it should not be taken to carry overtones of compliant reception; to be the recipient of the tourist/guest gaze can be uncomfortable and unwelcome for some receptionists, and can involve acts of resistance.

In the study, the receptionists were chosen for their ability to articulate the experiential quality of their work. The interview of the receptionist begins by asking each receptionist to recount

an episode from their everyday practice that illustrates a significant element of their experience. The researcher asks the question: 'What happened?' This invites the informant to describe the event in her own words contextualizing the narrative as far as possible in the locality, people involved, issue in question and sequence of events. The researcher then asks a second question: 'What was the experience like?' In responding to this question the receptionist is encouraged to leave out as much as possible, pre-conceived understandings, notions and explanations about the experience. This is achieved by inviting the receptionist to express the experiential quality of her experience in colourful metaphorical language. This contemplative 'dwelling on' the experience, has a strong foundation in the expressive-phenomenological approach, which seeks to provide a textual representation of the so-called 'whatness' (what it was like) aspect of the specific experience. The researcher and the researched then collaborate to craft a vivid narrative account of the receptionist's experience.

Finally, the researcher asks the question: 'What sense do you make of your experience?' The way the receptionist made sense of her experience is then interpreted through hermeneutic analysis. Hermeneutics seeks to find significant patterns in the way people interpret events in their everyday experiences. These personalized meanings are then linked to relevant social discourses. Hermeneutics can be used to illumine the socially embedded nature of human consciousness, and has the ability to bring out elements of the episodes of reception work that may have been overlooked or repressed by the powerful agents of society. Being the recipient of the tourist/guest gaze, it is suggested here is one such significant element (Willis, 1999).

Portrayal of the tourist/guest gaze

The following narrative account describes the experience of a Trainee Hotel Receptionist in a five-star hotel in Sri Lanka, referred to here as *The Goldmark* (pseudonym). Part of our induction into the job at the Goldmark involved learning its style in personal grooming in order to ensure our image met the requirements of the corporate hospitality image of feminized attractive receptionist, e.g. we wore pink uniforms, which made us look very feminine and docile. We were expected to look attractive at all times; we were often sent back to the locker rooms to put on make-up if we came plain-faced or if we wore a lipstick colour that our manager thought was too bold or too pale; we were reprimanded if we wore flat shoes or didn't wear stockings. Although, what follows is an extreme example of the predatory gaze, it represents a commonly encountered element in the receptionist experience. All names and locations have been allocated pseudonyms to respect confidentiality.

The long-staying guests would often come around for a chat in the late evenings as most of the receptionists were generally on top of the administrative work by then and were waiting to receive guests. The conversation would sometimes revert to mild joking and teasing by guests, but not many receptionists were comfortable with this form of communication because of the social distance between the guests and the receptionists. The following story explores an uncomfortable episode for a receptionist subjected to the gaze of an affluent, long-staying guest at the hotel called Mr Abubakar. The story is recounted in the words of the receptionist involved.

Portrayal – The gaze of Mr Abubakar

Mr Abubakar was a well-to-do business man who stayed at the Goldmark hotel for extended times. He often behaved as if he owned the hotel and all of us in it; he would strut across the lobby and, direct us to change the background music, or adjust the air-conditioning; sometimes he would re-arrange the furniture in the lobby to suit his needs. He expected that rules would be broken for him. He often took his guests to house guests-only areas (such as the gym) or would go to the restaurant without a booking and expect to be served. Sometimes he would enter our back-office or behind-the-counter as if to test the limits of his privileged position within the hotel.

I found Mr Abubakar very intrusive on my personal space. He always peeped at me and breathed into my face, sometimes he would blow cigarette smoke into my face, making me really mad inside. His eyes had a sleazy, shrewd quality to it and it made my skin creep

especially as his eyes would move up and down my body as if I was a tasty morsel that he'd like to savour. Often I caught him, trying to look deeper into my cleavage through the deep-cut neck of our uniform. He was a shrewd man who would try to break my defences by poking his tongue at me, or sometimes even winking as if we shared a secret.

He always approached nearer than was necessary, so that I could almost smell his breath. He would sometimes blow cigarette smoke into my face and say 'have you got a smile for me, sexy eyes?' Occasionally he would reach over to brush off something from my face or pick imaginary lint off my blouse, making me very tense. He intimidated me with petty intimate nicknames, like 'cheeky face', 'miss prim and proper' and 'sexy eyes'. Mr Abubakar was never too explicit in his sexual comments, so I felt that I did not have any concrete evidence to take to management to complain against his harassment. Moreover, I wasn't even sure whether management would do anything about it given the fact that he and his cronies were valued customers. I also didn't have much confidence about such a claim because other receptionists didn't seem offended by him. They often said, 'well he is only a looker! Oh! He gropes sometimes, but it's not that bad as he'll pays you well for it after'. Hence, I was not sure whether I was over-reacting even though I knew he was harassing me.

On the day I recall, he came over to the counter in the early evening and I was on my own behind the counter. There were no other guests waiting for service. I saw him approach from afar, and tried to look very small and blend into the surroundings, hoping that he would not notice me; but I had no such luck. As he came towards the counter, as usual, his eyes moved slowly up and down scanning my face and body while holding my gaze; it was as if he was mentally undressing me, or as if I was a pawn in some distorted game he was playing. His gaze was not only lingering, but was penetrating with a leering quality, the fear of which caused goose bumps in my skin. I felt trapped in his intense gaze, with no way to exit. It was as if I was a rabbit confronted by the headlights of a car, unable to move away and acutely aware of his presence and power.

Still holding my gaze, he came to stand very close to me. I got a gush of his strong after-shave and looked-up more closely to scrutinize him, I noticed then, that he was wearing a shimmering black shirt, with black pants; his slicked hair was combed to the side, he wore a gold watch and was carrying his mobile phone and wallet in his left hand; and of course, it went without saying that he was smoking one of those strange cigars, that perhaps only the rich could afford. He looked like he was ready to go somewhere. I looked at him with suspicion trying to ascertain his intention and predict his next move.

As he came to the counter, I knew that I would be in trouble if I didn't look up at him and acknowledge him with a steady greeting; so I greeted him as usual and then lowered my eyes very quickly, to look down at my computer screen. My defence was to pretend to look very busy by focusing intently on my computer monitor, hoping he would get the signal that I was very busy, and leave, cutting his visit short. But again I had no such luck. He reached over the counter and bent over to the computer monitor.

'What are you doing?' he asked, blowing a cloud of smoke into my face. 'I am making some reservations,' I replied, without looking up.

'Busy day?'

'Yes, very.'

'What time did you start?'

'Three.'

A few seconds passed. He was silent as he stood there his gaze still fixed on me. I felt like a butterfly pinned to a board, as he held me in his gaze. This went on for some time, as the battle of our wills continued. Then I felt his fingers reaching over and lifting my chin up.

'Look up at me when you talk. This is no way to treat a customer now is it!', he reprimanded in a half serious, half teasing tone. I looked up at him . . .

'Now that's better' he said, and then he peeped closer at my face with a leering smile.

'You do have the most sexy eyes you know'. At this, I started to lower my eyes again, but he caught me off-guard by issuing an order, 'Print my bill!' Then as I looked up at him, he smiled and continued, 'I have come to settle my bill; and if you are good, who knows, I might even give you a tip. Now you would like that wouldn't you my dear?'

. . . The story continues . . .

This episode of Mr Abubakar illustrates some of the ways in which the receptionist is a recipient of the male predatory gaze. What follows next is a poetized reflection of being the object of this predatory gaze.

Portrayal through poetized reflection

Seedy eyes skewing
these clothes of mine;
Slimy eyes penetrating
this body of mine;
Swollen eyes groping
this skin of mine;

I am trapped with no escape,
like a butterfly, with broken wings;
I cannot flee, I cannot see,
like a rabbit in the light;

I have no face,
I have no name,
I am nothing, but a cardboard pawn!

The above poem expresses the feelings experienced by the receptionist during this episode. These are: feeling emotionally vulnerable and exposed, fear of feeling trapped, a sense of confusion and powerlessness, as well as anger at being seen as just an object to leer upon.

Portrayal through metaphors

The above narrative excerpt has brought a significant yet typical episode of practice clearly to mind, which is to do with the fluidity and precariousness of receptionist–guest relations. The researcher then collaborates with the researched (receptionist) to focus on this event-made-present *as an experience* by using a phenomenological approach, which develops metaphors to bring out the typical elements in her experience. Crotty (1996) has provided a number of 'sentence stems' through which the researcher and the researched could collaborate to generate a vivid expressive text. Examples of these sentence stems, which are to be completed carefully, avoiding analytical or explanatory comments, are:

Being gazed at in receptionist work in this episode of practice is like ....

Being gazed at in receptionist work reveals itself to me in this episode as ....

The experience of reception practice in the episode described above had several powerful dimensions, which the receptionist expressed in colourful metaphor summarized in the following points:

I visualise being the recipient of the tourist gaze, as being a display of candy in an open jar that is exposed for visual appreciation, but not for touching or tasting.

I perceive receiving the tourist gaze in reception work like being an ornament in a shop that customers might think they could pay for and possess.

I picture the predatory gaze in reception work as being like a rabbit confronted by the headlights of a car.

The feeling of the predatory gaze is like being a butterfly pinned to a board.

Being gazed at is like being scrutinised through an X-Ray machine.

Distilling the Phenomenon – Interpretation

The following are examples of some of the interpretative themes that were distilled from the portrayal of Mr Abubakar's episode:

- **Teasing the senses: 'lovely to look, but don't touch'.**
  Receiving the tourist gaze in reception work is like being treated as an inanimate thing, like an ornament on display. It has a sense of teasing the guests' senses, beckoning and saying, 'look but do not touch!' It is like being a dish of food to be smelled and appreciated visually, but not to be consumed. Receiving the tourist gaze in reception work is like being on display, like a dish of food, like candy in an open jar vulnerable to the temptation of guests.
- **Exposed and vulnerable.**
  Receiving the tourist gaze in reception work is like being a rabbit caught in a trap.
- **Being shaped into response.**
  Receiving the tourist gaze is like being offered a defining garment to wear and

accepting or modifying it in the act of putting it on.

Linking the Significance of the Phenomenon with Social Discourse

Exploration of power relations

As can be seen from the above accounts, the gaze of a guest can be received favourably by the host who offers invitations to sample certain services and suggests possibilities for other leisure pursuits. At the same time, the gaze of the guest can be seen as an 'intrusive eye' by the host who may react with a 'resisting gaze'. The resisting gaze is necessarily subtle given the asymmetry of power relations between the male guest who comes from an affluent social context and the female receptionist from a third world country who is in a subservient labour context.

The fact that Mr Abubakar was a valued guest held the receptionist back from wanting to complain about him to management. Interestingly, these sentiments are echoed by a number of service workers who experienced sexual harassment from customers: 'It's not really suitable to blurt out what you think in front of the guest. Waiters or receptionists are not supposed to react like that, even if they are really upset' (Folgero and Fjeldstad, 1995, p. 307). Folgero and Fjeldstad report that workers have felt that 'telling off' (scolding) customers for sexual harassment would constitute unprofessional conduct. Some workers were afraid to say anything because they did not want to jeopardize their job. Some felt it was part and parcel of the job, '. . . if you work in a reception you play the receptionist. Then you've got to take what comes, and make the best of it' (Folgero and Fjeldstad, 1995, p. 308). Folgero and Fjeldstad observe that some workers viewed their service role as being similar to that of an actor/actress in a theatrical performance whereby they were expected to act out a particular script. In this acting role 'the actor [sic] is like the whore who feels nothing for the man she is with, but lets herself go in his arms anyway as a demonstration of her professional competence' (Diderot, 1773, as cited in Roach, 1985, p. 138).

In Sri Lanka, women were employed in marginal jobs, the best of which is working as a receptionist and waitress, where they are easily made submissive to the manager's demands. Samarasuriya states that in fact women are sought after in these occupations because of their perceived 'submissiveness to authority and their lack of organizational background' (1982, p. 81), which allows hotels to exercise power over them to bend and form them whichever way management want.

Receptionists are also called upon to tolerate situations they would not normally tolerate, e.g. tolerating a guest who is verbally abusive. This involves not retaliating and holding back anger and frustration. This frustration is succinctly expressed by the following stanza:

> you've pinched me into submission,
> your breath reeking of insolence,
> neither blusters nor whispers but hangs
> inaudibly like an English oil.
>
> (Marcus, 1995, p. 251)

Next, the poet captures the resigned way in which workers live through the turmoil of not being able to express their true emotions:

> You are an insult to
> yourself because you request that
> which you are unable to bear.
> But you are forgiving, for what use
> is a great emotion?

The withholding of one's own emotions so that one neatly fits into the job description is the focus here.

Sexualization of the role

Urry argues that the male gaze, the male look is a kind of voyeuristic 'porno-tropics' and that 'tourism is often about the body-as-seen, displaying, performing and seducing visitors with skill, charm, strength, sexuality and so on' (2002, p. 156). In this study, the feminized and sexualized presentation of the receptionist is made available for the visual consumption as a well presented appetizing meal that is offered for visual appreciation.

Mason (1988) agrees that the typical image of a receptionist as an attractive female is promoted by male executives in the hospitality

industry who are seeking to capitalize and 'cash in' on the sexual appeal and sense of fantasy the image promotes. He also points out how this image is created and communicated to the public through advertising:

> on the cover of the Swallow Hotel's tariff the female Receptionist has her shoulder length hair in ringlets, she is wearing a wedding ring, make-up and a smile which displays her white teeth. With her wing collar shirt and puffed sleeves and her hand on the computer terminal she is both feminine, contemporary and efficient . . . and the decanter suggests that a warm welcome awaits the businessman in his home away from home!
>
> (Mason, 1988, pp. 286–287)

Mason shows how the weaving of this image is designed to lure the fantasy of businessmen. The female receptionist, who is presented as a social hostess, is 'someone who is made up to look beautiful in the eyes of men, and coupled with the appeal of a mother, appears domesticated, organized and an object of sexual gratification' (Mason, 1988, pp. 245–246). However, Mason believes that the projection of women in the reception role:

> . . . is nothing more than a softener, a placid and superficial projection of an image, created by men for other men . . . The image of receptionists becomes an advertisement for all that can be expected, it becomes a commodity itself: 'come to our hotel to buy our product and this is what will await you'.
>
> (Mason, 1988, pp. 245–246)

Adkins, in her study of female workers in the tourism and hospitality industries, established that the sexualization of women by the industry extends far beyond just sexual harassment:

> the conditions and controls which operated in relation to the appearance of women workers operated to sexualise them and to define them primarily in terms of their sexual attractiveness. This reduced their status as workers. The systematic sexualization of women and the conditions and regulations to which they were subject placed them in a situation where they were defined primarily in relation to their sexual attractiveness, and turned them into sexual commodities. These processes prevented women having any choice in relation to this definition (in how they were defined) . . . Failure to be sexually attractive (to be a sexual commodity) led to

dismissal, but it meant that the work they did and their skills went largely unnoticed.

(Adkins, 1995, p. 134)

The fact that women who did not package themselves as sexual commodities were not given recognition or appreciation of their work is fairly disturbing.

It is evident from what has been presented so far that the social engineering and packaging of receptionists in the hospitality industry provides a fertile soil for customers for fantasizing and stretching the conventional limits of service. In the anthology titled *For a Living: the Poetry of Work* (Fulton, 1995), a number of female workers speak out about how their gender is offered as a commodity to the public through their work. They describe how their looks, deportment, dress and tone of voice while representing a saleable feature of their work are used to lure customers to their side (Fulton, 1995, p. xviii). Similarly, workers on the reception desk as shown by the example discussed here were expected to perform aesthetic labour (Witz *et al.*, 1998) 'dolling' themselves up by wearing make-up, doing their nails and wearing tight fitting suits. Receptionists had to wear stockings even in the warm tropical weather so that they would not 'put customers off' by revealing any body hair. In *The Body*, Maxine Scates (1995, pp. 288–290) describes how she was vulnerable in her female body, and uniform of 'gold hip-length toga and calf-high boots with their gold trim':

> When I interviewed for my first job
> as an usherette at the Fabulous Forum,
> the interviewer asked, referring
> to the scanty toga I would wear,
> 'How would you handle a drunk?'

In this poem, Scates describes how she waited tensely not knowing the customer's intentions, and silently endured the unseen violation on her person, all in the name of her professional code of conduct:

> And when the men did approach,
> when they walked the cement steps
> down through the loges,
> the double letters of the alphabet,
> to where we stood, backs to the railing,
> we never knew if he needed to know
> where his seat was
> or if he was going to lean suddenly,
> whisper lewdly – but if he did,

> I took pride in knowing how to do my job.
> I exhibited restraint in the public arena
> where no one had to know what he was saying
> where he got to say what he wanted to say.
> After all, I was a Forum girl.

Sexual harassment is a significant part of the hospitality reception work experience because of the contested nature of relations between receptionists and guests. In a study of sexual harassment in the hospitality industry, Gilbert *et al.* (1998) state that it is very difficult to define sexual harassment, as individuals have different perceptions and thresholds of what constitutes sexual harassment. This is certainly true in relation to the experience portrayed here with Mr Abubakar, where the receptionist was uncertain whether his behaviour constituted sexual harassment because other receptionists did not find his behaviour offensive. The European Commission Code of Practice defines sexual harassment very simply as, 'unwanted conduct of a sexual nature, or other conduct based on sex affecting the dignity of women and men at work. This can include unwelcome physical, verbal or non-verbal conduct' (Gilbert *et al.*, 1998, p. 48).

Implications for Practice and the Professional Development of Receptionists

The implications of the study discussed here help understanding of the experience of reception practice in terms of what receptionists are required to do in the industry, why they are feeling the way they are feeling, and the skills, competencies, roles, personal attributes and dispositions that are needed to do this challenging work. The episode of practice explored herein has illustrated the fluidity, boundlessness and contradictory nature of relations in the receptionist–guest role. It brings into focus the fact that long-term, high-spending guests can sometimes think that the money they are spending can be used to stretch the boundaries of the hotel's offerings.

It also illustrates the gendered nature and sexualized element of reception work and the invitation to be compliant guests. The *invitational* character of hospitality has its risks, such as hoping that the guests will benefit from a hotel's offering, whilst knowing that what occurs cannot be wholly controlled or predicted; it involves being subjected to unknown ultimatums – rebuke, reward or camouflage/masking of behaviour by strangers/guests. Engaging in hospitality reception work is like accepting the risks and enrichment of inviting a stranger into friendship, while accepting the risk that the friend can also turn out to be an enemy. Similarly, if the guests are not properly schooled and converted, especially when they first check-in, then hostility can lurk in the background and guests can turn into enemies – angry, demanding, unhappy and manipulative. This can lead to tensions in the receptionist–guest relationship, as in the episode discussed here. Guests such as Mr Abubakar, who have slipped from being properly schooled in the culture of the accommodation establishment and who have not been converted into compliant guests, can become difficult to handle. They are not players and remain outside the game, making demands based on their own terms.

As every hospitality reception practice is embodied within a specific personal, social, cultural, environmental and commercial/occupational setting, each of these forces has many and varied possibilities for the experience to take shape, and each of these aspects have implications for achieving the challenge of converting strangers to guests.

Conclusion

This chapter explored the role of arts-based textual genre as an alternative approach to doing research. In the crafting of the episode, even though much effort was taken to retain the expressive nature of the themes, inevitably a certain amount of analysing took place, as the experience was translated into words and labelled and categorized. However, much thought was put into crafting the portrayal so that the experience of the receptionist could be brought to life in a way that readers could recognize the experience as a possible one, and create that 'aha, so, that is what it is like!' moment. The standpoint from which I speak in this study as a practitioner, relates to my positioning in the industry at the time. The receptionist presented here is a young, non-white, well-presented female, from a socially reserved culture (which tended to inhibit women's communication with people, particularly men not known to them) engaged in an occupational category that was perceived to have a low status. Her youth, femininity, non-whiteness, well-presentedness, non-social initiative taking and lowly occupation may in fact be a recognizable pattern for some guests – a particular mix of exotic, desirability and opportunity.

The story portrayed here, together with those depicted in the full research study are intersections of different personalities, cultural types and roles. These social and cultural factors had an important influence on the structure of the embodied nature of the receptionist's experience. The vignette discussed here reveals the feminized and sexualized nature of reception work, since the receptionist was expected to look feminine and display so-called female qualities such as nurturing, being attentive and sympathetic. When taken together with the wider findings, it is clear that the female receptionists studied were vulnerable to the way in which their sexuality and physical attractiveness were employed by the industry to tease and attract the senses of male customers and provide a focus for their fantasies. Overall, the issues raised by the experience portrayed here cannot be ignored.

References

Adib, A. and Guerrier, Y. (2003) The interlocking of gender with nationality, race, ethnicity and class: the narratives of women in hotel work. *Gender, Work and Organisation* 10, 413–432.

Adkins, L. (1995) *Gendered Work: Sexuality, Family and the Labour Market*. Open University Press, Buckingham.

Baden-Semper, A.R.N. (2002) The eyes have it. Available at: http://www.we-love-poems.net/readpoem. asp?Ref=9101 (Accessed 18 May 2009).

Berger, J. (1972) *Ways of Seeing. London*. BBC/Penguin: London/Harmondsworth.

Carel, H. (2008) *Illness*. Acumen, London.

Carlzton, J. (1987) *Moments of Truth*. Harper and Row, New York.

Crotty, M. (1996) Doing phenomenology. In: Willis, P. and Neville, B. (eds) *Qualitative Research Practice in Adult Education*. David Lovell Publishing, Melbourne, pp. 265–276.

Czepiel, J.A., Solomon, M.R., Surprenant, C.F. and Gutman, E.G. (eds) (1985) *Service Encounters: an Overview.* Lexington Books, Lexington, MA.

Enloe, S. (1983) *Making Feminist Sense of International Politics: Bananas, Beaches and Bases.* University of California Press, London.

Folgero, I.S. and Fjeldstad, I.H. (1995) On duty – off guard: cultural norms and sexual harassment in service organizations. *Organisational Studies* 16, 299–313.

Fulton, A. (1995) Fictions of the feminine: quasi-carnal creatures from the cloud decks of Venus – the cocktail waitress. In: Coles, N. and Oresick, P. (eds) *For a Living: the Poetry of Work.* University of Illinois Press, Chicago, IL, pp. 162–163.

Gilbert, D., Guerrier, Y. and Guy, J. (1998) Sexual harassment issues in the hospitality industry. *International Journal of Contemporary Hospitality Management* 10, 48–53.

Guerrier, Y. and Adib, A. (2000) Working in the hospitality industry. In: Lashley, C. and Morrison, A. (eds) *In Search of Hospitality: Theoretical Perspectives and Debates.* Butterworth Heinemann, Melbourne, pp. 255–275.

Hall, E.J. (1993) Smiling, deferring, and flirting: doing gender by giving 'good service'. *Work and Occupations* 20, 452–471.

Hofstede, G. (1979) Value systems in forty countries. In Eckensberger, L., Lonner, W. and Poortinga, Y. (eds) *Cross-cultural Contributions to Psychology.* Swetes & Zeitlinger, Lisse.

Leidner, R. (1993) *Fast Food Fast Talk: Service Work and the Routinization of Everyday Life.* University of California Press, Berkeley, CA.

Marcus, S. (1995) At the office. In: Coles, N. and Oresick, P. (eds) *For a Living: the Poetry of Work.* University of Illinois Press, Chicago, IL, pp. 251–252.

Mars, G. and Nicod, M. (1984) *The World of Waiters.* Allen & Unwin, London.

Mason, S.D. (1988) Technology and change in the hotel industry: the case of the hotel receptionist. Unpublished PhD thesis, The University of Durham.

Messaris, P. (1997) *Visual Persuasion: The Role of Images in Advertising.* Sage, London.

Metelka, C.J. (1990) *The Dictionary of Hospitality, Travel and Tourism.* Delmar Pub. Inc., New York.

Novarra, V. (1980) *Men's Work, Women's Work.* Marion Boyars, London.

Parasuraman, A. (Ed.) (1995) *Measuring and Monitoring Service Quality.* John Wiley & Sons, Chichester.

Parry, D.C. and Johnson, C.W. (2007) Contextualising leisure research to encompass complexity in lived leisure experience: the need for creative analytic practice. *Leisure Sciences* 29, 119–130.

Picot, D. (1993) *Hotel Reservations.* Robson Books, London.

Ritzer, G. (1996) *The McDonaldization of Society,* revised edn. Pine Forge Press, Thousand Oaks, CA.

Roach, J.R. (1985) *The Player's Passion, Studies in the Science of Acting.* University of Delaware Press, Newark, DE.

Samarasuriya, S. (1982) *Who Needs Tourism? Employment for Women in the Holiday-Industry of Sudugama, Sri Lanka.* Research project women and development, Colombo.

Scates, M. (1995) *The Body.* In: Coles, N. and Oresick, P. (eds) *For a Living: The Poetry of Work.* The University of Illinois Press, Chicago, IL, pp. 288–290.

Schroeder, J.E. (1998) Consuming representation: a visual approach to consumer research. In: Stern, B.B. (ed.) *Representing Consumers: Voices, Views and Visions.* Routledge, London.

Springgay, I. and Wilson, K.S. (2005) A/r/tophraphy as living inquiry through art and text. *Qualitative Inquiry* 11, 897–912.

Telfer, E. (2000) The philosophy of hospitableness. In: Lashley, C. and Morrison, A. (eds) *In Search of Hospitality: Theoretical Perspectives and Debates.* Butterworth Heinemann, Melbourne, pp. 38–55.

Urdang, L. (ed.) (1991) *The Oxford Thesaurus.* Clarendon Press, Oxford.

Urry, J. (1990) *The Tourist Gaze: Leisure and Travel in Contemporary Societies.* Sage, London.

Urry, J. (2002) *The Tourist Gaze: Leisure and Travel in Contemporary Societies,* 2nd edn. Sage, London.

van Manen, M. (1990) *Researching Lived Experience: Human Science for an Action Sensitive Pedagogy.* State University of New York Press, New York.

Warhurst, C. and Nickson, D. (2007) Employee experiences of aesthetic labour in retail and hospitality. *Work, Employment and Society* 21, 103–120.

Wijesinghe, G. (2001) Taking cultural differences into account in the delivery of emotional labour in the tourism and hospitality industry. Paper presented at the Australia and New Zealand Academy of Management (ANZAM) Conference, Auckland, 5–8 December.

Wijesinghe, G. (2007) How may I serve you? Women receptionists' lived experience in the hospitality industry. Unpublished thesis, University of South Australia, Adelaide.

Willis, P. (1999) Looking for what it's really like: phenomenology in reflective practice. *Studies in Continuing Education* 21, 91–112.

Witz, A., Warhurst, C., Nickson, D. and Cullen, A.-M. (1998) 'Human Hardware'? Aesthetic labour, the labour of aesthetics and the aesthetics of organization. Paper presented at the Work, Employment and Society Conference, Cambridge.

Youell, R. (1998) *Tourism: an Introduction*. Addison Wesley Longman, Harlow.

13 Seeing the Sites: Tourism as Perceptual Experience

James Moir

School of Social & Health Sciences, University of Abertay Dundee

Introduction

One of the defining aspects of tourism is that it involves sightseeing and capturing images of what has been seen. As John Urry points outs, the tourist gaze is a 'strategy for the accumulation of photographs' (1990, p. 139). This chapter provides a social constructionist perspective on the visuality of tourism and explores the ways in which it is located within an inner/outer dualism with respect to a mind that tries to apprehend, grasp, understand or make sense of sites that are visited. This kind of perceptual-cognitivism is a cultural commonplace, actively maintained in the accomplishment of a range of social practices, including the construction of tourism as one of visual encounter. However, the tourist gaze is also borne out of a separation between labour and leisure, one in which a view of the world is literally framed through acting out *being* a tourist (Osborne, 2000).

The advent of a mass tourist industry has been accompanied by a burgeoning popular tourist literature and media in the form of various guides, brochures and websites that contain a wealth of information about sightseeing. These commonly provide the prospective tourist with images that can be seen on-site in tourist destinations. Within this literature is an overarching ideology of tourism as primarily a psychological experience rooted in seeing. The tourist travels to be somewhere else, to see it

and to gain some sort of beneficial personal 'experience' from having seen. For most people, this is associated with a holiday and therefore what can be seen is often framed in terms of the temporal nature of the tourist's stay, ranging from the must-see short stay attractions to more extensive longer stay touring.

Popular tourist literature therefore conveys a sense of how other places can be experienced, understood and seen. And within this context, it is often framed in terms of seeing sites through which personal enjoyment is an outcome that is expected. This sense of enjoyment is related to the notion of the psychology of the tourist as visiting somewhere different in order to break with routine life and gain some recreative experience by sightseeing. Therefore, there is an underlying assumption of a psychology that drives what the tourist industry and its associated literature is about. The assumption is made that there are two realms: an external reality that acts as 'raw material' and the 'input' for a psychological system, which operates upon this in some way to produce an 'output' such as a perception or feeling which becomes treated as an 'experience' or memory to be drawn upon translated into talk and text. This decoupling of cognitive activity and social practices preserves an ideology of tourism and an economy of tourism as rooted in psychological discourse, and in particular the notion of personal enjoyment through sightseeing.

Sightseeing as Imagination

Much of the tourist guide literature refers to sightseeing and includes photographs of what are presented as notable places to visit. Therefore, the visual world for the tourist is a major aspect of the holiday experience. Such sites might include buildings, religious sites, natural scenery and so on. Some may be listed as 'must-see' whilst others are included in terms of a more leisurely or wider interest. Imagination is therefore a key aspect of these guides in terms of the presentation of photographs and descriptions for the would-be tourist to project a mental image of visiting a destination.

In other words, sightseeing as a form of visual rhetoric is founded upon an association between 'inner mind' and 'outer reality'. In this way, a major dualism is maintained in the popular tourist literature: a mind that tries to apprehend, grasp, understand or make sense or an experienced reality from page to place. This kind of perceptual-cognitivism is a cultural commonplace, actively maintained in the accomplishment of a range of social practices.

Although much of psychology is based upon a perceptual-cognitivist model of the person, it can also be found in less explicit ways within other, more unlikely, realms that accord more theoretical weight to social practice. As Potter and Edwards (2001) point out, the social theorist Pierre Bourdieu may be considered an unlikely advocate of cognitivism but his theorization of habitus (e.g. Bourdieu, 1977, 1992) trades on an unreflexive 'inner/outer' dichotomy. This presupposes the development of a psychological system in which dispositions associated with membership of social and cultural groups come to generate practices, perceptions and attitudes. This system is then able to produce 'meaning' (i.e. make sense), store and process it. Now whilst Bourdieu gives more precedence to social practice and culture than that of cognitive psychology, he cannot rid himself of this 'inner/outer' dualism and the reification of 'mind' as a perceptual system.

Whilst academic disciplines such as psychology and sociology trade on this dualism it is also, of course, constructed and maintained in less formal academic ways as part-and-parcel of everyday social practices, including tourism. Much of this is accomplished discursively in people's conversations and rememberings about their tourist experiences and in popular guides. Making tourism a visual event in this literature is therefore a means of maintaining the construction of a cultural 'inner/outer' dualism and the location of tourism within it.

Anti-cognitivism and Anti-foundationalism

In order to explore this issue, it would be unhelpful to start from the assumption that such a dualism exists, that there is a psychological system that operates upon an external reality. For one thing, such an assumption is not necessarily a cultural universal, and for another people themselves do not exclusively make reference to such a dualism in terms of 'sense making' as they engage in various social practices. This is not to say that it does not exist but rather that for the purpose of studying how people make use of this dualism within the world of tourism, we need not start from a cognitivist position. But why? The reason for adopting a non-cognitivist approach is that my focus is on how this inner/outer dualism is pressed into service as part of social practice that is constructed as tourism, and specifically within popular tourism literature. In other words, my focus will be on reality construction as part of what people do as tourists.

It would also be absurd to begin from a point of doing what I intend to study, i.e. how 'reality' and 'mind' are associated in order to do something or other. To take these as givens would be to fall back on 'experiential reality' as a 'bottom line' instead of examining what this dualism is used to do. The analytical pay-off for this is in terms of achieving a means of dealing with its sheer pervasiveness as a means of accomplishing a range of social practices. So my starting point is to adopt an analytically agnostic stance with regard to the 'inner mind' and 'external reality' and instead adopt an epistemologically relativist, or anti-foundationalist, position, i.e. to examine how versions of 'reality' are produced as part of what people do, and in particular as related to tourism.

This may all seem a bit abstract and part of some philosophically arcane debate on how we can 'know' what is 'real'. But the significance of such an analytical move is that it allows the focus of study to become how the relationship between 'mind' and 'reality' is not, for most people, some philosophical issue but a rather a practical sociological construction as they go about the business of constituting tourism as a certain kind of sightseeing activity. Much has been written recently about the discursive means by which people construct such an association (e.g. Edwards and Potter, 1992; Potter, 1996 ; Edwards, 1997) but there is much less of a discussion as to how this is accomplished through visual means as part of what constitutes tourism. The upshot of this kind of construction is that it is built around a certain notion of what the tourist 'experience' is about in terms of sightseeing.

This is what I wish to concentrate upon in the remainder of this chapter. In doing so, I wish to *draw attention* to two ways in which this is accomplished (a visual metaphor which *shows* how we routinely make use of the inner/outer dualism). One kind of move involves the use of visual rhetoric as a means of persuasion, as a 'reality-fixing' practice associated with a mental world of 'belief'. The other works in the opposite direction and involves the establishment of a person's state of 'mind' by the visual presentation of some aspect of their actions.

Making Tourist Destinations Visual Encounters

Let us take the first of these then, the means by which making something visual is presented as a way of constituting its existence in a particular way and that it should be 'believed' to be so. Within the sociology of scientific knowledge, there have been a number of studies (e.g. Lynch and Woolgar, 1990; Goodwin, 1995) of the ways in which much of scientific *practice* involves observation and the visual constitution of 'facts'. For example, in biology, scientists may present evidence in terms of images obtained from microscope slides as indicative of a particular pattern of say bacterial growth. In this way, 'growth' is constituted a biological phenomenon but of course there is nothing that is pre-conceptual or pre-discursive about this.

This process therefore involves constituting and labelling a phenomenon, which is then placed prior to this process as an already-existing feature of the world.

But whilst this form of constituting facts is the stock-in-trade of scientific practice, it is also a major part of the *modus operandi* of the tourist industry. Tourist guides and brochures commonly use visual images to establish the *nature* of places and sites of interest. The assumption is that people will employ their 'mental processes' to operate upon this material in order to 'understand' these places prior to visiting them. In this way, tourist sites are placed prior to this operation, as being a certain way and needing to be part of a sightseeing itinerary. In this communication model, there is a realm of places and tourist sites and a realm of mental operations requiring to be brought together. Photographic images are taken as enhancing this process, helping the reader to apprehend or grasp the nature of these sites. In this way the selection and active constitution of tourism as a social practice is occluded through the reification of 'reality' and 'mind', through the 'external' world of place that needs to be 'understood' by an inner mental processing system that 'perceives' that outer reality. It also creates a version of temporality in which the tourist destination becomes historically reified as something that has to be seen in a particular way.

Nowhere more apparent is this association between visual presentation and mental operation than photographs that are presented of 'must-see' emblematic sights. These are often associated with a mythology associated with 'inner' states such appreciation, wonder and awe. The accompanying text constructs these must-see sights as being of critical importance to *being* a tourist in these regions. However, some photographs may be used to stimulate sympathy, sadness or even a sense of outrage with respect to some sites that tourist should see (e.g. cemeteries, concentration camps, etc.). These sights are again presented as emblematic tourist destinations.

In this way, the visual and discursive are intertwined to maintain the old adage that a 'picture speaks a thousand words', that a photographic image provokes an active 'inner' response of imagination, of being a tourist at a given locale. Here then the use of photographs and accompanying text is associated with the psychological notion of provoking a reaction in terms of inner 'thoughts' and 'feelings', and the construction of oneself as a tourist. In this way, the inner/outer dualism is maintained as a pervasive discursive cultural common place, of the need to experience being a tourist through seeing these sites. In each case, the construction of 'mind' as 'working on' what is seen in order to constitute a tourist 'experience' is actively pursued. Here the individual brings his or her mind to bear upon the place that has been travelled to, thus preserving intact the notion of the tourist as primarily a psychological individual. The constitution of this dualism through the use of sightseeing is therefore a powerful and pervasive cultural feature, which is implicated in the exportation of tourism as a perceptual experience. It is the visual experience that is taken as provoking notions of a psychological 'reaction'.

In this sense, the reader of such tourist guides and brochures literature is positioned as 'outside' of the experience and needing to be 'drawn in' to being active participant, to see it with one's own eyes. Perhaps this is why these guides literally guide tourism as a form of sightseeing; they position the reader as having to be guided as to what to sites to go to and what to see in order to have a certain kind of psychological experience.

The Tourist Capturing the Image and the Image of the Tourist

I now want to turn to how the tourist is made visible through the very images captured when on site. It would be unthinkable for most us to be a tourist somewhere without a camera or camcorder. People want to have their own photographs and images of the sites they have visited. This desire to capture the image can be so strong that, despite 'No Photography' signs at certain sites (e.g. religious sites, palace interiors, museums etc.) people will routinely ignore these and attempt to photograph or video record what they see. There is therefore a sense in which being a tourist involves not only seeing for oneself but also of capturing images. Indeed as many tourists will know, it is often possible to spend more time actually capturing these images

when on-site that actually seeing things fully. It is also the case that people take photographs and images of themselves 'experiencing' being a tourist at particular sites and of 'enjoying' themselves. Here the focus is not on the place in itself but of photographs of tourists as being there. The socially constructed nature of tourism, as having 'been there, seen it and done it' effectively ensures its constitution as rooted in the psychology of the individual. Close-up photographs of smiling faces again serve to maintain tourism as a means of personal enjoyment.

These photographs and video recorded images are used back home to show to others or to remember what was seen. They also in some sense raise the visibility of the person as having been a tourist by virtue of having seen these sites/sights. In other words, people can point to these photographs and images as markers of their psychological experiences and enjoyment. It is a means of recalling being in *situ* and of *having* these experiences as a result that these images are used as a social practice of remembering and recounting.

Conclusion

The notion of these two separate realms that interact and where there is a process of influence going on between the two is therefore a major rhetorical feature, which is incorporated into the constitution of tourism as a visual encounter. It provides a means of trading on notions of 'understanding' as well as the portrayal of people's 'inner' mental states and processes states as related to their actions. Popular tourist literature presents a world of sightseeing in order to provoke an 'inner' reaction of wanting to be there. And for whatever else 'seeing' is in terms of requiring biological apparatus, it is nonetheless a social practice in which 'perception' is claimed to be its outcome, that is, an 'inner' mental operation on what is 'seen'.

Tourism studies could well engage with this examination of the ways in which an inner/outer dichotomy is constituted as tourism. I have briefly outlined a few ways in which this could be explored but a more thoroughgoing project could be incorporated into this field. For example, tourist sites of natural beauty are often seen in terms of provoking a sense of awe and of being struck by seeing them. There is often a kind of humanism at work here in which people look out onto nature as appreciation. What I have tried to argue in this chapter is that inner/outer dualism is a rich untapped area of work in tourism studies in terms of examining how tourism trades upon the notion of a psychological individual who brings his or her mental realm to the world of sightseeing. This in turn drives much of the tourist economy as people flock to places to see certain sites as constituting the very nature of the destinations they visit.

References

Bourdieu, P. (1977) *Outline of a Theory of Practice*. Cambridge University Press, Cambridge.

Bourdieu, P. (1992) *Language and Symbolic Power*. Polity Press, Cambridge.

Edwards, D. (1997) *Discourse and Cognition*. Sage, London.

Edwards, D. and Potter, J. (1992) *Discursive Psychology*. Sage, London.

Goodwin, C. (1995) Seeing in depth. *Social Studies of Science* 25, 237–274.

Lynch, M. and Woolgar, S. (eds) (1990) *Representation in Scientific Practice*. MIT Press, Cambridge, MA.

Osborne, P.D. (2000) *Travelling Light: Photography, Travel and Visual Culture*. Manchester University Press, Manchester.

Potter, J. (1996) *Representing Reality: Discourse Rhetoric and Social Construction*. Sage, London.

Potter, J. and Edwards, D. (2001) Sociolinguistics, cognitivism and discursive psychology. In: Coupland, N., Sarangi, S. and Candlin, C.N. (eds) *Sociolinguistics and Social Theory*. Pearson Education, Harlow.

Urry, J. (1990) *The Tourist Gaze: Leisure and Travel in Contemporary Societies*. Sage, London.

14 Goods of Desire: Visual and Other Aspects of Western Exoticism in Postcolonial Hong Kong

Hilary du Cros
Institute for Tourism Studies, Macao SAR, China

Introduction

The income levels of Chinese tourists have risen since the 1990s when they first started to travel en masse outside of China (Wong and Law, 2003). The rise of materialism and conspicuous consumption of Western luxury items is also becoming evident in trade council and media reports about China's more affluent groups, some of whom target Hong Kong and Macao for their shopping activities [e.g. HKTDC, 2007; *South China Morning Post (SCMP) Magazine*, 25 February 2007]. In the last ten years, marketers from Western countries have focused on China as a highly desirable growth market for their brands. Marketers of luxury brands are particularly interested in China's rapidly expanding urban middle class and their appetite for consumer high-end goods. Even the lower segment of this market is relatively affluent given that living costs and accommodation are still heavily subsidized by the government (Schiffman and Kanuk, 2007). These consumer goods are then displayed as visual affirmations of success: wealth defined by brands.

For many years, these consumers have spent their discretionary income on locally produced fakes and copies of Western items occasionally purchasing the real thing. Now they are no longer

interested in these articles, preferring instead to seek out the genuine articles while travelling. Why? Is it because these tourists are rediscovering new aspects of Western culture after the insulation of the communist regime or is this phenomenon a new phase in appreciating it? This chapter will first investigate the nature of desire for certain Western luxury goods in relation to the visual presentation to mainland Chinese tourists of one of the most consistently popular items: Western-made timepieces. Then it will examine the current situation with Hong Kong mainland tourist shopping experiences as a way of understanding how these tourists are starting to consume Western culture independently now they have more freedom of movement and the economic means.

China's First Western Luxury Consumer Goods of Desire: Clocks

Said's work has been instrumental in the analysis of the nature of Orientalism in the Western mind (Said, 1978). He cites the Treaty of Nanking in 1842 as a key turning point in Western trade penetration into China in that more ports were opened up and interaction could be carried on outside of official intermediaries of the Hongs.[1]

---

[1]These intermediaries were Chinese or Eurasian *compradores* (merchants) that were the people authorized by Qing dynasty to work between Western traders and mandarin officials, particularly as traders were discouraged from learning Chinese because of the imperial decree that foreigners should not be taught it. The lack

© CAB International 2010. *Tourism and Visual Culture*, Volume 1
(eds P. Burns, C. Palmer and J-A. Lester)

However, it is unlikely that even during the Ming dynasty that China was ever totally cut off. Trade had shifted from the Silk Road to the Silk Maritime Trade Route around South-east Asia and India. Direct contact was limited to adventurers, such as Marco Polo and Jesuit missionaries, many of whom based themselves intermittently in Macao with the Portuguese enclave from 1557. Some limited trade was established from this time that led to a greater awareness in the West of the quality of Chinese goods.

But what about the development of the reverse of Orientalism that might be described as Chinese notions of Occidentalism or Western Exoticism? What did China first want from the West, after being insulated behind its walls for many years after the demise of the Silk Road? There has been little formal study of this on the Chinese side but studies have occurred elsewhere in Asia into this issue, mainly in relation to consumerism in Japan or Hong Kong (Tobin, 1992; Mathews and Lui, 2001).

One of the few studies of the history of Chinese consumption of foreign articles comes from Beijing. There is a long history of Chinese appreciation of clocks and other timepieces, which has been documented. Researchers inside and outside the country are starting to publish articles on this history in English as they recognize that it is an important part of East–West relations. Pagani (2001) notes that this interest took off in 1987 when the Forbidden City Palace Museum sent an example of its collection of early European mechanical clocks to the USA as a travelling exhibition in 1987. It also included examples of early Chinese copies of these clocks with a high standard of artistry and embellishment. Although China had been developing mechanical clocks to replace water-powered ones, the Western mechanical clocks that arrived with missionaries derailed the process and then were imitated. The accuracy and performance aspects of the Western clocks were too attractive.

The Jesuit missionaries from Macao, who first introduced Western clocks to China, realized very quickly how desirable these items were to the Chinese. They recognized that these gifts were integral to gaining trust of the people at all levels. Matteo Ricci, a Jesuit leader in 1598 asked the Vatican for two specially decorated clocks to sway Emperor Wanli. The clocks were the beginning of the extensive Imperial Clock Collection (now in the Forbidden City Museum) and the reason for the construction of a clock tower for the largest clock within the city in the emperor's private garden. The Ming dynasty court enjoyed hearing the clocks strike or chime and clock appreciation became a fashionable pastime. Ricci also used clocks and the knowledge of their maintenance and construction to assist in converting to Christianity various Chinese mandarins interested in Western science and technology (Peterson, 1994). In doing so, he unintentionally achieved almost godlike status by being hailed as the Chinese originating master of clock and watch makers (Shucun, 2004).

The knowledge of clock manufacture was soon passed on as part of the diplomatic process with the expected result that many local versions would be produced. The first timepieces were much smaller than the Western-made originals, perhaps foreshadowing the advent of copy watches in the 20th century. The Qing dynasty continued the interest in clock making by subsidizing the local industry (Pagani, 2001). It is likely that many skilled watchmakers from Shanghai and Nanjing left China after the Second World War and subsequent upheavals leaving a local industry that is still regaining its name in terms of designing quality locally made items. Most copy watches and clocks of Western brands for sale in Hong Kong, as such, can be sourced to factories on the mainland where quality is sometimes dubious. Hong Kong now has a quality endorsement scheme that is set up to promote quality assurance for tourists, particularly with regard to the acquisition of Western brand name items.[2] Overall, the legacy of this interest in clocks and watches can be seen today in the high ratio of watch shops to other shops in most shopping malls in Hong Kong and the high number of advertisements in Chinese and English language media.

---

of direct dealings made trading less efficient and more costly for traders, who pressured for change (Garrett, 2002).

[2]It is called the Quality Services Scheme, but it is still unable to control the antics of camera salesmen on Nathan Road, who are notorious for their buy and swap scams (*SCMP*, 13 April 2007).

Shopping in Hong Kong and Modern Goods of Desire

Tourists from the People's Republic of China (referred to here as mainland Chinese tourists) are increasingly experiencing more travel freedom as groups and individuals than ever before. Since trips to Hong Kong and Macao were officially allowed in 1983 and 1984, respectively, outbound travel has bloomed. Leisure tourism has also become sanctioned and easier as a growing number of destinations have been added to the Approved Destination Scheme (ADS) with Thailand, Singapore and Malaysia attracting the most groups (Zhang et al., 2003). In addition to this programme, the Individual Visitor Scheme (IVS) was initiated after SARS to boost tourism to Hong Kong and Macao for leisure tourists with individual visas and the opportunity for more freedom of movement.

However, no other destinations beside Hong Kong and Macao have been approved for IVS at this stage by the national government. It is also inevitable that mainland tourists will develop their own way of experiencing Western culture that goes beyond what was sanctioned by tightly controlled tour itineraries to other destinations. Shopping (which will include walking and gazing in the malls) has emerged as a key activity and motivation for trips outside of China.

Initially, when finances are still tight most people will purchase the locally available copies and fakes in China, but as incomes rise there is a certain status attached to travelling outside China to purchase the real thing: a visual manifestation of wealth. Sometimes this acquisition will occur with some kind of proof taken, even if it is a photograph of the store in which it was purchased. Wong and Law's (2003) survey of tourists' shopping satisfaction levels in Hong Kong found that mainland tourists stood out from the rest as a group that was significantly concerned about quality of goods with higher expectations than any other group (Wong and Law, 2003).

However, some Hong Kong Chinese designers are trying to change the nature of shopping in Hong Kong away from just being a hub for Western derived brands at overblown prices in many cases. One such case is that of G.O.D (which stands for Goods of Desire). Its eye-catching brand name and attention to detail in the goods at a reasonable price have still a way

to go to be desirable to mainlander tourists who are fixated on luxury Western brands. The chief executive and co-founder of the firm, Douglas Young Chi-chiu, has tried to use Western-derived expertise in marketing and design to rework Chinese traditional craft designs for household furnishings. In this, his approach is not dissimilar to certain brands in Japan mentioned in case studies by Tobin (1992). Young's view is that his G.O.D. brand signifies goods that 'have a unique design of their own that will incorporate Eastern philosophy, practicality, aesthetics and value for money' (SCMP, 3 March 2007). However, at present his goods are more popular with Hong Kong Chinese and Westerners, who are more open to appreciating their ingenuity than with mainland Chinese tourists.

Western Exoticism and Tourism Research

Urry (1990) mentioned Orientalism in his work on The Tourist Gaze. However, he said very little about Occidentalism or Western exoticism. The latter term is a more recent concept than Occidentalism and occurs more in tourism studies (du Cros, 2002, 2005). The concept also appears in some studies of Chinese outbound tourism (Arlt, 2008). Western exoticism for the mainland Chinese tourist will not be generated by the 'Suzie Wong' orientalist flavour (that some Western tourists still see as exotic), but more from observing/participating in an experience, such as the Hong Kong leisure, shopping, gazing and arts district in Lan Kwai Fong. Indeed, the latter has been the subject of another study by anthropologist Cheng (2001) who found that even local Chinese find this district exotic and beyond their normal experience. Efforts to replicate Lan Kwai Fong across the border (du Cros, 2006) are not quite as successful as they lack the Western cultural underpinnings that have allowed the former to flourish freely as an 'icon of cosmopolitan consumption in Hong Kong since the 1980s' (Cheng, 2001, p. 237).

Arlt (2008) also emphasizes the role that popular culture and consumer goods from the West play in the expectations and perceptions of outbound Chinese tourists. He notes that because of this, Europe is likely to be viewed 'as a big open-air ethnological museum with shops attached'. This view is not the mirror image of what early Western travellers to Shanghai and Beijing perceived and depicted in early travelogues. It suggests that Chinese tourists are likely to require a shallow experience, which will not conflict with what is possibly a liminal state that they enter whilst in 'Elsewhereland'.

Liminality in tourism is usually associated with a process that the act of travelling inspires whereby a tourist leaves a familiar place (separation) to a destination (liminality in that it feels more dreamlike than the more familiar homespace) and then returns to the familiar place (reintegration) (McKercher and Bauer, 2003). The dreamlike state described by Arlt (2008) could be a mechanism that these Chinese mainland tourists use as a way of dealing with its strangeness and sense of cultural distance, or because they first experienced Western culture through theme parks in their own country not having access to outbound travel, or they are just there to shop and enter that state as part of it. Once in a liminal state, it is fascinating as a non-participating observer to watch how and what the mainland tourist gaze alights on in postcolonial Hong Kong!

Methodology

The main way of gathering data at this stage was through observing mainland tourists shopping behaviour as a non-participant. This observation was carried out over the month of March 2007 with interviews conducted several weeks after Chinese New Year in order to observe and gather data when shopping malls were less busy. Midweek was also a quieter time with most of the local Chinese at work making the mainland tourists more obvious by their shopping behaviour and clothes worn.[3] Some tour groups, it was observed were 'dropped off' by buses to wander freely and then picked up later at another point.

Both tour groups and independent tourists (under the IVS) were discreetly watched as to where they went and what they did. Shopping mall staff and guides were also interviewed.

Data was gathered by making notes, taking digital images and videos of behaviour and movement. This kind of data is not commonly available through undertaking interviews, travel diary recording or analysis of Internet text in blogs or forums. The results, however, were complemented by interviews with tourists, guides, shopping mall information desk staff, Hong Kong Tourism Board staff and shop assistants. Analysis of available tour brochures and tour operator websites was also made. A more extensive survey of tourists in Hong Kong and Macao is the subject of further study. Further data are also being gathered for both cities using travel blogs and chat room threads on specific issues in English and Chinese.

Results: Trawling the Malls and Markets in Hong Kong

Five of the key modern shopping malls and two tourist precincts were targeted for site observation. The shopping malls comprised the newest and most expensive, which were The Landmark, IFC (International Finance Centre) and Pacific Place (Hong Kong Island), and Harbour City and Festival Walk (Kowloon). There are a number of smaller and less salubrious shopping malls, but these are either likely to include more Chinese wares or copies (very discreetly as they are illegal in Hong Kong).[4] The two precincts, Stanley Markets and Lan Kwai Fong (both of which occur on Hong Kong Island), are both promoted heavily to all kinds of tourists by the Hong Kong Tourism Board. The results are presented in Table 14.1.

---

[3]Hong Kong Chinese colleagues devised a ten-point checklist of common mainland body language, grooming and fashion trends so that if the tourist has two or three of the key ones and a number of the lesser ones marks them as from the mainland. This list came in very useful as many Guangdong mainland tourists speak Cantonese and not Mandarin, so discreet eavesdropping does not always work as a way of identification of origin. As conditions change on the mainland and these tourists become more experienced travellers, it will be harder to make this distinction in the region.

[4]Although copies and fakes are technically illegal on the Mainland too, there has been little interest at the government level in cracking down on the industry as it could affect social stability and tourism. This is much to the disgust of many Western manufacturers, whom are concerned about intellectual property violations and subsequent loss of income.

Table 14.1. Summary of observations at Hong Kong Island and Kowloon shopping malls and precincts.

Place	Groups	Independent	Goods Available	Comments
Harbour City, Tsim Sha Tsui next to China Ferry Terminal	Yes – many	Yes – many	Almost entirely Western high-end designer fashion stores, watches, clocks and jewellery. One or two Japanese designer shops	Male tourists observed shopping for watches and female jewellery (for gifts); female tourists interested in cosmetics, clothes, shoes, handbags, jewellery and watches
Festival Walk, Next to Kowloon Tong MTR subway station	Yes – some	Yes – low to moderate number	Mix of Western, and Hong Kong high-end designer fashion stores (including G.O.D), Western watches and clocks and Western and Asian jewellery	Special Festival Walk Shopping Promotion in March/April moderately increased its profile with tourists as this is the most distant mall from popular mainland hotels; male tourists observed shopping for watches
IFC (Phase 1 and 2). Above Hong Kong Airport Express Station and close to Central MTR, buses, ferries, trams etc.	Yes – not many	Yes – a moderate number; some noted in Italian cafes too	Almost entirely Western high end designer fashion stores, watches and clocks, and jewellery. One or two Japanese designer shops	Male tourists window shopping for clothes, particularly Italian suits; some buying shoes; luggage was popular too; watches and jewellery
The Landmark, near Central MTR, buses, trams etc.	Yes – moderate number with some resting in the air conditioning around fountain on ground floor	Yes – moderate number of couples and singles	Entirely Western high-end fashion, watches, jewellery and some exclusive stores not found elsewhere (e.g. Harvey Nichols); and temporary store for Rugby Sevens in the basement	Female independent tourists focusing on clothes, cosmetics and shoes; male tourists on watches and suits; some group tourists just sightseeing and window shopping
Pacific Place, near Admiralty MTR subway station; buses, taxis etc.	Yes – some	Yes – some tourists with a higher ratio of male tourists, who were in groups together (business tourists?)	Almost entirely Western high-end fashion, watches, jewellery with local high-end department stores; Hong Kong designer fashions (e.g. only Shanghai Tang store in a shopping mall)[5]	Male tourists mostly who were on a mission to buy Italian suits, shoes and watches

(Continued)

[5]Worn by Angelina Jolie in the second *Tomb Raider* film with location scenes filmed in Hong Kong (for those who are interested in film-induced tourism).

Table 14.1. *continued*

Place	Groups	Independent	Goods Available	Comments
Lan Kwai Fong Precinct, Central MTR, buses etc.	Yes – some groups that were dropped off before or after dinner	Yes – moderate number of couples or small groups that were mostly window-clubbing	Small designer shops either side of precinct and mixed in with bars, clubs and restaurants; watches and handbags	Only shop that drew consistent interest was the new watch shop. Group tourists went inside and also took photos outside with staff
Stanley Markets, Stanley on south side of Hong Kong Island, buses and taxis only	Yes – only a few tours	Yes – but only a few tourists	Markets and small shopping mall that include mainly gifts, Chinese souvenirs, Western paintings/ prints, not much jewellery or watches	This is a Western tourist spot which has mainly Chinese/Asian goods but some Western clothes, sports shoes and other items; even so, some Mandarin speaking tours do come here to shop

From the table, it appears that the Kowloon shopping malls are the most popular, particularly with group tourists from nearby Guangdong province coming by ferry or train and who speak Cantonese. The Hong Kong Island malls are close to the airport express train station and are within close walking distance to most of the international five-star hotels. More independent tourists were observed in Hong Kong Island malls throughout the day; however, group tours visited Lan Kwai Fong and Stanley Markets at specific times. Without surveying tourists about their respective income levels and type of accommodation booked, it is difficult to be sure that there was a concentration of wealthier tourists targeting the Hong Kong Island malls, although it seems likely.

The independent tourists observed also visited more Western designer and exclusive shops (small and department) than group tourists. Shop assistants confirmed that their Western brand name stores tend to attract the wealthier independent tourists for purchases of gifts and fashion items, and not the group tourists who window-shop.[6] There were differences observed by shop assistants and the author regarding what male and female independent tourists were inspecting or buying. Male tourists were especially focused on Western watches, suits[7] and shoes intended for themselves as business apparel. Female tourists seemed to be more interested in Western brand designer clothes, shoes, luggage and watches as well as jewellery and cosmetics. Italian, French and English brands seemed to attract the most interest, while reputable Asian and Hong Kong brands were much less popular with this type of tourist. American brands seemed popular with younger tourists, e.g. designer Levi's jeans. All these stores (except the Asian designers) use Western models in shopfront and promotion photographs and as manikins. All these goods are objects for displays of visual, conspicuous consumption.

Watches were popular with everyone and were the busiest shops in Harbour City and Lan Kwai Fong. The photo-taking behaviour to verify genuine purchase was noted at the

[6]Budget tour groups tend to be taken to outlets and shops that pay the guide a commission as this is the guide's only way of earning an income out of the trip that is sold to tourists at a rock bottom price. The Hong Kong Tourism Board is trying to discourage this kind of tour, but it is still popular with first time travellers with limited resources and those who want to spend almost all their money on shopping.

[7]These are usually worn without ties as few offices are air-conditioned. Lack of tie-wearing with a suit is on the spot-the-mainlander checklist for male tourists, along with sports t-shirt with suit pants and shoes (again because of the air-conditioning issue).

Fig. 14.1. An Armani watch store with small windows to focus attention and indicate exclusiveness.

latter, which the author has only ever seen before online in Internet blogs. Jewellery shops were the next most popular. Both types of shops stand out in malls and shopping precincts visually as the most brightly lit, sometimes with the smallest display windows (e.g. Cartier) indicating rarity and exclusiveness (Fig. 14.1).

Many shops and cafes also stressed their longevity as businesses with foundation dates above doors (Fig. 14.2). The Levi shop in Harbour City was especially notable for its over-the-top attempt at this aspect in its display window. It had extensive text about the history of the brand and in its role in American culture and history. It is likely that some marketers have realized that businesses that have been prosperous continually attract some respect from many Chinese people aware of how difficult it is to keep enterprises going through political and social upheavals. Businesses with a long history are still found in Guangdong, but so few that they are sometimes celebrated with a type of heritage listing (du Cros and Lee, 2007). Interviews with shop assistants and managers indicate that this marketing ploy is also aimed at cementing the idea of the brand's iconism in the consumer's mind.

It is also common in Asia to find Hollywood movie stars endorsing designer fashion items, e.g. Brad Pitt for Tag Heuer watches, which they would not do as blatantly in the West (Fig. 14.3). Even if mainland tourists have not heard of these people, the glamorous photographs add to their enjoyment of the Western exoticism of the shopping experience. This is particularly the case for those who are only window-shopping on one trip, but who may come back to shop seriously on a later one.

Western tourists were evident at most shopping places, but were most numerous at Stanley Markets. The precinct was added as a control in the study, because it carries mainly Chinese souvenirs of interest to Orientalists or Western tourists. It was observed that window-shopping at Stanley Markets also involved some mainland tourists watching what the more numerous Western tourists did and bought. Later in the day, mainland tourists were observed going off to also photograph Western historical buildings nearby, such as Murray House, as well.

Finally, all the new modern shopping malls are noted for having up-scale Western style

Fig. 14.2. An Italian coffee bar at IFC on Hong Kong Island makes the point very strongly that it is a continuously run business and genuine.

Fig. 14.3. An example of a Western celebrity doing an endorsement to add glamour and credibility to a Western product in Asia. Brad Pitt endorses Tag Heuer watches.

restaurants and cafes where weary shoppers can rest and refresh. The mall with the most mainland tourists, Harbour City in Kowloon, listed these establishments on its store location map as 'Western Delicacies', which is a very literal translation into English of the Chinese category name on the same signboard.

Discussion

One argument for mainland Chinese tourist gaze focusing on Western luxury goods is that they are now fashionable as a class of consumer item useful for displaying status by China's increasingly upwardly mobile middle-class. It has already been observed that societies that retain some underlying Confucian values often link consumption to 'face' and status for both the individual and family. Wong and Ahuvia (1998) were the first to note this in their cross-cultural study of luxury consumption. More recent research into the hierarchical nature of such societies indicates that conspicuous consumption of luxury items is one way of promoting one's status to the rest of the community and affirming success (Yeung, 2000). Shopping bags bearing designer goods logos or the display of the goods themselves relay this message as a symbol of class identification or specific personal attributes to observers.

The emerging nouveau riche and middle-class mainland professionals have been seeking to purchase luxury goods in higher quantities than previously before (despite the current economic crisis) including; Western luxury cars, timepieces, home furnishings, designer handbags, luggage and clothes. This is not just one monolithic market: it could be divided further by age and income into at least two sub-categories. An older generation of entrepreneurs and economic pioneers who are starting to retire that are distinct from younger professionals who grew up and started their careers during China's economic reforms after 1980. Both are interested in luxury Western brands, but for slightly different reasons. The key characteristics of this latter younger group can be termed the 'Three Highs' in typical mainland Chinese fashion: high rank, high education and high income levels. A recent Hong Kong Trade Development Council report (2007) notes that this group is a,

> . . . new generation of mainland consumers (that) is typically leading a stressful life and thus they crave for a leisurely and carefree lifestyle . . . . They would buy luxury items, frequent high class venues, drink red wine, play golf, buy collectibles and travel overseas to reward themselves for working hard and to reaffirm their self worth.
>
> (HKTDC, 2007, p. ii)

The report also notes that this generation does not go after Western luxury products blindly, but with reference to their own hopes and aspirations. The youngest of this group are known in China as the *balinghou* or the '80s generation', born after the economic reforms began. Their attitudes to consumerist culture are totally different to that of many of their forebears (*SCMP*, 30 January 2008).

Conclusions

There are currently two general groups of mainland tourists featured in this discussion: group tours and independent tourists (who are more likely to be *balinghou*). It is likely that these could be broken down into more sub-groups with further research (e.g. overseas-educated returnees, experienced business travellers, first time travellers, anglophiles and extreme shopping tourists). Each would have a different way of appreciating Western culture and its centrality to their trip to postcolonial Hong Kong. However, it is clear that the brands marketed in the larger shopping malls know their target market well and are good at encouraging a liminal shopping experience with the clever use of Western trappings. Visual aspects of the experience include, but are not limited to, the nature of the displays, lighting, promotional photography, historical symbolism, iconography and even glamorous associations with film stars. The shopping experience can comprise window shopping, sometimes purchasing, watching other tourists, buying drinks, eating in Western style cafes and photographing Western historic buildings nearby.

Other factors yet to be appreciated are the impact of travel to Western destinations for non-leisure related reasons and how the China outbound market develops generally, as the Chinese middle class become more experienced travellers and consumers. These factors may have an influence on what is desired in the future by such tourists. Tastes may develop in a similar direction to those of Hong Kong Chinese, who are more comfortable with postcolonial Hong Kong designer brands, such as G.O.D. and Shanghai Tang, which are local/Asian brands with Western marketing influences. Alternatively, as the mainland Chinese outbound tourist market develops, it could be influenced by other countries' marketing in the region. Japanese and Korean luxury fashion brands could also become more popular with the younger Chinese market. Marketers of shopping malls with predominantly Western brands and the shops themselves will have to be aware of these trends too and others as China travels. In the meantime, most Chinese mainland tourists are still likely to be very interested in (genuine) Western-made watches!

Acknowledgements

Thanks should be accorded to Chin Ee Ong first for his assistance in translating and locating relevant travel blogs and signboards for this project. Also I would like to thank my Hong Kong colleagues, Euphemia Chow and Ceda Leung, who assisted me in devising a checklist for identifying mainlander tourists, so I could be sure I was observing the right people discreetly.

References

Arlt, W. (2008) Chinese tourists in 'elsewhereland': behaviour and perceptions of mainland Chinese Tourists at different destinations. In Cochrane, J. (ed.) *Asian Tourism: Growth and Change*. Elsevier, London.

Cheng, S.L. (2001) Consuming places in Hong Kong: experiencing Lan Kwai Fong. In Mathews, G. and Lui, T.L. (eds) *Consuming Hong Kong*. Hong Kong University Press, Hong Kong, pp. 237–262.

du Cros, H. (2002) The 'culture' in cultural tourism experiences: is exoticism dead or is it out shopping? In: Chon, K., Zhang, H. and Xie, Y. (eds) *Asia Pacific Tourism Conference 2002 Conference Proceedings*, Dalian, China, pp. 278–281.

du Cros, H. (2005) The concept of western exoticism and its utility in the development of cultural tourism products for Asian tourists in Asian destinations. Regional Branding Conference IFT/Purdue, December 2005.

du Cros H. (2006) The 'romantic European culture island' with a turbulent history: the intrinsic and extrinsic values of Shamian Island, Guangzhou. *China Tourism Research* (Chinese and English), 193–220.

du Cros, H. and Lee, F. (2007) *Cultural Heritage Management in China: Preserving the Pearl River Delta Cities*. Routledge, London.

Garrett, V. (2002) *Heaven is High, the Emperor is Far Away. Merchants and Mandarins in Old Canton*. Oxford University Press, Hong Kong.

Hong Kong Trade Development Council (2007) *New Generation of Mainland Consumers*. Hong Kong Trade Development Council, Hong Kong.

Mathews, G. and Lui, T.L. (2001) *Consuming Hong Kong*. Hong Kong University Press, Hong Kong.

McKercher, B. and Bauer, T. (2003) Conceptual framework of the nexus between sex and tourism. In: McKercher, B. and Bauer, T. (eds) *Sex and Tourism. Journeys of Romance, Love and Lust*. The Haworth Hospitality Press, Binghamton, NY, pp. 3–18.

Pagani, C. (2001) *Eastern Magnificence and European Ingenuity: Clocks of Late Imperial China*. University of Michigan, Ann Arbor, MI.

Peterson, W. (1994) Why did they become Christians? Yang Tingjun, Li Jizao and Xu Guangqi. *Review of Culture* 2, 95–110.

Said, E.W. (1978) *Orientalism*. Peregrin Books, London.

Schiffman, L.G. and Kanuk, L.L. (2007) *Consumer Behavior*, 9th edn. Dorley Kindersley, New Delhi.

Shucun, W. (2004) *Chinese Gods of Old Trades*. Foreign Languages Press, Beijing.

South China Morning Post, 30 January 2008, p. C5.

South China Morning Post, 13 April 2007, p. C1.

South China Morning Classified Post, 3 March 2007, p. 8.

South China Morning Post Magazine, 25 February 2007, pp. 16–20.

Tobin, J. (1992) *Re-made in Japan: Everyday Life and Consumer Taste in a Changing Society*. Yale University Press, New Haven, CT.

Urry, J. (1990) *The Tourist Gaze: Leisure and Travel in Contemporary Societies*. Sage, London.

Wong, N.Y. and Ahuvia, A.C. (1998) Personal taste and family face: Luxury consumption in Confucian and western societies. *Psychology and Marketing* 15, 423–441.

Wong, J. and Law, R (2003) Diference in shopping satisfaction levels: a study of tourists in Hong Kong. *Tourism Management* 24, 401–410.

Yeung, L. (2000) Consuming designer fashion in Hong Kong. *The Hong Kong Anthropologist* 13, 34–41.

Zhang, Q.H., Jenkins, C. and Qu, H. (2003) Mainland Chinese outbound travel to Hong Kong and its implications. In: Lew, A. Yu, L. Ap, J. and Zhang, G. (eds) *Tourism in China*. The Haworth Press, Binghamton, NY, pp. 277–296.

15 Mauritanian Guestbook: Shaping Culture while Displaying it

Maria Cardeira da Silva

Center for Research in Anthropology, Universidade Nova de Lisboa, Lisboa, Portugal

Introduction

Tourism, heritage and cultural display confirm that the present era is nothing if not an age of resilience and tough modernity. However, this does not imply an essentialized view of touristic encounters and culture displays. It merely affirms that the gaze of others is bound up in the West's historical way of seeing, as scientific examination, optical entertainment and aesthetical contemplation – as Bennett (1988) and Urry (1991) put it, following Foucault – imposing the visual gaze as a pervasive way of recognizing and organizing the world. Yet, simultaneously, and because of the pervasiveness of this gaze, it is possible nowadays to discover a variety of ploys by which it is enacted, as well as different ways of dealing with it. For this reason, I favour a comparative dialogue among different ethnographies of touristic and other sites of display of culture, a comparative trend that anthropology has neglected, when culture as *monographicable* substance came under criticism from the 1970s. My theoretical setting will thus be that of Mitchell (1991) and Bennett (1988) and their exhibitionary complexes,

arguing that cultural displays – often created by colonial impulse or other asymmetrical conjunctures – make people feel culturally knowledgeable and thereby cultured themselves. At the same time, in order to pursue my statement above, I will argue that sites of cultural display enacted by tourism are a good basis for comparative experimentation, precisely because, while sharing this universal and inescapable subordination to the visual gaze, they respond differently and imaginatively to it, in accordance with their partners, who mutually gaze at each other. To understand 'local touristic culture', you cannot ignore the economic, social, racial, and gender and other identity differentiation frameworks, within which it is produced and reproduced.

In order to illustrate this, I will take two main sites of cultural transaction and display in Ouadane – an emerging oasis on the new tourist routes of the Adrar in Mauritania – where I undertook fieldwork for 3 years (between 2003 and 2006).[1] These will be: (i) the exhibitionary procedures of local 'museums' that are mushrooming in response to the increasing touristic demand; and (ii) guestbooks and placards exhibiting tourist experiences

[1]The research was conducted within the framework of the project *Portuguese Castles I* (http://castelos-a-bombordo.tiddlyspot.com) and more recently of the project *Portuguese Castles II. On Heritage, Tourism and Portuguese Cultural Cooperation in African Context*, which I am currently co-ordinating. This article benefited from a teamwork spirit, which encouraged shared information among all the researchers, whom I would like to thank here. Both projects are funded by the Portuguese Foundation for Science and Technology.

and photos at Mauritanian guesthouses. This will also allow me to consider together two aspects of touristic sites, which, as Bell Dicks has already suggested, are inseparable: visibility and visitability.

Ouadane and its routes

Ouadane, a small oasis of some 2300 inhabitants in the desolate Adrar, has recently entered the touristic routes of the Mauritanian desert. Ouadane belongs to the route of holy libraries – along with Chinguetti, Tichitt and Oualata – and shares with these other towns the symbolic capital of knowledge and religiosity gathered during centuries of pilgrimage flow, coming from the south on their way to Mecca. This symbolic capital, together with its architectonic materialization, has recently attracted the first impulses of patrimonialization in contemporary Mauritania.

It is true that Mauritania, and the Adrar in particular, is rich in archaeological remains and other heritage, most of it yet to be explored. Its symbolic value was raised and charted by romantic perambulations like those of Théodore Monod and Odette du Pigaudeau and, of course, Saint Éxupèry. Desert, ruins, enigmatic stones, unexplored caves, pre-historic paintings and Neolithic ateliers lost in the sand, maritime fossils 500 miles away from the coast . . . All seem to have been lying buried in the sand until the fever of patrimonialization broke out in the 1990s. French colonization cared less about this patrimony than, for instance, its Moroccan heritage. After all, Mauritania, and particularly the Adrar, in the north of the country, was seen mostly as a military, sandy and harsh district of its Central African (rhetorically *less* Arab) possessions. But in due course, as culture became an important resource all over the world, Ouadane, Chinguetti, Tichitt and Oualata achieved the classification of World Heritage (UNESCO, 1996), by the hand of the Mauritanian *Fondation Nationale pour la Sauvegarde des Villes Anciennes*.

Although colonial France did not invest that much in this scattered heritage concealed in Mauritania, its 'empty' and sandy space was early on domesticated and charted with automobile rallies, which regularly crossed distance and time, propelling modernity, continuing up to the present, indifferent to cultural borders or historical events, such as decolonization. The Paris–Dakar rally – which has now recently moved to South America because of attacks that stopped the last rally from taking place[2] – has naturally played an important role in divulging the attractions of the Mauritanian landscape. Nevertheless, in order to understand the recent development of touristic impulse, an apparently less relevant event should be considered: the making of *Fort Sagan* – a film directed by Alain Corneau in 1984 (Fig. 15.1).

The way in which this film promoted Mauritanian landscape and Mauritanian people, staged or unstaged, would be another interesting topic to develop here. However, I will take another path. This is because *Fort Sagan* has not only shaped Western representations of Mauritania (as did the Paris–Dakar rally), but also provided the first infrastructural means to launch a small burgeoning industry in the north of Mauritania. Local memory of the origins of tourism in Mauritania states that the first local tour company – the *Adrar Voyages* – was formed from the remnants of automobiles and other foreign engines, networks, ideas and expertise left behind the making of *Fort Sagan*.

It was only 10 years later that the Mauritanian government began to control touristic activities. This left enough time for informal activities and businesses to rise and to mushroom. Local people began to build lodges and inns in the oasis to welcome the emergent routes of *meharists* or walking tourists now crossing the white dunes guided by Bedouins who had previously herded cattle or had been traders. The number of tourists increased as the first charter flights began to land, every Sunday, in Attar, the capital of the district of Adrar. During the tourist season of 2004–2005 (from October to April) 9923 tourists of 39 nationalities (but mainly French) landed in Attar. Numbers kept rising until the attacks that justified the Paris–Dakar transfer to South America, in 2007.

Spontaneous Museums

It is from Attar that the majority of tourists arrive at Ouadane, walking, riding a camel or driving

---

[2]And this clearly affected tourism fluxes in Mauritania.

Fig. 15.1.   Fort Sagan inspiration. Copyright Maria Cardeira da Silva, CEAS/CRIA, FCT.

a four-wheel drive. They come inspired, among other things, by the illusion of a bare desert landscape, unaware of the warning signs that bound it.

However, to some of them, the desert itself no longer provides an inexhaustible motivation, or the exclusive inspiration for their journey, as it might have been for romantic travellers. (And I shall not mention here those for whom Africa has become a gym of sorts, the challenging continent where you test your physical endurance and push your own limits.)

Presently, sightseeing increasingly involves the search for cultural meaning. And since culture is not antithetical to sightseeing and other touristic activities, heritage has become a shared agenda in Ouadane as elsewhere.

As Kieshenblatt-Gimblett (1998) puts it, sites of display aim to reduce the amount of down time and dead space between high points. Local 'spontaneous' museums in Ouadane, as in the surrounding desert, have overcome the danger of cultural insignificance, where cultural evidence is hard to locate and to consume (Fig. 15.2).

The proliferation of local museums, their exhibitionary options, the selection of artefacts for display and the performance of chosen objects allows us to visualize the way local culture is being produced and reproduced through its materialized exhibition, and ordered through imported categories and market demand. Local patrimonialization and local 'museum' procedures respond mainly to the impulse of salvation that motivates tourists and, because of that, exhibits culture as a total, pristine, fragile and anachronous, therefore external, product. But, ironically, although local owners strive to classify and display culture in a thematic and chronological way – as it is represented in a conventional museum – their lack of museographic means and skills makes them, unadvisedly, replicate some postmodernist approaches adopted in exhibition displays, juxtaposing different items together with fragments and other cultural detritus, to be reinterpreted.

In reducing the amount of down time and dead cultural space between high points, spontaneous museums trace the new routes of tourist caravans. They thus help to include new spots in these routes. On the other hand, in places like Ouadane, these museums can make tourists spend more time in the town and, eventually, encourage them to spend the night in one of its guesthouses.

Fig. 15.2.   Desert displays. Copyright Maria Cardeira da Silva, CEAS/CRIA, FCT.

In the specific case of Ouadane, something else has contributed to its touristic capitalization and to place it on the tourist route: this was the construction of the walls around the ruins of the *ancienne ville* (Figs 15.3 and 15.4).

The construction of these walls was subsidized under the scope of a bilateral co-operation agreement signed by the Portuguese and the Mauritanian governments. Such co-operation was inspired by the idea that the Portuguese had built a trading post there in the 15th century in order to intercept the caravans of Saharan merchants (something still to be archaeologically confirmed). In fact, the construction of the walls has played an important role in the touristic promotion of Ouadane, since it permitted a new reading of the landscape: something which used to be a pile of stones became 'ruins' and earned a symbolic density that enabled it to be transformed into a touristic attraction. A touristic attraction that appeals to the preservationist rationale, the salvage impulse (Butcher, 2003) that leads most tourists to Ouadane. Those ruins are the remains of a past that deserves all efforts to preserve it, since it supports the identity of cultures: remains of culture. What most tourists are not aware of is that,

although Ouadane has obviously its own history that it strives to save – and now to display as merchandise for tourists – the type of construction that the walls signal and preserve – a *ksur* – was not necessarily enclosed by walls (Cheikh *et al.*, 2002). This type of urban gathering was adapted to the seasonal rhythms and flows of its inhabitants who lived mostly from long-distance trade and grazing and, therefore, a *ksur* was made of perishable constructions, since its population was relatively mobile. Constructions and ruins were intertwined. In any given moment, the ruins made part of the present of the town, whose inhabitants did not waste much effort rebuilding what time or the unpredictable force of the river (*uad*) destroyed every year. Moreover, the several drought periods (in the 1960s and 1980s) and subsequent urban migration, the war between Mauritania and Senegal in 1989 and, with more direct effects over Ouadane, the Sahara war, all contributed to its *natural urban decadence* (at that time, Ouadane had barely over 100 inhabitants). And when, at the beginning of the 1990s, some of the country's more distinguished patricians returned, in part attracted by the cultural capitalization of their homeland, they were

Fig. 15.3. *Ancienne ville*. Walls give sense to ruins. Copyright Maria Cardeira da Silva, CEAS/CRIA, FCT.

Fig. 15.4. International politics of heritage. Copyright Maria Cardeira da Silva, CEAS/CRIA, FCT.

more committed to developing the new part of the town than repopulating the ancient nucleus.

Consequently, preservationist worries that today make part of daily ideology and practices in Ouadane seem relatively recent and imported. The ruins (*ghariba*), nowadays circumscribed by the walls built with the help of Portuguese funding – testify to a much more recent past (and therefore, from a semantic point of view, much more insignificant) than tourists can imagine. They possess, nonetheless, a fundamental worth – rightly accrued by the circumscription that has improved its display – since, in the eyes of the visitor, they claim the need to preserve, or shall I say, to salvage local patrimony. In the eyes of the tourist, ruins are the witnesses to a signalled endangered authenticity that you need to preserve at all cost (Fig. 15.5).

By now, you can surmise an ironic movement in this touristic encounter: museums, walls, routes that have been painstakingly planned to ensure the comfort and safety of the new nomadic tourists, contrive the paradoxical sedentarization of an essentially nomad culture. Daily travelling objects, scarce and fugacious – tents, rifles, camel milk gourds, saddles – are

captured, accumulated and held still to be classified side by side with Neolithic blade and arrowheads (Fig. 15.6).

Like distance, time is annihilated in a field of cultural remains. But this is the only way of providing consumable visibility to a culture that is too fluid because of its mobility and too opaque because of its exoticism. The next step, still at an early stage in Ouadane but already emerging in larger towns such as Attar or turistified ones such as Chinguetti, is to re-semantize the objects through more sophisticated narratives that provide them with a cultural meaning, such as those made by more experienced guides, or the curators of museums and libraries. These narratives are now obviously in motion and are produced in the dialogue and negotiations with the tourists that stop and have a chat with them. As elsewhere, culture displayed is always intertextual and tailored to the audience expectations. For the time being, their museographic ineptitude is more adaptable to collage, pastiche, irony and fragmentation, which constitute a trend that differs from the techniques of interpretation and theming of classical museography (although, in fact, that is the one they crave). For now, the result is ironically closer to some displays that

Fig. 15.5. Japanese tourists at the *ancienne ville*. Copyright Maria Cardeira da Silva, CEAS/CRIA, FCT.

Fig. 15.6. Local museums, displaying cultural stratigraphy and complexity. Copyright Maria Cardeira da Silva, CEAS/CRIA, FCT.

juxtapose different items together, quoting fragments and disjointed narratives characteristic of some postmodernist approaches.

The irony and paradox of these encounters are not innocuous nor shall they be carelessly equated with mere recreational optimism so characteristically postmodern. Touristic encounters must be taken as seriously as any other intercultural encounter. Furthermore, while these happen in an atmosphere of leisure and ephemerality for some – which might justify the thoughtlessness of some theoretical approaches – they actually imply hard work for others. Accordingly, you need to go beyond the mere ideal of a mutual gaze. The effects of the mutual gaze are not only reciprocal or, even less so, symmetrical.

Guestbooks and placards

The results of touristic encounters for local cultural reconstruction are better observed by micro-ethnographies that witness them at the level of identity negotiations currently going on. This is so because, in order to understand 'local culture', you cannot ignore the economic, social, racial, and gender and other identity differentiation frameworks, within which it is produced and reproduced. Now, a fine mirror of that microscopic negotiation is precisely the guestbooks and placards displayed in the small lodges that have mushroomed in response to the new opportunities that nomads/tourists have brought.

Although some classic anthropology has perhaps exaggerated the importance – by reifying it – of hospitality in Arab and Mediterranean societies, it cannot be dismissed in a framework such as the one we encounter in Mauritanian tourism. In fact, recapturing its importance, after the undertow of hypercriticism of the 1980s, may be one of the key elements to understand some apparently surprising contemporary phenomena.

To find a shortcut to a process that is very hard to summarize, I shall follow the case of Zeida – a young black woman, divorced and mother of two – who, in the adverse context of the Adrar, which is eminently male, Moorish and where age is one of the main sources for status, has won respect, admiration and prestige because of her successful business. In less than 3 years, Zeida alone managed to establish the most successful lodge in Ouadane today.

I have only time here to make a stop together with you – too short a one, alas – at her guestbook and the placard she displays in the canteen of her lodge with an eye informed by her life history that I could not here describe in detail (Fig. 15.7).

In both guestbook and placard, what Zeida displays by means of messages, photos sent by tourists, friends and visitors is, before anything else, irrecusably, her racial complexion, and after that her smile, her coolness 'like an oasis', her force in face of adversity, her ability to work. Zeida's photos emerge in the middle of maps and a panoply of images that advertise Mauritania as a tourist destination, and she sees herself (tacitly there, but explicitly while having a chat with me) as part of the 'landscape', or shall I say, as an attraction in a landscape that, as we have already seen, the semiotic battalions of tourists come to consume (Zeida did not have to read Urry or MacCannel to understand that). At the same time, she displays her legality and professionalism: diplomas, statutes, local legal framing for

her lodge. This legality and entrepreneurship have attracted members of humanitarian NGOs, regular customers, of her lodge who have often asked her to tell the history of her success and to participate as mediator in the implementation of local development projects. That interest in her life history has her toying with the idea of writing it in French to display it – as a leaflet – for the tourists that visit her lodge. 'Tourists get interested by that' – she said to me (probably recalling that I was a tourist as well).

Behind Zeida's virtues – that are totally deserving and which she does not shy from knowingly taking advantage of – there is something enigmatic that enhances them and that explains even better her magnetism for tourists, members of NGOs and unprepared anthropologists. I believe it is the frailty raised by the fact that she belongs to a minority – being a woman, black, divorced and living in an environment that endangers all those characteristics – that has earned her admiration and invites solidarity. These features appeal to the same conservationist and redeeming spirit tourists experience in view of ruins, the past, the Environment and endangered cultures (Butcher, 2003). From

Fig. 15.7. Placards: fragments, memories, mirrors, visual resources to build narratives and identities. Copyright Maria Cardeira da Silva, CEAS/CRIA, FCT.

most of the tourists' point of view, Zeida is twice 'endangered': she belongs to a fragile group (to several fragile groups: black people, women, young people) within an endangered culture (Mauritanian). And, although she has always been aware of her multiple subordinate positions in a highly stratified social setting, she's displaying now – wisely and elegantly – what used to be a handicap and has become a resource.

I have already mentioned that hospitality may not be neglected in these new contexts of touristic emergence. In order to understand Zeida's success, as well as to explain how this sort of women and some socially underprivileged groups are now in the informal run for the development of tourism, you have to take into account that, unlike dominant white Moorish groups (*beidan*), they do not consider hospitality an uncomfortable obligation. Having people in their homes, and charging them for it, does not affect their honour as it would affect a *beidan*. In that sense, socially – and not culturally in an essentialist fashion – these fragile and minority groups have more capacity to grab the opportunities offered by tourism in this context. In order to do that, and precisely due to their subordinate and subsidiary position, these people have developed working skills and expertises that, in a traditional framework, would socially undervalue the members – particularly the women – of other groups. From that point of view, we can say that Zeida's *frailty* and subordination in a traditional framework has become a twofold added value in the touristic encounter framework: because, culturally, it responds perfectly to tourist stereotypeness; because, socially, it has trained her for an adverse labour market.

None of this would go much beyond a simple record of the effects of mutual gaze if, at least, I could not leave here some clues to shed light on how much these effects may influence the more intimate negotiations of personal identity and show how they can contribute to clarify some shady contours of the cultural dialogues that are established in touristic encounters.

Frailty as attraction

Zeida's placards and guestbooks – which she displays for tourists' sake, returning to them fragments of their frivolous perceptions (which she simultaneously stimulates) – are like the museums that capture objects in time and space without taking into account what gives them meaning to be better reinterpreted and/or consumed, by displaying them in an unintentionally postmodernist fashion. However, this placard and guestbook concern Zeida and her home. And not a *culture* that belongs to everyone, without belonging to anyone and that, in spite of the efforts of some, is now prey to plunder. In my opinion, the stories and negotiations that are happening in parallel with – although not alien to – what is happening on the stage of touristic encounters are precisely what give even more cultural meaning to the effects of these encounters. I shall mention here some elements of it that, in spite of being persuasive, would deserve a more detailed explanation.

Zeida's hard life history, and the dramatic changes that tourism has inflicted on it, strengthen a reflexive and careful attitude in face of her actions, her femininity and her morality. Her social survival – and success – depends locally and largely on that. Traditionally, Zeida's symbolic capital would be so insignificant that the double contact with foreign people in her house, that on top of all are mostly men – something demanded by her professional activity – might be considered neglectful. However, she not only takes economic advantage of her former handicap, but she also seems to want to use it as a platform to assert her social and individual status, by ways that are alternative to local tradition. The idiom that she has found to convey that was, as for so many other women in contexts of social transformation, the idiom of Islam. Zeida often asks an *'alim* to ascertain the Islamic legitimacy of the money she receives from non-Muslim tourists: whether it is unclean and because of that prevents her from using it for the pilgrimage she intends to do to Meca or from paying the *zakat*. But, at the same time, when a policeman stopped her on the street because she was alone accompanying male tourists, Zeida stated that: first, he had never met her and she was an honoured working woman ('If it is forbidden to work in order to survive, you tell me it is forbidden to go with the tourists. I don't work with tourists to find a husband'); second, that she was Muslim like him but he would not 'burn in hell' if that ever happened, which she thought was highly improbable; and thirdly that anyway in Mauritania those that need to be careful are the *tubab* (foreigners) because they are not in their own country. With her final touch, the message Zeida was conveying to the policeman, subverting the criticism he had made her, was that she had nothing to fear because she expected the men in her country would always protect their Muslim women, even from any eventual danger arising from the *tubab*. These, conversely, were the ones unprotected in a country that was not their own.

Zeida's case shows us how an individual interpretation of Islam can offer alternative legitimacy for individual behaviour within rigid and paralysing social codifications unready for quick social changes, such as the ones produced by tourism. In her interpretation of Islam, female visibility and visitability does not necessarily affect her honour, which boundaries she carefully redefines publicly appealing to *fiqh* (Islamic jurisprudence). And this is why, and how, she allows her image to be used in her placard, in touristic sites of NGOs, at the Internet, and versions of her story to be told on conferences and papers on anthropology.

References

Bennett, T. (1988) The *exhibitionary* complex. *New Formations* 4, 73–102.
Butcher, J. (2003) *The Moralisation of Tourism. Sun, Sand. . .and Saving the World*. Routledge, London.
Cheikh, A.W.O., Lamarche, B., Vernet, R. and Durou, J.-M. (2002) *Sahara. L'Adrar de Mauritanie. Sur les Traces de Théodore Monod*. Vents de Sable, Paris.
Kirshenblatt-Gimblett, B. (1998) *Destination Culture. Tourism, Museums and Heritage*. University of California Press, Berkeley, CA.
Mitchell, T. (1991) *Colonizing Egypt*. University of California Press, Berkeley, CA.
Urry, J. (1991) *The Tourist Gaze: Leisure and Travel in Contemporary Society*. Sage, Newbury Park, CA.

16 Transforming Taste(s) into Sights: Gazing and Grazing with Television's Culinary Tourists

David Dunn

School of Drama and Creative Industries, Queen Margaret University, Edinburgh, UK

Soups delicately coloured like summer dresses, coral, ivory, or pale green . . .

(Elizabeth David)

Television travelogues have struggled with taste. The gaze of the camera is predisposed to privileging the scopic of tourism; and however significant the other senses have become for an understanding of the diversity of contemporary touristic practice, and whatever the importance of food for many tourists, the taste of food is, in the main, mediated on the television screen by words. As holiday programmes have waned, new lifestyle strands address the aspirations of viewers, reflecting in the process the growing convergence between mobility, leisure and tourism. Not least amongst these are cookery programmes, with the television chef, liberated from the domestic space of his or her kitchen, able to make cooks' tours of varying purpose; cookery demonstrations *in situ*, narratives of food heritage, searches for 'authentic' local ingredients, personal quests by celebrity chefs.[1]

This chapter is about the culinary travelogue, about the ways in which television can evoke flavour, and deploy visual signifiers of

location and ingredients to authenticate and validate gastronomic journeys. It considers two British television series, *Rick Stein's French Odyssey*, shown on BBC2 in 2005, and *Jamie's Great Italian Escape*, Jamie Oliver's self-reenergizing pilgrimage through Italy shown on C4 also in 2005. It will suggest that both owe much to the legacy of the food writer Elizabeth David, whose work Mennell (1985, p. 271) argues 'might be considered gastronomic literature as much as cookery books'.[2] The culinary travelogue has some kinship with travel writing, and owes at least some of its signifying practices to the ways in which she, and the gastro-literary tradition that she created, evoked the taste of food through vivid, almost painterly, descriptions of the raw and the cooked, and celebrated food as the signifier of a landscape and the history of its people. Both of these series reflect David's construction of the Mediterranean as a prelapsarian Eden, culturally and gastronomically, and offer examples of how the television camera focuses on location and ingredients *in situ* to authenticate and validate aspirational journeys which both stand for the taste of things and which flatter by association the tastes of

---

[1]See Strange (1998) for a typology of cookery programmes; Cookery-Educative, Personality, Tour-Educative, Raw-Educative.

[2]Mennell (1985) cites Jane Grigson, herself a *protégée* of David as the other influential figure. See also Jones and Taylor (2001), for a comparative study of their quests for authenticity in the kitchen, and Floyd (2004) on the (im)practicalities of David's culinary articulations with her readership.

viewers,[3] journeys about the performance of distinction.

The Legacy of Elizabeth David

In 1950, Elizabeth David published *A Book of Mediterranean Food*. It was written for readers who wanted 'to bring a flavour of those blessed lands of sun and sea and olive trees' into the colourless austerity of post-war Britain (*MF*, Introduction[4]). Her subsequent books, *French Country Cooking* (1951), *Italian Food* (1954), *Summer Cooking* (1955) and *French Provincial Cooking* (1960), and her journalistic work, consolidated her reputation. She touched the dawning aspirational *zeitgeist* of increasing travel and cultural mobility, and, in the words of her 'official' biographer Artemis Cooper (1999, p. xii),[5] described food 'in such a way as to make people dream of it and want to cook it'. Her recipes are full of flavour and detail; but it is the detail of place, not the detail of the cookery class. In the first of the discursive pieces which form an introduction to *French Provincial Cooking*, David writes of her favourite Mediterranean region,

> Provence is a country to which I am always returning, next week, next year, any day now, as soon as I can get on to a train. Here in London it is an effort of will to believe in the existence of such a place at all. But now and again the vision of golden tiles on a round southern roof, or of some warm, stony, herb-scented hillside will rise out of my kitchen pots with the smell of a piece of orange peel scenting a beef stew.
> (*FP*, p. 23)

The emphasis on colour and smell as signifiers of place, of memories catalysed by a scent or an image, is a constant in her writing. So too is her representation of the Mediterranean as the English traveller's proper destination, a place of heightened senses and sensuality; yet one which

made little concession to her public's insular sensibilities, to the ears, eyes and nostrils. David positions her readers within the continuity of the generations of privileged English tourists who had made The Grand Tour. As she wrote for her post-war readers not yet protected from the realities and importunities of Mediterranean markets by the 'environmental bubble'[6] of the package tour,

> the butchers' stalls are festooned with every imaginable portion of the inside of every edible animal (anyone who has lived for long in Greece will be familiar with the sound of air gruesomely whistling through sheep's lungs frying in oil).
> (*MF*, pp. 9–10)

Visual evocation is an important aspect of David's work, and she was, of course, writing at a time when colour photographs were rare in cookery books. In the case of *French Country Cooking*, she insisted of John Minton's illustrations that they convey information, not just atmosphere (Chaney, 1998, p. 275). Yet what is of equal interest to the boldly stroked-in ingredients, the *batterie de cuisine* and the occasional 'sultry French peasants and [...] jovial bourgeois family at lunch' (Cooper, 1999, p. 156), is the neo-romantic view through an open window to a pastoral or urban scene. One might as easily be looking at a travel poster, save for the absence of colour, as a cookery book. Yet these illustrations offer a reminder of what the French call *goût de terroir*, that *nexus* of place and produce held to define flavour as a unique and place-specific taste (Trubek, 2005).

Weary of her own life in England, where, after youthful studies in Paris and Munich, she had worked as an actress and as an assistant in the fashion house of Worth, David and her lover Charles Gibson Cowan had set sail for Marseilles *en route* for Greece in July 1939 in the yacht which they had bought largely with money provided by her Uncle Jasper. The outbreak of war made them refugees, and after fleeing

---

[3]See Barthes (1957) and Bourdieu (1989) on the links between food and the expression of taste.
[4]David's texts cited in this chapter are abbreviated as follows: *MF*: *A Book of Mediterranean Food* (1950); *IF*: *Italian Food* (1954); *FP*: *French Provincial Cooking* (1960). See the references for details of the subsequent editions cited here.
[5]The description 'authorised', Cooper suggests, meant merely that she was given full access to David's papers, not that she was subject to any censorship (Cooper, p. xv).
[6]See Cohen (1972) on the tourist's need for the familiar when in unfamiliar places.

France, and subsequent arrest as well as the loss of the yacht and their possessions in Italy, they arrived in Athens in July 1940. They settled on the island of Syros where, according to Cooper (1999, p. 79), 'she learnt how to rely on the ancient, basic foods of the Mediterranean'. What Cooper describes as a 'primitive Mediterranean idyll' ended when the Germans occupied Greece in April 1941, and the couple, once more refugees, fled to Egypt. Her relationship with Charles at an end, Elizabeth spent the remainder of the war in Egypt, working first in Alexandria and then in the Ministry of Information in Cairo.

There she came to know the writers Robin Fedden and Lawrence Durrell, who with the poet Bernard Spencer edited the quarterly *Personal Landscape*. Bolton (1997, p. xii) describes this as 'a record of group experience, of responses to, among other things, world war, exile, and the Levantine landscape, culture and art.' The sense of exile they felt was exile from Greece, their perceived centre of western culture, not England. Elizabeth's other biographer Lisa Chaney (1998, pp. 180–181) suggests that

> Elizabeth might not have benefited from the rigorous classical education of Spencer or Fedden, but like Durrell she identified entirely with their sense of exile and was party to many late-night conversations emanating from the same principles inspiring *Personal Landscapes*.

For these writers, Bolton argues, Egypt was a country bleached of colour by the sun.

> This white and colourless landscape became [...] a kind of emblem of blankness, erasure and emptiness – the very antithesis of the colourful and irregular contours found in the topography of Greece.
>
> (Bolton, 1997, p. 61)

At the same time, Durrell was formulating his belief that characters were functions of landscape, a belief that would find its fullest expression in the four novels of *The Alexandria Quartet*, but also one that would inform much of his travel writing.

> [A]s you get to know Europe slowly, tasting the wine, cheeses and characters of the different countries you begin to realize that the important

determinant of any culture is after all – the spirit of place. Just as one particular vineyard will always give you a special wine with discernible characteristics so a Spain, an Italy, a Greece will always give you the same type of culture – will express itself through the human being just as it does through its wild flowers.
>
> (Durrell, 1969, p. 156)

For David, it would be the food of a landscape that above all expressed the spirit of place. In her work, the life of the country was articulated by its food and by its people's encounters with that food, and was signified not just by tastes and smells, but by the sight of ingredients and dishes, by provenance, and by the memories of eating, of shared meals.

Food and Celebrity Serendipity:
Rick Stein's French Odyssey

Rick Stein's French Odyssey was shown on BBC2 in 2005. It charted a serendipitous barge journey through the canals of South West France in search of traditional recipes and a culinary way of life, which reflected the *terroir* and the unchanging spirit of place of a rural, implicitly peasant, landscape. As traveller's tales on television go, however, this one appeared to be singularly lacking in travail. Rick Stein, a chef in later middle age with a string of television series in search and celebration of regional produce[7] is seen lounging on a sofa in the barge's cabin. 'I just love the movement,' he muses. 'Isn't it nice when you're just going along only at four miles an hour. Because life suddenly assumes a peacefulness, and that's what barge life's like.' Underpinning Stein's travels in search of a more authentic way of life is the ambivalence implicit towards his chosen mode of transport, the 100-year-old steel barge *Rosa* and then, for the second leg of the voyage, her younger sister *Anjodi*. The pair's stately pace and girth appear to cause the film crew much unspecified grief, perhaps since they cannot easily be reversed along the canal for re-takes. Stein muses on the problems of seeing beyond the unending screen of towpath trees that lines the canal[8] and begins to

---

[7]See Randall (1999) for a detailed analysis of *Rick Stein's Taste of the Sea* (BBC2 1996).
[8]*Rick Stein's French Odyssey*, Episode 2 (August 2005).

wonder whether this is a good way to discover France until he announces, 'Hang on, I'm in my own secret moving garden, where I can stand up and stare and smell the joys of rural France.' Subsequently, in the book of the series, he contrasts *Rosa* and her breed with the ubiquitous and not to be taken seriously flotillas of fibre glass hire craft, which his camera shows to line the towpaths and clog up the locks, 'On a barge, you are the correct form of canal transport and you feel superior to those over-cheerful Noddy-boaters getting in the way. It's total bliss' (Stein, 2005, pp. 12–13).

The barge becomes a signifier of taste and of difference and also a signifier of an authentic journey; of continuity between pre-industrial past and post-industrial present, of a gentler life attuned to the rhythms of season and landscape, of the taste and distinction[9] that mark out Stein's quest of gastronomic discovery as being at least figuratively 'off the beaten track' (Buzard, 1993) of the hordes of fellow British holidaymakers who, it is implied, merely skim the surface of a French canal and its life. Yet existing in tension with this is the series' generally unspoken confusion about exactly what constitutes past and present, what is 'heritage' and what is the life still lived along the Canal du Midi. This 'long village'[10] of locals and the many Anglophone incomers, whom Stein and his camera seek out for lazy lunches, their calling card his celebrity and television's power to guarantee an open door, is a World Heritage Site whose purpose has, as a consequence, been appropriated and redefined. The steel hulled barges whose authenticity, sanctified by time and usage and aesthetic, and whose superiority over the plastic Noddy boats Stein lauds, are themselves comparative newcomers to a waterway old enough to have known wooden hulls and horse traction. Above all is the paradox that steel, associated with cities and industrialism, here becomes a symbol if not of pre-industrialism then of a timeless rural tradition.

Over two decades earlier, Stein's producer David Pritchard had, when working with chef Keith Floyd, established the convention of filming cooking on location. Freeing them from the constraints and the safety of the studio brought a new immediacy and a new authenticity to cookery programmes. Hall *et al.* (2003) draw parallels with the concept of *goût de terroir* to suggest that there is a unique combination of the physical, cultural and natural environment, which gives each region its distinctive touristic appeal, its *touristic terroir*.

> The French have long used the term *terroir* to describe the phenomenon of the place characteristics of food products – a term which defies a literal translation into English, but which is the 'almost mystical' combination of all aspects of soil, climate and landscape present . . .
> (Hall *et al.*, 2003, p. 35)

This series' use of 'real' locations as background to a cookery demonstration offers visual references to the touristic and culinary *terroir* of each recipe and its ingredients, compounded by the use of the barge to heighten that sense of *terroir* and to underpin and authenticate the sense of a voyage of culinary discovery. Yet within days, it became clear that tensions between the television chef and *Rosa*'s chef meant that the barge's galley was off limits for filming,[11] and Stein was required to recreate his newly discovered recipes back home in his own kitchen in Cornwall, or else to occupy, cuckoo-like, the kitchens of those whose homes bordered the canal. The galley had offered little visual potential, with its modern fitted units and cramped space, and it was clear that for the purposes of aesthetic and culinary authenticity, canal-side homes like that of American food writer Kate Hill offered more.

The name of her house, the *Relais des Longues Jours*, referred to the carters, the men who hauled the barges by horse, worked long days and who moored up at night, stabled the horses and cooked food in what was then their rest house.[12] She authenticates it with the words,

---

[9]See Bourdieu (1989) and Palmer (2004).
[10]The Canal is so named by American food writer Kate Hill in Episode 2.
[11]*Rick Stein's French Odyssey*, Episode 2 (August 2005).
[12]*Rick Stein's French Odyssey*, Episode 4 (September 2005).

'So somebody's been barging and eating here since the middle eighteen hundreds.' The slow pace of Stein's diesel-powered barge offers a further visual metaphor for the slow cooking of the region. As a dish of duck breasts is prepared by Stein and his hostess, the television camera frames, in the close-ups so suited to domestic viewing,[13] bunches of garlic, raw duck breasts crusted with herbs and pepper, a dice of crisp fried duck fat piled in a glazed clay bowl, crystals of salt sprinkled over the surface, the blackened patina of an *hachoire*, that crescent shaped blade with a handle at each end for chopping onions and herbs. Underpinning the historical continuities of the meal there is a close-up of a well-aged and knife-scored wooden table top on which Stein lays a piece of toast before spreading it with pâté. He is shown standing in front of the house, whose warm stone, trailing vine and wooden shutters are further visual signifiers contributing to the continuity of a culinary tradition and to the totality of the *goût de terroir*, which Stein is communicating to his viewers. The sensuousness of the sequence is heightened by a satisfying crunch on the soundtrack as Stein takes an indulgent bite of a piece of toast laden with pâté. Central to Stein's voyaging and celebration of food are meals shared with his hosts, invitations to which his viewers can only, enviously, aspire.

Food to Re-energize a Celebrity: *Jamie's Great Italian Escape*

Stein acknowledged his debt to Elizabeth David by reading to camera a passage from *French Provincial Cooking*, which celebrated the produce of French markets and suggested their potential superiority as a tourist sight over the local *château*. She is also one of the dedicatees of the more iconoclastic Jamie Oliver's book of his series, *Jamie's Great Italian Escape* (Oliver, 2005). Oliver, younger, streetwise, is more driven than the laid-back Stein, his series being a self-proclaimed attempt to take time off from

his celebrity lifestyle and television appearances. He appears to be unaware of the irony that a television crew will accompany him on this journey of self re-energizing. Like Stein, he equates authenticity with the rural, but this Italian journey is not about the well-trodden beat of Chiantishire, but the less touristically developed south. In creating a second layer of authenticity to his series by travelling rather more literally than Stein 'off the beaten track', he positions himself in the camp of the anti-tourist. For Buzard (1993), such competitiveness first emerged in the years after the Napoleonic Wars as Europe was opened up to more and more tourists.

> [T]he authentic 'culture' of *places* – the *genius loci* – was represented as lurking in secret precincts 'off the beaten track' where it could be discovered only by the sensitive 'traveller', not the vulgar tourist.
> (Buzard, 1993, p. 6)

This is underpinned by Oliver's choice of transport, a battered old camper van, whose tendency to break down at opportune moments for the camera brings the appropriate amount of travail to his travels as well as occasioning tirades whose four letter words, bleeped out for pre-watershed viewing, suggest that there is not always an obvious correlation between sensitivity and being a traveller.

At the beginning of the first episode,[14] he makes clear his culinary purpose. 'Even though I've cooked Italian food for 12 years, I've never lived there and I don't even speak the language. I want to find out why Italian families are so passionate about food. I also want to find out why the average Italian family eats so well when millions of British families eat such scrote.' He addresses the camera from the wheel of his van, 'I'm going to be learning from the people that can, the working-class, builders, and . . . you know . . . the *cucina povera*, the poor man's cooking. It's almost like day one of college all over again. I'm just so excited, I can't possibly tell you. I guess it's the unexpected; that's what travelling's supposed to be all about. You know,

[13]See Ellis (1990) on the correlation between domestic viewing of television and choice of shot size, and Wheatley (2004) on the increasing audio-visual pleasures to be had as screen size and picture quality improve.
[14]*Jamie's Great Italian Escape*, Episode 1 (October 2005).

not always knowing exactly where you're going.' Implicit in this is that the business of food, of harvesting and cooking and shared meals, provides signifiers of the continuity and the bonds of 'real' family life, and throughout a series ostensibly about the raw and the cooked, the widely reported instabilities of Oliver's own marriage will disrupt the narrative and function intertextually as a counterpoint to his encounter with older certainties signified by older tastes.

Oliver is a celebrity. Celebrities, Rojek (2001, p. 51ff) argues, are elevated above their public, have quasi-religious powers.[15] Jamie discovers that Italian culinary attitudes are ultra-conservative, firmly rooted within the region, and hostile to embracing the recipes of neighbours. Thus, whatever his claims to be in Italy to learn from the older ways, to be their celebrant, he sets out instead to re-educate the palates of others. In a narrative of overcoming adversity, he uses ingredients and recipes as his weapons in his crusade to win the approval of the locals and bestow on them the enlightenment of Jamie's 'new' authentic Italian cooking. Whether in a working-class market in Palermo,[16] where he overcomes the locals' distaste for adding flavourings of orange and rosemary to freshly grilled fish, or in a farm in The Marches,[17] where he insists on stuffing the local lamb with a neighbouring Tuscan mix of rosemary and pine nuts and wins approval from his hunter hosts even although he has failed to respect the traditions of the region, Jamie complains about the dead hand of whichever granny or *nonna* rules the kitchen and attempts to inhibit his creativity. Heldke (2005, p. 388) argues that 'there is no such thing as a cuisine untouched by "outside influences"' and that what we identify as authentic is often simply what is new to us, and

it may be that Oliver, or his producer, is being disingenuous in talking up his narratively convenient critical encounters with the grannies.[18]

There is, however, a rare getting of wisdom when Oliver has to come to terms with the logic of his pursuit of the freshest of produce, and loving close-ups of lemons all knobbly and unwaxed on a tree high above the sea, of purple artichokes in a Palermo market, of heady clumps of basil in a monastery garden are replaced by the flash of a slaughterman's knife and blood. These uncomfortable signifiers of 'real' food accompany Oliver's own 'blooding' as his hosts, hunters in the muddy, misty wildness of an Italy little visited, invite him to kill a lamb for their feast. 'I'm quite interested while I'm in Le Marche to get to grips with the whole hunting wild food, you know, sustainable living and all that sort of business, living off the land. Something that in England in a normal sense has disappeared, you know.' Standing in a field, Jamie looks off-camera. 'No I don't know if I can kill a lamb. I've never done that before.' He looks around and hesitates. 'I mean . . . I, I . . . well not with a knife anyway.' There is a shot of men trussing a live sheep, while he looks on before joining them to bind its front feet. There is a cut to his host Massimo and Jamie carrying it out by the feet and in voice over Jamie adds, 'It's not quite like Sainsbury's[19] is it? I don't know what to do.' The camera tracks behind them as they carry it down the field. There is a shot of the sheep on grass, its neck in the centre of the frame, then a close-up of a knife in someone's hand. Jamie and Massimo are with the sheep. 'It's first time? Si,' Massimo asks, then indicates the spot and puts Jamie's hand to it. There is a close-up of Jamie blinking. 'Un momento,' he half laughs, half cries. Massimo's hand cuffs him gently. There is a close-up of the sheep, with Massimo's hand on it, then a shot of

---

[15]See Horton and Wohl (1956) on the complexity of the audience's relationship with media performers, and also Langer (1981).

[16]*Jamie's Great Italian Escape*, Episode 1 (October 2005).

[17]*Jamie's Great Italian Escape*, Episode 4 (November 2005).

[18]See also Sutton (2001, pp. 144ff) who identifies a myth of 'harmonious community' apparent in much current cookery writing which idealizes tradition and articulates it in recipes which become culinary memoirs, and Barthes (1997, p. 24), who argues that French food permitted a daily communion with a national and unchanging past.

[19]The intertextuality of this would not have gone unnoticed by viewers familiar with Oliver's role in promoting premium food lines for that supermarket.

Jamie looking around, then a close-up of Jamie's hand with the knife. Massimo puts his hand over Jamie's and the knife goes in. The camera zooms fast into Jamie's face as he turns away while bearing down on the knife, then a long shot as the sheep bleeds over the grass, and Jamie continues to look away. He screws up his eyes and then Massimo whispers 'OK'. Jamie looks up to the camera, 'That was horrific, but I don't know what's more horrific, a nation full of raving idiots that couldn't give a crap about the lives of thousands of animals that get treated like s**t, or an animal that has a most fantastic life, gets treated well, as you say natural, natural . . .'. There is a cut to a cat lapping up blood from grass, then to a wide shot of a field with sheep grazing. After this brief encounter with the business of death, pastoral calm is restored. As he skins and butchers the carcass, it starts to look more like meat that he recognizes, and he says that, however beautiful an animal it was, it will also taste fantastic and that 'we're at the top of the food chain'. Such are its signifiers, and, if only for a moment, the imperatives of the balance of nature have shifted Jamie from celebrity chef to a player in an older, more grounded game.

Conclusion

Oliver is dismissive of the eating habits of millions of his fellow citizens, dismissing their diet as 'scrote'. Stein too, while more measured, regularly compares and contrasts attitudes to food on either side of the Channel, suggesting that the lovingly crafted displays of produce in French markets set them apart from British farmers' markets,[20] that the importance of good wine and plenty of it in the sauce is 'something that we don't do in Britain'.[21] In conversation with a young French female member of *Rosa*'s crew,[22] he asks about her visits to England and the food she ate in Grimsby. She tells him that she enjoyed fish

and chips. He surmises that that was the only dish that she enjoyed. She equivocates. 'English food is quite special. That's my opinion.' Stein, surprised, counters with 'I don't think you mean special.' She is unclear. 'Sorry?' Stein adds 'Oh dear . . .'. However such an encounter might flatter those aspirational viewers for whom Mediterranean tastes are deployed as signifiers of taste, it sends an at best ambivalent message to others.

If Oliver and Stein both reflect Elizabeth David's belief that the Mediterranean is the proper destination of the food lover, their television journeys also reflect the discourse that food is an element of heritage tourism, which sets great store by old recipes, country traditions and natural products in their environment. Leitch (2000) has identified in cookery writing the phenomenon of 'Tuscanopia [. . .] in which Tuscan peasant cuisines . . . and picturesque rurality . . . seem to have become key fantasy spaces of modern urban alienation' (cited in Sutton, 2001, p. 148). In such a context, the work of Morley and Robins (1995, p. 20) has particular resonance. Reflecting on a European identity torn between nationalism and 2000 years of Greece, Rome and Christianity, they suggest a third allegiance through small, local identities to set against encroaching globalization, arguing that 'the appeal of this Europe of the *Heimats* – Basque, Lombard, Breton, Corsican and others – is to a more 'authentic' way of belonging.' While they admit to a danger of 'introverted and nostalgic historicism and heritage fixation', Morley and Robins remain optimistic that in the new mobility 'a critical regional or local culture must necessarily be in dialogue with global culture' and it is perhaps significant that both Stein and Oliver adapt, and are allowed to adapt, once sacrosanct regional recipes to a measure of local popular acclaim. Stein 'invents' a bargeman's stew, a mix of pork, beans, garlic and parsley, which while not traditional is something that he can imagine bargees eating on cold days.[23] He tries it out on the crewmember Julie who liked fish and chips,

---

[20]*Rick Stein's French Odyssey*, Episode 2 (August 2005).
[21]*Rick Stein's French Odyssey*, Episode 3 (August 2005).
[22]*Rick Stein's French Odyssey*, Episode 2 (August 2005).
[23]*Rick Stein's French Odyssey*, Episode 3 (August 2005).

who thinks it nice but in need of more salt. Oliver, more confrontational, wins over his sceptical Italian hosts in each episode with *bravura* displays of culinary promiscuity.

Culinary journeys are about distinction, about cultural capital (Bourdieu, 1989) and displays of taste 'off the beaten track' (Buzard, 1993) as well as about the sense of taste. Television's current obsession with celebrity and first person narratives[24] means that the mediation of any sense is secondary to the positioning of the presenter. Stein is constructed as urbane traveller and *bon viveur* rather than a tourist, with a network of contacts acquired *ex officio* as a travelling celebrity, while Oliver is allowed to work out his relationship with his craft and his family by going through a series of quasi-Herculean labours where the produce and culinary culture of the *terroir* are the tools and the sites of those labours. Nevertheless, in their choices of ingredients and dishes as signifiers – the gaze of Oliver's and Stein's cameras function less to add detail to the business of cooking than to add culinary detail to authenticate and illustrate programmes which are about travel and

aspiration – they share much with Elizabeth David's eye for the sensuous detail.

> Of all the spectacular food markets in Italy, the one near the Rialto in Venice must be the most remarkable. The light of a Venetian dawn in early summer – you must be about at four o'clock in the morning to see the market coming to life – is so limpid and so still that it makes every separate vegetable and fruit and fish luminous with a life of its own, with unnaturally heightened colours and clear stencilled outlines. Here the cabbages are cobalt blue, the beetroots deep rose, the lettuces pure green, sharp as glass.
>
> (*IF*, p. 169)

Yet reading these words, with their painterly ability to evoke a scene and to engage the senses, serves as a reminder that for all that television is reputed to be a visual medium, its signifying processes are generally illustrative rather than allusive. For all the close-up detail of Stein or Oliver's camera, lingering on a lemon here, a bunch of herbs there, the cliché that one picture is worth a thousand words does not always hold good in enhancing the culinary tourist's gaze.

References

Barthes, R. (1957) Ornamental cooking. In his *Mythologies*, trans. Annette Lavers (1972). Cape, London, pp. 78–80.
Barthes, R. (1997) Towards a psychosociology of contemporary food consumption. In Counihan, C. and van Esterik, P. (eds) *Food and Culture: A Reader*. Routledge, London, pp: 20–27.
Bolton, J. (1997) *Personal Landscapes: British Poets in Egypt During the Second World War*. Macmillan, London.
Bonner, F. (2003) *Ordinary Television: Analyzing Popular TV*. Sage, London.
Bourdieu, P. (1989) *Distinction*. Routledge, London.
Buzard, J. (1993) *The Beaten Track: European Tourism, Literature, and the Ways to 'Culture'*. Clarendon Press, Oxford.
Chaney, L. (1998) *Elizabeth David: A Biography*. Macmillan, London.
Cohen, E. (1972) Towards a sociology of international tourism. *Social Research* 39, 164–182.
Cooper, A. (2000) *Writing at the Kitchen Table: the Authorised Biography of Elizabeth David*. Penguin, Harmondsworth.
David, E. (1950) *A Book of Mediterranean Food*. John Lehmann, London. Republished 1952, Penguin, Harmondsworth.
David, E. (1951) *French Country Cooking*. John Lehmann, London. Republished 1959 and subsequently, Penguin, Harmondsworth.

[24]See Bonner (2003), Dovey (2000), Dunn (2005, 2006), Macdonald (2003) and Rojek (2001) on television as 'theatre of the ordinary' and on the importance of first person narratives, whether celebrity or 'ordinary people' in lifestyle programmes.

David, E. (1954) *Italian Food*. Macdonald, London. Republished 1963 and subsequently, Penguin, Harmondsworth.

David, E. (1955) *Summer Cooking*. Museum Press, London. Republished 1965 and subsequently, Penguin, Harmondsworth.

David, E. (1960) *French Provincial Cooking*. Michael Joseph, London. Reprinted 1964 and subsequently, Penguin, Harmondsworth.

Dovey, J. (2000) *Freakshow: First Person Media and Factual Television*. Pluto, London.

Dunn, D. (2005) 'We are not here to make a film about Italy, we are here to make a film about ME . . .': British television holiday programmes' representations of the tourist destination. In: Crouch, D., Thompson, F. and Jackson, R. (eds) *The Media and the Tourist Imagination: Converging Cultures*. Routledge, London, pp. 154–169.

Dunn, D. (2006) Singular encounters: mediating the tourist destination in British television holiday programme. *Tourist Studies* 6, 37–58.

Durrell, L. (1969) Landscape and character. In: *Spirit of Place: Letters and Essays on Travel*. Faber, London, pp. 156–163.

Ellis, J. (1990) *Visible Fictions*. Routledge, London.

Floyd, J. (2004) Coming out of the kitchen: texts, contexts and debates. *Cultural Geographies* 10, 61–73.

Hall, C.M., Mitchell, R. and Sharples, L. (2003) Consuming places: the role of food, wine and tourism in regional development. In: Hall, C.M., Sharples, L., Mitchell, R., Macionis, N. and Cambourne, B. (eds) *Food Tourism Around the World: Development, Management and Markets*. Elsevier, Oxford, pp. 25–59.

Heldke, L. (2005) But is it authentic? Culinary travel and the search for the 'genuine article'. In: Korsmeyer, C. (ed.) *The Taste Culture Reader: Experiencing Food and Drink*. Berg, Oxford, pp. 385–394.

Horton, D. and Wohl, R. (1956) Mass communication as para-social interaction: observations on intimacy at a distance. *Psychiatry* 19, 215–229. Reprinted in John Corner and John Hawthorn (eds) (1993) *Communication Studies*, 4th edn. Arnold, London, pp. 156–164.

Jones, S. and Taylor, B. (2001) Food writing and food cultures: the case of Elizabeth David and Jane Grigson. *European Journal of Cultural Studies* 4, 171–188.

Langer, J. (1981) Television's 'personality system'. *Media, Culture and Society* 4, 351–365.

Leitch, A. (2000) The social life of *Lardo*: slow food in fast times. *The Asia Pacific Journal of Anthropology* 1, 103–182.

Macdonald, M. (2003) *Exploring Media Discourse*. Arnold, London.

Mennell, S. (1985) *All Manners of Food: Eating and Taste in England and France from the Middle Ages to the Present*. Blackwell, Oxford.

Morley, D. and Robins, K. (1995) *Spaces of Identity: Global Media, Electronic Landscapes and Cultural Boundaries*. Routledge, London.

Oliver, J. (2005) *Jamie's Italy*. Penguin/Michael Joseph, London.

Palmer, G. (2004) 'The new you': class and transformation in lifestyle television. In: Holmes, S. and Jermyn, D. (eds) *Understanding Reality Television*. Routledge, London, pp. 173–190.

Randall, S. (1999) Television representations of food: a case study. *International Journal of Tourism and Hospitality Research* 1, 41–53.

Rojek, C. (2001) *Celebrity*. Reaktion Books, London.

Stein, R. (2005) *Rick Stein's French Odyssey: Over 100 New Recipes Inspired by the Flavours of France*. BBC Books, London.

Strange, N. (1998) Perform, educate, entertain: ingredients of the cookery programme genre. In: Geraghty, C. and Lusted, D. (eds) *The Television Studies Reader*. Arnold, London, pp. 301–312.

Sutton, D. (2001) *Remembrance of Repasts: An Anthropology of Food and Memory*. Berg, Oxford.

Trubek, A. (2005) Place matters. In: Korsmeyer, C. (ed.) *The Taste Culture Reader: Experiencing Food and Drink*. Berg, Oxford, pp. 260–271.

Wheatley, H. (2004) The limits of television? Natural history programming and the transformation of public service broadcasting. *European Journal of Cultural Studies* 7, 325–339.

17 World in One City: Surrealist Geography and Time–Space Compression in Alex Cox's Liverpool

Les Roberts

The University of Liverpool School of Architecture, Liverpool, UK

No face is surrealistic to the same degree as the true face of the city.

(Walter Benjamin, quoted in Abbas, 2003, p. 148)

Liverpool®: On the Brandwagon

To begin with a well-worn cliché: this is a tale of two cities. Cities that share the same geographical co-ordinates but that in other respects defy conventional processes of mapping and the semiotic inscription of place and identity. The provincial city of Liverpool in the northwest region of England is a place undergoing dramatic urban, economic, social and cultural transformation. Its confidence having been given a considerable boost by the events and activities surrounding its status as European Capital of Culture in 2008, in 2009 Liverpool nevertheless remains within peering distance of an economic abyss, the unfathomed depths of which resound with the clamour of a global capitalist economy in the throes of crisis.

In a report published in January 2009, Liverpool was cited as one of the UK cities likely to be worst hit by the global economic recession.[1]

For a city long struggling with the social and economic impacts of post-industrial decline, the wisdom of putting all its economic eggs in the same 'regenerative basket' of culture-led urban renewal (centred on tourism, leisure and consumption) reflects a policy that warrants closer – and evermore urgent – critical scrutiny (Jones and Wilks-Heeg, 2004).

In this chapter, I start by examining the role of moving image discourses in the branding of Liverpool's urban landscape as a postmodern 'consumerscape': a representational space in which local urban specificity is refined and repackaged (and, as I argue, ultimately dispensed with) to serve the rapacious demands of the global consumer economy. In 2002, the promotional film *Liverpool: World in One City* was produced as part of the city's campaign bid to become European Capital of Culture 2008.[2] Taking its title from the marketing tag-line for the bid, 'The World in One City', the 8-min film, commissioned by Liverpool Council, is a postmodern city symphony composed of a largely fast-cut montage of iconic buildings, famous street signs, corporate brand logos, and colourful festivals and performers. The vibrant image of a global, multi-cultural city, confident and at ease with

---

[1]See the Cities Outlook Report 2009, published in January 2009 by the independent urban policy research group Centre for Cities: www.centreforcities.org/outlook09.
[2]The other cities competing for the coveted prize were Birmingham, Bristol, Cardiff, Newcastle/Gateshead and Oxford.

itself, was far removed from the hitherto more negative representations of Liverpool as a post-industrial city dogged by unemployment, economic decline and social and racial tension. However, despite, or perhaps because of its rich semiotic plenitude, the film's densely packed urban melange maps a curiously absent or dislocated sense of place. What is particularly striking is the extent to which the unique landmarks and architectural iconography that had formerly dominated Liverpool's representational spaces have in large part been supplanted by a super-abundance of signs: street signs, shop signs, famous music venues and global brand logos, foregrounding the act of consumption as the pre-eminent marker of the city's urban renaissance. As a consequence, the symbolic (and actual) navigation of these spaces prompts a heightened sense of urban disorientation: the city disappearing underfoot as the semiotic fabric of the urban imaginary spirals further down the wormholes of the global symbolic economy.

Against this corporate vision of a post-industrial city caught in the 'irradiating gaze' (Augé, 1996, p. 179) of global capital, swept up by what Jonathan Meades refers to as the 'brandwagon' of the 'regeneration industry',[3] we can perhaps envisage another city, one that lurks somewhere beneath the shiny veneer and neo-liberal facades of 'culture-capital', a city whose landscapes are dwarfed by the corporate edifices epitomized by the Liverpool One development: Grosvenor's eponymous 'Paradise Project'[4] (after Paradise Street in the City Centre South where it is located), at the time of writing the largest retail development in Europe. Within these alternative spaces of the city, a qualitatively different set of urban mobilities becomes evident. Excavating and indeed embracing the spaces of disorientation that define the de-localized geographies of consumption and globalization, artists and film-makers seek new pathways through these landscapes, psychogeographic and surreal journeys, which, in their wake, expose the inert and socially neutered qualities of the urban fabric that define large areas of cities such as Liverpool today. It is these alternative spatial practices that are explored in the second part of this article. Against the contextual backdrop of Liverpool as 'world in one city', I set out to navigate the surreal urban geographies mapped in British director Alex Cox's 1998 'Liverpool film' *Three Businessmen*. The film, or more precisely the cinematic geographies it maps (in which travellers around Liverpool pass through locations in Rotterdam, Hong Kong and Tokyo) serve to initiate a wider discussion on the heterotopic nature of the city as a global space of deterritorialization, consumption and 'time–space compression' (Harvey, 1990). Taking the form of a Buñuelian travelogue or odyssey, the film narrates an uncertain space of urban *flâneurie* marked by disorientation, ellipses and thwarted desires of consumption. In this regard the film may be read as a psychogeographic counterpoint to the deliriously consumerist vision of Liverpool promoted in *Liverpool: World in One City*.

Liverpool®: Culture-Capital

If Liverpool is the 'Pool of Life',[5] its culture ripples throughout the world: an outward expression of vitality, talent, innovation,

---

[3] 'Jonathan Meades Abroad Again: On the Brandwagon', BBC2, 16 May 2007.

[4] See www.grosvenor.com/Portfolio/Liverpool+One.htm.

[5] A gift to the city by the Swiss psychologist Carl Gustav Jung, the phrase 'Liverpool the Pool of Life', while a boon to city marketeers, has wider resonance amongst local community groups and artists that is suggestive of a broader set of meanings and associations than those appropriated by the regeneration industry in Liverpool. In his 1961 book *Memories, Dreams, Reflections*, Jung famously recounted a dream in which he found himself wandering amongst the 'dirty, sooty' landscapes of a nocturnal city, in the centre of which was a 'broad square dimly lit . . . into which many streets converged. In the centre was a round pool, and in the middle of it a small island' (quoted in Jones and Wilks-Heeg, 2007, p. 209). As Jones and Wilks-Heeg have shown, the idea of a 'pool of life' into which 'many streets converged' played an influential role in the establishment of Peter O'Halligan's 'Liverpool School of Language, Music, Dream and Pun', an influential alternative arts and cultural venue. Inspired by his own dream of a spring bubbling out of a manhole cover on Mathew Street, O'Halligan identified a point where, at the point of converge of several streets (East Mathew Street, West Mathew Street, Button Street, Rainford Square and Temple Street), there was indeed a manhole cover. Convinced this

fashions, music, humour, an unmistakable cultural identity; the world in one city . . .

Commissioned by Liverpool Culture Company, the body set up by Liverpool Council to manage the city's Capital of Culture activities,[6] *Liverpool: World in One City* was made in 2002 by River Media, one of Liverpool's leading media production companies. Founded in 1998 by Jon Corner and Paul Rodgers, the company has played an influential role in shaping much of the visual communication and marketing discourses of the city as a place of regeneration, culture and tourism, both in the lead up to and aftermath of the city's successful bid in 2003 to become Capital of Culture 2008. On its website (www.river-media.com), River Media highlights the company's philosophy and service provision, foregrounding *communication* as its principal raison d'être: 'The whole point is to *connect* with audiences . . . put simply – that's what we'll help *you* to achieve'.[7]

The message conveyed in *Liverpool: World in One City* is one comprised of both affective and semiotic structures of communication (Anderson and Holden, 2008), with a veritable glut of fast-cut imagery, overlain with a musical collage (delivered at a breakneck pace) of an 'inclusive' mix of the classic and popular, and a commentary (by the actress Cathy Tyson) composed less of narration *per se*, as a list of keywords designed to trigger immediate and positive associations: Vitality; Talent; Innovation; Fashions; Music; *Unmistakable Cultural Identity*. The image accompanying the latter phrase is a panorama shot of Liverpool Waterfront viewed from the Wirral side of the River Mersey (in fast motion – the Mersey a projectile force of nature, throwing itself to the four corners of the globe). Featuring prominent landmarks such as St John's Beacon tower, the two cathedrals, the 'Three Graces' (the Liver, Cunard and Port of Liverpool buildings), the image frames an iconic cityscape which, as perhaps the most recognizable of all Liverpool 'brands', has long served to communicate an instant

and 'legible' image of the city to the outside world (Lynch, 1960; Roberts and Koeck, 2007; Roberts, 2010a).

 . . . Diversity of Peoples; Influences; Unique Culture; World-Class; Heritage; Stunning; Beautiful; Jewel on Europe's Cultural Map; Outstanding; Diverse; Excellent; Ecumenical Leadership . . .

At pains to declare its strong commitment to issues of cultural diversity and inclusivity, this 8-min visual message is replete with symbols and icons that bombard the senses, washing over the viewer with the same force as the cascading river, flooding (or drowning) the cultural landscapes of the city with an aesthetic designed not so much to extrude specificity of place and identity, as to ensure that all conceivable pockets or lacunae (whether cultural, ethnic or religious) are representatively 'filled' (Fig. 17.1).

Such is the sweep of cultural and civic references recounted in the film (both visually and textually) that viewers could be forgiven for thinking that its diligent attention to matters of 'diversity' and 'inclusivity' extends to all the social landscapes that make up Liverpool's conglomerate urban form. This is of course not the case at all. As the predominant use of qualitative and affective adjectives suggests, the cultural offer that is promoted in the film is one premised on an exclusively consumer and competitive model of urban cultural identity (Bristow, 2005). Akin to any other commodity circulating in the global market place; brand Liverpool is packaged and sold on the strength of its attributes as a place and space of consumption. Whether proclaiming itself as 'Guinness Official World Capital of Pop', a place of 'Lifelong Learning', 'Communities', 'Beacon Schools', 'Centres of Excellence', 'World-class Institutions' and so on, the conceptual parameters of what may be regarded as 'culture' in this context are such that the material spatial practices that make up the everyday geographies of the

---

was the location in Jung's dream, in the late 1970s he purchased a disused warehouse on the site and established what was originally known as 'Aunt Twacky's', soon to become 'the hub of an emerging avant-garde cultural scene in Liverpool' (Jones and Wilks-Heeg, 2007, p. 212).
[6]See http://www.liverpool08.com/.
[7]www.river-media.com (Accessed 1 May 2009).

Fig. 17.1. Still from Liverpool: World in One City (2002) (courtesy of River Media Ltd).

city are not merely pushed to the margins of the urban imaginary; they are conspicuous by their very absence.

Paradoxically then, the sustained semiotic saturation that *Liverpool: World in One City* confers on the city, far from mapping the sort of urban lacunae to which such representations might otherwise lay claim, renders Liverpool a curiously deterritorialized zone; its 'culture' contingent on necessarily *de-localized* patterns of symbolic consumption. Moreover, maintaining the neo-liberal illusion that everyone has equal access to these 'material and symbolic' landscapes (Highmore, 2005), the film ostensibly reads like an instrument of New Labour cultural policy. Despite large-scale regeneration of the city centre, many areas of Liverpool have seen little in the way of material improvement; the dilapidated and boarded-up dwellings that punctuate the urban landscape providing a stark counterpoint to the glossy, 'vibrant' images of glass and steel that characterize the new areas of development. As spatial and material expressions of the regenerative accumulations of capital that accolades such as the Capital of Culture status help cement, it is not altogether surprising that urban developments like the Liverpool One complex and other of the city's revamped spaces of consumption should feature so prominently in marketing discourses aimed at tourists, shoppers and venture capitalists alike. However, by the same token the very persistence of material expressions of the city's slow and painful urban decline – inscribed in graffiti-sprayed bricks and crumbling mortar – provides at least some acknowledgement of the socially embedded cultures and everyday tactics (de Certeau, 1984) of those whose stake in the city (or lack of it) has remained less readily visible in official narratives; a representational analogue of the uneven nature of post-industrial capitalist development. Against this socio-economic backdrop, it is instructive to note that, unlike the childhood homes of John Lennon and Paul McCartney, both of which are firmly on the tourist map of Liverpool (located in the middle-class areas of Woolton and Allerton, respectively), the home of Ringo Starr, who grew up in a working-class terrace house in the Welsh Streets area of Toxteth, is roundly ignored. One could perhaps

Fig. 17.2.   9 Madryn Street, Toxteth, Liverpool 8, birthplace and childhood home of Ringo Starr. A stone's throw from the Grade II listed Princes Park, Madryn Street is in a prime gentrification zone (author's photo, May 2009).

speculate as to whether this is because of Starr's least-liked Beatle status or that 9 Madryn Street, like most of the other properties in the strongly multi-cultural neighbourhood (an area which, following the riots of 1981, continues to prompt largely negative associations) has been allowed to fall into dereliction by Liverpool Council, and is condemned to be demolished as part of proposed 'regeneration' (or gentrification) plans for the area (Fig. 17.2).[8]

> . . . Vibrant; Unique; Unparalleled; Dynamic; Creative; Forward-looking; Great; Diverse; Excellent; Exciting; Vibrant; Unrivalled; SUPERCHARGED, COSMOPOLITAN, CULTURAL CAPITAL . . .

Perhaps mindful of the fact that the depiction of the city in *Liverpool: World in One City* might sit uneasily with some Liverpudlians (although it should be noted that the film's intended audience was the business and 'regeneration industry'

rather than the general public), the producers seek to reassure the viewer that despite the film's corporate and instrumentalist message, it is still able to display a 'cutting edge', reflexive awareness of the semiotic mine-field through which the film-makers are required to gingerly tread. The inclusion of a 6-s sequence consisting of a crudely animated image of the Liverpool actor Ricky Tomlinson in a mocked up version of the BBC test card graphics,[9] accompanied by the 'Gallery Theme' music from the 1960s–70s children television's programme *Vision On* (Fig. 17.3), is suggestive of a certain playful disregard for the film's own formal and aesthetic conventions, while at the same time referencing the iconoclasm and sense of humour of popular Scouse mythology. Similarly, the staggeringly insincere celebrity endorsements of the Capital of Culture bid in the film (from the likes of Atomic Kitten, Blue, Status Quo, Lionel Ritchie) appear almost wilfully chosen for their

---

[8]John Lennon and Paul McCartney's childhood homes are now maintained by the National Trust, which organizes tours of the properties (www.nationaltrust.org.uk/main/w-the_beatles.htm). Campaigners trying to save 9 Madryn Street from demolition have petitioned the National Trust also to preserve Starr's former home in the interest of British heritage and national tourism (see www.petitiononline.com/ringo/petition – accessed 4 May 2009).
[9]The BBC test card was a static image that appeared during periods when no programmes were being broadcast to confirm reception of the signal.

Fig. 17.3.   Still from Liverpool: World in One City (2002) (courtesy of River Media Ltd).

ironic rather than 'star' appeal. The inability of Craig Phillips, a former winner of the reality TV programme Big Brother, to even complete the phrase 'Good luck to Liverpool for Capital of Culture' (the viewer is shown several toe-curling takes of him trying to get it right) is no doubt intended to convey an inclusive, 'democratiz-ing' message that all Liverpudlians, irrespective of class, educational background, or communi-cation skills, have a stake in the Capital of Cul-ture enterprise (Phillips' bungling performance is inter-cut with a word-perfect endorsement by the conductor of the Liverpool Philharmonic Orchestra). However, it could just as easily be read in a more cynical light: the vacuity of 'celebrity culture' becoming synonymous with that of city branding and 'place marketing cul-ture'. The clearly prompted nature of the celeb-rity endorsements, as if reading from a cue card (which they probably were), does not exactly convey the kind of assured, heartfelt and authentic sense of civic belonging and solidarity that one might otherwise expect from a down-trodden city fighting its corner in the rough and tumble world of place competition.

The narrator goes on to observe that 'Liv-erpool is the most filmed city in Britain, after London', noting that '141 films alone last year' were shot in the city. While this statement is true, what it does not acknowledge is that, in the case of the majority of film productions based in the city, Liverpool all too rarely 'plays itself'; that is, the productions are not place-specific to the extent that landmarks and loca-tions are expressive of the city's own on-screen identity and urban character. Not so much the 'star' as 'body double' (Brown, 1995, p. 10), Liverpool's architecture and locations are more prominently exploited as backdrops for narra-tives set in other cities and historical periods. Suggesting an altogether different take on the theme of 'world in one city', Liverpool's cine-matic geographies have served as a stand-in for, amongst others, Cannes, Vienna, Moscow, St Petersburg, Dublin, Amsterdam, Rome, New York, Chicago, Paris, London and war-time Germany (Roberts, 2008, p. 201).

In 2002, the same year as the Capital of Culture bid, Liverpool Council's tourism unit in association with Liverpool Film Office (the UK's

Fig. 17.4. Liverpool Movie and Television Map (2002) (courtesy of Liverpool Council).

first dedicated city film commission) published 'Boomtown!', a map showing locations featured in a range of film and television productions based in the city (Fig. 17.4). The 'movie map' was part of a wider marketing campaign aimed at promoting Liverpool – its architecture, landscape and locations – as a desirable destination for tourists and film-makers alike. I have elsewhere conducted a more detailed exploration of the relationship between the film and tourist industries in Liverpool and other destinations, and the increasingly prominent role of film in the marketing of cityscapes as sites of spectacular consumption (Roberts, 2008). In the present context, and in light of the discussions around globalization, visuality and urban space that I pick up in the next section, Liverpool's preeminent status as 'world in one city' is well illustrated in the following quote from the producer of the Jacqueline de Pré biopic, *Hilary and Jackie* (Anand Tucker, 1998):

> I came looking for a beach and they sold me the whole city. International concert halls, Moscow hotels, Parisian apartments, golden synagogues, civic buildings, sand dunes and stately homes.
> (Andy Patterson, producer of *Hilary and Jackie*, quoted in

'Boomtown! Liverpool Movie and Television Map', 2002; Fig. 17.4)

This endorsement, which would not look out of place on a tour operator brochure, reinforces the central message that the bludgeoning aesthetics of *Liverpool: World in One City* are designed to instil in the would-be consumer of brand Liverpool. Consisting of upward of 525 individual shots, the 500-s marketing missive rushes towards a vertiginous crescendo of rapid-fire images, the narrator's Powerpoint-style bullet intonation firing home the message that Liverpool = Culture = Entrepreneurial City = Consumer City:

> . . . Energy; Diversity; Imagination; Expression; Risk-takers; Pioneers; Entrepreneurs; Inventors; Writers; Reformers; a Place for Doing, Changing, Trying and Learning; an Extraordinary City; a City for the World; a Cultural City; The World IN One City.

World in One City: Alex Cox's Liverpool

After the heady sugar rush that is *Liverpool: World in One City*, the slow-paced and largely conversational scenes that make up Alex Cox's

Three Businessmen (1998) offer a welcome respite. Mostly composed of sequence shots – long, continuous takes, which often feature the actors moving through, and interrelating with, largely empty cityscapes – the film can perhaps best be described as a surreal urban travelogue: a journey or odyssey that takes many unexpected (and sometimes unnoticed) twists and turns as the characters traverse a Borgesian global landscape governed by few, if any of the rational, Euclidean properties of vernacular urban space.

By way of brief synopsis, the plot centres for almost the entirety of the film on the urban adventures of two businessmen, Benny, a garrulous American (played by Miguel Sandoval) and his coy, initially reluctant interlocutor, Frank (played by Cox himself). Both are art dealers visiting Liverpool. They meet in the city's legendary Adelphi Hotel where an unsuccessful attempt to secure a meal in the vast and deserted hotel dining room precipitates their downtown quest in search of a restaurant. Scripted by Cox's partner Tod Davies, the film is in no small part inspired by the Spanish director Luis Buñuel's surrealist classic *The Discreet Charm of the Bourgeoisie* (1972).[10] Like the characters in Buñuel's film, Frank and Benny's attempts to dine are continually thwarted, although, unlike the Buñuelean tale, these are for a variety of mostly banal reasons.

The Liverpool sequences of the film (geographically at least, in diegetic terms they never actually leave the place they call 'Liverpool') provide the stage for some comic and philosophical musings on the history and geography of the city, with the British character Frank acting as both foil and tourist guide to the unremittingly inquisitive Benny. Topics range from Liverpool's involvement in the slave trade, the Beatles, the significance of Carl Jung's statue in Mathew Street, and speculations, based around their understandings of the social demography of the city, as to the likely clientele of a Mercedes car dealership they pass (they settle on drug dealers).

A series of mysterious flyers bearing the name and image of someone called 'Daddy Z' connect the different areas of the city through which they pass, unwittingly en route to what is later revealed to be a place of pilgrimage (where, moreover, they finally get to eat). Now joined by a third businessman, Leroy (Robert Wisdom), who has lost his way somewhere in Chicago, the travellers' quest ends in a desert (somewhere off Mathew Street), in actuality one of the Spanish locations used in Sergio Leone's iconic spaghetti westerns. Their hunger finally appeased, the three businessmen (or Three Kings as we now understand them to be) seem to find their bearings once more. The film ends with a sense of the miraculous: a psychic deliverance from the mundane and homogenized world from which they have stumbled. As Frank and Benny head off in the direction of Mathew Street, however, it is unclear to what extent their journey might have shaken them out of their somnambulance and disconnection from the global corporate-scapes (Appadurai, 1996) they seem forever destined to wander.

Described by one critic as a 'corporate road movie' (Davies, 2000, p. 170), *Three Businessmen* is in many respects the cinematic antidote to the 'idea' of Liverpool on offer in *Liverpool: World in One City*. As I have already alluded, in terms of their formal composition one of the more striking differences between the two films lies in the radically divergent nature of their editing. The 525+ edits that comprise the 8-min marketing film establishes a pace that makes the 120-shot, 83-min *Three Businessmen* seem positively glacial in comparison. Yet although they both 'map' ostensibly the same city, the stylistic adherence to the sequence shot or long take in Cox's film allows the viewer to dwell in representational spaces, which, privileging spatial contiguity and the uninterrupted unfolding of real time, allow closer engagement with the *materiality* of the urban landscape, and, by extension, the *situatedness* of human actors within this landscape. This is not to say that Cox's Liverpool is any less constructed, any less a cinematic assemblage of images and sounds. The essential 'messiness' (Till, 2009) of lived space necessitates a certain creative ordering (not to mention contractual and logistical compliance) when it comes to location filming in cities. In the case of *Three Businessmen*, this ordering appears principally geared towards the exclusion of people and traffic. In keeping with the alienating urban geographies portrayed in the film, the city is mostly depopulated, its empty spaces heightening the sense of solipsistic

---

[10]Cox and Davies' production company is called Exterminating Angel, in homage to Buñuel's 1962 film of the same name.

abstraction that characterizes Frank and Benny's urban peregrinations. The more practical considerations of shooting in busy locations such as Mathew Street, a popular tourist attraction and mecca for night-time revellers, demanded the services of two burly security guards who joined the production crew on the Liverpool shoot. As Cox describes in his book *X Films* (2008), this was partly to keep drunken on-lookers from disrupting certain scenes (a quiet word in a doorway with the offending culprit would usually suffice), but more importantly to stop the theft of production equipment, a problem for which the otherwise film-friendly city had acquired something of a reputation (Cox, 2008, p. 220).[11]

In the context of the present discussion therefore, the cinematic geography of *Three Businessmen* is approached not in terms of its realism or its perceived 'urban verisimilitude' (of which, by implication, *Liverpool: World in One City* is in some way deficient), but rather – as a *surrealist travelogue* – its unique spatial and temporal dynamics, and the ways in which these prefigure, articulate or map some of the experiential disjunctures in space and time wrought by globalization and the neo-liberal expansion of multinational capital. In this regard, and against the contextual backdrop of *Liverpool: World in One City*, Frank and Benny's frustrated gastro tour of 'Liverpool locations' – a spatial narrative of thwarted or unsated consumption – raises salient questions about the role and complicity of the moving image in the production of postmodern urban space. Furthermore, the film's navigation of these frequently bewildering landscapes points to alternative forms of aesthetic, social and cultural practice which 'go against the grain' of hegemonic spatio-temporal ordering. These psychogeographic modes of critical urban praxis both map and disrupt the abstract spaces of consumer capital, infusing them with a poetics of the absurd; the marvellous; the serendipitous and enchanted (Selwyn, 2007). Cultivating the layered topographies of an affective geography, the psychogeographer, or 'critical urban wayfarer' (Roberts, 2010b), creates the imaginative possibility of an embodied and authentic reclamation of everyday urban space.

The oft-cited definition of 'psychogeography', a termed coined by the Situationist guru Guy Debord, is '[t]he study of the special effects of the geographical environment, consciously organized or not, on the emotions and behaviour of individuals' (Debord in Coverley, 2006, p. 10). As a critical aesthetic response to the rationalization of (post)modern urban space, the psychogeographic practice of the *dérive*, or 'urban drift', is more latterly associated with the work of the writer and film-maker Iain Sinclair. Noting that '[w]alking is the best way to explore and exploit the city', Sinclair suggests that '[d]rifting purposefully is the recommended mode, tramping asphalted earth in alert reverie, allowing the fiction of an underlying pattern to reveal itself' (1997, p. 4).

As a pithy distillation of the rationale surrounding the 'doing' of psychogeography, Sinclair's reflections seem particularly well-observed. However, they do not lend themselves all that readily to the characters of Frank and Benny, who appear less consciously aware of the 'underlying pattern' which their global tour of Liverpool is laying bare. 'Drifting purposefully' in search of a meal, Frank and Benny's journey narrates a spatial fiction from which they themselves seem somehow disconnected. The 'impossible' geographical ellipses that mark the points of transition between different (global) locations, while disorientating and perplexing for the travellers as they try and regain their bearings, are not ever questioned or seen in any way to be out of the norm (or 'out of place'). For Frank and Benny, they are merely navigating a world to which they have long grown accustomed. An environment all too crushingly familiar in their workaday, corporate existence as travelling businessmen. However, as a (purposefully) *psychogeographic* encounter with (or drift through) Liverpool's urban landscape, their journey is experienced vicariously, by us, the viewer.

Or is it. . .?

What Cox and writer Tod Davies subtly convey in *Three Businessmen* is the close correspondence between, on the one hand, the navigation and architecture of cinematic space, and, on the other, that of the consumer city, which shapes and demands evermore globalized

---

[11]Despite the security precautions, equipment was stolen on three separate occasions during the Liverpool shoot (Cox, 2008, pp. 222–228).

structures of cognitive mapping (Cairns, 2006, p. 199). 'Travelling' the deterritorialized spaces of Cox's Liverpool, the viewer, like the would-be consumer and tourist targeted by *Liverpool: World in One City*, moves seamlessly between an array of image-spaces, each a virtual brick in the composite wall of representation that mediates – or obscures – material forms of engagement with the city. Navigating the city in film, the spectator finds his or her embodied urban analogue in the figure of the tourist (or business traveller) who wanders a landscape composed of architectural 'jump cuts' and ellipses (Koeck, 2008). This de-localized configuration of urban 'markers' (MacCannell, 1976, pp. 109-133) refines a post-industrial cityscape that is increasingly unable to articulate its own grounded (Smith and Katz, 1993) sense of place and identity. Indeed, '[o]n the ground', as Cairns suggests, 'this [misalignment of the virtual and material] generates conditions that mingle hyperreal zones of spectacle, surveillance, and control with the left-over, derelict, fallow spaces of material and economic entropy that are found in the wake of capital's evacuation from one place and its concentration in another' (2006, p. 197). For a clear illustration of this, we need only consider the relationship between the phantasmagoric spatialities of the new Liverpool One retail complex and those pockets of dereliction that are found in the surrounding inner-urban area.

In *X Films*, Cox recalls comments made by audience members at an early screening of *Three Businessmen*, noting that many seemed to genuinely not pick up on the fact that, despite the very obvious visual clues, Frank and Benny were travelling between transnational urban locations (Liverpool, Rotterdam, Hong Kong and Tokyo) (Figs 17.5 and 17.6):

> Consider the scenes with Benny and Frank aboard the Metro. While we're aboard the train, it's pretty similar to the Liverpool Merseyrail: a Metro interior is a Metro interior after all. The train that Miguel and I board in Liverpool was painted yellow; the train we emerged in Rotterdam was green . . . Yet almost no one in the audience noticed it. This taught me that people watch films on a shot-by-shot basis. What they see now, they accept as 'reality' within the frame, what was on screen five minutes ago is already forgotten.
>
> (Cox, 2008, p. 242)

Similarly, in an interview with Maximillian Le Cain, Davies vents her frustration at the way the film, or rather the film's geographies, are often (mis)read by audiences (Fig. 17.7):

> [I]t's very dispiriting when you have people at the end of the screening who actually think there is a Japanese garden that looks like Tokyo in Liverpool! It gets depressing when people come up to you and say 'Where is that Japanese garden in Liverpool?' and you're like 'There were thousands of Japanese people on

Fig. 17.5. Frank and Benny board the metro at Liverpool . . . (courtesy of Exterminating Angel Films).

Fig. 17.6.   . . . and alight in Rotterdam (courtesy of Exterminating Angel Films).

Fig. 17.7.   Visiting the Japanese Gardens in Liverpool (courtesy of Exterminating Angel Films).

the screen, there were big screen televisions, do you really think that's what it was?' But that is what the point was: anything that you're told you just take in as truth, you don't ever evaluate it and you should start evaluating it.

(Le Cain, 2003)

Observations such as these lend support to Lefebvre's critique of film as an 'incriminated medium', which, in its abstraction from the experiential flux of everyday urban spaces, is ill-equipped to reveal the inherent contradictions

that make up these spaces (1991, p. 97). Given that these very contradictions and tensions lie at the heart of what, thematically and conceptually, *Three Businessmen* is all about, audience responses such as those Cox and Davies describe above are suggestive of a critically muted, and overly spectacularized engagement with the film's representational spaces. The viewer (or at least these particular viewers) seem to navigate the cinematic spaces of *Three Businessmen* in the same abstract and disorientated fashion as their diegetic counterparts, Frank and Benny. In this regard, the film would provide an interesting case study for audience-based research on perceptions and readings of urban landscapes in film, and the extent to which these are imbricated within the wider symbolic economy of cities such as Liverpool. Playing on pervasive ideas of a 'global consumer village', Cox and Davies' Liverpool is a space caught in the homogenizing web of global consumerism. A space in which the valorization and reification of the *act* of consumption eclipses all semblance of local urban and cultural specificity. The 'Liverpool' we encounter in *Three Businessmen* is thus both a mirror and a sustained spatial critique of the idea of Liverpool promoted in *Liverpool: World in One City*.[12]

Liverpool: Spectacular City/Disappearing City

[I]mages fragment; they are themselves fragments of space. Cutting things up and rearranging them, *découpage* and *montage* – these are the alpha and omega of the art of image-making . . . It fetishizes abstraction and imposes it on the norm. It detaches the pure form from its impure content – from lived time, everyday time, and from bodies with their opacity and solidity, their warmth, their life and their death. After its fashion, the image kills.
(Lefebvre, 1991, p. 97)

In his later work on social rhythms and temporality, Lefebvre explores the dynamic interactions between space, time and the body. Putting forward the case for 'rhythmanalysis' (2004) as a mode of critical urban praxis, Lefebvre's theorizations on time and 'rhythmicity' (Highmore, 2005; Wunderlich, 2008) are intricately entwined with his writings on space and everyday life (Mendieta, 2008, p. 150). As indicated in the above quote (from *The Production of Space*, his most-cited work), for Lefebvre time and space are inseparable: co-originary and co-determining (Mendieta, 2008, p. 151). The semiotic excess of an image-saturated space of representation, detached from the embodied

and temporal dynamics of space as it is lived, further informs processes of urban 'spectacularization' or 'cinematization': a condition diagnosed by Guy Debord in the Situationist classic *Society of the Spectacle* (1992). *After its fashion, the image kills.*

As writers such as Highmore (2005) and others have demonstrated, a shift in attention towards the study of social and cultural *rhythms* provides a productive framework by which to navigate cultural texts as embedded elements in the production and consumption of everyday urban landscapes. The rhythms of *Liverpool: World in One City* and *Three Businessmen* are key to our reading and mapping of these texts as *spatial practices*. As we have seen, the MTV-style montage aesthetics of the Capital of Culture marketing film structure a temporal geography that inhibits 'lingering' or 'dwelling'. A preponderance of signs and rapid visual sound bites (or 'site bites' to quote Jonathan Meades[13]) construct the immaterial architecture of a city being primed for hyper-consumption and touristic spectacle. The short, fleeting, contractual encounters with the mostly a-spatial and non-place-specific image-spaces on screen define an urban experience increasingly subject to what Abbas (1997, p. 28) refers to as a 'new localism', where the local is rendered mutable, dislocated and semiotically unstable by the seemingly unstoppable encroachment of corporate globalization.

By contrast, Frank and Benny's more ponderous navigations of the city unfold in 'anthropological space' (de Certeau, 1984, p. 117). Placing human actors within the deterritorialized spaces of the city, the spatio-temporal structuring of the sequence shot draws closer attention to the embodied interactions of the travellers as they journey through a dislocated urban landscape. The 'peripatetic' mode of spatial practice which underpins the cinematic geographies of *Three Businessmen*, as with the travel and journey films of Theo Angelopoulos, a director renowned for his use of long, complex sequence shots (e.g. *The Travelling Players*, 1973), privileges the affective and embodied act of walking (Wallace, 1993; Roberts, 2005). As a consequence, the spectator is drawn into

---

[12]For a discussion of the role of film as a spatial/architectural critique, see Keiller (2007).
[13]See note 3.

closer proximity with the material spaces and non-places (Augé, 1995) of the city, and with the transitory zones of interconnection (or local 'slippage') that frame the de-localized globality of Frank and Benny's urban tour.

In terms of its intrinsic homogeneity, the city which the businessmen traverse bears close resemblance to what the architect Rem Koolhaas' describes as the 'Generic City': 'the city without history . . . like a Hollywood studio lot, it can produce a new identity every Monday morning' (in Abbas, 2003, p. 147). Adaptive to the fickle and ever-shifting demands of the global consumer, Liverpool: Generic City is a place where everyone, irrespective of nationality, domicile or culture, becomes a tourist, where the material and virtual merge in global consumerscapes that are increasingly difficult to differentiate from the transitory spaces which connect the city to other cityscapes and urban locations. In *Three Businessmen*, the interstitial zones of public transportation that punctuate Frank and Benny's urban odyssey become the points of transition between various global locations: Liverpool to Rotterdam (one metro stop); Rotterdam to Hong Kong (a short tram ride); a ferry trip 'back across the Mersey' (Frank reasons they have unwittingly crossed the river and are somewhere in Birkenhead, rather than, as is the case, Hong Kong harbour); a bus or tram to Tokyo; and a taxi ride from Tokyo to the Spanish desert region of Almería.

Equipped with a tourist guidebook to Liverpool (their 'master narrative'), Frank and Benny's culturally myopic orientations prevent them from confronting the state of existential homelessless (Berger *et al.*, 1973) which has engulfed them, casting them adrift in a featureless corporate world from which they have grown evermore alienated. In a curious inversion of Kevin Lynch's arguments on the importance of 'imageability' and 'legibility' in the framing of a coherent (i.e. marketable) 'image of the city' (1960), the sheer overabundance of imagery and visual stimuli in representations of the

postmodern city has rendered these spaces all *too* legible or, indeed, *illegible*: as interchangeable with or undistinguishable from any other global Generic City (Cairns, 2006, p. 201; Roberts and Koeck, 2007, p. 8). Finding distraction amongst the various miscellany and props that structure their day-to-day lives (Frank's newspaper and computer; Benny's Plutonium Card, the ultimate in customer loyalty cards, offering 'dismemberment insurance', 'product replacement guarantee' and 'total salvation') the (three) businessmen wander the cityscapes of the world without ever knowing exactly where they are, their desires for consumption never fully satisfied:

> Benny and Frank walk and take public transport all the way around the world, in total ignorance. They think Rotterdam is Liverpool. They think Shinjuku in Tokyo is Liverpool's famed 'Japanese Garden'.[14] They think the desert is a city. They wake up in generic hotel rooms, with no idea where they are, or why they're there. One of *Three Businessmen*'s earliest enthusiasts was a United Airlines flight attendant: he understood exactly what was going on.
>
> (Cox, 2008, p. 242)

The geographer David Harvey argues that '[t]ime-space compression always exacts its toll on our capacity to grapple with the realities unfolding around us' (1990, p. 306). The shrinkage of geographical scale through innovations in transport and telecommunications technology has, according to Harvey, precipitated a growing sense of anxiety and disorientation:

> As space appears to shrink to a 'global village' of telecommunications and a 'spaceship earth' of economic and ecological interdependences . . . and as time horizons shorten to the point where the present is all there is . . . so we have to learn how to cope with an overwhelming sense of *compression* of our spatial and temporal worlds.
>
> (Harvey, 1990, p. 240, emphasis in original)

If sight-seeing in Liverpool is akin to visiting the 'world in one city' then the idea of tourism as a geographic practice begins to fall apart. The

---

[14]Referring to his Liverpool tourist guide, Frank mistakes a floral landscape in Tokyo for the Japanese Garden that was designed for the Liverpool International Garden Festival in 1984. The site of the festival (at Dingle in the south docks area of Liverpool) has long since fallen into dereliction, and all that remains of the Japanese Garden is an old tourist map, with Japanese and English text, which is still visible amongst the overgrown trees and flora which have consumed the abandoned spaces of the festival site. For a discussion of the 1984 Garden Festival and culture-led regeneration in Liverpool, see Roberts (2010b).

uniqueness and 'legibility' of cities as a complex conglomeration of people and place comes to reflect the uniqueness and legibility of *deterritorialized* cultural forms to which the city lays claim. With the more circumscribed practices of 'tourism' being subsumed within a broader theoretical framework of 'mobility' (Cresswell, 2006; Urry, 2007), the figure of 'the tourist' similarly loses its specificity if the structuring premise of *distance* is no longer a given. Responding to these theoretical re-routings in the sociological study of tourism, Franklin and Crang call for a 'sedentary tourism of the everyday' (2001, p. 9), in which, as Rojek and Urry point out, '[i]t is now clear that people tour cultures; and that cultures and objects themselves travel' (1997, p. 1). Viewed in this light, Frank and Benny's journey becomes a sedentary form of travel: the world shifts around them, while they themselves remain fixed, as if distractedly surfing the Internet or travelling the virtual spaces of film and television. The passivity inscribed in this particular mode of 'travel' leaves little room for the contingent and serendipitous. In the same way that *Liverpool: World in One City* is designed to communicate a specific (and unambiguous) message, the world which Frank and Benny inhabit steers them (and the inattentive viewer) through a cultural landscape dominated by various 'signage' that maps a reassuringly familiar if dull urban imaginary.

In *X Films*, Cox describes a painting by Otto Dix of an office clerk who has just hanged himself. Sitting in a chair beside the corpse, the ghost of the hanged man is reading a newspaper, unaware that he's dead (2008, p. 243). This is Frank's predicament: he is unaware of his condition. Culturally inured to the corporatized spaces that dominate his world, he is oblivious to the fact that amidst all the signage and semiotic excess exists a city that is gradually disappearing.

Conclusion: Surreal City

Inasmuch as the act of seeing and what is seen are confused, both become impotent . . . That which is merely seen (and merely visible) is hard to see.
(Lefebvre, 1991, p. 286; Abbas, 1997, p. 48)

Reinforcing Lefebvre's critical perspective on visuality and space, Ackbar Abbas notes that 'the more abstract and ungraspable space becomes the greater the importance of the image' (1997, p. 690). *Liverpool: World in One City* maps a virtualized space whose overabundant – and overexposed (Abbas, 1997) – imagery functions to stabilize a legible (or 'branded') space of representation, the instrumental goal of which is to reframe a more marketable signifier of place to entice tourists, shoppers and the service-based industries to 'take a closer look' (to quote from the film) at the Culture-Capital and its 'cultural offer'.

The downside of this is that the further the city is abstracted and virtualized, the further it undermines the anthropological dimensionality of urban space (the city as lived space), hastening the processes of fragmentation, dissolution and time–space compression which Cox and Davies so effectively map in their surreal, slightly dystopic urban travelogue. The cognitive rendering of a city as merely the sum of its semiotic parts, each delivered in a cacophonous (or rapturous) assemblage of visual site-bites, contributes towards what Abbas refers to as the 'cinematization of space', where direct observation gives way to the authority and primacy of the media image (1997, p. 41). Writing on Hong Kong cinema of the 1980s and 1990s, Abbas argues that ghost films such as *Rouge* (Stanley Kwan, 1988) crystallize a certain spatial anxiety tied up with an acute sense of loss and disappearance (*déjà disparu*) at a critical point in the history of the former British colony. According to Abbas, the ghost story, in which different periods of Hong Kong's history are brought together, evokes Harvey's concept of time–space compression, serving as a tropic device that enables the director (Kwan) to represent and critically explore the space of the *déjà disparu* (Abbas, 1997, pp. 41, 47).

Drawing on the work of Isozaki and Asada (1992), Abbas distinguishes three types of urban space: real cities (historically contextual), surreal cities (hybridized urban forms, without historical context) and hyperreal or simulated cities (televisual, theme-park cities). All three of these types of urban space can be found in Liverpool, yet it is the second, the surreal city, that has most bearing upon the present discussion. Encouraging a 'regime of the subliminal, uncanny and half-seen' (Abbas, p. 77), the geographies of the surreal city dominate the virtual landscape of *Liverpool: World in One City*. Mapping ostensibly the same space (or configuration of spaces), Cox's Liverpool embraces this surreality but allows it to manifest itself in different, more subversive ways. Whereas the surrealism of *Liverpool: World in One City* is functionally predicated on the marketing of Liverpool as a consumer paradise, Cox's surrealism – pared down and nurtured in real time (and real space) – is altogether more radically and tactically deployed. Allowing the spatial logic of global corporate capitalism to unravel itself, *Three Businessmen*'s surrealist aesthetics reframe the idea of 'world in one city' as a spatial expression of, to paraphrase Jameson, the visual and spectacular logic of late capitalism (1984).

In this regard, *Three Businessmen* may itself be read as a critical exercise in cognitive mapping, contributing to wider debates on the politics of globalization and multinational capitalism, and furnishing a cultural space that allows us to secure positionality, both spatially and politically, within the everyday consumerscapes that dominate global urban environments. As a cognitive map, therefore, *Three Businessmen* plays its part in instilling a critical spatial imagination in which we can 'begin to grasp our position as individual and collective subjects and regain a capacity to act and struggle which is at present neutralized by our spatial as well as our social confusion' (Jameson, 1995, in Cairns, 2006, p. 199).

As I have argued, the rhythmanalytical dissection of media texts and consumer spaces reveals the underlying structures and tensions shaping the representation of cities, and, by extension, the increasingly dissonant spatialities underpinning many contemporary urban formations. The glitzy sheen and HD cinematography of the neo-liberal city symphony has never been more out of step with our times. After all, why travel to Liverpool unless to shop? And if the act of shopping – conceived in terms of consumption for the sake of consumption – has proved to be not quite the urban panacea that the regeneration industry had foretold, then why travel at all?

Yet if the aesthetics and pace of these representations seems out of synch with the experiential fabric of everyday urban living, then the critical observance of such is not to argue for a counter 'realist' aesthetic of film, or to necessarily posit the case for a more 'authentic' form of spatio-visual engagement. That is not to say that these represent arguments that should not be made, but rather that my more immediate focus of analysis has been the ways in which specific cinematic geographies shape cognitive understandings of post-industrial global cityscapes, and to reflect on some of the urgent spatio-political considerations prompted by the virtual domination of everyday social spaces.

Acknowledgements

I am grateful to the UK Arts and Humanities Research Council who funded the research on which this article draws.

References

Abbas, A. (1997) *Hong Kong: Culture and the Politics of Disappearance*. University of Minnesota Press, Minneapolis, MN.

Abbas, A. (2003) Cinema, the city and the cinematic. In: Krause, L. and Petro, P. (eds) *Global Cities: Cinema, Architecture, and Urbanism in a Digital Age*. Rutgers University Press, London.

Anderson, B. and Holden, A. (2008) Affective urbanism and the event of hope. *Space and Culture* 11, 142–159.

Appadurai, A. (1996) *Modernity at Large: Cultural Dimensions of Globalization*. University of Minnesota Press, Minneapolis, MN.

Augé, M. (1995) *Non-Places: Introduction to an Anthropology of Supermodernity*. Verso, London.

Augé, M. (1996) Paris and the ethnography of the contemporary world. In: M Sheringham (ed.) *Parisian Fields*. Reaktion Books, London.

Berger, P., Berger, B. and Kellner, H. (1973) *The Homeless Mind: Modernization and Consciousness*. Penguin, Harmondsworth.

Bristow, G. (2005) Everyone's a 'winner': problematising the discourse of regional competitiveness. *Journal of Economic Geography* 5, 285–304.

Brown, T. (1995) Everytown, nowhere city: location filming and the British city. Unpublished MA dissertation, Birkbeck College, University of London.

Cairns, S. (2006) Cognitive mapping and the dispersed city. In: Lindner, C. (ed.) *Urban Space and Cityscapes: Perspectives from Modern and Contemporary Culture*. Routledge, London.

Coverley, M. (2006) *Psychogeography*. Pocket Essentials, London.

Cox, A. (2008) *X Films: True Confessions of a Radical Filmmaker*. I.B. Taurus, London.

Cresswell, T. (2006) *On the Move: Mobility in the Modern Western World*. Routledge, London.

Davies, S.P. (2000) *Alex Cox: Film Anarchist*. Batsford, London.

Debord, G. (1992) *The Society of the Spectacle*. Rebel Press, London.

de Certeau, M. (1984. *The Practice of Everyday Life*. University of California Press, London.

Franklin, A .and Crang, M. (2001) The trouble with tourism and travel theory? *Tourist Studies* 1, 5–22.

Harvey, D. (1990) *The Condition of Postmodernity: An Enquiry into the Origins of Cultural Change*. Blackwell, Oxford.

Highmore, B. (2005) *Cityscapes: Cultural Readings in the Material and Symbolic City*. Palgrave Macmillan, Basingstoke.

Jameson, F. (1984) Postmodernism, or, the cultural logic of late capitalism. *New Left Review* 146, 53–92.

Jones, P. and Wilks-Heeg, S. (2004) Capitalising culture: Liverpool 2008. *Local Economy* 19, 341–360.

Jones, P. and Wilks-Heeg, S. (2007) Packaging culture, regulating cultures: the re-branded city. In: Grunenberg, C. and Knifton, R. (eds) *Centre of the Creative Universe: Liverpool and the Avant-Garde*. Liverpool University Press, Liverpool, pp. 202–219.

Keiller, P. (2007) Film as spatial critique. In: Rendall, J., Hill, J., Dorrian, M. and Fraser, M. (eds) *Critical Architecture*. Routledge, London.

Koeck, R. (2008) Cine-tecture: a filmic reading and critique of architecture in cities. In: Hallam, J., Koeck, R., Kronenburg, R. and Roberts, L. (eds) *Cities in Film: Architecture, Urban Space and the Moving Image. Conference Proceedings*. Liverpool School of Architecture, Liverpool, pp. 108–114.

Le Cain, M. (2003) Interview with Alex Cox and Tod Davies. In: *Senses of Cinema*: www.sensesofcinema.com

Lefebvre, H. (1991) *The Production of Space*. Blackwell, Oxford.

Lefebvre, H. (2004) *Rhythmanalysis: Space, Time and Everyday Life*. Continuum, London.

Lynch, K. (1960). *The Image of the City*. The MIT Press, Cambridge, MA.

MacCannell, D. (1976). *The Tourist: A New Theory of the Leisure Class*. Macmillan, London.

Mendieta, E. (2008) The production of urban space in the age of transnational mega-urbes: Lefebvre's rhythm-analysis or Henri Lefebvre: the philosopher of May '68'. *City* 12, 148–153.

Roberts, L. (2005) Non-places in the mist: mapping the spatial turn in Theo Angelopoulos' peripatetic modernism. In: Everett, W. and Goodbody, A. (eds) *Space and Place in European Cinema*. Peter Lang, Oxford.

Roberts, L. (2008) Cinematic cartography: movies, maps and the consumption of place. In: Hallam, J., Koeck, R., Kronenburg, R. and Roberts, L. (eds) *Cities in Film: Architecture, Urban Space and the Moving Image*. Conference Proceedings. Liverpool School of Architecture, Liverpool, pp. 194–202.

Roberts, L. (2010a) Dis/embedded geographies of film: virtual panoramas and the touristic consumption of Liverpool waterfront. *Space and Culture* 13(1). In press.

Roberts, L. (2010b) Regeneration, mobility and contested space: cultural reflections on a city in transition. In: Harris, J. and Williams, R. (eds) *Regenerating Culture and Society: Art, Architecture and Urban Style within the Global Politics of City-Branding*. Liverpool University Press, Liverpool.

Roberts, L. and Koeck, R. (2007) The archive city: reading Liverpool's urban landscape through film. In: Grunenberg, C. and Knifton, R. (eds) *Centre of the Creative Universe: Liverpool and the Avant-Garde*. Liverpool University Press, Liverpool, pp. 84–93.

Rojek, C. and Urry, J. (1997) Transformations of travel and theory. In: Rojek, C. and Urry, J. (eds) *Touring Cultures: Transformations in Travel and Theory*. Routledge, London.

Selwyn, T. (2007) The political economy of enchantment: formations in the anthropology of tourism. *Suomen Antropologi: Journal of the Finnish Anthropological Society* 32, 48–70.

Smith, N. and Katz, C. (1993) Grounding metaphor: towards a spatialised politics. In: Keith, M. and Pile, S. (eds) *Place and the Politics of Identity*. Routledge, London.

Sinclair, I. (1997) *Lights out for the Territory*. Granta Books, London.

Till, J. (2009) *Architecture Depends*. MIT Press, Cambridge, MA.

Urry, J. (2007) *Mobilities*. Polity, Cambridge.

Wallace, A.D. (1993) *Walking, Literature and English Culture: The Origins and Uses of Peripatetic in the Nineteenth Century*. Clarendon Press, Oxford.

Wunderlich, F.M. (2008) Walking and rhythmicity: sensing urban space. *Journal of Urban Design* 13, 31–44.

Index

Page numbers followed by '*n*', e.g., 109*n*, indicate footnotes.